HEATH
COMMUNICATION
*HAND*BOOK

TEACHER'S PLANNING GUIDE

AUTHORS

Donna Alvermann
Linda Miller Cleary
Kenneth Donelson
James Fliakas
Donald Gallo
Alice Haskins
J. Howard Johnston
John Lounsbury
Alleen Pace Nilsen
Robert Pavlik
Jewell Parker Rhodes
Alberto Alvaro Ríos
Sandra Schurr
Lyndon Searfoss
Julia Thomason
Max Thompson
Carl Zon

TEACHER CONSULTANTS

Lucretia Pannozzo, John Jay Middle School, Katonah, New York
Tom Tufts, Conniston Middle School, West Palm Beach, Florida

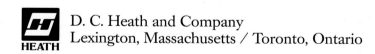

D. C. Heath and Company
Lexington, Massachusetts / Toronto, Ontario

Teacher's Edition Design: Chris Hammill Paul

Copyright ©1995 by D. C. Heath and Company

Published simultaneously in Canada

Printed in the United States of America

International Standard Book Number: 0-669-32176-1

3 4 5 6 7 8 9 10-VHP-99 98 97 96

Heath Communication Handbook
Pupil Edition and Teacher's Planning Guide

Additional Resources

U N I T S	C O N T E N T

Unit I   You as a Communicator

Introduction to the three basic kinds of projects	• You as a writer • You as a speaker • You as a visual communicator

Unit II   Communication Strategies and Projects

Instruction and assignments focusing on seven specific strategies of communication, with three projects (and many options) for each	• Telling about yourself • Describing, observing • Telling a story • Explaining • Giving your opinion, persuading • Evaluating • Reporting

Unit III   Language Resources

Guidelines on the building blocks of writing, plus grammar, usage, and mechanics	• Types of paragraphs • Sentences for specific purposes • Writing style and diction • Parts of speech • Phrases and clauses • Anatomy of sentences • Correct usage • Punctuation, capitalization, and manuscript form

Unit IV   Additional Resources

Advice on the use of technology, correct spelling, vocabulary improvement, letter writing, study skills, test taking, research, and critical thinking	• Using a computer • On-line and CD-ROM resources • Improving your spelling • Writing personal and business letters • Study skills and test taking • Elements of critical thinking

Unit V   Evaluation and Assessment

Ways to assess students' performance	• Assessment issues and tips • Portfolio assessment • Performance assessment

PRACTICE BOOKS

• One *Practice Book* for each grade–6, 7, and 8
• Increase in level of difficulty according to grade, with grade 8 dealing with all skills.
• Special emphasis on taking tests and editing written work

HEATH MIDDLE LEVEL LITERATURE

The *Heath Communication Handbook* is an ideal companion volume to the *Heath Middle Level Literature* series.

MINI-LESSONS

Designed specifically to supplement the *Heath Middle Level Literature* series, *Mini-Lesson* copymasters and transparencies focus on many of the skills covered in the *Handbook*.

CONTENTS

Introduction T6

Unit I You as a Communicator T8

    Chapter 1 You as a Writer T11

    Chapter 2 You as a Speaker and Visual Communicator T13

Unit II Communication Strategies and Projects T15

    Chapter 3 Communicating About Yourself–Communicating About Others T15

    Chapter 4 Communicating to Describe T18

    Chapter 5 Communicating to Tell a Story T21

    Chapter 6 Communicating to Explain T24

    Chapter 7 Communicating to Give Your Opinion T27

    Chapter 8 Communicating to Evaluate T30

    Chapter 9 Communicating to Report T33

Unit III Language Resources T36

    Building Blocks of Writing

    Chapter 10 Paragraphs T36

    Chapter 11 Writing Style T37

    Grammar

    Chapter 12 Parts of Speech T38

    Chapter 13 Phrases and Clauses T39

    Chapter 14 Sentences T40

Usage

Chapter 15 Using Verbs T41

Chapter 16 Using Pronouns T42

Chapter 17 Subject-Verb Agreement T43

Chapter 18 Using Adjectives and Adverbs T44

Chapter 19 Glossary of Usage T45

Mechanics

Chapter 20 Punctuation T46

Chapter 21 Capitalization T47

Chapter 22 Italics, Numbers, and Abbreviations T48

Unit IV Additional Resources

Unit IV Additional Resources T49

Chapter 23 Technology T49

Chapter 24 Spelling T50

Chapter 25 Vocabulary T51

Chapter 26 Letter Writing T52

Chapter 27 Test, Study, and Research Skills T53

Chapter 28 Critical Thinking Skills T54

Unit V Evaluation and Assessment

Unit V Evaluation and Assessment T55

The Assessment Process T55

Dealing with the Paper Load T61

Writing Folder Assessment T62

Performance Assessment T63

Literary Terms and Techniques T64

Introduction

If you were to ask your students how they would communicate an important message to as many people as possible, what answer would they give? A hundred years ago, students would probably have answered, "Write a newspaper story." Today, however, students know that people get much of their information from nonprint media—radio, television, movies, and computer networks. As the shapers of the future, your students need to know how to use all of these communications modes. Although effective writing remains an irreplaceable skill, language arts textbooks need to reflect the impact of twentieth-century technology on all of our lives—particularly on those lives reaching far into the next century.

Communications Technology

- **Radio:** In the 1920s, radio made the spoken word immediately accessible to millions of people for the first time.
- **Movies:** Also in the 1920s, movies added sound to their visual pictures, communicating the most realistic images of experience ever known.
- **Television:** In the 1950s, television combined movies' visual and sound images with radio's ability to broadcast messages instantaneously to millions of people.
- **Computers:** Since the 1970s, computers have affected all other modes of communication.
- **Computer technology** even promises to merge other media with one unifying communications mode: the global information superhighway.

The *Heath Communication Handbook* reflects these contemporary realities in the language arts. Therefore, it deals not only with writing—although it strongly emphasizes written communication—but also covers the full spectrum of modern communication.

Features of the Heath Communication Handbook

- *One handbook for three years.* The *Heath Communication Handbook* is designed to be used by students throughout the middle-school or junior-high years.
- *Many projects and options.* A wealth of activities allows you to pick and choose those most suitable for your students in these grades. Students should understand that they are not going to be asked to do everything in the book in one year.
- *Grade-specific* **Practice Books.** Separate *Practice Books* are available for students at the sixth-, seventh-, and eighth-grade levels. These helpful, workbook-format ancillaries are recommended but are not required for successful use of the *Heath Communication Handbook.*
- *Holistic focus.* The *Heath Communication Handbook* focuses on communication as a whole. It concentrates on four aspects of getting one's message across:

1. Thinking.
If your students are to write well, speak effectively, and produce strong visual presentations, they must be able to think clearly and imaginatively. The *Heath Communication Handbook* demands critical and creative thinking in every activity.

2. Writing process.
In the past, students typically were handed assignments, shown models of professional writing, and told to write essays on their own without much additional guidance. By contrast, each writing project in the *Heath Communication Handbook* takes students through the writing process, with guidance at the following stages:
- Prewriting
- Drafting
- Revising
- Editing
- Publishing

3. Speaking and listening.
Not too long ago, textbooks presented speaking and listening activities almost as afterthoughts, in the form of brief handbook chapters or alternative projects to writing assignments. The *Heath Communication Handbook* recognizes the primary importance of speaking and listening skills. Each of the seven chapters in Unit II, "Communication Strategies and Projects," includes a separate and challenging treatment of speaking and listening.

4. Visual communication.
Instruction and practice in visual communication have become essential today, since your students receive so many messages via visual images in television programs, movies, videotapes, and CD-ROM disks. This *Handbook* includes a visual project for every one of the seven chapters devoted to "Communication Strategies and Projects." These activities will open up the world of visual communication to students who too often have remained passive recipients of new technology and visual arts.

UNIT 1 You as a Communicator

You may ask yourself, "Will all my students be able to handle these diverse strategies and projects?" After all, students themselves are so diverse, with many different skills and preferences.

Three Kinds of Student Abilities

• Writing Ability: Some students enjoy writing and expressing their ideas in essays, stories, and poems–and are good at it.
• Speaking Ability: Some students express themselves best in speeches, stories, jokes, and other forms of oral communication.
• Visual Ability: Some students excel in creating and interpreting visual images–drawing, making posters and collages, creating charts and graphs, responding to televised and filmed images.

These different abilities draw on different kinds of intelligence. A well-rounded communications program encourages students to apply different intelligences to the work they do. The built-in versatility of the *Heath Communication Handbook* and the excitement it can generate in your students will become increasingly evident as you glance through this *Teacher's Planning Guide* and as you use the *Handbook* itself.

Different Kinds of Intelligence

Dr. Howard E. Gardner of Harvard's Project Zero has proposed a theory of multiple intelligences, suggesting that the concept of "intelligence" is actually much broader than the traditional view of the subject. Here are the different intelligences that he identifies, all of them applicable in some way to communication.
• Musical/Rhythmic Intelligence: People with this kind of intelligence have an inborn sensitivity to music and sound. They can use this special ability to solve problems (for example, finding a rhythm to help them memorize something) and to create and communicate meaning (for example, through choral reading, composing, and singing).
• Verbal/Linguistic Intelligence: Those with a special sensitivity to language remember words more easily than others and respond more quickly to the meaning and form of verbal communications. They also have a deep appreciation for the emotional power of language. They show these special gifts in speaking and listening, reading and writing.

- Visual/Spatial Intelligence: Individuals with visual intelligence respond more readily to representations-to pictures, patterns, and graphs, for example. They also use visual images to solve problems and to create and communicate meaning in such activities as making photographs and films, designing, decorating, drawing, painting, sculpting, and sewing.
- Logical/Mathematical Intelligence: People with an innate awareness of logic and mathematics have an exceptional ability to grasp numerical patterns and relationships. They recognize logical connections between items or events and are comfortable with abstract thinking. They can create and communicate meaning using mathematical formulas, scientific proofs, syllogisms, logical treatises, and arguments.
- Body/Kinesthetic Intelligence: Individuals who exhibit a special sense of the body and its movement use this type of intelligence to solve problems and express themselves (for example, through physical exploration, competition, athletics, and dance). They also create and communicate meaning through role-playing and physical or practical demonstrations.
- Interpersonal Intelligence: Those with special interpersonal abilities connect more readily with other people. They recognize the goals, strengths, weaknesses, and strategies of other people. They create and communicate meaning in group activities through cooperating, leading, and negotiating.
- Intrapersonal Intelligence: People with intrapersonal intelligence have an innate sense of their own goals, strengths, and weaknesses. They can extend this understanding of themselves to empathize with others, creating and communicating meaning in such activities as healing, consulting, and meditating.

Introductory

Games and Activities

Use these quizzes for fun and as a whimsical way for students to discover their own preferences and special intelligences. Where different types of intelligences are suggested in the answers below, you and your students may well come up with your own responses.

The *What's Your Favorite Flavor?* Quiz

Students will probably enjoy this quiz, especially since there are no right or wrong answers. When they finish, ask them which one of the activities they liked the best. Their favorite activity may indicate their own particular kind of intelligence.

- If I could be any flavor, I would be ___ because ___.
  (Suggested intelligences: Intrapersonal, Body/Kinesthetic)

- Where would you look to find five of your favorite flavors?
  (Suggested intelligences: Body/Kinesthetic, Logical/Mathematical)
- Draw pictures of five foods with flavors you like. Label each picture.
  (Suggested intelligences: Visual/Spatial, Verbal/Linguistic)
- In a few sentences, describe a flavor without naming it.
  (Suggested intelligences: Verbal/Linguistic, Intrapersonal)
- List five flavors and create a sound or song for each one.
  (Suggested intelligences: Verbal/Linguistic, Musical/Rhythmic)
- Write a short dialogue between yourself and a friend, beginning with the question, "Tell me, what is your favorite flavor?"
  (Suggested intelligences: Verbal/Linguistic, Interpersonal)
- In a few sentences, suggest a plan to identify an unknown flavor.
  (Suggested intelligences: Verbal/Linguistic, Logical/Mathematical)

The *What Would You Like To Do?* Quiz

Use this quiz as an entertaining way for students to pinpoint personal preferences and aptitudes. After they've chosen their five activities, help them to interpret these choices in the light of the different intelligences. Ask which choices reflect the same type of intelligence–clues to their special aptitudes. Explain that their preferences may change as they get older and learn more about themselves and the world.

List in your journal the five activities from the following list that you would most like to do.
- Work on a jigsaw puzzle. (Logical/Mathematical, Visual/Spatial)
- Interview a local celebrity. (Verbal/Linguistic, Interpersonal)
- Produce a slide show. (Visual/Spatial, Logical/Mathematical)
- Tell a joke. (Verbal/Linguistic, Interpersonal)
- Decorate a room. (Visual/Spatial, Intrapersonal)
- Conduct an experiment. (Logical/Mathematical, Body/Kinesthetic)
- Read a book or short story. (Intrapersonal, Verbal/Linguistic)
- Run around the track. (Body/Kinesthetic)
- Sing in a choir. (Musical/Rhythmic, Body/Kinesthetic)
- Write a poem. (Verbal/Linguistic, Musical/Rhythmic, Intrapersonal)
- Draw a map. (Visual/Spatial, Logical/Mathematical)
- Design a coat. (Visual/Spatial, Body/Kinesthetic, Logical/Mathematical)
- Break a secret code. (Verbal/Linguistic, Logical/Mathematical)
- Direct a play. (Interpersonal, Body/Kinesthetic, Visual/Spatial)
- Play a video game. (Visual/Spatial, Logical/Mathematical)
- Play a team sport. (Body/Kinesthetic, Interpersonal, Logical/Mathematical)

The *What's Your Style?* Quiz

This quiz may encourage your students to expand their horizons and try something that they had never thought of doing. Students who are comfortable writing, for example, may challenge themselves to try giving a speech or creating a visual product. Students who love to talk may work on improving their writing, and the visual learners in your class may take this opportunity to try more writing or speaking. The idea is that all students will discover their comfort zones and will be motivated to work on areas that are more difficult for them.

• If you could choose any person–living or dead, famous or not–to learn more about, what person would you choose?

   Ask your students the following: What kind of person did you choose? A musician? Athlete? Movie producer? The kind of person you choose to learn about is probably in a field that interests you and for which you have talent.

• What are three sources you might use to learn about the life of that person?

   Ask your students the following: What kind of sources did you choose? Seeing a movie? Talking to people? Listening to music? Reading books? Your choice of sources can tell you how you like to go about discovering knowledge.

• In presenting the information you learned to your class, would you rather write a composition? Give a talk? Prepare a slide or video show?

   Ask your students the following: How would you present your information? Did you choose more than one way? Your choice or choices may indicate a preference, but why not experiment with a presentation you might not have considered?

Chapter 1 You as a Writer

(Handbook Pages 8-25)

This chapter provides an overview of the writing process. It asks students to think about their own special skills and abilities and then moves on to the writing process: prewriting, drafting, revising, editing, and publishing. Before your students begin the activities and projects in the chapter, you may want to introduce two basic tools they will be creating and using in the course.

Journals and Writing Folders

• *Journals.* Journal-writing opportunities begin early in the *Heath Communication Handbook.* Each student will need a notebook to maintain as a journal. You may wish to specify the type of notebook–8½ x 11 spiral-bound, for example–or you may prefer to leave the choice up to the student. In many classrooms, students are allowed to carry their journals with them. Again, the choice is yours.

• ***Writing Folders.*** The writing folder is a student-generated file. Ordinarily, it will be a manila folder marked with the student's name. You, the teacher, will specify which writing samples go into the folder. Suggestions appear in this *Handbook,* but these need not be viewed as mandates. Writing folders usually remain in the classroom throughout the year.

Tips on Classroom Management for Writing

Just as writing is intensely personal, so are the methods of teaching writing. Still, your students have to know what to expect in class–and what you expect from them.

Establishing Guidelines

■ 1. Allot specific blocks of time for writing.
Make these blocks long enough to allow students to immerse themselves in the writing process. One or two classroom periods a week may be adequate, depending upon how you structure your language arts program.

■ 2. Maintain a "communication-safe" writing environment.
You may wish to have your students comment on other students' writing. This interaction can be tremendously helpful, but it can also be damaging. Therefore, you should make it clear to students from the beginning that they must respect other writers' efforts.

Their criticisms and comments should be well thought out and expressed clearly, and all comments should include positive suggestions for improvement.

■ 3. Establish guidelines for written work.
Ideally, every student should submit his or her writing in typewritten form, double-spaced, on plain white 8½ x 11 paper. If that is unlikely or impossible, set a reasonable standard that all students can meet.

Dealing with Varying Ability Levels

Sometimes students with widely varying abilities require special classroom arrangements.

• *Whole-class instruction.* In general, whole-class instruction works well when
  • You are introducing entirely new concepts.
  • You are explaining essential information or basic guidelines.
  • You are describing or reviewing a basic skill that everyone needs to improve.

• *Individual and small group instruction.* Because the writing process requires quiet time, it also gives you many opportunities to provide for individual differences by offering one-on-one or small-group help that is tailored to students' differing abilities.

• *Hold one-on-one writing conferences.* While other students are busy writing, discuss the problems or concerns of individual students who need special help.

• *Use peer review of papers.* Students are often more receptive to a classmate's reaction to their work than to a teacher's. All students have something to offer each other. Have students with complementary abilities review one another's writing and suggest improvements. You might consider matching up "verbal" students with "visual" students, for example, or "logical" students with "musical" students. Consider especially drawing on the "people" skills of students with interpersonal and intrapersonal abilities.

• *Create a workshop environment by organizing small groups.* Small-group projects enable student writers to support, encourage, and help one another and to recognize and supplement each other's strengths. The *Heath Communication Handbook* suggests small writing groups for many activities. As with peer-review pairs, try to create a constructive "mix" when you organize small groups in your classroom. In each group, include students with complementary intelligences, as well as one or more students with interpersonal abilities.

Practice Books:

Grade 6	pages 1-5
Grade 7	pages 1-4
Grade 8	pages 1-4

Chapter ❷ You as a Speaker and Visual Communicator

(Handbook Pages 26-37)

Writing is a major part of the communication process, but only one part. Students love to talk and sometimes seem to talk incessantly–even when you would rather they didn't. They also watch a great deal of television, as countless studies have shown.

Student Communication Time

Ask students to draw a pie chart showing how they spend their time during a typical school day. Suggest that they include separate segments for these activities:

> writing (in school, at home, on a computer)
>
> speaking and listening (in school, on the bus, at home)
>
> reading (in school, on the bus, at home)
>
> viewing (television, movies, computer games)
>
> eating (regular meals, snacks)
>
> sleeping (at home—not in school!)

The students' pie charts will help remind them of the importance of speaking and listening and visual communication in their daily lives. If speaking and listening and visual interaction consume a high percentage of their time, it will be easy for you to document the need for learning the techniques of effective speaking and listening and the need for exploring the world of visual communication.

Tips on Classroom Management

Speaking in public can be intimidating even for adults. Professional actors wait nervously for reviews of their performance. Small wonder that teenagers feel uncomfortable in the same situations. What can you do to lessen their fears?

Maintaining a "Communication-Safe" Classroom Environment

■ 1. Be positive.
Students who feel you are on their side will perform with greater ease and confidence than they will if they fear rejection or failure.

■ 2. Be informal.
Some teachers are naturally more informal than others. For students in high-stress circumstances, such as speaking before the class or presenting an original photo essay, an informal atmosphere in class can be an important confidence builder. You, as a teacher, have the opportunity to create a communication-safe environment.

■ 3. Make your expectations clear.
Your students have probably had more experience with writing assignments than with projects that involve speaking and listening or visual communication. When you start a project in Chapter 2 (as well as the numerous speaking and listening and visual projects in Unit II)

- Explain how the final product will be presented.
- Use the *Handbook,* but don't be limited by it. The *Handbook* offers specific suggestions, but you will want to explain the expected outcome. Let students know exactly what constitutes success.

Practice Books:

Grade 6	pages 6-7
Grade 7	pages 5-6
Grade 8	pages 5-6

Evaluation and Assessment
(See pages T55–T63.)

UNIT II Communication Strategies and Projects

Chapter ❸ Communicating About Yourself— Communicating About Others

(Handbook Pages 40–73)

In this chapter your students will

write a personal narrative
write and perform a reader's theater production
create a self-portrait or a collage

Throughout this chapter your students will find models of each kind of writing project, speaking project, and visual communication project. These models are the work of middle-school students, not professional writers. Encourage your students to pay close attention to the models. They are good illustrations of the level of performance toward which your students should strive.

The Writing Project:

Personal Narrative (Handbook pages 42-57).

Remind your students that, no matter what specific writing project they are working on, they will always progress through the same five stages of the writing process: prewriting, drafting, revising, editing, publishing. Remind them also that this writing process is recursive. That is, at various stages in the writing process, they may find themselves returning to earlier stages— doing some new prewriting, for example, as a result of a discovery made during revising.

1. Stress the importance of an authentic purpose and a real audience. Mention that no one ever writes without a reason. This *Handbook* places a strong emphasis on
   • discovering a genuine, personal reason for writing
   • focusing on an actual and credible audience for the finished paper.

2. Concentrate on a few characteristics of good writing at a time. Tell students about this strategy, so they will know that you may purposely overlook some aspects of writing (and some errors) on any given paper.

3. Point out that even though you may sometimes ignore specific matters of grammar, usage, and mechanics, the students themselves should not. Chapters 12 through 22 in the *Handbook* deal with grammar, usage, and mechanics. Advise students to refer to the information in these chapters whenever necessary.

TEACHING TIP

Your students may not have thought much about their family background. Yet it is an interesting subject to most people, and it is directly related to the writing project in this chapter. Ask your students to list the names of their parents, grandparents, and, if possible, great-grandparents. Suggest that they find photographs of as many as they can. Where did these people live? What did they do for a living? What were their hobbies or outside interests? Did any of them have unusual lives or jobs? The answers to such questions may provide topics for a personal narrative, or they may supply details that add vitality and interest to your students' projects.

Practice Books:

Grade 6	pages 8-9
Grade 7	pages 7-8
Grade 8	pages 7-8

Mini-Lessons:

Grade 6 Mini-Lessons 66-72
Grade 7 Mini-Lessons 73-78
Grade 8 Mini-Lessons 74-79

Assessment

Encourage students to think carefully about each of their responses on the Self-Evaluation Form (*Handbook* page 57). Suggest that the best kind of revising, editing, and evaluating is that which the writer does himself or herself. You will want to decide for yourself what to concentrate on in the evaluation process.

Here are some options.

Characteristics of a Good Personal Narrative

1. The audience is clearly defined.
- Assess the style and tone of the student's narrative and state how well suited you think it is to its intended audience.
- Indicate places in the paper where the audience may need more information to understand the people and events being described.

2. The writing includes details.
- Praise the writer for including specific details; they are the life blood of narration and description.
- Suggest the addition of details in specific places where they are lacking.

- Advise against needless repetition, if the student has made that common error.

■■3. The paper is neat.
- Point out that neatness counts.
- Specify how many handwritten changes and corrections (if any) you will accept without penalty in future papers.

■■4. The punctuation of introductory phrases is correct.
- Mark any errors in the use of commas with introductory phrases (see *Handbook* Chapter 20, pages 368-369).

For additional teacher guidelines on evaluation, see pages T56-T63.

The Speaking Project:

Reader's Theater Production
(Handbook pages 58-67).

Play for your students a cassette recording of a radio drama from the golden age of radio—*The Green Hornet, The Shadow*, or a similar program. Hearing this recording will give them a first-hand idea of the basic requirements for an effective reader's theater production. Be sure to preview any vintage radio shows before using them in class. Sexism, racism, ageism, and so on were more tolerated fifty years ago than they are today.

The Visual Project:

Self-Portrait/Collage (Handbook pages 68-73).

Encourage students to attempt a self-portrait, even if they say, "I can't draw." Have them look at Chris Cloke's drawings on page 69, noticing how he used his imagination to add a touch of humor to his work. A self-portrait can be realistic, of course, but it can also be pure fun.

- Advise students that they can work from a photograph of themselves, if they wish; many professional portrait painters use photos.
- As the *Handbook* suggests, students can also generate a computer portrait.

Your suggestions for a self-portrait may be more successful with some students than others. Invite some students to do the collage (*Handbook* pages 70-73) as an alternative. Artistic students may want to do both. Point out for students doing the collages that

- The collage in this project is a kind of self-portrait.
- A good collage takes time, selectivity, and organization.
- A collage, like any other creative endeavor, can benefit from revision.

Chapter ④ Communicating to Describe or Observe Something or Someone

(Handbook Pages 74-101)

In this chapter your students will

write a description based on personal observation

write and deliver a descriptive speech

create a photo essay of a community place

You may want to begin by saying that close observation is the key to good description. In order to describe something with accuracy and imagination, a writer, speaker, or illustrator must first *see* it in all its varied detail. Even if they have indeed observed something carefully, however, students may forget a particularly significant element or detail. Since your students are already keeping journals (*Handbook* page 4), point out to them that a journal can be an especially valuable resource in working with description. That one telling detail, that one perfect phrase, that one fleeting insight: these are easily lost in the rush of schoolwork and outside activities. Jotting down such observations in a journal makes them readily available for later use.

TEACHING TIP

To illustrate how easy it is for students not to observe a familiar scene, try this experiment: Remove from your classroom (or hide) five items that are ordinarily in plain view of class members every day. Ask them to identify the five missing items. If they identify any of them, follow up by asking for a description of each missing item—size, shape, color, texture, and so on. Conclude by pointing out how important careful observation is to effective description.

The Writing Project:

Description of a Community Place
(Handbook pages 76-89).

As you know, descriptive writing is common in good literature, and–like the student's effort in "The Tastee Diner"–good descriptive writing is worth studying for its technique. Following are two worthwhile activities you may want to ask some of your better students to pursue while they work on their descriptive essays. Both activities can make use of the *Heath Middle Level Literature* series.

1. Mention to students that authors

of stories frequently describe a main character or setting in a paragraph or two. Have students search for an example of this kind of description and bring it to class. For manageability, these examples should be handwritten, typewritten, or photocopied. You may want to review the descriptions or appoint a student committee to review them. Then have a student or students read several of the best descriptions in class and comment on what makes them effective. (Save all these descriptions for the following search, if you intend to assign it.)

2. In Chapter 4, page 86, you will find definitions of simile, metaphor, and hyperbole. Ask students to search for one example in literature of each of these figures of speech. They may find one or more of them in the descriptions they have already brought to class. If not, advise them that they can use examples from poetry as well as prose. Have students read aloud the examples they find. Concentrate first on simile, then metaphor, then hyperbole.

- Encourage students to use original figures of speech in their own descriptive writing.
- Remind them that most clichés are overworked similes and should be avoided (see page 294).

Practice Books:

Grade 6	pages 10-11
Grade 7	pages 9-10
Grade 8	pages 9-10

TEACHING TIP

You may find it useful to show students how to handle spatial order in descriptive writing. Display a large photographic poster of a scene in class, or else use a reproduction of a landscape or still-life painting. Ask students to suggest what they would put first in their description of the scene, what would go second, and so on. Write their suggestions on the chalkboard. Number them, but be prepared to renumber them if the class decides that a different order would be better. Emphasize that some kind of organization (left-to-right, near-to-far) is usually needed in order to make a written description clear and understandable.

Mini-Lessons:

Grade 6 Mini-Lessons 73-79
Grade 7 Mini-Lessons 79-86
Grade 8 Mini-Lessons 80-87

Assessment

Encourage students to think carefully about each of their responses to the Evaluation Activity (*Handbook* Chapter 4, page 89). You'll want to decide for yourself what you want to emphasize in the evaluation process. Here are some options.

Characteristics of Good Descriptive Writing

■■ 1. The paper is well organized.
- Question any aspect of the description that is unclear.
- Use arrows to suggest how blocks of text might be moved.
- Point out where better transitions would help.

■■ 2. Figurative language is appropriate and original.
- Mark all (or most) of the figures of speech to show that you have noticed them. Praise those that deserve it.
- Comment specifically on the effectiveness of the student's use of figurative language.

■■ 3. Verb tenses are used consistently.
- Give your reactions to the student's overall choice of verb tense.
- Mark and explain any inappropriate shifts in tense in the student's paper (see *Handbook* Chapter 15, pages 337-344).

The Speaking Project:

Descriptive Speech
(Handbook pages 90-95).

The *Handbook* suggests using a journal as a source of ideas for writing a descriptive speech (page 92). You may want to extend that suggestion by building an "Ideas for Speeches" bulletin board. Ask each student to bring in a clipping from a newspaper or magazine. Each clipping should be on a topic that might appeal to someone in class as an idea for a descriptive speech. Have a committee choose and post what they consider the most interesting possibilities. Encourage students to use the bulletin board as a source for their descriptive speeches.

The Visual Project:

Photo Essay
(Handbook pages 96-101).

You will want to emphasize from the start that a photo essay is more than a random collection of photographs on a particular topic. A photo essay
- is an organized sequence of visual images
- has no glaring gaps that will distract or confuse the viewer
- creates a consistent mood; it should not contain some images that are funny and others that are serious
- can be accompanied by captions, spoken narrative, or music, if desired.

Not every student will have access to a camera. For those who do, this project should be highly appealing. For those who don't, an essay consisting of published photos can still be challenging and rewarding. Students who are assembling published photos by others should be reminded of these points:
- The finished essay should meet all the criteria above.

- The essay must be original–that is, based on several sources–not merely picked up from an already published photo essay.
- Permission should be obtained before cutting photos from magazines or newspapers.

- Photos that cannot be clipped can be photocopied (using a setting for "light" on the machine's darkness scale).

Chapter **5** Communicating to Tell a Story

(Handbook Pages 102-133)

In this chapter your students will

write an original short story

write and present a tall tale

develop and display a storyboard

Students like to tell stories, and many of them are very good at it. This chapter will help them improve their performance in an already enjoyable activity. It will get them to think consciously about the many elements of a successful story–purpose, opening "hook," point of view, characterization, setting, and plot.

The Writing Project:

Short Story (Handbook pages 104-117).

Even very good storytellers can become better storytellers with specific instruction. This *Handbook* provides a step-by-step guide to creating an original short story.

1. "Where do you get your ideas?" is a question students frequently ask professional writers. Often an author answers, "From my own life," or, sometimes, "From the daily news." Ask students where *they* get their ideas for stories. Form small groups to discuss the sources of story ideas. Have each group report its findings. Write each new suggestion on the board.

2. Emphasize the importance of a story's opening (the "hook") and its ending (the final impression). Mention these two points.

- Writers sometimes draft their endings first. By doing so, they know from the outset exactly where their story is going.
- Writers sometimes create a story's hook after writing the first

draft. The reason is that the hook is often easier to write after the story as a whole has taken shape.

3. Have students find and bring to class examples of two or three hooks and two or three final paragraphs from short stories they have enjoyed. These excerpts should be handwritten, typewritten, or photocopied. Discuss what makes each one effective.

- Encourage students to observe and apply the techniques used by published writers.
- Point out that using another writer's *technique* is perfectly acceptable; using another writer's *exact words* is plagiarism.

TEACHING TIP

Ask your students to find, cut out, and bring to class one nonviolent news story from the local newspaper that they think could be developed into an interesting short story. Note and comment on the number of students who choose the same stories. Ask students to discuss their choices, explaining what aspect of the story caught their attention.

Practice Books:

Grade 6	pages 12-13
Grade 7	pages 11-12
Grade 8	pages 11-12

Mini-Lessons:

Grade 6 Mini-Lessons 80-86
Grade 7 Mini-Lessons 87-93
Grade 8 Mini-Lessons 88-94

Assessment

It isn't always easy for students to judge their own stories. Peer assessment is a particularly good idea for this chapter, because other students are likely to have a clear understanding of the characters' motives and concerns. When you evaluate the finished story yourself,

- Try to react to the story as an interested reader rather than as a critic or a teacher.
- In general, use your marginal notes to ask questions, rather than making demands.
- End on a positive note. Don't be dishonest, but do praise whatever seems most praiseworthy about the story.

Refer to pages T55-T63 (Unit V, Evaluation and Assessment) in this *Teacher's Planning Guide* for additional advice on judging students' writing. In evaluating the stories students produce for this chapter, you may want to emphasize the following criteria:

Characteristics of a Good Story

1. The story has a clear and coherent plot.
- Evaluate the effectiveness of the opening lines of the story.

- Comment on the conflict between or within main characters.
- Consider the suitability of the ending.
- If appropriate, suggest ways in which the plot might be improved.

2. The characters in the story are well developed and believable.
- See how well you can picture the characters.
- Note whether the characters have individual personalities.
- Evaluate the dialogue for realism.

3. The story has few or no clichés.
- Mark any overworked expressions you find.
- If the clichés are figures of speech, ask the student to think of more original comparisons.

4. The dialogue is punctuated correctly.
- Make sure a new paragraph starts when the speaker changes.
- Check to see that quotation marks enclose all direct quotations.
- Mark any punctuation or capitalization errors you see in the dialogue.

The Speaking Project:

Tall Tale (Handbook pages 118-125).

To introduce this oral project, "Making Up a Tall Tale," you may want to read aloud in class or play a recording of a tall tale about Paul Bunyan or Mike Fink. Have students listen carefully and list the obvious features of a tall tale—exaggerated events, larger-than-life characters, humor, often a frontier setting. Mention to students that they will use the same basic techniques in their own tall tales, although the settings of their stories do not have to be the American frontier. The setting should, however, be a real place, not a science-fiction or space-travel destination. Have them notice the true-to-life setting in Mac Brodt's "Paul the Dragon Tamer" (*Handbook* page 119).

The Visual Project:

Storyboard (Handbook pages 126-133).

This project will appeal very much to students who like to draw. On the other hand, as the *Handbook* suggests, it may worry some of those who have limited artistic skills. One way to deal with the concerns of the less artistic is to assign the project to small groups, each including at least one person who is willing to do the sketching. Other solutions for individual students include
- drawing cartoonlike or simple stick figures with descriptive labels
- taking color or black-and-white photos
- using pictures from magazines or newspapers.

Regardless of the type of presentation, your evaluation (and the students' self-evaluation) of the storyboard should take into consideration the artistic merit of the result. The *Handbook* recognizes that different kinds of intelligences exist. One of these is visual/spatial intelligence. A student or small group showing special skill in the visual/spatial presentation of information should be rewarded for it, just as you reward students for exceptional verbal skills in the writing projects.

Chapter 6 Communicating to Explain

(Handbook Pages 134-167)

In this chapter your students will

write an expository essay

prepare and deliver a demonstration speech

create an explanatory chart

Each project in this chapter requires your students to explain something to others. The technical term for this type of communication is *exposition.* Exposition, whether written, spoken, or visual, informs the audience of something. Few types of communication are more familiar to your students than exposition. Ask them to point out examples of exposition in the classroom. No matter where they point, they can hardly miss finding something. For instance, the *Heath Communication Handbook* is an example of written exposition, as are most textbooks. Your classroom teaching is spoken exposition. Charts, diagrams, maps, and graphs are examples of visual exposition. In essence, exposition is instruction. When your students write, speak, or use visual media to explain something, they become instructors.

TEACHING TIP

The following activity applies to any of the three kinds of projects, but especially to writing and speaking. Ask for a volunteer. Have him or her read a page or two from a textbook in another subject—social studies or science, for example. Next ask the student to teach the material in class. Tell the other students to keep notes on any questions they have about the subject. Discuss the student-teacher's presentation, asking students to identify three or four of the most important elements of good exposition. Possibilities include

• organization of the material

• definition of key terms

• clarity of the presentation

No doubt other elements will be mentioned, too. Advise students to keep these in mind as they work on the projects in the chapter.

The Writing Project:

Expository Essay (Handbook pages 136-149).

Ask students to think of some kinds of exposition that are often interesting, such as
- biographies of sports figures or rock stars
- science articles in magazines aimed at general audiences
- recipes for favorite dishes.

1. In discussing the various examples of expository writing, you may want to stress how widespread this kind of writing is. It seems to be everywhere. Because of its abundance and also because of its practicality you can easily make the point that learning how to do expository writing is worth the effort.

2. The *Heath Communication Handbook* goes into considerable detail about organizing an expository essay. Help your students understand that time spent organizing the paper saves time later. Following a well-thought-out plan reduces the time they will need to revise their essays. In the long run, skipping or slighting the note-taking and outlining stages would make them lose time.

3. Remind your students again that even the most experienced writers have to revise their first drafts. Tell them to pay close attention to the Checklist for Revising an Expository Essay on *Handbook* page 146. In addition to the points on the list, they should be on guard against
- *Inaccuracy.* Factual errors are easier to make than to spot, but those that are missed will detract from the essay.
- *Wordiness.* Common culprits are needless repetition, unnecessary phrases, and too many adjectives or adverbs.

Practice Books:

Grade 6	pages 14-15
Grade 7	pages 13-14
Grade 8	pages 13-14

Mini-Lessons:

Grade 6 Mini-Lessons 87-93
Grade 7 Mini-Lessons 94-102
Grade 8 Mini-Lessons 95-103

Assessment

You will find a number of general guidelines for evaluation and assessment on pages T55-T63. In deciding what to emphasize when grading your students' expository essays, review what the class as a whole is having difficulty mastering. Take into account, too, the specific aspects of writing that have been stressed in this project. Following are some features that you may wish to focus on.

Characteristics of a Good Expository Essay

■■ 1. The paragraphs are properly developed and set off.
- Be sure all paragraphs are indented.
- Mark any place where you think a new paragraph should begin or where two existing paragraphs should be combined.
- Comment on the adequacy of paragraph development.

■■ 2. The writer builds and sustains interest.
- Note the effectiveness of the opening paragraph.
- Check the middle of the essay to make sure your interest doesn't start to wane.

■■ 3. Transitions provide smooth movement from one thought to the next.
- See how well the writer uses transitional words, phrases, and sentences to make the writing fluent and coherent.
- Mark any gaps in the development of ideas.

■■ 4. The writer has avoided run-on sentences.
- Be sure every sentence begins with a capital letter and ends with a period, question mark, or exclamation point.
- Watch out for the use of commas where semicolons or periods are needed.

The Speaking Project:

Demonstration Speech
(Handbook pages 150-159).

Point out to students that the demonstration speech they are to prepare and deliver will not include charts and graphs (the focus of the next project). The speech can, however, include an actual physical demonstration—making a salad, playing a cello, creating a costume. Throughout the work on this project, you will want to stress the importance of clarity. The sole purpose of a demonstration speech is to show the audience how to do something. Its success has to be judged primarily by how well the audience understands the explanation.

The Visual Project:

Explanatory Chart
(Handbook pages 160-167).

You may want to paraphrase the old axiom by suggesting to your students that "a good chart is worth a thousand words." As the visual presentation of information becomes more common, spurred by television and computers, it becomes increasingly important for students to learn how to produce charts and other visual aids that help convey knowledge. To give students a clear picture of what charts can accomplish, you may want to post a few commercially produced charts on the bulletin board and discuss what makes them effective.

Chapter **7** Communicating to Give Your Opinion

(Handbook Pages 168-205)

In this chapter your students will

write an editorial

prepare and present a persuasive speech

create a public service poster

As the *Heath Communication Handbook* indicates, your students will find opinions expressed in many print forms—newspaper editorials, columns, letters to the editor, pages, magazine articles, books, advertisements. On radio and television they will encounter opinions in editorials, talk-show discussions, political roundtables, and so on. Professional opinion-shapers can be experts at blurring the line between fact and opinion. Your students need to know how to recognize opinion as well as how to produce it.

TEACHING TIP

Separating fact from opinion can be tricky. Write the following statements on the board, and ask your students to identify which are facts and which are opinions. Then ask students to indicate what clues they used to separate the facts from the opinions. (Clues are given in parentheses.)

1. John F. Kennedy's Inaugural Address is included in many textbooks today. (Fact: The information can be verified in the public record.)

2. John F. Kennedy was a very eloquent speaker. (Opinion: The subjective term *eloquent* indicates an opinion is being expressed.)

3. The reduction of crime should be the first concern of government today. (Opinion: *Should* signals an opinion.)

4. In a recent poll, more Americans chose crime reduction as their chief concern than any other issue. (Fact: Polls can be verified.)

Help students see that a given piece of writing is likely to include both fact and opinion. For example, Statements 1 and 2 could appear in an article about John F. Kennedy, with the fact in Statement 1 being used to support the opinion in Statement 2. The same holds true for the opinion in Statement 3 and the fact in Statement 4. Remind students that a good communicator must separate opinion from fact and should use facts to support opinions.

The Writing Project:

Editorial (Handbook pages 170-185).

Since your students already have opinions on many topics, they should find it easy and enjoyable to choose a topic for an editorial. Gathering the facts to back up a particular opinion, however, can be challenging.

1. Your students need to know where they can find reliable facts. Ask them to name some sources they think can be counted on to provide accurate facts. (As the *Heath Communication Handbook* notes, students can usually rely on encyclopedias, almanacs, and standard reference books, which are catalogued in the library under "Reference." They can also rely on most on-line databases.) In assembling their facts, students should be wary of merely repeating the opinions of others, which may or may not be backed by genuine facts.

2. Suggest that students use the following format to guide their thinking in expressing their opinions in the editorial:

Topic:
    What I believe:
    1.
    2. (and so on)

    What others believe
    (both pro and con):
    1.
    2. (and so on)

3. As the *Handbook* states, most of the facts a student assembles will go into the body of his or her editorial. You may want to mention, though, that a single startling fact can sometimes be a knockout opener. For example, a student editorial arguing that Texas is too big begins, "By law, the state of Texas could divide itself into five separate states tomorrow if Texans wanted to do it."

4. Caution your students, as the *Handbook* does, against exaggerating or overstating. An editorial is usually more persuasive if it makes its case calmly and factually, without relying on questionable superlatives or dire predictions that only time will prove true or false.

Practice Books:

Grade 6	pages 16-17
Grade 7	pages 15-16
Grade 8	pages 15-16

Mini-Lessons:

Grade 6 Mini-Lessons 94-97
Grade 7 Mini-Lessons 103-108
Grade 8 Mini-Lessons 104-109

Assessment

The assessment activity for this project is a self-evaluation form. Depending on the method of publication, you may want to have a classroom discussion about one or more of the editorials. Students whose views differ from those of the editorial writer may have valid criticisms that might not otherwise come up. Students who agree with the writer may add facts and examples to support the editorial. Along the way, you can make the important point that conflicting views are to be expected in a democratic society. Pages T55-T63 (Unit V, Evaluation and Assessment) offer additional advice on how to grade student papers. For the editorial-writing project, you may want to stress the following:

Characteristics of a Good Editorial

1. The main idea is stated clearly and briefly.
- Check to see that the statement is limited to a single, well-expressed idea.
- Make sure the editorial has unity—that it sticks to the main idea without going off on a tangent.

2. The editorial shows a continuing awareness of its audience.
- See that the vocabulary is appropriate for the audience.
- Assess the tone of the writing, marking any passages that you think might not be persuasive.
- Note whether the writer tries to anticipate opponents' arguments—always a plus.

3. The writer has included enough facts to support his or her opinion.
- Be sure the facts in the editorial do support the opinion.
- Watch out for repetition of the same facts.
- Indicate if you are personally persuaded by the editorial, and tell why.

4. The sentence structure is varied and interesting.
- Praise students for the effective use of sentence-starting phrases and clauses.
- See that long sentences alternate with shorter sentences.
- Comment favorably on the imaginative use of varied sentences.

The Speaking Project:

Persuasive Speech (Handbook pages 186-197).

Most of your students have seen political speeches, either on television or in person. Political speeches are written to persuade. Ask your students what they expect in a political speech. Information? Ideas? Controversy? Inspiration? Which politicians do they consider to be good speakers? The President? The governor? A senator? The mayor? What do they think makes a speech effective? You may want to suggest that just as student athletes can learn from watching professionals in action, so can student speakers learn from the pros.

The Visual Project:

Public Service Poster (Handbook pages 198-205).

A public service poster is a form of persuasion. Bring in or identify a few examples of public service posters (there are probably several posted around the school—announcements, requests for volunteers, and so on). Ask students if they remember any public service posters they have seen. Mention that some posters are memorable and have become classics, such as the army recruiting poster in which Uncle Sam points toward the viewer and says, "I want you." If students can bring to class some posters or reproductions of posters with a message, they may generate some ideas, graphic or textual, for their own public service posters.

Chapter ⑧ Communicating to Evaluate

(Handbook Pages 206-247)

In this chapter your students will

write a book review

prepare and deliver a spoken movie review

create a book jacket

The *Heath Communication Handbook* suggests some strategies for choosing material to review or publicize. You may want to point out to students that if they choose a book or movie from a recommended list—yours or someone else's—they are working from a prescreened group of choices. The works on such a list have already been rated highly by critics or professional reviewers. Although prescreening doesn't mean that students will necessarily like all the books or movies, it does make favorable reviews far more likely than if students make random choices of their own.

TEACHING TIP

Suggest to your students that the class assemble "top ten" lists of favorite books and films at the end of the projects in this chapter. Tell them to begin by asking other students about books and movies they have enjoyed. In choosing books they may also get helpful advice from a school or public librarian, who will be aware of what books students their age have liked best; someone who works in a videotape rental store may have some ideas about the movies rented most frequently by people in this age group. Appoint a committee to "review the reviews" as the projects are completed. Have the committee submit recommended "top ten" book and movie lists to the class for discussion and possible revision. Post the final lists.

The Writing Project:

Book Review (Handbook pages 208-225).

Many of your students will have written book reviews before, but they may not have gone about the task in the careful, step-by-step way the *Heath Communication Handbook* does. Assure them that the writing-process approach used here will give them a firm foundation for doing other book reviews later.

1. Remind the school librarian that your students will be working on book-review projects. That way, if students ask for advice on what to read, the librarian will be prepared. If you are planning to have them assemble a "top ten" list, advise the librarian of that, too, so that his or her recommendations will be in line with the plan.

2. If your students have done the short story project (*Handbook* Chapter 5, pages 104-117), tell them that many of the elements they worked on for that project—characters, setting, plot, point of view, theme—are the same elements they will be observing and assessing in a published work of fiction. They should have gained some valuable insights into the shaping of those elements, insights they can now apply to their book reviews. In fact, this is a good time to mention that the mastery of writing is a cumulative process. Every student's writing builds on his or her previous writing. In that sense, none of the projects in

this *Handbook* is an isolated exercise; they are intertwined.

3. Stress the importance of note-taking to the task of reviewing a book. No matter how good a student's memory may be, it is impossible to remember all the thoughts and questions that come to mind when reading a book. Since any of those thoughts or questions may prove valuable when drafting a review, your students should write them down on note cards or keep "sticky notes" on the actual book pages (*Handbook* pages 214-215).

Practice Books:

Grade 6	pages 18-19
Grade 7	pages 17-18
Grade 8	pages 17-18

Mini-Lessons:

Grade 6 Mini-Lessons 98-100
Grade 7 Mini-Lessons 109-115
Grade 8 Mini-Lessons 110-116

Assessment

Encourage students to pay close attention to the reader evaluation of their book reviews (*Handbook* page 225). Although these evaluations follow publication, your students will be doing more of this kind of writing in the future, and any help they get now should be useful to them then. As you go over the reviews yourself, you will decide what you want to emphasize. Here are four options.

Characteristics of a Good Book Review

1. The review contains basic factual information about the book.
- Title (with subtitle, if any)
- Author (or authors)
- Publisher and date of publication (from title page)
- (Optional): Number of pages and price.

2. The review presents a clear picture of the content of the book.
- Comment on how well the reader gets to know the people, places, and events described in the book.
- Be sure the plot summary doesn't take over and become the substance of the review.

3. The review offers a clear judgment about the book.
- Check to see that the writer has evaluated the book.
- Make sure the writer has backed up his or her evaluation with examples or other information from the book.

4. The review uses the present tense to refer to events in the book.
- Make sure the writer uses the present tense throughout in regard to events in the book: e.g., "Anne movingly *describes* her fears. . . ."
- Note, however, that the past tense is correctly used for the reviewer's own reactions: e.g., "Reading it *made* me feel anger, pity, and sorrow. . . ."

The Speaking Project:

Spoken Movie Review (Handbook pages 226-239).

Your students may be more familiar with movies than with books. You may want to introduce this project with a brief classroom discussion of motion pictures. What kind of films do your students like best? Why? Who are their favorite actors? Have your students watched movie reviewers on television? If so, what do they think of the reviews they have seen? Point out, as the *Handbook* does, that everyone who sees a movie becomes a critic in a way, since all viewers make judgments about the films they see. This project is designed to make such judgments more thoughtful.

The Visual Project:

Book Jacket (Handbook pages 240-247).

To introduce this project, you may want to bring to class three or four books for teenagers that have especially attractive jackets. Bring varied titles, because books written about different subjects will appeal to different readers and thus will vary widely in the style of their jackets. Go over the elements of the book jackets—the front, the back, the spine, the flaps—to show students what they will be doing. On the front, discuss the placement, size, and type used for the title and author. On the back, note testimonials, excerpts from the book, information about the author. You may want to read the flap copy from one of the books to give students a preview of what copywriters include about the contents of the book. Point out that book jackets offer great scope for the imagination.

Chapter ❾ Communicating to Report

(Handbook Pages 248-285)

In this chapter your students will

write a research paper

write and deliver a news report

create a videotaped presentation

A fairly high percentage of your students will eventually have to prepare reports of one kind or another: written, oral, or multimedia. You may want to ask your students how many of their parents have to prepare reports on the job, either routinely or occasionally. Quite likely this kind of communication is the most widespread of the seven types covered in Unit II.

The Writing Project:

Research Paper (Handbook pages 250-269).

In this chapter your students will write a brief research report, using a variety of sources. You may want to point out to them that a single encyclopedia article, or any other single source no matter how detailed, cannot be the sole basis of their research. The essence of research is finding out as much as possible about the topic from different points of view.

TEACHING TIP

In this chapter, the student writer Laliev Ben Avraham discovers that one of his "facts"—that dinosaurs died out during the Ice Age—is incorrect. Your students have probably made similar mistakes. Everyone has. Discuss with them the subject "facts that weren't facts." Ask them to give examples of "facts" they once thought to be true but later learned were untrue. The discussion can include childhood misperceptions, disproven scientific theories (like the Ptolemaic system), ridiculous articles in supermarket checkout-line tabloids, and hoaxes like the Piltdown Man and the faked Loch Ness Monster photo.

1. Be sure to inform your school librarian that your students will be working on research projects.

2. Since your students are new to the research process, you'll want to stress the importance of getting quotations exactly right. Here are a couple of techniques your students can use to ensure the accuracy of the quotations they include:

- Tell students to make photocopies of the longer passages they expect to quote. That way, the longer quotations in their final draft can be checked against their sources, not against handwritten notes.
- If students have access to a tape recorder, advise them to tape any interviews they conduct. Then they can listen to the speaker's exact words at their leisure, rather than jot down quotations hurriedly (and perhaps inaccurately) during the interview.

3. Evaluating sources can be tough even for experienced researchers. An interesting and worthwhile activity is to have students read and evaluate in class three fairly short, widely divergent reports on the same topic. You can either find these reports yourself or assign students to find them. After students have read and discussed the reports, ask them which one they consider the most authoritative, and why.

Practice Books:

Grade 6   pages 20-21
Grade 7   pages 19-20
Grade 8   pages 19-20

Mini-Lessons:

Grade 6 Mini-Lessons 101-109
Grade 7 Mini-Lessons 116-124
Grade 8 Mini-Lessons 117-125

Assessment

The self-evaluation in this chapter is a written survey of the audience. When you evaluate your students' reports, you'll want to keep the following criteria in mind. You may wish to add others as well.

Characteristics of a Good Report

■■ 1. The report makes effective use of sources.
- Check the student's list of sources. It should contain at least three or four items, even if the topic is very limited.
- Make sure the student hasn't overused one source.
- Check the form of the student's citations. They should follow the form indicated in the *Handbook* on page 263.
- Be sure the factual information in the report is accurate, as far as you can tell.

▪▪ 2. The report is well-developed and balanced.

- The report should have enough evidence to back up the main idea convincingly. At the same time, it should not be padded. Watch out for needless repetition.
- Evaluate balance. Some writers have an irresistible urge to put too much emphasis on certain parts of a report—usually the parts where they found a wealth of information.

▪▪ 3. The report has a clearly defined opening and conclusion.

- Praise openings that are especially appealing. The model report by Laliev Ben Avraham gets off to a rousing start.
- See if the conclusion conveys a sense of finality. Some reports simply trail off, without really tying the information together or restating the main idea.

▪▪ 4. Sentences are clear and precise.

- Mark any sentences that do not say what the student seems to have had in mind.
- Indicate any ambiguous sentences you see.

The Speaking Project:

News Report (Handbook pages 270-277).

In this project, your students become local news reporters. To introduce the process, ask your students to bring to class several leads from a television station's news broadcast. Use these examples to help students determine the characteristics of a good lead. Your discussion will also show what qualifies as news at the station. If some students monitor a national news broadcast while others monitor a local broadcast, you can also point out the differences that result from different audiences. You'll want to stress that the project they will be doing involves a school or community event or issue.

The Visual Project:

Videotape (Handbook pages 278-285).

As students prepare to do a videotaped presentation, review the various kinds of equipment with them. If the school or district has a media specialist, he or she may be willing to give your students some pointers on what they can accomplish with the school's equipment. Encourage students to explore the potential of the new technologies. As shown in the example in the *Handbook* (pages 279-280), it is helpful to prepare a rough script of the presentation. Consider a storyboard as an alternative.

UNIT III Language Resources

Chapter 10 Paragraphs

(Handbook Pages 288-293)

The *Heath Communication Handbook* organizes paragraphing into two categories:

- ***Types of Paragraphs***. Make the point that different kinds of writing require different kinds of paragraph development. When your students write, they have to keep these differences in mind. Mention that *purpose* determines the kind of sentences in a paragraph, as well as the order of the sentences.

- ***Parts of Paragraphs***. You may want to note that a topic sentence, important as it is, is only the starting point for a well-developed paragraph. Appropriate and effective supporting sentences are crucial, as are good transitional sentences and concluding sentences.

Practice Books:

Grade 6	pages 22-28
Grade 7	pages 21-25
Grade 8	pages 21-25

Mini-Lessons:

Grade 6 Mini-Lessons 113-133
Grade 7 Mini-Lessons 128-148
Grade 8 Mini-Lessons 129-149

Chapter 11 Writing Style

(Handbook Pages 294-298)

You may want to quote Jonathan Swift, the author of *Gulliver's Travels,* on writing style:

Proper words in proper places make the true definition of a style.

The *Heath Communication Handbook* offers students several stylistic *do's* and *don'ts.*

- *Do*
  - use a consistent point of view
  - choose words with care
  - adjust the tone of writing according to audience and purpose
- *Don't*
  - use clichés
  - use mixed metaphors
  - needlessly repeat words, phrases, or ideas

TEACHING TIP

Remember that most of today's clichés are figurative language that was once vivid. To teenagers, a cliché may therefore still *seem* imaginative and effective. To help students understand clichés, conduct a Cliché Roundup in class. Ask students to identify clichés that they themselves use: "pale as a ghost," "sell like hot cakes," "shaking like a leaf." The list is almost endless. Encourage students to consult books on the subject, such as Eric Partridge's *Dictionary of Clichés.* You may also want to ask for a sampling of mixed metaphors: "The window of opportunity appeared—I had to grasp it while I could." "There is no such thing as smooth sailing on the rocky road to success." Advise students that although everyone uses clichés from time to time—and although mixed metaphors are often hilarious, both clichés and mixed metaphors are considered flaws in most kinds of writing.

Practice Books:

Grade 6	pages 29-34
Grade 7	pages 26-30
Grade 8	pages 26-30

Mini-Lessons:

Grade 6 Mini-Lessons 113-133
Grade 7 Mini-Lessons 128-148
Grade 8 Mini-Lessons 129-149

Chapter ⑫ Parts of Speech

(Handbook Pages 299-313)

The goal of this chapter is to show your students how to identify the eight parts of speech: nouns, pronouns, verbs, adjectives, adverbs, prepositions, conjunctions, and interjections. One basic principle you will want to stress is that the part of speech of a word is determined by the way it is used in a sentence. To make this point, write the following examples on the board.

1. The settlers dug a <u>well</u>. (noun)
2. She looks sad; her eyes <u>well</u> with tears. (verb)
3. Conchata plays softball <u>well</u>. (adverb)
4. After his bout with flu, Sid seems to be <u>well</u>. (adjective)
5. <u>Well</u>! I never expected a party. (interjection)

Practice Books:

Grade 6	pages 35-51
Grade 7	pages 31-48
Grade 8	pages 31-48

Mini-Lessons:

Grade 6 Mini-Lessons 159-164
Grade 7 Mini-Lessons 175-178
Grade 8 Mini-Lesson 172

TEACHING TIP

Students sometimes wonder what the parts of speech have to do with effective writing. To show the relevance, you may want to discuss the following teachers' marginal notes on students' writing.

- "*Idealism* is too abstract a word. Use a more concrete noun." Abstract Nouns (*Handbook* page 300)
- "The word *it* has no antecedent." Pronouns (*Handbook* page 301)
- "How about a more vivid verb?" Action Verbs (*Handbook* page 304)
- "You need to capitalize *Irish*." Proper Adjectives (*Handbook* page 309)
- "Replace *good* with an adverb." Adverbs (*Handbook* pages 309-310)
- "Is *of* the right preposition?" Prepositions (*Handbook* pages 311-312)
- "Don't start a sentence with *And*." Conjunctions (*Handbook* page 312)
- "Too many *Wows*!" Interjections (*Handbook* page 313)

Chapter 🔢 Phrases and Clauses

(Handbook Pages 314-321)

The easiest way for students to classify a related group of words is to look for a subject and a verb. If a related word group lacks a subject or verb, it is probably a phrase.

- *Phrases:*   into the darkness

                  had been missing

                  walking the dog

You may want to point out, however, that not every related word group is a phrase. Compound nouns, such as *White Sulphur Springs* and *Los Angeles International Airport,* for example, are not classified as phrases.

If a related word group has both subject and verb, the group of words is a clause:

- *Clauses:*   which <u>she</u> <u>discovered</u> this morning

                  as the <u>planes</u> <u>landed</u>

Of course, a clause may also be a complete sentence. (See Independent Clauses, *Handbook* pages 319-320.)

TEACHING TIP

Sentence combining is a technique that asks students to combine short sentences into longer, varied sentences. (See Sentences, page 336.) The procedure usually involves making an independent clause into a subordinate clause, a phrase, or even a single word. To create a sentence-combining exercise of your own, choose a poorly written paragraph from a past student composition (you will want to use a composition from a student not in this particular class). Use a paragraph that uses very simple, subject-verb-object sentences. Ask your students to combine the simple sentences on their own, in any way they wish, to produce a more mature-sounding paragraph, with greater sentence variety. After they finish this sentence-combining activity, they may be interested to see how closely their paragraphs match their classmates'.

Practice Books:

Grade 6	pages 52-55
Grade 7	pages 49-58
Grade 8	pages 49-58

Mini-Lessons:

Grade 6 Mini-Lesson 165
Grade 7 Mini-Lessons 179,182
Grade 8 Mini-Lessons 173,177-
               178

Chapter 14 Sentences

(Handbook Pages 322-336)

The more your students know about the structure, types, and purposes of sentences, the better their own sentences should be. This chapter is a good place to make the point (if you haven't done so already) that a knowledge of grammar will give students a vocabulary with which to discuss the craft of writing. Also, mention to students that word order is very important in English. Not only does word order help to determine the meaning of a sentence, it has a major impact on the power of the sentence. Every sentence requires careful, thoughtful construction. In this chapter, your students will learn a number of ways to increase the effectiveness of their sentences.

TEACHING TIP

Keep grammar lessons short and specific. One useful kind of mini-lesson is to take a single sentence from a student's paper and have the class analyze it grammatically. For example: *Anne Frank: The Diary of a Young Girl* is an important, interesting, and very moving book.

Ask students:

1. Is this a simple, compound, or complex sentence? (simple sentence)

2. Is it a declarative, imperative, interrogative, or exclamatory sentence? (declarative sentence)

3. What is the subject of the sentence? (*Anne Frank: The Diary of a Young Girl*)

4. How is the word *book* used in the sentence? (predicate nominative)

5. What part of speech is the word *important*? (adjective)

Note: When choosing students' sentences for analysis, be selective. Some of their sentences can have remarkably complicated syntax. (You may even want to use one or two very difficult student sentences just to impress on students how sophisticated their use of language really is.)

Practice Books:

Grade 6	pages 56-73
Grade 7	pages 59-78
Grade 8	pages 59-78

Mini-Lessons:

Grade 6 Mini-Lessons 166-168
Grade 7 Mini-Lessons 180-181, 183-186
Grade 8 Mini-Lessons 174-176, 179-183

Chapter ⑮ Using Verbs

(Handbook Pages 337-344)

Now and then, your students undoubtedly make a few common errors with verbs. The most frequent difficulties arise in these three areas:

- *Irregular verbs.* Even when students know the principal parts of irregular verbs, they may continue to make errors with those verbs in their daily speech. Repeated oral practice with irregular verb forms will often help.
- *Shifts in tense.* Tense indicates time. In writing, your students' goal is to maintain consistency in the tense of verbs. Problems arise when the time of the action differs from the time indicated by the basic verb tense being used. You will want to concentrate on only the most obviously incorrect shifts.
- *Active and passive voice.* Encourage your students to use the active voice of verbs whenever possible. They should use passive voice primarily when the doer of the action is either unknown or unimportant: *Waste paper was strewn everywhere.*

Although you will find errors in verb usage in your students' writing, an equally damaging flaw is the use of dull, lifeless verbs. Point out to students that one of the surest ways to add life to their writing is to use specific, colorful action verbs in the active voice.

TEACHING TIP

Since the proper and effective use of verbs is a skill learned mainly through listening and reading, encourage your students to listen carefully to people who speak standard English. Radio and television newscasters are generally good models. Most of the errors students make with verbs come from hearing those same errors repeated by others. Listening to speakers who do not make such errors may encourage students to change their habits. In class, concentrate on oral practice, using standard English.

Practice Books:

Grade 6   pages 74-86
Grade 7   pages 79-89
Grade 8   pages 79-89

Mini-Lessons:

Grade 6 Mini-Lesson 169
Grade 7 Mini-Lesson 187
Grade 8 Mini-Lesson 184

Chapter 16 Using Pronouns

(Handbook Pages 345-351)

A literary critic once wrote, "Beware of pronouns–they are devils." Since even accomplished writers get into tangles with pronouns, you can expect your students to have similar difficulties. This chapter deals with the three cases of pronouns (nominative, objective, possessive) and with the antecedents of pronouns. It also explores the perennial perplexities of *who, whom,* and *whose.* Written practice with pronoun problems can be useful. As always, you should direct your assignments toward the mistakes your students are actually making. A brief pretest based on pronoun errors you have found in student compositions can help you pinpoint areas of concern. Here is a sample (answers are in italics).

1. (*We*, Us) cheerleaders arrived early.
2. Carla told her brother and (I, *me*) a ghost story.
3. For (who, *whom*) are the flowers intended?
4. We were delighted at (*his*, him) agreeing to speak.
5. (Its, *It's*) time to give the cat (*its*, it's) dinner.
6. The honored guests at the party were (*they*, them.)
7. Two players, (*he*, him) and (*I*, me), will accept the award.
8. Each student must do (their, *his or her*) own work.
9. We all wondered (*who*, whom) would run for president.
10. One of the girls brought (her, their) cassette player.

TEACHING TIP

To help your students solve usage problems when a pronoun is part of a compound subject or object, show them how to "split the compounds." Write on the board a few sentences like numbers 2 and 7 above. Have them try two techniques:

- Divide each sentence into two separate sentences; then choose the proper pronoun for each new sentence.

- Cover one half of each compound part; then choose the proper pronoun by considering it in isolation from the other noun or pronoun.

Practice Books:

Grade 6	pages 87-93
Grade 7	pages 90-97
Grade 8	pages 90-97

Mini-Lessons:

Grade 6 Mini-Lesson 170
Grade 8 Mini-Lesson 185

Chapter ⑰ Subject-Verb Agreement

(Handbook Pages 352-355)

Understandably, questions about subject-verb agreement tend to get harder as your students become better writers. As their sentences become longer and more complex, students may include elements that make it harder for them to isolate the subject and verb in order to make them agree. Using interrupted words, inverted word order, compound subjects, and indefinite pronouns all complicate the choice of the proper verb form. This is the basic rule for your students to remember:

Watch the subject of every clause. The subject of the clause determines the number of the verb.

- In deciding which verb form to use with a subject, ignore interrupting words or groups of words, including prepositional phrases. (Exceptions are prepositional phrases after fractions and after the words *some, all*, or *most.* In these exceptional cases, the object of the preposition determines the number of the verb. For example: "Some of the glass was broken"; *but* "Some of the glasses were broken.")
- Mentally place inverted sentences in normal word order, in order to identify the subject and so choose the correct verb form.

TEACHING TIP

As an exercise in peer evaluation of one of the writing projects, ask students to exchange papers and look for errors in subject-verb agreement. Tell them to look at nothing else—just subject-verb agreement in every sentence. Have each student write down, uncorrected, any such errors that he or she finds. Assemble at least ten of the errors yourself, or appoint a student committee to collect errors. Put the sentences on the board; have the class, individually or as a group, rewrite the sentences, correcting all the subject-verb agreement errors they find.

Practice Books:

Grade 6	pages 94-100
Grade 7	pages 98-105
Grade 8	pages 98-105

Mini-Lessons:

Grade 6 Mini-Lesson 171
Grade 7 Mini-Lesson 188
Grade 8 Mini-Lesson 186

Chapter ⑱ Using Adjectives and Adverbs

(Handbook Pages 356-359)

Some of your students may find themselves confused by certain aspects of adjective and adverb usage. The *Heath Communication Handbook* divides the likely difficulties into two main categories:

- **Comparisons.** Point out that even regular comparisons can raise questions about when to use *-er* and *-est,* as opposed to *more* and *most.* These questions usually stem from the number of syllables in a particular adjective or adverb; longer modifiers tend to use *more* and *most.* Irregular and negative irregular comparisons, by contrast, require a major change in form: e.g., *good-better-best; little-less-least.*

- **Double troubles.** Point out that double comparisons *(more better)* and double negatives *(don't expect no favors)* are always considered incorrect.

The issue of *good* versus *well,* like pronoun problems with *who* and *whom,* is long-standing and tricky, partly because of many speakers' use of good as an adverb, and partly because the word *well* can function correctly as either an adverb or an adjective.

TEACHING TIP

Certain usage choices that are frowned on in language arts classes are quite common in ordinary conversation and on television. Have your students spend a few days collecting examples of usage errors (not necessarily restricted to adjectives and adverbs) that they hear on the school bus, on television, or anywhere else in their daily life. This activity can lead to a discussion of the importance of usage. Since many celebrities, even many rock stars, seem to pay little attention to standard usage, and yet have multimillion-dollar incomes, students may need some reassurance that at least in the everyday world of school and work, usage *does* matter.

Practice Books:

Grade 6	pages 101-106
Grade 7	pages 106-110
Grade 8	pages 106-110

Mini-Lessons:

Grade 6	Mini-Lesson	172
Grade 7	Mini-Lesson	189
Grade 8	Mini-Lesson	187

Chapter ⑲ Glossary of Usage

(Handbook Pages 360-365)

Your students may be surprised to hear that book-length glossaries of usage sell briskly in bookstores and by mail. Many people in business and the professions need advice on English usage, and since the days of Samuel Johnson's classic *A Dictionary of the English Language (1755)*, many dictionaries have included usage notes or usage labels. The best-known book on usage is probably H. W. Fowler's *A Dictionary of Modern English Usage (1926)*, the latest edition of which is still in print. Many other usage guides can be found today in the reference sections of libraries and bookstores.

Practice Books:

Grade 6	pages 107-109
Grade 7	pages 111-112
Grade 8	pages 111-112

TEACHING TIP

The *Heath Communication Handbook*'s Glossary of Usage is primarily a reference for your students to consult as they work on the projects in Units I and II. The Glossary is designed to answer specific usage questions clearly and concisely. If you wish to use the Glossary for teaching purposes, consider taking this approach: Assign between five and ten usage items at a time. Give a quiz on those items after students have had a week or so to go over them. As you assign later groups of Glossary items, you may want to make one or more of your quizzes cumulative. That way, earlier items will not be forgotten or ignored as time passes.

Chapter ⑳ Punctuation

(Handbook Pages 366-380)

Your students may view this chapter as simply a list of standard rules. There is some truth to that, although in fact the rules of punctuation vary somewhat from one resource to another. The style sheet of a newspaper, for example, differs from that of a university press. This *Heath Communication Handbook* offers advice for middle school students on the use of

- end marks (periods, question marks, exclamation points)
- commas (which have just two main uses: to set off and to enclose)
- semicolons (common in academic writing, little used elsewhere)
- colons (to introduce lists, with a few other specialized uses)
- quotation marks (for direct quotations, dialogue, and certain titles)
- hyphens (to divide a word at the end of a line)
- apostrophes (for possessives, contractions, and some plurals)
- parentheses and dashes (interrupters with somewhat similar uses)

Encourage your students to refer to this chapter whenever they have questions about punctuation.

TEACHING TIP

In evaluating students' writing, you may want to check the use of one or more marks of punctuation for each project. If so, add punctuation to the three or four items on the "Characteristics of . . ." list in the *Teacher's Planning Guide*. Here is a possible way to match projects with punctuation marks.

- Chapter 3: Personal Narrative — End Marks
- Chapter 4: Descriptive Essay — Commas
- Chapter 5: Short Story — Quotation Marks, Apostrophes
- Chapter 6: Expository Essay — End Marks, Commas
- Chapter 7: Editorial — Hyphens, Apostrophes, Dashes, Parentheses
- Chapter 8: Book Review — Commas, Quotation Marks
- Chapter 9: Research Paper — All Marks of Punctuation

Practice Books:

Grade 6	pages 110-129
Grade 7	pages 113-131
Grade 9	pages 113-131

Mini-Lessons:

Grade 6 Mini-Lessons 173-177
Grade 7 Mini-Lessons 190-193
Grade 8 Mini-Lessons 188-191

Chapter **21** Capitalization

(Handbook Pages 381-387)

This chapter explains the basic rules of capitalization. These rules are fairly easy for most students to master. Applying the rules, however, can be perplexing. What do you say when a student asks, "Is it french fries or French fries?" "Is it the Westin Hotel or the Westin hotel?" "Is it Bayer aspirin or Bayer Aspirin?" Sometimes, as with French fries, a dictionary may help. But the correct capitalization of certain trade names may be hard to determine, even when you know the basic rules. One place students should not look for answers is in printed advertisements. Advertising copywriters employ capital letters mostly for visual effect. These difficulties aside, this chapter covers most of the specifics of capitalization that your students will need in working on their projects.

TEACHING TIP

An occasional classroom discussion of capitalization—one that is brief and focused—can be more helpful than random written exercises. A good way to handle capitalization instruction is to keep a list of mistakes from students' compositions and discuss the ones that come up most frequently. You may want to limit each of these discussions to a look at three or four errors so as not to overload your students with rules. Be very clear in explaining what the error is. Tell why it is an error, show how it should be corrected, and indicate how serious you consider it to be.

Practice Books:

Grade 6	pages 130-135
Grade 7	pages 132-137
Grade 8	pages 132-137

Mini-Lessons:

Grade 6 Mini-Lesson 178
Grade 7 Mini-Lesson 194

Chapter 22 Italics, Numbers, and Abbreviations

(Handbook Pages 388-391)

This chapter, like the previous two, provides a quick reference for your students on specific matters of mechanics. Some of the rules in the chapter apply mainly to particular kinds of writing. The use of italics for titles, for example, is fairly frequent in research papers and book reviews but less common in other kinds of writing. Your students will use abbreviations only occasionally in their writing projects, even though their use is widespread in everyday life and business.

- *Italics.* Not long ago, students always used underlining to indicate italics. Now, with computer printers, they may be able to print italics.

- *Numbers.* You may want to tell students that, as a general rule, they will spell out all numbers under one hundred and write those above one hundred as numerals.

- *Abbreviations.* Perhaps the most prevalent problem with abbreviations concerns whether or not to include periods. The Postal Service wants no periods in state abbreviations: *NY, CA.* Government agencies also want no periods in abbreviations: *CIA, NASA.* Many company abbreviations use no periods: *GE, IBM.* Advise your students to check the dictionary for the correct form of nonbusiness abbreviations.

TEACHING TIP

As you review your students' writing, notice the kinds of problems they have with italics, numbers, and abbreviations. Keep a list of the errors you find. In class, write several of the incorrect examples on the board. Ask students to identify the mistakes and tell how they should be corrected. In this activity, and others like it, encourage students to refer to the Language Resources section of the *Heath Communication Handbook* for help.

Practice Books:

Grade 6	pages 136-139
Grade 7	pages 138-141
Grade 8	pages 138-141

UNIT IV Additional Resources

Chapter 23 Technology

(Handbook Pages 394-404)

The use you make of this chapter will depend to some extent on the electronic hardware and software your school has available. The information in the chapter is valuable to students even if your school lacks certain equipment. Ideally, though, you will be able to show and demonstrate (or have had demonstrated by the librarian or computer specialist) several methods of communication that use modern technology. Your school may have some of the following items:

Hardware
- Computers
- CD-ROM drives (on computers)
- On-line catalogs (library)
- FAX machines

Software
- Word processor(s)
- Desktop publishing
- On-line databases
- Other programs
  - on hard disks
  - on CD-ROM disks
  - on 3.5-inch disks
  - on 5.25-inch floppies

You will want to familiarize yourself with any new electronic equipment, programs, and services that become available to your school.

Practice Books:

Grade 6	page 140
Grade 7	page 142
Grade 8	page 142

Mini-Lessons:

Grade 6 Mini-Lesson 147
Grade 7 Mini-Lesson 163
Grade 8 Mini-Lesson 160

TEACHING TIP

Since word processing and desktop publishing have such a direct connection to writing, you will want your students to be aware of what equipment and programs are available for their use. Invite the school or district's computer specialist to give a demonstration to your classes, showing students how to make use of the available hardware and software. Encourage students to submit their writing projects in the most professional form possible, whether multifont laser printing, old-fashioned typewriting, or neat, legible handwriting. If students use a dot-matrix printer at home, ask them to be sure the ribbon isn't so worn that the printing is too light to be readable.

Chapter ㉔ Spelling

(Handbook Pages 405-417)

You may be using a published spelling program as part of the language arts curriculum. If so, the material in this chapter will serve mainly as a handy reference guide for your students. It presents in a concise form the main spelling rules, lists one hundred frequently misspelled words, and suggests strategies that students can use to improve their spelling. Here are two ways for students to check their spelling:

- *Dictionaries.* Encourage students to use the dictionary to check the spelling of any words of which they are unsure. Misspellings should be minimal after a paper has been revised, edited, and proofread.
- *Computer spelling-checkers.* These software programs are very popular with shaky spellers. However, they are not infallible. Mention to students that (among other errors) the computer program will *not* spot mistakes with homonyms, words that are pronounced the same but spelled differently—for example, *there, their, they're.* The computer's problem is that it has no idea what the words mean. It knows that all three are possible spellings and therefore accepts any one of them as correct.

TEACHING TIP

Have students keep cumulative lists of their own misspellings that you or peer evaluators point out on their writing projects. Ask students to pair off from time to time and test each other on their lists of misspellings up to that point.

Practice Books:

Grade 6	pages 141-149
Grade 7	pages 143-150
Grade 8	pages 143-150

Mini-Lessons:

Grade 6 Mini-Lessons 127-132
Grade 7 Mini-Lessons 142-147
Grade 8 Mini-Lessons 143-148

Chapter ㉕ Vocabulary

(Handbook Pages 418-427)

Wide and perceptive reading is undoubtedly the best way for students to improve their vocabularies. Even television viewing can be an excellent vocabulary builder, but only if the programs students watch feature speakers with wide-ranging vocabularies. In other words, MTV won't help them much, but PBS may. Some direct study of the vocabulary of English may also help. This chapter deals with

- word parts (roots, prefixes, suffixes)
- word origins (words from other languages, words from names)
- synonyms, antonyms, and homonyms
- denotation and connotation
- context clues (definitions, examples, comparison/contrast, tone)
- multiple meanings

The chapter also suggests several strategies and concludes with a number of activities for vocabulary building.

TEACHING TIP

One way to foster vocabulary building is to identify each day a fairly difficult but commonly used word from the news. Ask students to find a word in their daily newspaper that is unfamiliar to them. Have them bring the newspaper clipping to class, with the unfamiliar word underlined or highlighted. Ask a few students to read their articles in class, pointing out the unfamiliar word. Post one or more of the clippings on the bulletin board. Encourage students to use the highlighted words in an ongoing way. Periodically, you can give a brief quiz to see if students can define the words that have appeared on the bulletin board.

Practice Books:

Grade 6	pages 150-162
Grade 7	pages 151-161
Grade 8	pages 151-161

Mini-Lessons:

Grade 6 Mini-Lessons 1-11
Grade 7 Mini-Lessons 1-11
Grade 8 Mini-Lessons 1-12

Chapter 26 Letter Writing

(Handbook Pages 428-434)

Both personal and business matters are increasingly discussed on the telephone, by E-mail, through teleconferencing, on videocassette recordings, via electronic bulletin boards, and by other technological means. Nevertheless, letter writing remains an important skill to master. The introduction of the FAX machine may even have increased its importance. This chapter deals with the form and content of personal and business letters, including punctuation, capitalization, and the addressing of envelopes. You may want to point out some of the clear advantages of letter writing over electronic communications.

- *Low cost.* Even with rising postal rates, the cost of a first-class letter is very low compared to that of a long-distance phone call, which most electronic devices, such as FAX machines and computer modems, require.
- *Revision.* As the *Handbook* notes, you can edit a letter to get it just right. You can't do that with many forms of electronic communication.
- *Permanent record.* You have probably heard people protest, "Oh, no, I never said that." If they had said it on the telephone, there would probably be no way to settle the controversy one way or the other. If they had said it in a letter, however, the words would exist in black and white and could be verified.

Practice Books:

Grade 6   pages 163-164
Grade 7   pages 162-163
Grade 8   pages 162-163

Mini-Lessons:

Grade 6 Mini-Lessons 110-112
Grade 7 Mini-Lessons 125-127
Grade 8 Mini-Lessons 126-128

TEACHING TIP

Some local newspapers provide a forum for students' letters to the editor. This forum can be a powerful teaching tool, if your local paper provides, or can be persuaded to provide, editorial-page space for the views of students. In a daily paper, one day a week may be set aside for students. In a weekly paper, the editor may allow space for one student letter among the adult letters. In either case, the letters should be brief. Not only do letters to the editor require practice in the letter-writing process, they also demand carefully thought-out, persuasive prose of the kind explained in Chapter 7 of the *Heath Communication Handbook,* "Communicating to Give Your Opinion."

Chapter 27 Test, Study, and Research Skills

(Handbook Pages 435-454)

Studying and test taking are important skills for your students to master. More than ever before, success in school is measured by standardized tests, and you will want your students to be as well prepared for them as possible. This chapter presents some test-taking strategies and then looks at the two basic kinds of tests.

- *Objective tests.* These tests come in various forms. Multiple choice, fill in the blanks, and analogies are three of the most familiar kinds. Among the standardized tests your students will encounter are reading comprehension tests, which usually follow a multiple-choice format.

- *Essay tests.* The long-standing criticism of objective tests—that they are too cut-and-dried and encourage guessing—has led to a greater use of essay tests. Although essay tests are harder to score and the scorer's judgment is inevitably more subjective, essay tests do require students to organize and express their thoughts rather than just mark an answer sheet.

The chapter also covers note taking, memorizing, outlining, citing sources, and using the library.

TEACHING TIP

Mention to your students that outlining is both a useful research skill and a good way to study. To demonstrate its value as a study method, have students outline this chapter (Chapter 27), using the outline form shown on page 447. Tell them that while this format will be helpful to them in outlining, it will not furnish all the headings and subheadings they need for a detailed outline—nor will the format of their outline be the same as the *Handbook's*. When your students have finished the outlines, go over them in class, writing a final, agreed-upon version on the chalkboard.

Practice Books:

Grade 6   pages 165-177
Grade 7   pages 164-177
Grade 8   pages 164-177

Mini-Lessons:

Grade 6 Mini-Lessons 134-158
Grade 7 Mini-Lessons 149-174
Grade 8 Mini-Lessons 150-171

Chapter 28 Critical Thinking Skills

(Handbook Pages 455-464)

The arrival of the Information Age has brought a growing awareness of the importance of critical thinking. The jobs of tomorrow, for which your students are preparing today, will demand more flexibility and versatility than many jobs required in the past. To be flexible and versatile, your students will have to be able to think for themselves–thus, the new emphasis on critical thinking. The *Heath Communication Handbook* offers advice on the following aspects of critical thinking:

- observing cause and effect
- ordering information
  (by time, by location, by importance)
- drawing conclusions
- making generalizations
- evaluating information
- understanding point of view
- distinguishing between fact and opinion
- recognizing stereotypes
- determining an author's purpose
- classifying
- comparing and contrasting

TEACHING TIP

Conduct an informal debate on a topic of interest to your students. Choose a topic on which they are divided *pro* and *con* fairly evenly. You may want to have the students on each side of the debate sit on opposite sides of the room. You may moderate the debate yourself, unless you have a student who you believe can do a forceful yet impartial job. As the debate progresses, have a small committee, perhaps three students, take notes on the kinds of critical thinking being used. (It will help if you put the bulleted list on the left on the board for their reference.) After the debate, discuss not "winners" and "losers" but, rather, the nature of the arguments that were advanced. Limit the discussion to three or four specific kinds of critical thinking.

Point out to your students that they engage in these activities on an everyday basis, whether they realize it or not. To take a single example, they make generalizations all the time. The purpose of this chapter is to encourage them to make *better, more thoughtful* generalizations–and, on a broader scale, to get them to engage actively and consciously in all facets of critical thinking.

Practice Books:

Grade 6	pages 182-186
Grade 7	pages 182-186
Grade 8	pages 182-186

Mini-Lessons:

Grade 6 Mini-Lessons 12-29
Grade 7 Mini-Lessons 12-29
Grade 8 Mini-Lessons 13-30

UNIT V Evaluation and Assessment

As you know, evaluating and assessing your students' work is a highly individual process, one that you constantly fine-tune to meet different student needs. Your students want to know where they stand, and yet each responds differently to being evaluated. You may know some students who regard a critical comment as a challenge that spurs them on to better work. You may know others who resent any kind of criticism whatsoever. Then there is the difficult question of when to apply standards and what kinds of standards to apply. Sometimes using criteria that are too strict and not open-ended enough during the early stages of a work-in-progress blocks a student's flow of ideas. During the early stages of a paper or project, you may find that encouraging comments and concrete advice seem to work best; after students have finished their work, you can apply understandable, consistent criteria to evaluate the final product.

Students need to feel that they have met clear and worthwhile goals in their schoolwork. Your evaluations should provide usable helps and easily understood guidelines that will enable your students to set and achieve these goals.

The Assessment Process

Your evaluation of the work done by your students, the assessment process, should be both formative and summative:

Type	Formats	Purposes
Formative evaluations	Comments, questions, and concrete suggestions that guide students during the early or middle stages of a work-in-progress.	To encourage creative activity; to help focus ideas; to clarify goals.
Summative evaluations	Comments applying specific standards to a finished or nearly finished work. These standards, or **rubrics**, should be discussed with students early in the work process.	To give students an idea of how successful their work has been; to help students revise the work at hand and to improve future work.

Tips on Assessing Students' Work

The following tips will help you deal with three specific assessment modes: student-teacher conferences, written teacher evaluations, and peer conferences. You should use these tips in conjunction with the other self-evaluation activities and peer-group activities suggested throughout this *Handbook.*

TEACHER'S WRITTEN ASSESSMENTS

Evaluation Mode	Purposes	Strategies
Written assessment of final (or nearly final) products	To assess work holistically, applying mutually understood rubrics (standards) regarding content and form.	Use class discussions and conferences to make sure that the student understands and accepts the assessment rubrics. Use consistent rubrics to assess student work. Make sure the student regards the product as finished or nearly finished. Make holistic comments at the end of a paper or on a form that you use consistently. (See sample on the next page.)
	To comment specifically about details of content, language, grammar, usage, and mechanics.	Make specific comments in margins of papers. In the case of frequently recurring grammatical or mechanical errors, correct a few examples and refer to the recurrent problem at the end of your holistic comments.

SAMPLE TEACHER EVALUATION FORM (FINISHED PRODUCT)

Student:

Date:

Work Title:

Holistic Comments:

• Topic and ideas (validity, originality, relevance, audience interest)

• Focus (sense of purpose, specificity, adequacy of coverage, clarity)

• Organization (effectiveness, appropriateness to topic, consistency, coherence, unity)

• Style and tone (appropriateness to purpose, audience appeal, fluidity of sentence structure, liveliness, and appropriateness of word choice)

Additional Comments (if applicable):

• Grammar and usage (areas showing improvement; areas needing work)

• Spelling (areas showing improvement; areas needing work)

• Punctuation and capitalization (areas showing improvement; areas needing work)

Overall Evaluation/Assessment:

STUDENT-TEACHER CONFERENCES

Evaluation Mode	Purposes	Strategies
Student-teacher conferences	To maintain ongoing assessment of student work.	Meet regularly with each student (15 minutes a month). In addition, schedule special conferences in response to student requests or your perception of student needs.
	To offer guidance and encouragement for works-in-progress.	Use a standard form to document each session, recording ideas and problems discussed. (See sample below.)
	To help students set their own goals and sharpen their critical faculties.	

SAMPLE FORM FOR STUDENT-TEACHER CONFERENCES

Student:

Teacher:

Date of Conference:

1. Work(s) discussed:

2. Strong areas or areas showing improvement:

3. Areas needing attention:

4. Goals:

PEER CONFERENCES

Evaluation Mode	Purposes	Strategies
Peer conferences	To provide feedback students value because it comes from other students and so seems "reality based." To focus on works-in-progress or on finished work.	Consider using both small-group and partner peer conferences. Small-group conferences consist of three to six students meeting regularly. Each meeting should focus on the work of a single student, who is present during the conferences. Student comments should be constructive, focused on helping the author improve his or her work. Consider creating small groups to focus on specific issues. One group might specialize in sentence structure and grammar, another in organization. Such groups should include students who excel in the specialty. All students in the group should be familiar with the work to be evaluated. Group members may take turns commenting on the work. The author of the work should have opportunities to respond to comments. Partner peer conferences should occur between two students with comparable but not identical abilities that complement each other. Encourage students to lead with their strengths in such conferences. Students can deliver their peer evaluations orally; they can also mark up photocopies of a paper under discussion or record their comments on evaluation forms. (See sample on the next page.)

SAMPLE PEER EVALUATION FORM

Student:

Evaluator:

Date:

Work Title:

Holistic Comments:

• Ideas (Are the ideas original? Valid? Do they appeal to you as an audience? Why or why not?)

• Focus (Is the writer's purpose clear? Is the work focused enough, or is the writer trying to do too much?)

• Organization (What kind of organization has the writer used? Do you think this choice was the best one for this topic, purpose, and audience? Why or why not? Does the writer follow the organization plan consistently throughout the work?)

• Style and tone (Does the writer's style appeal to you as an audience? Does the style suit the apparent purpose of the work? Do the sentences flow or seem choppy? Has the writer chosen interesting, appropriate words?)

Additional Comments (if applicable):

• Grammar and Usage:

• Spelling:

• Punctuation and Capitalization:

Dealing with the Paper Load

You will probably be coordinating several different forms of assessment: your conferences with students, your written evaluations of their final products, small-group peer conferences, and partner peer conferences. You and your students may be reviewing work at various stages of completion; each type of review may also involve its own documentation or evaluation form. You'll need some well-planned methods for time management and record keeping.

Tips for Handling the Paper Load

- *Skim student papers.* When conferring with students during early stages of the writing process, you may be able to skim their papers, reading enough to get a sense of their ideas, focus, and organization.
- *Focus on a single element.* You may make assignments with a particular rubric in mind, such as organization, sense of audience, or sentence structure. During early stages of the writing process, your comments can focus on the targeted area.
- *Ask students to follow certain conventions in preparing papers.* Make sure that students use a word processor, type, or write their papers legibly, that they double-space their work, and that they leave ample room in the margins for comments.
- *Focus your attention where it's needed.* As the term progresses, you will become aware of each student's special strengths and weaknesses. In evaluating the work of students with recurrent problems, you should help the students focus on these problems without losing sight of their strengths. You may need to make more frequent evaluations of the work of these students. On the other hand, you may need less frequent evaluations of the work of students who do well on their own. Challenge such students to work independently and set new goals for themselves.
- *Allow students to share responsibility for evaluation and assessment.* Use peer conferencing, both small groups and partner conferences, to extend your own evaluations of each student's work. In addition, encourage your students to keep their own written records of their progress, using journal entries, self-evaluation forms, lists of areas for improvement, and portfolios saving progressive drafts of each project.

Writing Folder Assessment

Ask your students to keep a writing folder for the papers that you return to them. Encourage them to review the folder in preparation for their monthly conferences with you. Reviewing the writing folder will give you both specific reference points when you discuss the perceived strengths and weaknesses in your students' writing. The review will also help to clear up any questions or confusions the students may have. At certain points in the school year, plan to assess each student's work as a body. The following procedure will help you assess students' writing folders:

1. Announce a few weeks ahead of time when you will collect the writing folders. Continue to remind students as the review date approaches.

2. Tell students that they may choose a certain number (for example, eight) pieces of writing to be evaluated as a body.

3. Invite students to revise previously completed assignments, according to your comments and those of their peers. (They should include the original version on which you commented, in addition to the revision.)

4. In evaluating a student's writing folder, focus particularly on the progress you have seen over the course of several months.

5. Help the student identify what he or she did to make that progress (for example, spending more time prewriting, or allowing for one extra draft of each paper).

6. Point out one or two areas for further improvement, but keep the focus and tone of the discussion as positive as possible.

Performance Assessment

Performance assessment refers to the evaluation of a student's finished work according to certain widely accepted rubrics, or standards against which achievement is measured. In developing these standards for your own students, you may want to draw on the rubrics used by your school or district, or those used by other school systems throughout the country. Following is a sample list of rubrics for communications papers and projects.

SAMPLE RUBRICS FOR COMMUNICATIONS PAPERS/PROJECTS

CRITERIA   **RATING 1-5 (5 = HIGHEST)**

Content

1. Treats an appropriate, interesting topic. _____
2. Focuses the topic sufficiently for satisfactory coverage. _____
3. Presents a clear and valid thesis, or central idea about the topic. _____
4. Has a well-defined, achievable purpose. _____
5. Exhibits a clear sense of audience. _____
6. Includes sufficient material to support the thesis. _____
7. States all ideas clearly and develops them satisfactorily. _____
8. Includes only material appropriate to the topic, purpose, and audience. _____

Form

1. Begins with an introduction that presents the topic and thesis effectively. _____
2. Contains a body that is organized in a logical, effective manner. _____
3. Ends with a satisfying, appropriate conclusion. _____
4. For projects: Is made up of parts all of which build logically upon one another. _____
   For papers only: Contains well-developed paragraphs that build logically upon each other. _____
5. Includes transitions to improve coherence. _____
6. Includes sentences with varied structures. _____
7. Uses lively, precise, audience-appropriate language. _____
8. Follows an appropriate physical format and includes any expected conventions. _____

Grammar, Usage, and Mechanics (for papers only)

1. Uses correct grammar throughout. _____
2. Contains no usage errors. _____
3. Contains no errors in spelling or capitalization. _____
4. Uses correct punctuation throughout. _____

Overall Evaluation:

Literary Terms and Techniques

(Handbook Pages 465-477)

The teaching of literary terms is typically a part of the reading/literature component of the language arts curriculum. You will find most of the terms in this chapter defined and exemplified in the *Heath Middle Level Literature* series and its ancillaries, including copymasters and transparencies. What this final section in the *Heath Communication Handbook* provides is a brief, handy reference to the literary terms and their definitions. Your students will explore these terms and techniques in literature for a long time–throughout their middle years, into their high school years, and well beyond, if they go to college.

TEACHING TIP

Most likely you will decide to focus on these terms only when they come up in the writing, speaking, or visual communication projects. Chapter 5, "Communicating to Tell a Story," is one place where several of these terms are introduced. You may find yourself referring to certain terms, such as cliché, metaphor, and tone, with almost any kind of project. But since middle-school literature programs contain a wealth of activities involving these terms, you will probably wish to concentrate on them there.

Mini-Lessons:

Grade 6 Mini-Lessons 30-65
Grade 7 Mini-Lessons 30-72
Grade 8 Mini-Lessons 31-73

HEATH

COMMUNICATION

*HAND*BOOK

AUTHORS

Donna Alvermann
Linda Miller Cleary
Kenneth Donelson
James Fliakas
Donald Gallo
Alice Haskins
J. Howard Johnston
John Lounsbury
Alleen Pace Nilsen
Robert Pavlik
Jewell Parker Rhodes
Alberto Alvaro Ríos
Sandra Schurr
Lyndon Searfoss
Julia Thomason
Max Thompson
Carl Zon

D. C. Heath and Company
Lexington, Massachusetts / Toronto, Ontario

EDITORIAL

Susan Belt Cogley, DeVona Dors, Christopher Johnson, JoAnne B. Sgroi, Owen Shows, Rita M. Sullivan, Patricia B. Weiler

DESIGN

Format: Ronn Campisi

Book: Daniel Derdula, Robin Herr, Michele Locatelli, Martha Podren, David Rieffel, Angela Sciaraffa, Bonnie Chayes Yousefian

PHOTO RESEARCH

Martha Friedman, Carmen Johnson, Gillian Speeth

PRODUCTION

Patrick Connolly

Cover: Lois Schlowsky Computer Imagery
Cover Design: Angela Sciaraffa

Published simultaneously in Canada
Printed in the United States of America
International Standard Book Number: 0-669-38184-5
  2 3 4 5 6 7 8 9 10-VHP-99 98 97 96 95

MIDDLE LEVEL AUTHORS

Donna Alvermann, University of Georgia
Alice Haskins, Howard County Public Schools, Maryland
J. Howard Johnston, University of South Florida
John Lounsbury, Georgia College
Sandra Schurr, University of South Florida
Julia Thomason, Appalachian State University
Max Thompson, Appalachian State University
Carl Zon, California Assessment Collaborative

LITERATURE AND LANGUAGE ARTS AUTHORS

Linda Miller Cleary, University of Minnesota
Kenneth Donelson, Arizona State University
James Fliakas, Montgomery County Public Schools, Maryland
Donald Gallo, Central Connecticut State University
Alleen Pace Nilsen, Arizona State University
Robert Pavlik, Cardinal Stritch College, Milwaukee
Jewell Parker Rhodes, Arizona State University
Alberto Alvaro Ríos, Arizona State University
Lyndon Searfoss, Arizona State University

TEACHER CONSULTANTS

Suzanne Aubin, Patapsco Middle School, Ellicott City, Maryland
Lorraine Gerhart, Elmbrook Middle School, Elm Grove, Wisconsin
Marilyn Jurgenson, Crocker Middle School, Hillsborough, California
Lucretia Pannozzo, John Jay Middle School, Katonah, New York
Carol Schultz, Jerling Junior High, Orland Park, Illinois
Tom Tufts, Conniston Middle School, West Palm Beach, Florida

Contents

INTRODUCTION 1

Unit I   You as a Communicator   6

Chapter 1 You as a Writer 8

The Writing Process   9
    Prewriting   10
    Drafting   16
    Revising   20
    Editing   21
    Publishing   25

Chapter 2 You as a Speaker and Visual Communicator....26

You as a Speaker   27
    Getting Started   27
    Practicing and Revising   29
    Delivering   30
You as a Visual Communicator   31
    Predesigning   32
    Designing   34
    Revising and Getting Feedback   36
    Displaying   37
    Looking Back   37

Unit II   Communication Strategies and Projects   38

Chapter 3 Communicating About Yourself—
Communicating About Others 40

3.1 Writing Project:
    Writing a Personal Narrative   42
Prewriting   44
Drafting   49
    Applying Usage to Writing:
    Point of View   50
Revising   53
    Applying Technique to Writing:
    Transitions   54
Editing   55
    Applying Mechanics to Writing:
    Punctuating Introductory Phrases   56
Publishing   56
Evaluation Activity   57

3.2 Speaking Project:
    Writing and Performing Reader's Theater   58
Getting Started   61
Drafting Your Script   63
Rehearsing and Revising Your Script   64
    Applying Usage to Script Writing:
    Using Present Tense   64

Delivery 66
Performing Your Play 66
Evaluation Activity 67

3.3 Visual Project:
Creating a Self-Portrait or a Collage 68
Self-Portrait and Collage Ideas 70
Drafting Your Work 71
Revising Your Work 72
Exhibiting Your Work 72
Evaluation Activity 72

Chapter 4 Communicating to Describe........................ 74

4.1 Writing Project:
Describing a Community Place 76
Prewriting 78
Drafting 83
Revising 84
Applying Language to Writing:
Using Figurative Language 85
Editing 87
Applying Usage to Writing:
Maintaining Verb Tense 88
Publishing 89
Evaluation Activity 89

4.2 Speaking Project:
Writing and Giving a Descriptive Speech 90
Getting Started 92
Drafting Your Speech 93
Revising and Editing Your Speech 94
Practicing and Delivering Your Speech 94
Evaluating Your Performance 95

4.3 Visual Project:
Creating a Photo Essay of a Community Place 96
Pre-Viewing 98
Drafting, Revising, and Editing a Photo Essay 98

Presenting Your Photo Essay 100
Evaluation Activity 101

Chapter 5 Communicating to Tell a Story.................. 102

5.1 Writing Project:
Writing a Short Story 104
Prewriting 107
Drafting Your Story 110
Revising 114
Applying Usage to Writing:
Getting Rid of Clichés 115
Editing 115
Applying Mechanics to Writing:
Writing and Punctuating Dialogue 116
Publishing 116
Evaluation Activity 116

5.2 Speaking Project:
Making Up a Tall Tale 118
Getting Started 120
Drafting Your Tall Tale 121
Rehearsing and Revising Your Tall Tale 122
Editing 123
Delivering Your Tall Tale 123
What Did You Think? 125

5.3 Visual Project:
Developing a Storyboard 126
Pre-Viewing 130
Drafting Your Storyboard Panels 131
Revising Your Storyboard Panels 132
Applying Spelling to Storyboard Captions:
Spelling 133
Displaying Your Storyboard 133
Self-Evaluation 133

Chapter 6 Communicating to Explain 134

6.1 Writing Project:
Writing an Expository Essay ... 136
Prewriting ... 138
Drafting ... 144
Revising ... 145
Applying Language Resources to Writing:
Concluding Sentences ... 147
Editing ... 147
Applying Mechanics to Writing:
Avoiding Run-On Sentences ... 148
Publishing ... 148
Evaluation Activity ... 149

6.2 Speaking Project:
Giving a Demonstration Speech ... 150
Getting Started ... 152
Drafting and Practicing Your Speech ... 153
Applying Usage to Writing a Speech:
Colloquialism Versus Formal Diction ... 157
Revising Your Speech ... 157
Applying Grammar to Speech Writing:
Sentence Combining ... 158
Editing Your Speech ... 158
Delivering Your Speech ... 158
Evaluation Activity ... 159

6.3 Visual Project:
Creating an Explanatory Chart ... 160
Pre-Viewing Your Chart ... 162
Drafting and Designing Your Own Chart ... 164
Revising Your Chart ... 165
Editing Your Chart ... 166
Displaying Your Chart ... 167
Evaluation Activity ... 167

Chapter 7 Communicating to Give Your Opinion 168

7.1 Writing Project:
Writing an Editorial ... 170
Prewriting ... 172
Drafting ... 177
Revising ... 181
Applying Grammar to Writing:
Varying Your Sentence Structure ... 183
Editing ... 183
Applying Usage to Writing:
Making Good Transitions ... 184
Publishing ... 184
Evaluation Activity ... 185

7.2 Speaking Project:
Presenting a Persuasive Speech ... 186
Getting Started ... 188
Drafting Your Speech ... 192
Revising and Practicing Your Speech ... 194
Editing Your Speech ... 195
Applying Usage to Writing:
Pronoun Antecedents ... 196
Delivering Your Speech ... 197
Evaluation Activity ... 197

7.3 Visual Project:
Creating a Public Service Poster ... 198
Pre-Viewing Your Poster ... 200
Drafting and Designing Your Poster ... 202
Revising Your Poster ... 203
Editing Your Poster ... 204
Applying Spelling to Writing on a Poster:
Spelling Clues ... 204
Displaying Your Poster ... 205
Evaluation Activity ... 205

Chapter 8 Communicating to Evaluate 206

8.1 Writing Project:
Writing a Book Review   208
Prewriting   210
Drafting   218
Revising   222
Applying Usage to Writing:
Comparing with Adjectives   223
Editing   223
Applying Usage to Writing:
The Present Tense   223
Publishing   224
Evaluation Activity   225

8.2 Speaking Project:
Giving a Spoken Movie Review   226
Getting Started   228
Drafting and Practicing Your Spoken Review   233
Applying Usage to Speech Writing:
Slang   235
Revising Your Spoken Review   235
Applying Grammar to Speech Writing:
Prepositions   236
Editing Your Spoken Review   237
Delivering Your Spoken Review   237
Evaluation Activity   239

8.3 Visual Project:
Creating a Book Jacket   240
First Things First   242
Fashioning Your Book Jacket   245
Revising Your Book Jacket   246
Editing Your Book Jacket   246
Applying Spelling to Writing:
Spelling Strategies   246
Displaying Your Book Jacket   247
Evaluation Activity   247

Chapter 9 Communicating to Report 248

9.1 Writing Project:
Writing a Research Paper   250
Prewriting   252
Drafting   262
Revising   264
Applying Mechanics to Writing:
Using Quotation Marks Correctly   265
Editing   266
Applying Mechanics to Writing:
Using Capitalization Correctly   267
Publishing   268
Evaluation Activity   269

9.2 Speaking Project:
Giving a News Report   270
Gathering Information   272
Drafting   274
Revising, Rehearsing, and Editing   275
Delivering Your News Report   277
Evaluation Activity   277

9.3 Visual Project:
Preparing a Videotape   278
Planning a Videotape   280
Drafting and Filming   282
Revising/Editing   284
Presenting Your Videotape   285
Evaluation Activity   285

Unit III Language Resources 286

BUILDING BLOCKS OF WRITING

Chapter 10 Paragraphs 288

10.1 Types of Paragraphs 288
    10.1A Persuasive Paragraphs 288
    10.1B Descriptive Paragraphs 289
    10.1C Narrative Paragraphs 290
    10.1D Expository Paragraphs 291
10.2 Parts of Paragraphs 291
    10.2A Writing Topic Sentences 291
    10.2B Writing Supporting Sentences 292
    10.2C Writing Transitional Sentences 292
    10.2D Writing Concluding Sentences 293

Chapter 11 Writing Style 294

11.1 Style 294
    11.1A Clichés 294
    11.1B Mixed Metaphors 295
    11.1C Redundancy 295
    11.1D Point of View 296
11.2 Diction 297
11.3 Tone 297
    11.3A Word Choice 298
    11.3B Formality and Informality 298

GRAMMAR

Chapter 12 Parts of Speech 299

12.1 Nouns 299
    12.1A Proper and Common Nouns 299
    12.1B Concrete and Abstract Nouns 300
    12.1C Compound and Collective Nouns 300
12.2 Pronouns 301
    12.2A Personal Pronouns 302
    12.2B Reflexive Pronouns 302
    12.2C Possessive Pronouns 302
    12.2D Demonstrative Pronouns 303
    12.2E Indefinite Pronouns 303
    12.2F Interrogative Pronouns 304
12.3 Verbs 304
    12.3A Action Verbs 304
    12.3B Linking Verbs 305
    12.3C Verb Phrases 306
    12.3D Transitive and Intransitive Verbs 306
12.4 Adjectives 307
    12.4A Articles 308
    12.4B Position of Adjectives 308
    12.4C Nouns as Adjectives 308
    12.4D Proper Adjectives 309
12.5 Adverbs 309
    12.5A Interrogative Adverbs 310
    12.5B Negative Adverbs 310
12.6 Prepositions 311
    12.6A Compound Prepositions 311
    12.6B Adverbs or Prepositions 311
12.7 Conjunctions 312
    12.7A Coordinating Conjunctions 312
    12.7B Correlative Conjunctions 312
    12.7C Subordinating Conjunctions 313
12.8 Interjections 313

Chapter 13 Phrases and Clauses 314

13.1 Phrases 314
    13.1A Prepositional Phrases 314
    13.1B Verbals and Verbal Phrases 315
13.2 Clauses 319
    13.2A Subordinate Clauses 319
    13.2B Independent Clauses 319
    13.2C Adjective Clauses 320
    13.2D Relative Pronouns 320
    13.2E Adverb Clauses 321

13.2F Subordinating Conjunctions   321
13.2G Noun Clauses   321

Chapter 14 Sentences 322

14.1 Parts of a Sentence   322
   14.1A Subjects and Predicates   322
   14.1B Direct Objects and Indirect Objects   326
   14.1C Predicate Nominatives and Predicate
      Adjectives   327
14.2 Types of Sentences   328
   14.2A Simple Sentences   328
   14.2B Compound Sentences   328
   14.2C Complex Sentences   329
   14.2D Compound-Complex Sentences   329
14.3 Sentence Purposes   329
   14.3A Declarative Sentences   330
   14.3B Imperative Sentences   330
   14.3C Interrogative Sentences   330
   14.3D Exclamatory Sentences   330
14.4 Complete Sentences   331
   14.4A Fragments   331
   14.4B Run-On Sentences   332
14.5 Effective Sentences   332
   14.5A Coordination and Subordination   333
   14.5B Parallelism   334
   14.5C Sentence Variety   335
   14.5D Sentence Combining   336
   14.5E Length and Complexity of Sentences   336

USAGE

Chapter 15 Using Verbs 337

15.1 Parts of Verbs   337
   15.1A Regular Verbs   337
   15.1B Irregular Verbs   338

   15.1C Problem Verbs   339
15.2 Verb Tense   340
   15.2A Six Tenses   340
   15.2B Conjugation   341
   15.2C Avoiding Shifts in Tense   343
15.3 Active and Passive Voice   344

Chapter 16 Using Pronouns 345

16.1 Case   345
   16.1A Nominative Case   346
   16.1B Objective Case   347
   16.1C Possessive Case   348
   16.1D Problem Pronouns   348
16.2 Pronouns and Antecedents   349
   16.2A Number and Gender   349
   16.2B Indefinite Pronouns as Antecedents   350

Chapter 17 Subject-Verb Agreement 352

17.1 Singular and Plural   352
   17.1A You as Subject   352
   17.1B Verb Phrases   352
17.2 Common Agreement Problems   353
   17.2A Interrupting Words   353
   17.2B Inverted Order   353
   17.2C Compound Subjects   354
   17.2D Indefinite Pronouns   355
   17.2E Doesn't and Don't   355

Chapter 18 Using Adjectives and Adverbs 356

18.1 Comparison of Adjectives and Adverbs   356
   18.1A Regular Comparisons   357
   18.1B Irregular Comparisons   358
   18.1C Negative Comparisons   358
18.2 Problems with Modifiers   358
   18.2A Double Comparisons   358
   18.2B Double Negatives   359
   18.2C Good and Well   359

Chapter 19 Glossary of Usage 360

MECHANICS

Chapter 20 Punctuation 366

20.1 End Marks   366
   20.1A Periods   366
   20.1B Question Marks   366
   20.1C Exclamation Points   367
20.2 Commas   367
   20.2A Items in a Series   367
   20.2B Compound Sentences   368
   20.2C Separation of Adjectives   368
   20.2D Introductory Elements   368
   20.2E Interrupters   369
   20.2F Direct Address   369
   20.2G Appositives   370
   20.2H Nonessential Elements   371
   20.2I Dates   371
   20.2J Addresses   371
   20.2K Letters   372
20.3 Semicolons   372
   20.3A Compound Sentences   373
20.4 Colons   373
   20.4A Lists of Items   373
   20.4B Letters   374
   20.4C Time   374
20.5 Quotation Marks   374
   20.5A Direct Quotations   374
   20.5B Titles   375
20.6 Hyphens   375
   20.6A Word Division   376
   20.6B Compound Words   376
   20.6C Numbers and Fractions   376
   20.6D Prefixes and Suffixes   377
20.7 Apostrophes   377
   20.7A Possessive Forms of Nouns   377

20.7B Possessive Forms of Pronouns   378
20.7C Contractions   379
20.7D Special Plurals   379
20.8 Parentheses and Dashes   380
   20.8A Parentheses   380
   20.8B Dashes   380

Chapter 21 Capitalization 381

21.1 First Words and the Word I   381
   21.1A First Word of Sentence   381
   21.1B First Word of Direct Quotation 381
   21.1C The Word I   382
21.2 Proper Nouns   382
   21.2A Names   382
   21.2B Titles of People   386
21.3 Proper Adjectives   387

Chapter 22 Italics, Numbers, and Abbreviations ...388

22.1 Italics (Underlining)   388
   22.1A Words, Numbers, and Letters   388
   22.1B Titles   389
22.2 Numbers   389
   22.2A Numerals   389
   22.2B Ordinal Numbers   390
22.3 Abbreviations   390
   22.3A Use of Periods in Abbreviations 390
   22.3B Abbreviation of Some Titles   390
   22.3C Abbreviations for Time of Day
       and Year   391
   22.3D Abbreviations Without Periods   391

Unit IV Additional Resources 392

Chapter 23 Technology.................................394

23.1 **Using the Computer to Write**   394
    23.1A The Word on Word Processing   395
    23.1B Do-It-Yourself Desktop Publishing   396
23.2 **Storing and Getting Information**   397
    23.2A From Floppies to CD/ROMs   397
    23.2B The Basics of Databases   398
23.3 **Research the Modern Way**   400
    23.3A Technology in the Library   400
    23.3B On-Line Catalogs   401
23.4 **Using Technology to Communicate**   401
    23.4A The Facts About Fax   402
    23.4B Networking   402
    23.4C Technology for the Disabled   403
23.5 **The Scoop on Software**   403
23.6 **Do It Yourself: Technology Activities**   404

Chapter 24 Spelling 405

24.1 **Spelling Rules**   405
    24.1A Words with ie and ei   405
    24.1B Adding Prefixes   406
    24.1C Adding Suffixes   406
    24.1D Plurals of Nouns   407
    24.1E Spelling Homophones   409
24.2 **One Hundred Most Frequently Misspelled Words**   411
24.3 **Strategies to Improve Spelling Skills**   411
24.4 **Spelling and the Writing Process**   413
24.5 **Using Technology**   413
24.6 **Do It Yourself: Spelling Activities**   414

Chapter 25 Vocabulary.............................418

25.1 **Word Parts**   418
    25.1A Roots   418
    25.1B Prefixes   419
    25.1C Suffixes   419
25.2 **Word Origins**   420
    25.2A Words from Other Languages   420
    25.2B Words from Names of People and Places   421
25.3 **Synonyms, Antonyms, and Homonyms**   421
25.4 **Denotation and Connotation**   423
25.5 **Context Clues**   423
    25.5A Definitions   423
    25.5B Examples   424
    25.5C Comparison and Contrast   424
    25.5D General Idea or Tone   424
25.6 **Multiple Meanings**   424
25.7 **Strategies to Increase Vocabulary**   425
25.8 **Do It Yourself: Vocabulary Activities**   425

Chapter 26 Letter Writing.........................428

26.1 **Personal Letters**   429
    26.1A Friendly Letters   429
    26.1B Social Letters   430
26.2 **Business Letters**   431
    26.2A Letters of Application   431
    26.2B Other Business Letters   433
26.3 **Mechanics**   434
26.4 **Envelopes**   434
26.5 **Do It Yourself: Letter-Writing Activities**   434

Chapter 27 Test, Study, and Research Skills.........435

27.1 **Test-Taking Skills and Strategies**   435
    27.1A Preparing for Tests   436
    27.1B Objective Tests   437

27.1C Essay Tests 441
27.2 Taking Notes 443
27.2A Paraphrasing and Summarizing 444
27.3 Memorizing 446
27.4 Outlining 446
27.5 Bibliographical Forms 448
27.6 Using the Library/Media Center 451
27.7 Do It Yourself: Study-Skills Activities 453

Chapter 28 Critical Thinking Skills 455

28.1 Observation 455
28.2 Determining Cause and Effect 455
28.3 Ordering Information 456
28.4 Drawing Conclusions 457
28.5 Making Inferences 458
28.6 Making Generalizations 458
28.7 Evaluating Information 459
28.8 Point of View 459
28.9 Distinguishing Between Fact and Opinion 460
28.10 Stereotyping 461
28.11 Classifying 461
28.12 Compare and Contrast 462
28.13 Purpose and Audience 462
28.14 Do It Yourself: Critical Thinking Activities 463

Literary Terms and Techniques 465

Index 479

Acknowledgments...497

WELCOME

to the *Heath Communication Handbook!*

What exactly is communication? If you think about it, you'll realize that you communicate all the time—when you wave to a friend, write a letter, draw a picture, talk to your friends at lunch, give a speech, or use technology to send messages. The *Heath Communication Handbook* is filled with hundreds of useful ideas for making you a better communicator.

Unit I looks at the process of communicating. It contains all the steps you need to write, speak, and create visual products.

Unit II gives you the opportunity to learn and practice communication skills for seven different purposes. For each purpose, you can choose a written project, a speaking project, or a visual project.

Unit III contains language resources—the tools you need for writing effective sentences and paragraphs, using proper grammar, and understanding punctuation and capitalization.

Unit IV contains additional resources that will help you improve your spelling and vocabulary—and even support you as you master the art of communicating with technology.

The *Heath Communication Handbook* is also an easy-to-use reference tool. Look up what you need to know, choose a project, get familiar with each unit. Communicate!

What Kind of a Communicator Are You?

"We try to tell the story with light, and the director tells it with action.

William Daniels, Academy-Award-winning cinematographer

"Our teacher encourages us to write letters to the editor of the *Star-Ledger*. It was quite a thrill to have my letter on the dangers of smoking published—and to know it would be seen by nearly half a million people."

Debbie Lopez, seventh-grade student

"I especially enjoy creating visual images in my writing. It helps people get a better understanding of my complicated problems when I can paint them a picture of the situation."

Mary Sue Terry, Attorney General, State of Virginia

"I have to understand questions about electrical needs and be able to suggest the right kind of solution to my customers. They have to know what they're getting and how it will work."

Charles Minard, electrical contractor

"People express their ideas in different ways. I'm not a great writer or speaker. I communicate best through drawings, woodcuts, paintings—visual images."

Jeanine Di Nola, professional artist

"Maybe I'm a born politician. I like to run for class offices and make speeches. I think speaking is more fun than writing."

Britt McKeon, sixth-grade student

"I have to call on customers, write sales reports, and keep in touch with the home office. Sometimes I have to speak before groups. I use a slide projector or flip charts in my presentations. A sales rep that couldn't get her ideas across would be like a trout that couldn't swim."

Antonia Raebiger, sales representative

"As a black writer, I want to talk about my people. . . . The books come. They pour from me at a great rate. I can't see how any writer can ever stop. There is always one more story to tell, one more person whose life needs to be held up to the sun."

Walter Dean Myers, author of books for young adults

As you can see, people communicate in many different ways. Some prefer speech. They feel at home in conversation, on the telephone, in front of a group, on the stage. Others like to write. They express themselves best on paper—in notes, letters, stories, reports. Still others favor the visual or performing arts. They put their ideas most effectively into drawings, paintings, photographs, sculpture, music, or dance.

These different ways of presenting ideas suggest that people's minds work differently. Your style of thinking may not be the same as your friend's. Maybe you learn easily from reading and studying textbooks, while your friend learns more quickly from lectures or group discussions. Others in your class may prefer to learn through pictures or symbols, hands-on demonstrations or experiments, research or apprenticeships.

KEEPING A JOURNAL

Many of the people whose comments are on pages 2 and 3 keep journals. Although a journal is similar to a diary, it's not exactly the same. A diary is a daily record of thoughts and experiences. A journal is a source book of ideas for communicating. Keeping a journal will really help you to improve the ways you communicate. Use your journal to record striking phrases or sentences, brief anecdotes, and clever dialogue, and to save photographs or sketches that fascinate you. Use it to store anything you come across that might be useful to you later in writing, speaking, or creating a visual product.

Use your journal to help you discover what kind of a communicator *you* are. In your journal, respond to one or more of the following quizzes.

The *What's Your Favorite Flavor?* Quiz

- If I could be any flavor, I would be _____ because _____ .
- Where would you look to find five of your favorite flavors?
- Draw pictures of five foods with flavors you like. Label each picture.
- In a few sentences, describe a flavor without naming it.
- List five flavors you like and create a sound or song for each one.

 Write a short dialogue between you and a friend, beginning with the question, "Tell me, [name of friend], what is your favorite flavor?"

 In a few sentences, suggest a plan to identify an unknown flavor.

The *What Would You Like To Do?* Quiz

List in your journal the five activities from the following list that you would most like to do.

- Work on a jigsaw puzzle
- Interview the mayor
- Produce a slide show
- Tell a joke
- Decorate a room
- Conduct an experiment
- Read a book or short story
- Sing in a choir
- Write a poem
- Draw a map
- Design a coat
- Break a code
- Direct a play
- Play a video game

The *What's-Your-Style?* Quiz

 If you could choose any person—living or dead, famous or not—to learn more about, what person would you choose?

 What are three sources you might use to learn about the life of that person?

 In presenting the information you learned to your class, would you rather write a composition? Give a talk? Prepare a slide or video show?

JOURNAL WRITING

What do your answers to the quizzes on these pages tell you about yourself? What are you already good at? What would you like to be better at?

Unit I

You as a Communicator

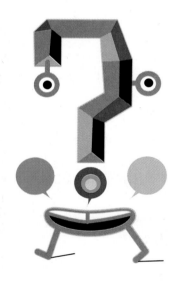

You're already a communicator. You have to be. Making yourself understood is a part of everyday life. You talk with friends and send them notes. You write stories for language arts, answer essay questions for social studies, prepare lab reports for science, and give speeches during school campaigns. You act in plays, draw pictures, take photographs, and create models and sculptures. You communicate with others not only in the classroom but in all areas of your life.

CONTENTS

CHAPTER 1 You as a Writer 8
CHAPTER 2 You as a Speaker and Visual Communicator 26

You as a Writer

Many people think that good writers are just born that way. That may be true of *great* writers such as Maya Angelou, Amy Tan, or William Shakespeare, but it's not true of *all* writers. In fact, *everyone* can learn to write. Why? Because learning to write is a process, like learning to ride a bicycle or learning to drive a car. These processes involve stages, or steps. Just learn the steps—and then take one step at a time.

THE WRITING PROCESS

Here are the stages of the writing process. These five stages aren't a magic formula, but they are a helpful guide. Use them whenever you're writing.

Stages of Writing

- ◎ **Prewriting** Prewriting is what you do *before* you write. You prewrite to gather and organize ideas. Techniques that help you prewrite include brainstorming, clustering, narrowing, and outlining.
- ◎ **Drafting** A draft is a sloppy copy. It's the first time that you write down what you've decided to say. If your ideas change as you draft, that's fine. Just go back to the drawing boards and do some more prewriting. A first draft *always* needs work, but it's a start.
- ◎ **Revising** When you revise, you look at your work *again*, get ideas *again*, and draft *again.*
- ◎ **Editing** Think of editing as polishing or fine tuning. When you edit, you correct errors in grammar, usage, mechanics, and spelling.
- ◎ **Publishing** Publishing means showing your work to the world—sharing your writing with other people.

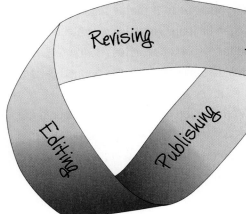

DO IT YOURSELF!

Which techniques work best for you? The only way to find out is to try one or two. But be selective. If your purpose for writing is to describe a memorable day in your life, the library is probably not the place to go. As you explore techniques, write about your experiences in your journal. Writing about writing is a great way to increase your skill.

PREWRITING

Picture this. You're in a class. It's the end of the period. Assignment time. You take out your notebook and listen. Your teacher speaks. She says, "For tonight's homework, I'd like you to write a one-page essay on a topic of your choice." Your heart sinks. Your palms grow sweaty. Questions whirl in your head—"What does she mean? What will I write about?" You pause for a moment and fear grips you as your inner voice screams, "BUT I HAVE NOTHING TO SAY."

Sound familiar? Well, take heart. Help is on the way. You really *do* have something to say. In fact, you probably have a lot to say most of the time. The trick is to discover what you will say for this particular assignment. Here's what you can do to make that discovery.

Finding Your Subject

"All right," you say. "I'm ready. How do I find my subject?" Actually there are many different techniques. Which ones work for you? The only way to find out is to experiment. So put aside your critical eye and open the doors to your imagination.

Ways to Find a Subject

- **Freewrite** Do you hate that blank sheet of paper in front of you? Then fill it up. Write down whatever comes into your head for five or ten minutes (no longer). If you hear a voice inside that says, "I'm not doing this right," put a muzzle on it.

- **Brainstorm** Perhaps you have a sheet of paper in front of you, but it's not totally blank. You've already written the glimmer of an idea or subject on it. Well, don't stop! Write everything you know, want to know, or can think of about that subject. Don't judge or evaluate what you write. Just write!

◎ **Cluster** This technique is similar to brainstorming, but the outcome is a diagram. A cluster looks very much like a spider web, with a central idea written in a circle in the middle. (In fact, clusters are sometimes called webs.) For both clusters and webs, write a subject in the middle of a blank sheet of paper and circle it. Then, around it, write down related ideas as they occur to you. Next, circle each related idea and connect it to the idea that made you think of it. Soon you'll have a page full of ideas—and probably one of them is a good subject.

◎ **Journal Writing** Try using a journal to capture ideas for writing. If you have an interesting conversation with a friend, write it down in your journal. Did something happen at the mall that upset you? Tell about it in your journal. How about the breakfast you ate this morning? Not very tasty or nourishing? Describe it in your journal. If you write in your journal on a regular basis, you'll soon have a rich source of ideas and subjects.

DO IT YOURSELF!

Find out what works for you. Try one or all of the techniques on this page. Work with a partner, if you like. When you've finished, see what you have. If you're keeping a journal, write about your experiences.

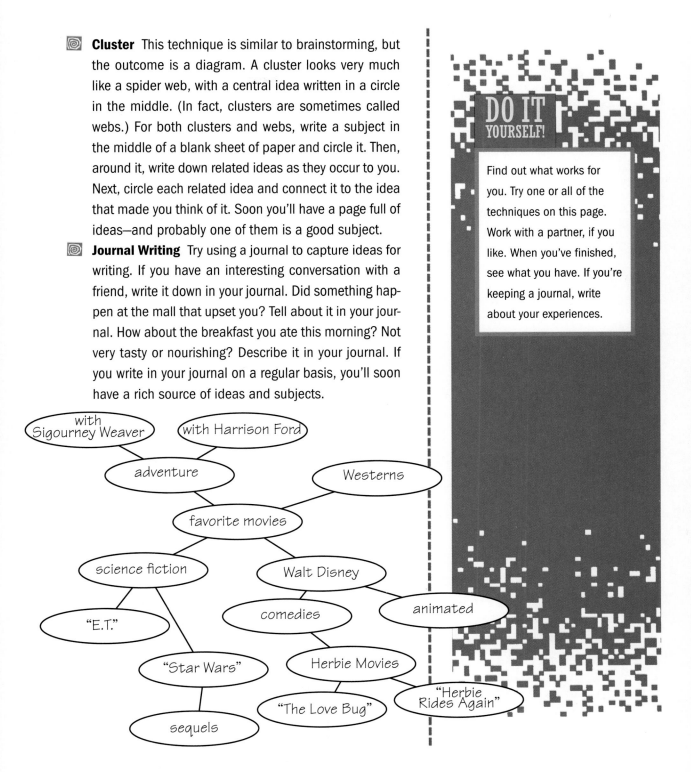

Writing for Your Reader

As you prewrite, keep in mind your audience—the person or people for whom you're writing. Is your audience a friend? A teacher? An adult? A child? Picture your audience in your mind as you plan. What do they know? What do they need to know? How will they respond if your tone is serious? Sarcastic? Informal?

Narrowing Your Subject

You can't write effectively about a general idea such as world history. But you can write effectively about a famous world leader, a specific time period, or a particular country. To get from a broad subject to a specific one, you have to do a bit more thinking and brainstorming. Here's how.

Think of a subject that interests you. Write it at the top of a blank sheet of paper. Then think of ideas that are related to it. For example, if you choose Baseball, you might quickly write *Houston Astros, perfect games, Nolan Ryan, Texas League, great hitters.* When you've written at least ten ideas related to baseball, choose one of them and limit it further. For example, under Nolan Ryan, you might write *Ryan's final game* or *the time when Corsicana beat Texarkana, 51-3.*

If you need more help, arrange your topics and subtopics in the form of an upside-down pyramid like the one shown. It really helps to see your big topics at the top and your smaller topics at the bottom.

Houston Astros

Nolan Ryan

Ryan's final game

Developing Your Subject

Ideas are the bedrock of communication, and—as with bedrock—you can build on them. In fact, you *must* build on them. The most disappointing examples of writing are those that start with good ideas—and go nowhere. Instead of giving vivid, precise details, the writer makes vague statements and repeats the same points over and over. Eventually, the bedrock turns to mush. Don't let this happen to you. Try some of these techniques to keep your bedrock solid.

Ideas for Developing Your Subject

- Take stock. Find out what you already know about your subject. Freewrite, brainstorm, cluster, or list. Circle ideas that you're not sure of. Cross off ideas that don't belong. Add topics that you need to explore.

- Stop, look, and listen. The world around you is a great source of information. Browse through bookstores. Listen to newscasts on television and on the radio. Do some people-watching at a mall or in school. If you've been keeping a journal, open it now. Who knows what delicious ideas and observations you'll find there! Finally, don't forget to talk to friends, relatives, and teachers about your topic. Find out what they know.

- Information, please. Collect information you need at the library. Use the library computer or the card catalog to search for books related to your topic. Skim through newspapers and magazines. Or use a computerized magazine index or the *Readers' Guide to Periodical Literature* to locate specific articles.

- Write it down. As you gather ideas and information, use note cards to record facts, examples, and quotations. There's nothing like a relevant fact, an interesting example, or a notable quotation to keep your writing focused.

NEED MORE HELP?

See Chapters 23.2 and 27.6 for tips on using the library. Also see Chapter 27.3 for tips on paraphrasing and summarizing.

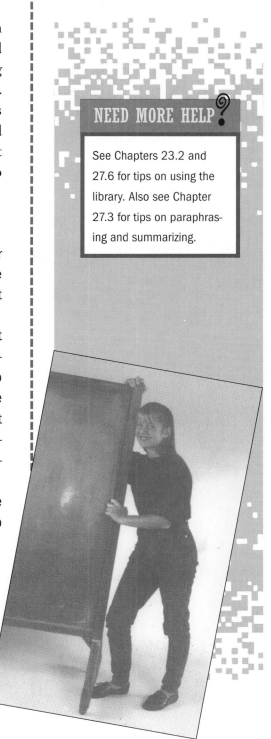

On June 28, 1914, an event took place in the Austro-Hungarian town of Sarajevo that triggered the start of World War I. (fact)

When World War I began in 1914, one British leader said to a friend, "The lamps are going out in Europe. We shall not see them again in our life-time." (quotation)

World War I was unlike any other in history. Before the war, most people believed that only men could handle certain jobs. During the war, however, people were forced to change their views as they watched women tackle jobs that were once considered men's work. (example)

Organizing Your Ideas

Before you write, you need a plan of action—a way to organize your incredible ideas, excellent examples, and fascinating facts. Here are a few tips to help you organize and plan.

Planning Ideas

- Say it up front. What's your purpose for writing? To describe your best friend? To explain how World War I began? To tell the story of your life? Who will be reading your writing? A teacher? Your classmates? A parent? Your friend? No one? Everyone? Try completing the following purpose statement before you write:
In this piece of writing, I'm going to write about (subject) in order to (purpose) for (audience).

- Sort and search. Before you write, select your main points and the details that support them. Gather your lists, clusters, and notes. Spread them out on a table. Choose your best ideas. (Remember your purpose statement.) Cross out ideas that don't belong. Add new ideas. If necessary, do some more research. If your topic shifts, change your purpose statement.

Choose an arrangement. How many times have you arranged and rearranged the items in your room, your desk, your locker, your life? Finding a good arrangement is also important in writing. Here are some ideas.

- **Order of Importance** If you're writing a persuasive letter or research report, you might choose to begin with your most convincing arguments or most important information. Or you might do the opposite—start with your least important ideas and use your best information to make a big splash at the end. Use phrases such as *most important* and *least important* as clues for your reader.

- **Chronological Order** Time order, or chronological order, is simply the order in which events occur. If you're writing a story, you can start at the beginning and cover the events straight through to the end. If you're writing a how-to-do-it piece, you can start with the first step and proceed in order to the end. Words like *first, next,* and *last* give your reader important time-order tips.

- **Spatial Order** If you're writing a description, you can arrange your details by location in space with the help of such expressions as *down, between,* or *next to.*

Outline your plan. An outline is an organized list of what you plan to write. It's also a guide that will keep you on track as you write. Remember your purpose statement? Write it at the top of your outline. Then list your main topics with Roman numerals, your subtopics with capital letters, and your details with numbers. Don't expect perfection the first time. You'll have a chance to fine-tune your outline as you draft and revise. See the example of an outline on the next page.

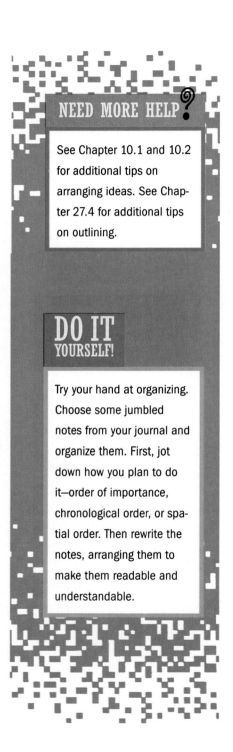

NEED MORE HELP

See Chapter 10.1 and 10.2 for additional tips on arranging ideas. See Chapter 27.4 for additional tips on outlining.

DO IT YOURSELF!

Try your hand at organizing. Choose some jumbled notes from your journal and organize them. First, jot down how you plan to do it—order of importance, chronological order, or spatial order. Then rewrite the notes, arranging them to make them readable and understandable.

How to Play Soccer

I. Kicking skills
   A. Methods of kicking
   B. Kicking for power
   C. Kicking for control
II. How to trap
   A. Purpose of trapping
      1. Wedging the ball
      2. Stopping the ball
   B. Skills needed
III. Techniques of heading
   A. Definition
   B. Two purposes of heading
      1. Passing
      2. Scoring
IV. Tackling in soccer
   A. Running or sliding to kick ball away
   B. Charging shoulder to shoulder

- **Draw your plan.** If you're a picture person, you might find that drawing a diagram or making a chart is a more useful way to do your plan.

DRAFTING

By the time you start drafting, you'll probably have a pretty good plan for writing. That's great, but when the time comes to write, you may find yourself wondering how to begin. Is there a tested and approved way to get going? Not really. The best approach may depend on your purpose for writing *and* what works for you, the writer. Here are some ideas to get you going.

Getting Started

- **Use your notes.** Gather your notes from prewriting. Use your clusters, brainstorming lists, purpose statement, and outlines as guides to get started.

◎ Go with the flow. Write your first draft quickly. Don't pause. Keep going! Even if you have second thoughts about your subject, don't throw up your hands in despair. The subject is probably all right. What you need is more confidence, not a new subject.

◎ Write from the heart. Picture your audience and talk directly to him, her, or them. Use words that your audience will understand and appreciate. Don't forget your purpose. Are you writing to persuade? Then choose words that will convince your teacher, mother, or friend. If you're writing to describe, brainstorm for adjectives and adverbs.

◎ *What*, not *how*. As you draft, focus on what you're saying, not on how you're saying it. Don't worry about errors in grammar, usage, spelling, and punctuation. You can deal with those later. Your first task is to get your ideas on paper.

◎ Keep an open mind. Include new thoughts, phrases, and details as they occur to you. Your outline and other notes are writing guides, not rules.

◎ Think positively. As you write, tell yourself, "This is terrific. I'm doing a great job." Have fun, explore, be creative. Writing is a process of discovery.

◎ Start anywhere. Sooner or later, your writing will have three distinct parts—an introduction, a body, and a conclusion. But you can begin a draft anywhere. If a great concluding statement comes to mind, start there. If you know what you want to say in the middle, write it down. Organize your writing in blocks (especially on the computer). You can cut and paste or copy and move later on.

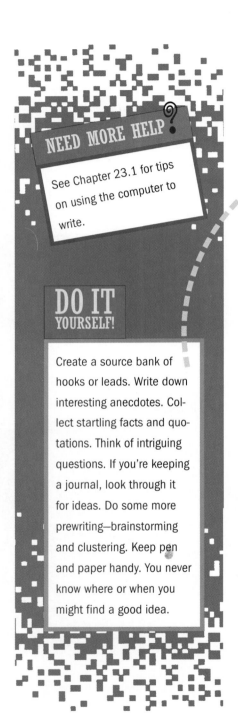

NEED MORE HELP?

See Chapter 23.1 for tips on using the computer to write.

DO IT YOURSELF!

Create a source bank of hooks or leads. Write down interesting anecdotes. Collect startling facts and quotations. Think of intriguing questions. If you're keeping a journal, look through it for ideas. Do some more prewriting—brainstorming and clustering. Keep pen and paper handy. You never know where or when you might find a good idea.

Ideas for Drafting Introductions

An old rule of writing says that an introduction tells readers what you're going to say. Sounds like sound advice—and it is. But you can tell them *and* entice them at the same time. For example, journalists pull in readers by writing interesting leads. Mystery writers hook their audiences with spooky starts. Here are several ways— followed by examples—to grab your audience's attention.

Attention Grabbers for Your Introduction

- **Startling Fact** *More Americans have died in automobile accidents than in all the American wars from the Revolutionary War to the Persian Gulf War.*

- **Quotation** *At the beginning of World War I, the kaiser of Germany told his troops, "You will be home before the leaves have fallen from the trees." He was wrong. The Great War lasted for four long years.*

- **Brief Anecdote** *Not all great athletes are well known. Take Eddie Feigner. You've probably never heard of him. He was a softball pitcher. Softball? That's right. Back in 1967, he pitched for a group of Hollywood celebrities in an exhibition game. He faced a lineup of baseball superstars that included Willie Mays, Willie McCovey, Brooks Robinson, Roberto Clemente, Maury Wills, and Harmon Killebrew. He struck them out—all six of them—in order.*

- **Questions** *Do you hate to clean your room? Have trouble organizing those piles? Wish you could push everything under a rug? Well, if you answered yes to these questions, don't despair. Help is on the way.*

Ideas for Drafting the Middle

Once your readers are hooked by your introduction, you have to keep them interested. To do that, you need to follow up your great beginning with a strong midsection—that is, the body of your writing. The body contains the ideas, facts, and details that develop your subject. Use the following suggestions to keep you on track.

Managing the Middle

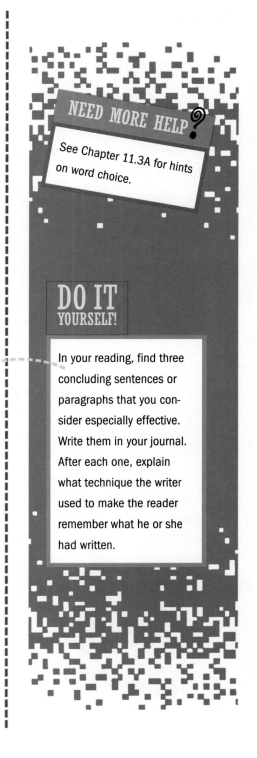

- Use your notes. Now is the time to retrieve your prewriting notes on developing your subject. Use these notes as a guide for drafting the body.
- Prewrite again. Don't hesitate to do some brainstorming or clustering. If you think of a new angle, include it in your draft. The main thing is to keep the flow going.
- Tap into your most expressive vocabulary words. Effective word choice is vital to effective communication. Use words that your audience will appreciate. Paint pictures that your audience can see. Create drama that your audience can feel.

Ideas for Conclusions

Tell them what you've said and then write THE END. Well, that's one way to conclude a piece of writing, but your reader probably won't like it very much. Try some of the following options for dynamic endings.

That's All, Folks

- Summarize. Summarize your main ideas—but don't repeat them word for word. Use phrases such as *in conclusion* to tell your reader that a summary will follow.
- Impress. Rather than summarizing what you've written, end with a single, powerful statement. You may want to make this statement the entire last paragraph.
- Echo. If you've written a strong opening, your readers will remember it. Reinforce your opening by repeating some part of it at the end.

NEED MORE HELP?

See Chapter 11.3A for hints on word choice.

DO IT YOURSELF!

In your reading, find three concluding sentences or paragraphs that you consider especially effective. Write them in your journal. After each one, explain what technique the writer used to make the reader remember what he or she had written.

-  Entertain. Short, entertaining stories are always appealing. If possible, use a brief anecdote that reinforces your main points.
- Quote. If you have a quotation that sums up your main points, use it (but don't forget to credit your source). Readers are often impressed by what someone else says, especially someone famous.
- Ask. Persuasion, in particular, can end with one or more questions. These questions don't require answers—they're thought-provoking ways of leaving a lasting impression.

REVISING

Revising is the *again* stage. You read again, write again, outline again, and arrange again. Every first draft needs to be improved or revised. The following strategies will help you.

Revising Strategies

- Wait a while. Let some time pass before you try to revise your draft. After a few days, you'll probably see many ways to improve what you've written. No one knows exactly why this time away from writing is so helpful, but it is.
- Find a fresh eye. Share your piece with a classmate, a parent, or a friend. Ask him or her to read your draft to you. As you listen, awkward passages may attack your ears. Sentence fragments may leave you hanging. Information that doesn't belong may make you jump.
- Reverse the process—with you as the reader and a friend or relative as the listener. What passages aren't clear to your friend? What sections don't make sense to your sister?

- Cut and paste. Review your outline and purpose statement. Use them as guides to move text. (A word processor is great for doing this!) Put your introduction first and your conclusion last. Check what you have in the middle. Is your information organized efficiently? Cut and paste some more. Get a smooth flow in place.

- Add copy. A first draft is sometimes too sketchy. It may need more specific details—more facts, more figures, more examples, more reasons, more illustration, more background, more explanation. When you revise, you must put yourself in the reader's shoes. What will he or she need in order to understand and be impressed by your writing?

- Stick to the point. Have you included details that don't belong? If so, get rid of them, no matter how interesting or amusing they seem.

- Connect copy. Getting smoothly from one idea to the next isn't always easy. To connect ideas, use transitional words and phrases. Keep your arrangement in mind.

- Check your style. Is your writing choppy? Dull? Do you need to add variety, zip, or precision? Sentence combining is one way to improve your writing style.

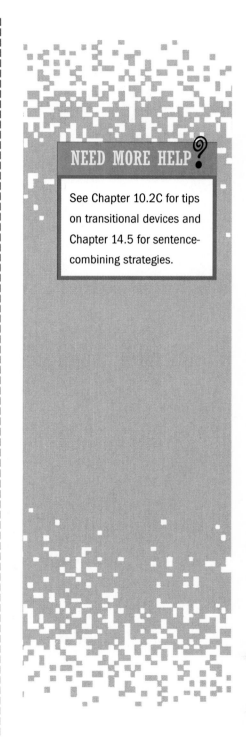

NEED MORE HELP?

See Chapter 10.2C for tips on transitional devices and Chapter 14.5 for sentence-combining strategies.

EDITING

Editing is the part you've all been waiting for. When you edit you *finally* get to look for and correct errors in punctuation, grammar, usage, and mechanics. Maybe you think the fun is over. But think again. Although editing may not be as creative and invigorating as prewriting and drafting, it can certainly be satisfying, especially if you're armed with a checklist and a plan.

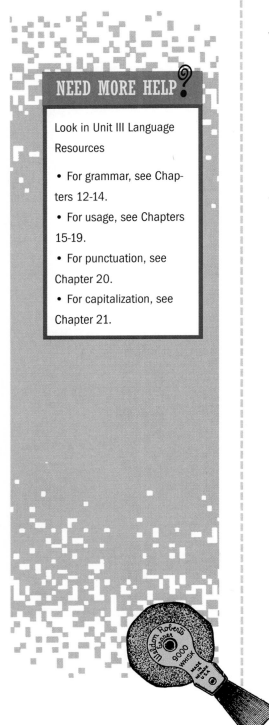

NEED MORE HELP?

Look in Unit III Language Resources

- For grammar, see Chapters 12-14.
- For usage, see Chapters 15-19.
- For punctuation, see Chapter 20.
- For capitalization, see Chapter 21.

Using Checklists

Jim Berg has a problem. He's been using a word processor since the fifth grade. He can type well, but for some reason he always types *fired* instead of *friend*. The spell check on his word processor is no help because *fired* is a correctly spelled word. It's just not the right word! When Jim edits, then, he pays special attention to that word. It's one of the entries on his oops! list—the personal mistake file that Jim keeps in a notebook. Like Jim, you too can create an oops! list in your notebook or your journal. Think about organizing items in your list in these categories.

Your Own Oops! List

- **Punctuation** Do you sometimes forget to use commas to set off items listed in a series? Put this problem under punctuation in your list.
- **Usage** Which is correct? "The boys and I ran home" or "The boys and me ran home"? If you don't know, put subject pronouns in your usage list.
- **Spelling** For your spelling oops! list, write down the words you frequently misspell.
- **Capitalization** Do you often forget to capitalize the name of a place? Do you sometimes forget to begin a sentence with a capital letter? Now's the time to put these in your capitalization list.
- **Grammar** Choose the correct word to fill in the blank. "An English teacher and a red pen (make, makes) a dangerous combination." If you're not sure which word is correct, put subject and verb agreement under grammar.

Making an Editing Plan

Now that you have a checklist, you need a plan. Try
this one.

Editing Plan

- Work with a classmate. It always helps to have another
  pair of eyes and ears checking your work.
- Do a quick read through, first silently and then aloud.
  What do you see that needs improvement? What do
  you hear that needs work? Mark your copy with notes
  and questions.
- Look for one type of error at a time. For example, read
  for spelling mistakes *only*. If you think a word is misspelled, look it up in a dictionary. Make the corrections
  immediately. Then go on to the next word in question.
  You'll feel a great sense of accomplishment when you
  cross spelling off your checklist.

Proofreading Techniques

Proofreading is the final
stage in prepar-
ing your written
work for publica-
tion. It's the final
check, the last
chance to catch mis-
takes. Interesting con-
tent can distract you
and keep you from
noticing mistakes. Use
the following techniques
to keep your mind on the
task at hand.

DO IT YOURSELF!

Choose a piece of writing from your journal or one that your teacher has asked you to edit. Using the proofreading techniques on this page, proofread your writing.

Proofreading Techniques

◎ Read the piece backwards. You'll be surprised at how errors pop out at you when you use this technique to go over what you've written. Read word by word, paying no attention to meaning.

◎ Cover the right half, then the left half. By using a piece of blank paper or cardboard to block out first one side of your paper, then the other, you'll read only for mistakes, not for content.

◎ Use a ruler. Go through your writing line by line, using a ruler to block out everything below the line you're reading. Concentrate only on that line. If you want, read each line backwards to avoid being distracted by content.

◎ Use the following proofreading marks as you edit your writing.

∧	insert	She'll give you a ^call^ later.
⌃	insert comma	Chet, Jan⌄ and I left for the day.
⊙	insert period	We stared at the speeding car⊙
℘	delete	Did you see ℘see℘ the eagle?
⁋	new paragraph	⁋ Another source of energy is oil.
....	let it stand	They'll always remember that exciting day!
⌗	add space	I'm studying for a science⌗test.
◡	close up	He's due back to⌒morrow.
∼	transpose	Simone rec∼ieved the news.
≡	capital letter	Her father's name is jos≡é.
/	lowercase letter	The Scouts helped with the /Cleanup.

Make a neat, final copy. Add a title or heading, put your name and date in a prominent place, and number your pages.

PUBLISHING

Whether you're writing a composition, preparing a speech, or working on a visual presentation, you'll want people to read, hear, or see the finished product. Publishing is the payoff. It's when an audience gets to experience the same excitement you felt in creating the work.

Any writing you produce using this book—a short story, a persuasive speech, a narrative essay—will have an assured audience of one—your teacher. But you may want a broader audience. Reaching an audience is important. You'll get increased satisfaction if several, dozens, or even hundreds of people read your work. Use one of the following ideas for going public.

Going Public

- Create a classroom or school magazine.
- Submit your work to a contest, magazine, or newspaper.
- Read your work aloud to friends, family, or others.
- Post your writing on the refrigerator at home.
- Make an audiotape of your work for friends, family members, or others.
- Make a poster that includes your writing.
- Use your writing to create a play.

DO IT YOURSELF!

Take something you've written and go public with it. Choose one of the ideas on this page or come up with your own publishing plan. Have fun as *you* the *writer* become *you* the *publisher*.

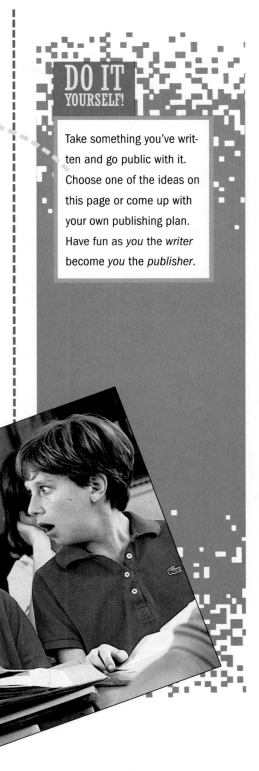

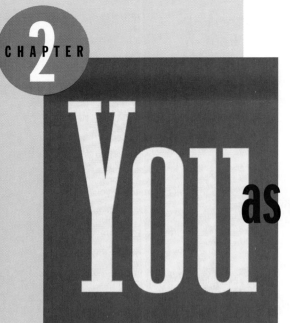

You as a Speaker and Visual Communicator

Terms to Know

Body language consists of the gestures and mannerisms that people use to communicate with one another.

You're being interviewed for a job. You describe your vacation to your friends. You tell a teacher exactly what happened when the science lab flooded. You explain how to change a tire. You express your opinion in a class discussion. You recommend a great movie. You deliver an oral report. These are all communications that are spoken and listened to rather than written and read. Such oral presentations might also include photographs, diagrams, charts, maps, demonstrations, even **body language**—these are visual elements that can make verbal communications clearer, more convincing, and more fun. In this chapter, you'll see how preparing oral and visual communications is like the writing process and how these modes offer unique opportunities and challenges.

YOU AS A SPEAKER

For most of us, speaking comes naturally. We ask questions, we express opinions, we argue, we chat, we laugh. The informal conversation that runs through our day is the most basic kind of oral communication. It is usually spontaneous. It usually involves other speakers.

But there's another kind of speaking. In an oral presentation, you're speaking to an audience to achieve a set purpose. You've prepared for this kind of speaking; you've rehearsed it; you've made many decisions about what you will say; you've made changes. In fact, an oral presentation will go through a process that is much like the writing process: getting started, organizing, practicing, improving, and delivering.

GETTING STARTED

An oral presentation is not just reading what you've written. If you settle for that, you'll miss important opportunities. For example, it's hard to laugh when you write. It's almost impossible to slow down, whisper, shout, move around, or take a long, dramatic pause.

Begin, as in writing, by choosing and narrowing a topic that interests you, using the prewriting suggestions on pages 10-16. As you do, consider what you can accomplish in an oral presentation that you can't in writing. For example, your facial expressions and body language will play large roles.

Define your audience and think about them as you plan your presentation. Most important, begin to define your main purpose. Is it to describe? To explain? To persuade? To inform? To evaluate? Finally, make sure that these elements—topic, audience, and purpose—work together and that an oral presentation is the best way to serve all three.

DO IT YOURSELF!

With a partner, think of a topic that would be suitable for a five- to ten-minute presentation. Look at the following ideas: television, children's toys, weather, musical instruments. Together, brainstorm what you might do in an oral presentation that you couldn't do in a piece of writing.

DO IT YOURSELF!

Imagine you've been asked to give a speech to your school's Student Council about the conditions in the cafeteria (or another commonly used area). With a partner, think of at least three catchy ways to grab your listeners' attention. Think of ways that wouldn't work if you were writing.

DO IT YOURSELF!

Imagine you're planning an oral presentation explaining a simple process: tying a shoe, making oatmeal, changing a tire, cleaning a fish tank. Make two note cards that will help you organize your ideas.

Getting Attention

Extra! Extra! Read all about it! Edison invents the light bulb! When folks heard newsboys shout the headlines of the day, they'd hurry to buy newspapers. Likewise, you can use your voice and a vivid detail to grab your listeners' attention. Use what you know about good beginnings, or hooks, in writing. Add your voice as an extra incentive. Maybe you want to whisper a scary descriptive detail, shout a shocking statistic, pose a serious question, or even—*Ha! Ha!*—tell a joke.

Planning and Organizing

Gather information for your oral presentation much as if you were prewriting. Choose a method of organization that suits your topic and purpose: order of importance, spatial order, or chronological order. Remember that theatrical elements—gestures, movements, volume, pacing, tone—can express meanings that written words cannot.

As you plan and organize, use note cards to write down your ideas. There's no need to write down every word you want to say—in fact, *Don't!* Make short notes, or cues, that will help you remember the order you want to use as well as key words. If you know a great deal about your subject, try to speak naturally with only a few notes. If you're presenting information that's new to you or full of facts and statistics, list the information on a card without writing it in complete sentences.

Note cards are handy for several reasons.

What's Good About Note Cards?

- You can easily rearrange their order.
- They're easy to hold while delivering your presentation.
- They fit in your pocket so you can practice while waiting for the bus!

Strong Endings

The last thing your audience hears will leave the most lasting impression, so save a gem for the end. Look at the suggestions for conclusions on pages 19-20 and think about how speaking offers different opportunities for a powerful last word. Ask for questions after you've paused for a few moments to let your ending sink in.

PRACTICING AND REVISING

Before you deliver a speech, you need to practice. And while you practice you'll probably find parts of your speech that need revising. Listen to yourself—on audiotape or videotape, if you can. You can also ask someone to listen to you and give suggestions.

Pace, Volume, and Tone

Pace refers to the speed at which you speak. Your pace can—and probably should—vary in different parts of your presentation.

What's Your Pace?

- **Fast** Forget fast pace when you're speaking to an audience. Never speak as quickly as you do in normal conversation. Your words will get lost.

- **Medium** Slow down and say each word distinctly. If you feel as if you're talking too slowly, you're probably speaking at just the right pace. Never rush. If you're pressed for time, cut. Don't ever speak quickly just to get it all in.

- **Slow** When you're climbing a difficult hill, you slow down. When you're presenting difficult or complicated information, slow down. Sometimes, it's good to repeat the most difficult sentences.

Like pace, volume can make or break your presentation. If your words can't be heard, what's the use? Just

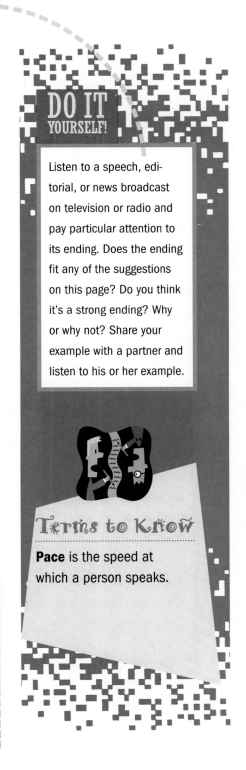

DO IT YOURSELF!

Listen to a speech, editorial, or news broadcast on television or radio and pay particular attention to its ending. Does the ending fit any of the suggestions on this page? Do you think it's a strong ending? Why or why not? Share your example with a partner and listen to his or her example.

Terms to Know

Pace is the speed at which a person speaks.

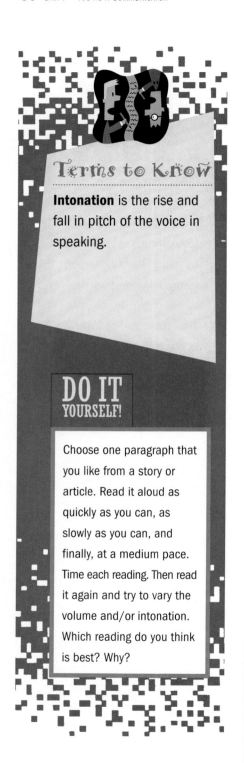

Terms to Know

Intonation is the rise and fall in pitch of the voice in speaking.

DO IT YOURSELF!

Choose one paragraph that you like from a story or article. Read it aloud as quickly as you can, as slowly as you can, and finally, at a medium pace. Time each reading. Then read it again and try to vary the volume and/or intonation. Which reading do you think is best? Why?

when you think you're speaking too loudly, you're probably just at the right volume. Speak as if you're talking to the person farthest from you, but make eye contact all around your audience.

Intonation refers to high or low pitch. In conversation, we change intonation to suit the mood or situation. Screams on the playground are high, but murmurs to a neighbor during class are low. As you practice your oral presentation, maintain a comfortable medium pitch unless you have good reason to vary it.

Practice, Improve, Practice, Improve

Whoever said, "Practice makes perfect," was certainly speaking of oral presentations. Practice as many times as you can. Practice in front of a long mirror or with a tape recorder or video recorder. Ask a friend or relative to listen at least once. Time yourself each time; once you've made final changes, try to keep your time consistent.

Practice over a period of several days. Your confidence will grow and your nervousness will decrease. As the final day approaches, try to practice at least once in the place where you will deliver your presentation.

If you can shorten your presentation without giving up essential information, *do it.* Your audience will appreciate your getting to the point, not repeating yourself, and not pausing too long between parts.

DELIVERING

OK. It's time. Wait until your audience is quiet and settled and take a deep breath before you begin. Speak loudly and slowly. Make eye contact. Smile. Keep going. Encourage your audience to hold their questions until you've finished.

Be mindful of your appearance. Wear comfortable clothes and shoes. Maintain a comfortable posture; use a podium or desk if it puts you at ease. Appear as natural and calm as you can. Remember that you're the expert on your topic, so speak with confidence!

Tips for Good Listeners

- Sit comfortably but stay alert.
- Try to concentrate on the speaker and what he or she is saying.
- Be as quiet and still as you can.
- Help the presenter by watching him or her at all times. Nod. Smile. Be encouraging and positive.
- Listen for key words. Write them down.
- If you are responsible for the information, take careful notes.
- Jot down questions as you think of them; ask them when the speaker is finished.
- Let the speaker know that he or she has done well. Applaud!

YOU AS A VISUAL COMMUNICATOR

Think of the number of **graphic images** you see every day in newspapers, magazines, and textbooks, on signs, posters, billboards, television and computer screens, and at the movies. They appear as photographs, charts, diagrams, paintings, drawings, maps, video displays. Let's face it—pictures are everywhere. And every one carries a meaning.

In addition to helping you become a better writer and speaker, this book offers you practice in visual communication. It includes

DO IT YOURSELF!

Choose a short poem that you like. Read it aloud; read it in front of a mirror; then read it for a friend. Time your readings. The next day, read it three times again—in front of a mirror, for a friend, and finally, to a tape recorder. Listen to your own voice. How did your reading and confidence change?

Terms to Know

Graphic images are the photos, pictures, charts, or diagrams that appear in written materials or in movies or TV.

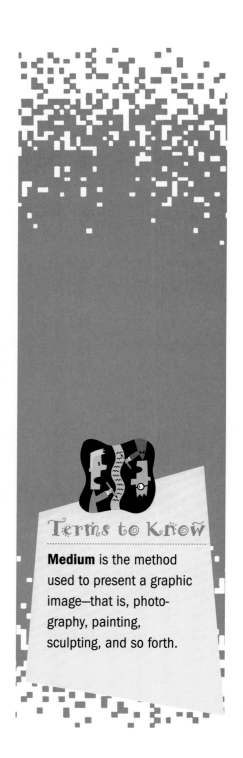

visual projects such as creating a storyboard, a photo essay, a public service poster and brochure, and a multimedia presentation. In these projects, you'll create graphic images—sometimes alone, sometimes in combination with words or text—that convey meaning. Some people say that a picture is worth a thousand words. Do you agree? You'll find out.

PREDESIGNING

Writing and speaking use words to convey meaning. In visual projects, you'll use graphic images—the process is called *graphic design*. In many ways, the designing process is like the writing process. First, you plan and make choices, gather information and brainstorm ideas. Then you begin to get images on paper (or screen). Next, you improve those images until you're satisfied. Finally, you share them with an audience.

You can use any or all of the prewriting techniques to get started on a visual design. Questions such as the ones that follow might help guide your thinking.

Starting a Visual Design

- What is the purpose of my design?
- Who will look at my design?
- Where will my design appear?
- How large will it be?
- How many colors can I use?
- Will my design include words or text? How many?

What Medium?

Medium in graphic design refers to the materials or methods used to create graphic images. For example, if you want to show a kitchen sink, you could paint a picture of one, photograph one, mold one out of clay, or import the image of a sink into a computer. Each of these methods–painting, photographing, sculpting, scanning–is a medium. Some people call the materials themselves–paint, ink, film, clay–**media** (the plural of *medium)*.

Deciding which medium to use is often the most important decision in the graphic design process. First, you must decide which ones are available to you. Then you must consider which ones you know how to use or enjoy most. Don't limit yourself to a medium you've used before. Learning to use a new medium can be one of the most rewarding activities you'll experience.

Doodling and Sketching

Have you ever doodled on a piece of paper? Lines and circles, squiggles, designs, arrows, dots? As you plan a visual communication, a blank piece of paper can be your best beginning. Let yourself go; release your imagination; don't worry that anyone will ever see it.

It may help to write some key words on the paper as you doodle. Let your mind free associate in much the same way as you do when you brainstorm (page 10) or make a cluster (page 11). At this point, don't stop yourself at all. Some of your best ideas might seem outrageous at first, but you can develop them into brilliant designs.

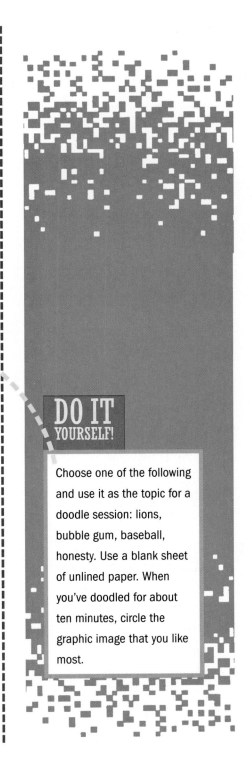

DO IT YOURSELF!

Choose one of the following and use it as the topic for a doodle session: lions, bubble gum, baseball, honesty. Use a blank sheet of unlined paper. When you've doodled for about ten minutes, circle the graphic image that you like most.

Doodling can turn into sketching once you hit on an idea that feels right. Sketching is like outlining. Start with a clean sheet of paper. Think about what your whole final product will look like and be shaped like. Then begin to draw in various parts. Think about their relative sizes and shapes and where they will be. Draw boxes to indicate where text will be if your design includes words. Look below at the sample of a sketch for this two-page spread in this book.

DESIGNING

Now it's time to do the work using the medium you've chosen. If your project involves photographs, it's time to get out the camera. If it involves computer-generated images, it's time to turn on the drive. This stage of the design process is like drafting.

Drafting Text

Many of the visual projects in this book also include text or words. If that's the case, go about drafting as you would any piece of writing.

The big difference, though, between other kinds of writing and *this* kind of writing (sometimes called **copywriting**) is this: here, graphic images will do some—preferably *most*—of the work. Here's a story that Benjamin Franklin told Thomas Jefferson. The story shows how powerful a graphic image can be.

When Franklin was a young man, his friend, John Thompson, decided to open his own hat shop. He needed a sign that would bring in the customers. His first version of the sign was a hat with the words "John Thompson, Hatter, makes and sells hats for ready money" underneath the hat.

To test the sign, Thompson decided to get opinions from his friends. One said he should eliminate "Hatter." Another said "makes" wasn't needed. A third advised Thompson to take out the words "for ready money," and a fourth said the words "sells hats" weren't necessary. What was left on the sign? The figure of a hat and the words "John Thompson." That's all he needed—the graphic of a hat and the maker's name told the whole story.

Laying It Out

Once you've gathered your combination of graphic images and text, it's time to do a **layout,** that is, a rough arrangement of the various elements of your design. Use the dimensions of your final product for your layout. At this stage, just "lay out" the various pieces without actually attaching them to anything. Then you can move them around easily and experiment with various arrangements. Think about the questions on the next page.

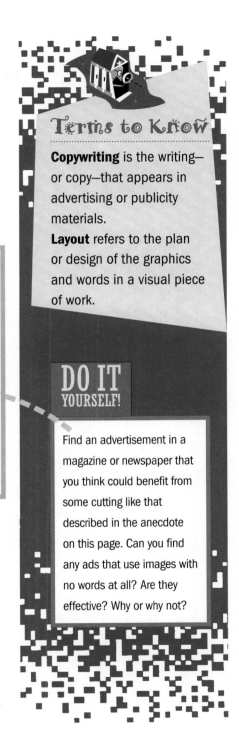

Terms to Know

Copywriting is the writing—or copy—that appears in advertising or publicity materials.

Layout refers to the plan or design of the graphics and words in a visual piece of work.

DO IT YOURSELF!

Find an advertisement in a magazine or newspaper that you think could benefit from some cutting like that described in the anecdote on this page. Can you find any ads that use images with no words at all? Are they effective? Why or why not?

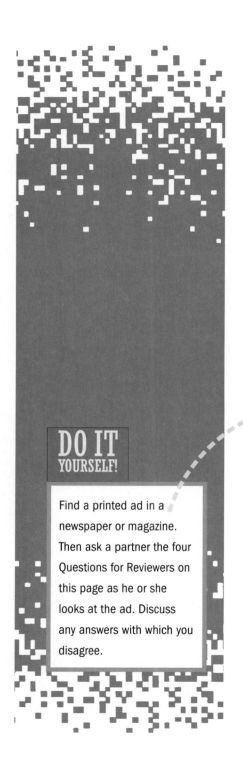

The Layout

- Which elements belong side by side?
- Which ones should be in the center? At the top?
- Which elements need more work? What needs to be done?

REVISING AND GETTING FEEDBACK

The Hatter, John Thompson, asked the advice of his friends and his sign improved as a result of their suggestions. You, too, should get reactions from one or two people as you begin to put the finishing touches on your design. Look at the list below for specific questions you could ask your reviewers.

Questions for Reviewers

- What does this design mean to you?
- What do you like most about this design?
- What do you like least?
- How would you suggest making improvements?

Making Improvements

Based on the comments of your friends, improve your design. Move some elements around. Eliminate what's unnecessary. Clean up rough edges. Make sure that any copy is grammatically and mechanically correct.

As with the writing process, it will help if you can let a few days pass as you make final decisions about your design. If possible, display it in a familiar place–in your locker, your room, or the inside of your notebook– someplace where you'll glance at it often. Try to imagine seeing it not as designer, but as your audience will. As you look at your design, ask yourself the questions that follow.

Questions About the Design

- Is it easy to understand?
- Is it enjoyable to look at?
- Does it make me think about something worthwhile?

DISPLAYING

Some kinds of visual products—such as movies, slides, filmstrips, videotapes, or computer graphics—will require special equipment for their presentation. Be sure you've tested the equipment beforehand and are comfortable with its operation.

Other products—such as photographs, posters, paintings, or sculptures—need an ample display area and proper lighting if they are to have their maximum effect. Find out who can help you arrange for the area and the lighting. Pay close attention to details.

Still other kinds of graphic designs—posters, murals, book jackets—demand nothing more than an audience willing to look at them. Make sure products like these are displayed in appropriate places where interested people can see, enjoy, and learn from them!

LOOKING BACK

Whenever you complete a visual communication project, step back and look at what you've done. Ask yourself questions such as the following.

Evaluation Questions

- Why is visual communication important?
- When do I need to communicate visually?
- What did I learn from this project?
- What are my strengths as a visual communicator?
- How can I improve my visual communication skills?

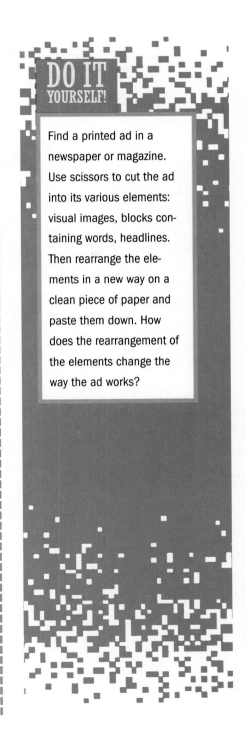

DO IT YOURSELF!

Find a printed ad in a newspaper or magazine. Use scissors to cut the ad into its various elements: visual images, blocks containing words, headlines. Then rearrange the elements in a new way on a clean piece of paper and paste them down. How does the rearrangement of the elements change the way the ad works?

Unit II

Communication Strategies and Projects

Wouldn't you like to become even better at communicating than you already are? This unit can help you. Take this opportunity to choose strategies for writing, speaking, and communicating visually. Each chapter has a particular communication focus–communicating about yourself or others, describing, telling a story, explaining, giving your opinion, evaluating, or reporting. You'll find practical hints for doing projects of your own. Let these strategies and projects open new doors of communication for you.

CONTENTS

CHAPTER 3 Communicating About Yourself—Communicating About Others......................40

CHAPTER 4 Communicating to Describe 74

CHAPTER 5 Communicating to Tell a Story 102

CHAPTER 6 Communicating to Explain 134

CHAPTER 7 Communicating to Give Your Opinion...168

CHAPTER 8 Communicating to Evaluate 206

CHAPTER 9 Communicating to Report..248

3

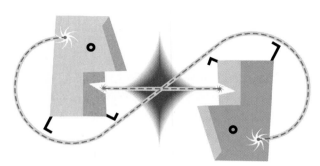

Communicating
About Yourself—
Communicating
About Others

- It's the first day of school, and you've just met the new student whose desk is next to yours. He's talked about the last school he went to and told you that his favorite sport is soccer. Now it's your turn to talk about yourself. What do you say?

- Your favorite aunt just showed up at your house for a visit. She wants to know how you are, what you've been doing, what's on your mind these days. How do you answer her questions?

- Your next-door neighbor is looking for someone to hire— a responsible young person who can do some yardwork. "You seem to be just the person I've been looking for," your neighbor says. "Tell me about yourself."

Why Communicate About Yourself or Others?

People communicate about themselves and others for many different reasons and in many different ways. Some people write autobiographies—accounts of their lives that help the readers get to know them better. Or they write biographies—accounts of the lives of others. People also communicate about themselves by talking. Famous people give television and radio interviews. You and your friends tell each other about scary, exciting, or confusing experiences.

Other people communicate about themselves without using words at all—through visual art. Artists may draw or paint self-portraits or communicate something about themselves through photography, video, or even computers. Look at this photographic self-portrait by the American artist/photographer Chansonetta Stanley Emmons. What does this picture tell you about the person who took it?

In the pages that follow, you'll have the chance to communicate about yourself in different ways. If writing is your specialty (or you'd like it to be), try your hand at creating a **personal narrative** about an event or experience in your life. If you like to perform in front of an audience and think you might make a good actor, then try creating and producing **reader's theater**. Finally, if you like art, then you might want to try your hand at a self-portrait or a **collage**. Whatever you choose, have fun and remember—*you* are on center stage.

LOOKING AHEAD

TO THE PROJECTS

3.1 Writing Project
Write a personal narrative, or story, about an important incident in your life (pages 42-57).

3.2 Speaking Project
Perform reader's theater based on an incident in your life (pages 58-67).

3.3 Visual Project
Create a self-portrait or a collage that communicates something important about you to other people (pages 68-73).

JOURNAL WRITING

Look at the photograph, a self-portrait by Chansonetta Stanley Emmons. Then, in your journal, write three questions that you would like to ask the person you see in the picture. If you like, you might also write the answers that you imagine she would give.

3.1 Writing Project

Writing a Personal Narrative

You'll be writing about an experience that you'd like to share with other people.

How many times have you been in a funny or unusual situation that you couldn't wait to tell your friends about? Perhaps you had a confusing experience when you were mistaken for someone else, or you got on the wrong bus by mistake. How can you communicate this experience to someone else— especially someone who lives far away, such as a relative or a friend who has moved away? There will probably be many times in your life when you'll want to write a personal narrative like this.

On the other hand, you may want to share with your family or friends an experience that taught you something about yourself. For instance, maybe you've moved far away from your grandparents and a visit to them has shown you how much they mean to you.

In this project, you'll write a personal narrative about an experience that you'd like to share with other people. Before you get started, however, you may find it helpful to see how another student your age wrote a personal narrative. Although you do not have to duplicate the model, reading another student's personal narrative will help you start thinking about how you might write your own.

STUDENT MODEL

A Trap for Cleland Dunkelberger
Anne Plummer, Grade 8

When I was eight years old, my least favorite person in the world was the boy next door. His name was Cleland Dunkelberger, and he was about a year older than I was. The main reason I didn't like him was that I thought he didn't like me. He kind of sneered whenever he saw me.

Cleland's best friend lived in the house behind ours, and when he went to his friend's house, Cleland would often cut through our backyard. It made me very angry to see him in our yard, because I thought of the yard as my special property. I told my mother about Cleland, expecting that she would also be angry. She said that she didn't mind and that it was safer for him to go that way than around by the streets. She made it clear that she wasn't going to stop him.

That answer did not satisfy me. As far as I was concerned, he still had to be stopped. Unfortunately, I could not just go out in the backyard and stop him. He was bigger than I was. I had to think of something else.

About that time, I was watching an old movie about settlers in a rain forest. Their settlement was being attacked at night by a large animal, so they decided to set a trap for it.

To make the trap, the settlers dug a large hole—I guess you would call it a pit—in the middle of the

animal's path. The pit was wide enough to hold the animal, and it was deep enough so that when the animal fell in, it would not be able to get out. Then they covered the pit with twigs and branches.

Sure enough, the trap caught the animal. It roared fiercely in the pit, and the settlers ran to see what kind of animal it was. But before they found out, I had turned off the television and was outside, tracing Cleland's usual path across the backyard. I had decided how to solve the Cleland Dunkelberger problem. I was going to capture him in a pit.

After carefully selecting a location for the pit, I got a shovel out of the garage and began digging. I could not dig very fast because I was careful to save the grass and to hide the dirt under the back porch so it wouldn't give the pit away. I also learned that digging was harder work than it had looked like in the movie. After an hour or so, I was tired out, and all I had to show for it was a hole six or eight inches deep and about a foot across.

It was hardly a pit, but it would have to do. I put some sticks across it and a lot of loose grass from the basket of the lawn mower.

I could see the trap from my room—that was part of the plan—so I went inside and waited by a window for Cleland to come by and fall into his trap. I waited until dinner time, and after dinner I waited again until it got dark, but Cleland did not come by. I was disappointed, but I was sure I would catch him sooner or later.

Continues ┈┈┈┈┈┈┈┈┈┈┈┈▶

Well, I caught somebody pretty soon, but it wasn't Cleland. It was the meter reader from the gas company. I was still in bed the next morning when I heard him yelling in the backyard. He sounded very upset. He had stepped into the hole and fallen flat on his face. It turned out that he wasn't hurt, just startled and probably frightened for an instant. But he sure was angry.

I told my mother that the trap was for Cleland and not the meter reader, but she didn't see that as much of an excuse. I had to fill in the hole and write an apology to the meter reader. Cleland came by while I was shoveling and asked why I was getting the dirt from under the porch, but I didn't answer him, and pretty soon he went away.

I was expecting some kind of punishment, but instead my mother sat me down for a long, serious talk. She told me how lucky we were that nobody—including Cleland—had been hurt. She pointed out that it was wrong to try to hurt people, no matter how annoying they might be. She said that there were always better ways to solve problems.

Terms to Know

Freewriting is a prewriting technique in which you write without stopping for a certain period of time, such as ten minutes. Freewriting lets you open a stream of thought about your personal experiences that will trigger other memories.

PREWRITING

Think back over your life to find a good experience for your narrative–an experience that taught you something valuable that you really want to write about. For example, think about a time you were frightened, a time when you had a particularly exciting experience, or a time when you had a problem to solve.

Freewriting: A Key to Your Memories

A great way to remember experiences is to use **freewriting.** Just write down events in your life without stopping to think about them. Don't tell stories; simply write a few words about each experience. Don't stop to choose (just yet) which experience would make the best writing topic. Just go with the flow of memories as they come to you.

As you freewrite, consider the kinds of memories listed on the next page.

Memories for Personal Narratives

- Important family events such as births, weddings, holiday celebrations, and vacations
- Times when family or friends pulled together to help someone
- Friends, and the good—or maybe not so good—times you've had with them
- The events and people that you've been reading about in books or magazines. Do these people and events remind you of your own experiences?
- Things you have done in school, starting in kindergarten or even earlier

Before Anne Plummer wrote "A Trap for Cleland Dunkelberger," on pages 43-44, she did quite a bit of planning. Here's her original freewriting that helped her think of a topic.

WORK IN PROGRESS

Fifth grade. Miss Prosser. Field trip to the dairy farm. Cows. Animals. Horses. Time the horse got loose in the school yard. Caught by Mr. Yamamoto. Caught. Trap. Cleland Dunkelberger trap. Mom. Mom's good advice.

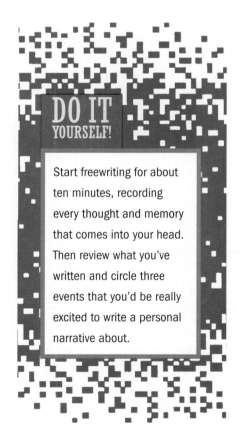

IDEAS FOR YOUR WRITING PROJECT

1. Write a letter describing an important incident from your life. Make it clear why the incident meant something to you.

2. Tell your story as if you were writing about someone else. Create a character with your name and identity, and then write about what happened to "him" or "her."

DO IT YOURSELF!

Start freewriting for about ten minutes, recording every thought and memory that comes into your head. Then review what you've written and circle three events that you'd be really excited to write a personal narrative about.

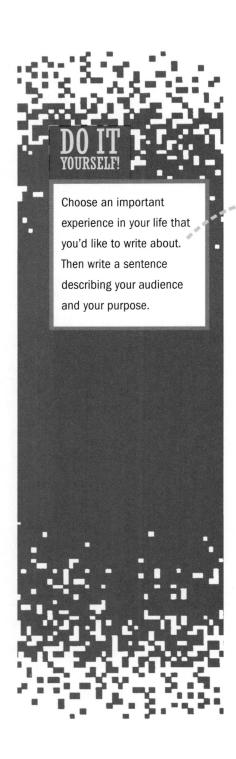

DO IT YOURSELF!

Choose an important experience in your life that you'd like to write about. Then write a sentence describing your audience and your purpose.

Choosing a Topic

Choose one of your freewriting ideas as the topic of your personal narrative. The following questions can help you decide which topic to choose.

Questions for Choosing a Topic

*   Which experience did you feel most strongly about?
*   Is it an experience that taught you something? For example, Anne Plummer learns that there are better ways of solving problems than trying to hurt people.
*   Do you remember enough about the experience to be able to write about it?

Purpose and Audience

After you've chosen an experience to write about, think about your audience—the people with whom you want to share your experience. You might write for a variety of audiences:

*   your friends and classmates
*   relatives
*   readers of a student magazine or newspaper

Then think about your purpose—*why* you want to reach this audience. Your purposes might include one or more of the following:

*   to entertain
*   to teach a lesson
*   to communicate something about yourself

Your purpose and your audience will determine the words you choose and the way you write, so consider them carefully. Make sure you know whom you want to reach and why.

Details, Details, Details!

What about the details–the sights, sounds, actions, and words that can bring an experience to life? You'll need to flesh your topic out with specific images and information.

A good way to remember details is to interview yourself about the experience. Write the answer to each of the following questions on a sheet of paper.

Questions for a Self-Interview

- How old was I when this experience happened?
- Where did the experience take place?
- Who was involved in the experience? What should I tell readers about these people?
- What was the central **conflict** in the experience?
- How did the experience unfold? What actually happened?
- What did I see, hear, smell, taste, and touch? How did I feel?
- In what order did the events take place?
- What did the experience teach me? Did I learn a lesson from it?

Terms to Know

A **conflict** is a problem that confronts a character in a narrative. In an external conflict, the character struggles against another character, nature, or society. In an internal conflict, the character struggles against himself or herself.

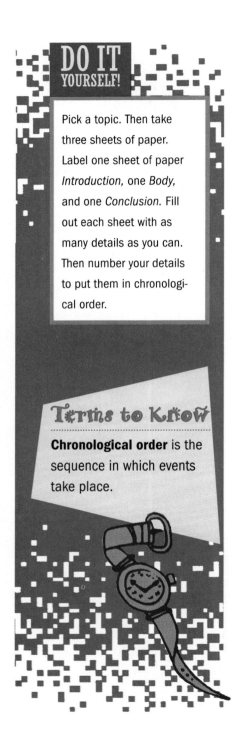

DO IT YOURSELF!

Pick a topic. Then take three sheets of paper. Label one sheet of paper *Introduction*, one *Body*, and one *Conclusion.* Fill out each sheet with as many details as you can. Then number your details to put them in chronological order.

Terms to Know

Chronological order is the sequence in which events take place.

Let's Get Organized

Now organize your details so that your narrative has a beginning (the introduction), a middle (the body), and an end (the conclusion). Use the following strategies to help you organize your personal narrative.

Strategies for Organizing Your Notes

Start by taking out three sheets of paper and labeling one sheet *Introduction*, one *Body,* and one *Conclusion.*

On the sheet labeled *Introduction*, write the details from your self-interview that deal with the beginning of the experience–how it got started. Include details that introduce the characters and setting and that explain how the conflict began.

> I. Introduction
>   A. Setting _____
>   B. Characters _____
>   C. Conflict_____

On the sheet labeled *Body*, write the details about how the experience developed. Put these details in **chronological order.** For example, in the middle of her personal narrative, Anne tells how she dug a hole to trap Cleland Dunkelberger and how the meter reader fell into that hole.

> II. Body
>   A. Detail 1 _____
>   Description _____
>   B. Detail 2 _____
>   Description _____

On the sheet labeled *Conclusion,* write about how the experience ended. The conclusion of a personal narrative has two main purposes. It resolves the conflict and it tells what you learned from the experience. For example, in her conclusion, Anne tells how her mother sat her down for a talk, and then Anne explains how she learned that it is wrong to try to hurt people.

III. Conclusion
   A. Resolution _____
   B. Lesson learned _____

DRAFTING

After you've done so much good planning, it's time to put it to use by writing your first draft.

Drafting the Introduction

Although you don't need to write it first, you might begin with the introduction—the beginning of your narrative. Your introduction should make the reader eager to read the rest of your narrative. Try these ideas when you draft your introduction.

Ideas for Attention-Getting Introductions

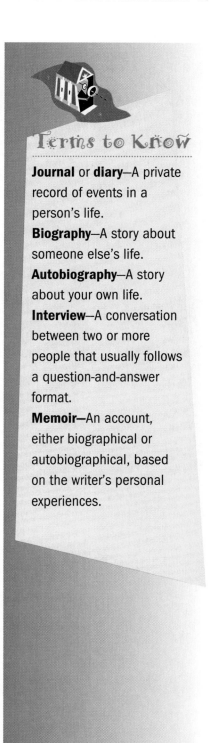

Begin with a sentence that arouses your readers' curiosity. Anne Plummer begins her narrative, "When I was eight years old, my least favorite person in the world was the boy next door." This sentence makes the reader wonder *why* Anne dislikes Cleland.

Terms to Know

Journal or **diary**—A private record of events in a person's life.
Biography—A story about someone else's life.
Autobiography—A story about your own life.
Interview—A conversation between two or more people that usually follows a question-and-answer format.
Memoir—An account, either biographical or autobiographical, based on the writer's personal experiences.

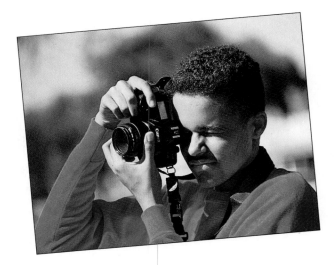 Introduce the main character of the narrative, whether it is you or someone else. In her introduction, Anne introduces Cleland and gives some key facts about him—that she didn't like him and that he was a year older than she.

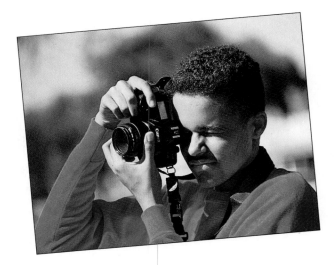 If there is a conflict in the narrative, introduce it as soon as possible. In her introduction, Anne doesn't waste any time introducing her conflict with Cleland.

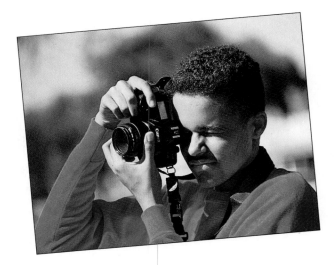 Give information about the setting of the narrative. For instance, it might be important to know whether the events took place in physical education class or on a camping trip.

APPLYING USAGE TO WRITING

Point of View

As you draft, use the first-person point of view. In other words, use *I* throughout to identify yourself as the narrator.

For more information on point of view, turn to Chapter 11.1D, Point of View.

Drafting the Body

Once you've grabbed your readers' attention with an interesting introduction, lead them through the body of your narrative as you tell how the events unfold. Above all, you should aim for good pacing, which means keeping the narrative lively and interesting. The following suggestions will help you pace your narrative well.

Suggestions for Good Pacing in a Narrative

- Tell the events in your story one step at a time and in chronological order.
- Keep the story on a straight track from beginning to end. Don't get distracted by some minor incident that doesn't carry your narrative forward to the next event.
- Add an element of suspense to your writing; that is, make readers eager to find out what will happen next. In addition, keep your readers in doubt about how things will turn out.
- Use lots of details. In the following passage from the model, notice how Anne makes you feel as if you're right there with her.

WORK
IN PROGRESS

> After carefully selecting a location for the pit, I got a shovel out of the garage and began digging. I could not dig very fast because I was careful to save the grass and to hide the dirt under the back porch so it wouldn't give the pit away.

- Begin each new development in your narrative with a new paragraph. Careful paragraphing will help the pacing. It'll also help your readers follow the action.

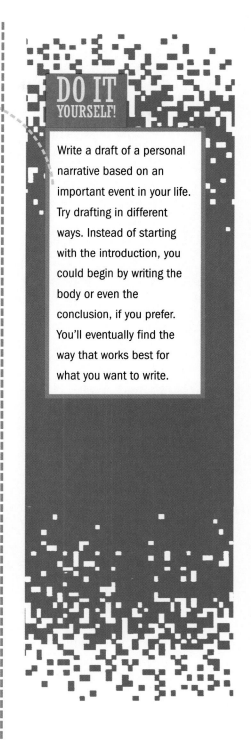

DO IT YOURSELF!

Write a draft of a personal narrative based on an important event in your life. Try drafting in different ways. Instead of starting with the introduction, you could begin by writing the body or even the conclusion, if you prefer. You'll eventually find the way that works best for what you want to write.

Drafting the Conclusion and Expressing the Theme

The conclusion resolves the conflict and helps readers understand what the experience means to the writer. Here are some suggestions for conclusions that your readers will remember.

Suggestions for Memorable Endings

- Resolve—or bring to an end—the conflict that you developed in the narrative. In her essay, Anne resolves the conflict by telling readers what finally happened: She had to fill in the hole and write an apology to the meter reader.
- Tell readers how you felt about the experience.
- Tell readers the theme of your narrative or the lesson you learned from the experience. You may state the theme directly in your narrative, as Anne does in her conclusion.

WORK IN PROGRESS

More important, she [Anne's mother] pointed out that it was wrong to try to hurt people, no matter how annoying they might be. She said that there were always better ways to solve problems.

REVISING

Good going! Now you've got your narrative down on paper. If possible, wait a few days before rereading the first draft. Then imagine you've never seen it before.

Improving Your Work

What would you like to change? The following checklist may help you decide what you'd like to improve about your narrative.

Checklist for Revising a Personal Narrative

- Is my story complete? Does the reader have all the information needed to understand what is going on?
- Does the narrative grab the reader's attention?
- Have I used transitions to connect my narrative? Is it written in chronological order? Does it have a clearly defined introduction, body, and conclusion?
- Does my narrative have good pacing? Does it build suspense?
- Does the narrative include information that is not important to the story?
- Does it wander far from the main story line? What unnecessary parts could I eliminate?
- Is it written from a consistent point of view and with consistent verb tense?
- Will it be clear to the reader why these events are important to me?
- Have I used details in telling the events in my narrative? Will my readers feel as if they are there with me?

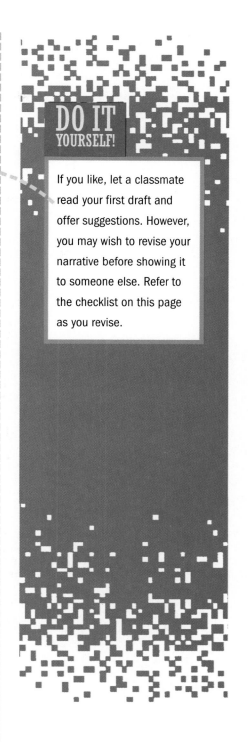

DO IT YOURSELF!

If you like, let a classmate read your first draft and offer suggestions. However, you may wish to revise your narrative before showing it to someone else. Refer to the checklist on this page as you revise.

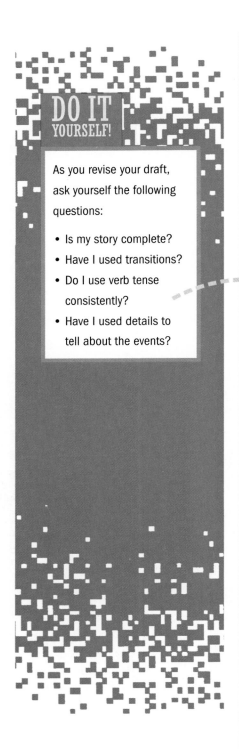

DO IT YOURSELF!

As you revise your draft, ask yourself the following questions:

- Is my story complete?
- Have I used transitions?
- Do I use verb tense consistently?
- Have I used details to tell about the events?

APPLYING TECHNIQUE TO WRITING

Transitions

To help your readers follow the events in your narrative, be sure to use transitions. Transitions are connecting words and phrases that lead readers smoothly from one event in your narrative to the next. They also show the passing of time and the sequence of events. Use transitions like these:

About that time, . . .

A few minutes later, . . .

Later that day, . . .

The next day, . . .

During the next few weeks, . . .

After seven years, . . .

For more information on transitions, turn to Chapter 10.2C, Writing Transitional Sentences.

Strategies for Revision

You can use several different strategies to evaluate and then revise your writing. Choose one or two of the following strategies to revise your personal narrative.

- Give your paper to someone else to read, such as a family member, a friend, or a neighbor. Ask that person to refer to the Revision Checklist while reading your paper. Then discuss the good features of your narrative as well as what needs to be changed.

- Read your paper aloud a few times to one or more of your classmates, asking your audience to listen for things that can be improved. Then ask your listeners to tell you what they liked, what they think needs a little more work, and what parts they didn't understand.

◎ Remember that you can always go back, freewrite, create new material, and add new ideas. Keep freewriting and drafting until your work is complete.

EDITING

When you edit, you give your paper a final polishing. Save editing until the content of your narrative is fairly set.

Polishing Your Work

Look for errors in grammar, usage, and mechanics, using the following procedure.

Suggestions for Editing a Narrative

◎ Read each sentence carefully and slowly to see if it makes sense.

◎ As you read, check the punctuation of your sentences.

◎ Also check for spelling errors. Circle words when you are unsure of the spelling.

◎ Watch out for transitions—are you using them correctly?

◎ Try reading your paper from the last sentence to the first sentence. You'll read the sentences more slowly because you'll be reading them in reverse order.

NEED MORE HELP?

For more information on punctuation, see Chapter 20, Punctuation. For more information on transitions, see Chapter 10.2C, Writing Transitional Sentences.

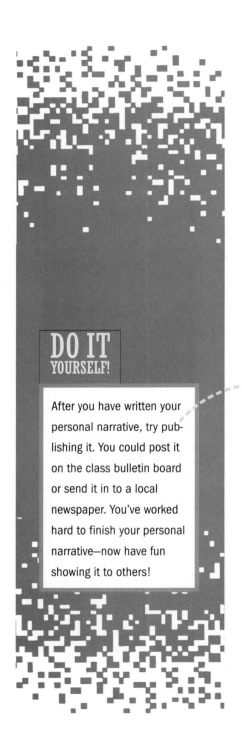

DO IT YOURSELF!

After you have written your personal narrative, try publishing it. You could post it on the class bulletin board or send it in to a local newspaper. You've worked hard to finish your personal narrative—now have fun showing it to others!

APPLYING MECHANICS TO WRITING

Punctuating Introductory Phrases

When Anne looked over her revision, she paid special attention to the punctuation that should follow introductory phrases. Look at the way she corrected some of her sentences.

WORK IN PROGRESS

> About that time, I was watching an old movie about settlers in a rain forest.
> Sure enough, the trap caught the animal.
> Well, I caught somebody pretty soon, but it wasn't Cleland.

For more information about using commas, turn to Chapter 20.2, Commas.

PUBLISHING

Now comes the payoff for your hard work—the chance to share your personal narrative with other people, your reading audience. Below are some ways of publishing your narrative. But if you think of another way to publish, by all means do it!

Ideas for Sharing the Wealth

- Arrange your chairs or desks in a circle and read your personal narrative aloud to your classmates. Be sure to read with enthusiasm and expression.

◎ Send photocopies of your narrative to friends or relatives who would be interested in the experience you've written about.

◎ Sometimes local newspapers invite readers to submit articles about personal experiences. If your newspaper has such a column, submit your narrative in typewritten form. Be sure it fits the length restrictions of the newspaper.

◎ Illustrate your narrative so that it becomes a "picture narrative" as well.

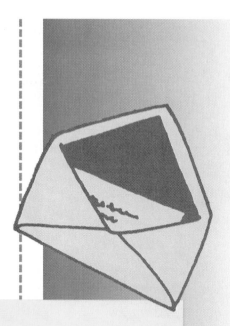

Evaluation

Evaluate your performance in writing your personal narrative, using the following questions as a guide.

Self-Evaluation Form

Type and purpose of writing:

1. Did I work hard on this assignment? Why or why not?
2. What do I like most about my paper?
3. What do I like least about my paper?
4. What did I learn that will help me in my next writing assignment?
5. Did I use transitions in my narrative?
6. What skills in grammar, usage, or mechanics did I learn about and apply to my writing?
7. What skills in grammar, usage, or mechanics will I apply to my next writing project?
8. I feel _____ about this paper because . . .

3.2 Speaking Project

You'll perform reader's theater about an incident in your life for an audience of your classmates.

Terms to Know

Dialogue is the speech and conversation of characters in a work of literature.

A **narrator** is the person or voice that tells a story.

A **reader's theater script** is the written version of what the characters and the narrator say.

Writing and Performing Reader's Theater

Take yourself back in time—to the 1940s, when there were no televisions or VCRs. Instead of watching programs on TV, people listened to radio dramas. A narrator described the setting, providing information that was not supplied by **dialogue.**

Imagine that it's 1946 and you are about to perform reader's theater. Reader's theater is a form of drama that is very much like a radio play. It is fun and easy to present. In reader's theater, there is no stage action, only a **narrator** and several actors who read the script.

For this project, you will create a script for reader's theater, based on a dramatic incident in your life—an incident that should reveal something about you. After writing the script, you'll direct the other actors through all the rehearsals until you're ready to perform your play before an audience of your classmates. You will also help out some of your classmates by acting in the plays that they have written.

Here is a **reader's theater script** based on "A Trap for Cleland Dunkelberger" on pages 43–44. Although you do not have to duplicate the model, reading a reader's theater script written by a student your age will help you when you write your own script.

The Trap That Worked Too Well
by Anne Plummer, Grade 8

NARRATOR: It's 8:45 A.M. on a sunny morning in spring as the meter reader enters the backyard of a house in Chicago and heads toward the back door.

METER READER: *(singing)* It's a beautiful day in the neighborhood . . .

NARRATOR: Suddenly the ground gives way beneath her foot.

METER READER: What in the world—

NARRATOR: She falls forward. First, her right knee hits the ground, then her right elbow, and then her right ear. She pushes herself into a sitting position and touches her ear.

METER READER: Ouch!

NARRATOR: . . . then her knee . . .

METER READER: Yaow!

NARRATOR: . . . and finally her elbow.

METER READER: YAOWEE!

NARRATOR: Looking at the ground to see what had made her fall, she discovers a small hole about six inches deep. Looking more closely at the hole, she realizes that it was cleverly concealed by a pile of grass clippings.

METER READER: What in the—

NARRATOR: A dignified middle-aged woman comes out the back door of the house.

MOTHER: What seems to be the problem? Are you all right? Is there anything I can do?

METER READER: Since when have you been setting traps in your backyard?

MOTHER: I beg your pardon?

METER READER: TRAPS! Holes in the ground to make innocent people trip and fall on their ears.

MOTHER: I'm afraid I don't understand.

METER READER: Look right there. See that hole? That's what made me fall.

MOTHER: Oh, dear. That wasn't there yesterday. But couldn't you have walked around it, or jumped over it, or—

METER READER: It was concealed. Hidden. Under dead grass. A trap!

MOTHER: Oh, *dear*! I *am* sorry. Are you hurt?

METER READER: Just some scrapes, I think. Maybe a little blood on my ear, but that's nothing. I don't think anything's broken. But about that trap—

MOTHER: Well, I don't know how it got there, but I certainly intend to find out. Now then, let me offer you a glass of iced tea.

METER READER: No, thanks. I think I'll be on my way—as soon as I've read your meter, which is what I came for in the first place.

Continues ⋯⋯⋯⋯▶

MOTHER: Of course. Right this way.

NARRATOR: As the meter reader goes into the house, Mother stares for a moment at the hole in the ground. Then she looks up at a bedroom window and says in a firm tone:

MOTHER: Winslow! Come here!

WINSLOW: I just got up.

MOTHER: That doesn't matter. Come here.

WINSLOW: I haven't brushed my teeth.

MOTHER: I don't care. Come here!

NARRATOR: After a moment, Winslow, a child of about eight, comes out the back door. The meter reader also comes out, right behind Winslow. She glares at Winslow and then disappears around the corner of the house.

MOTHER: Do you know who that was?

WINSLOW: No.

MOTHER: She is the meter reader for the gas company. Do you know why she looked at you that way?

WINSLOW: No.

MOTHER: Because she fell and hurt herself.

WINSLOW: Oh.

MOTHER: She fell because someone dug a hole in the backyard.

WINSLOW: Oh.

MOTHER: The hole was concealed under some cut grass.

WINSLOW: Uh-huh.

MOTHER: There is the hole. *(Pause)* Do you by any chance know how it got there?

WINSLOW: Yeah, uh, sort of . . . I mean kind of . . .

MOTHER: Does that mean that you, uh, sort of . . . kind of . . . dug it yourself?

WINSLOW: Uh, yes.

MOTHER: Can you tell me why you sort of . . . did it?

WINSLOW: Well, uh, well, to catch Cleland. To stop him from cutting across our yard.

MOTHER: What if it had sort of caught someone else instead?

WINSLOW: I never thought of that.

MOTHER: What if the person it caught—Cleland or anybody else—was—sort of— hurt?

WINSLOW: I guess that sort of was the idea.

MOTHER: I mean *really* hurt. A cast for weeks, maybe months. Maybe even permanent injury.

WINSLOW: I never thought of that. I guess I should have.

MOTHER: Yes, you should. There is never any point in trying to hurt people. Also, if you do hurt someone, we have to pay all the medical bills and maybe a lot more.

WINSLOW: OK. I get it. I'm sorry.

MOTHER: So fill in the hole. The next time you want to change something, try to find a more sensible way to do it.

NARRATOR: Mother goes back into the house. Winslow reaches under the back porch and pulls out a shovel. He begins shoveling dirt from under the porch into the hole, a small amount at a time. Cleland Dunkelberger enters from one side of the yard. He walks up to the hole and stares at it.

CLELAND: What's that?

WINSLOW: Never mind.

NARRATOR: Receiving no answer, Cleland shrugs his shoulders and continues across the yard. Winslow watches him go and resumes shoveling.

GETTING STARTED

The first step in creating a reader's theater is to decide on your topic. Think about an incident in your life that you'd like to dramatize. Pick an incident that is important, interesting, or funny to you. You can also create reader's theater from an existing story. If you're interested in a topic, chances are that your listeners will be interested in hearing about it.

Brainstorming

Begin by brainstorming, either alone or with others, about your life at home or at school. Jot down all the ideas that come to mind. At this point, don't worry about evaluating your ideas—just get as many ideas as possible on paper. You may want to brainstorm with a few classmates. Their ideas and memories may jog your memory. The following is an example of Anne's brainstorming ideas about her family life:

WORK IN PROGRESS

Get-togethers. Holidays. Uncle Bob and Mom dropping the turkey. Grandma's stuffing. Cousin Fred giving my father a jogging suit for his birthday. Birthdays. The birthday when I got my Rollerblades. First bike. My first major-league game. Terrible rain. The time the car broke down in a rainstorm. Rain. The hole in the roof. Hole. The trap for Cleland Dunkelberger.

Notice how the writer follows one memory to the next until she remembers digging the trap for Cleland.

IDEAS FOR YOUR SPEAKING PROJECT

1. Videotape or audiotape your reader's theater and play it for the class.

2. Interview someone who knew you when you were younger. Ask that person questions about your life and what you were like. Play a tape of the interview for the class.

DO IT YOURSELF!

Think of an incident in your life that you could develop into reader's theater. Begin by brainstorming for ideas for your play and writing them down on a sheet of paper. Cross out any ideas that you think won't work until you've selected two or three of your best ideas.

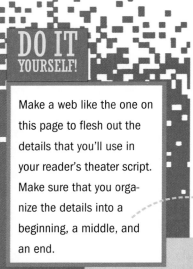

DO IT YOURSELF!

Make a web like the one on this page to flesh out the details that you'll use in your reader's theater script. Make sure that you organize the details into a beginning, a middle, and an end.

Choosing an Idea

To choose the best idea, create a web in which you place one idea in a circle. Around this idea, write the names of the characters, the setting where the incident took place, and the events that led up to and followed the incident. Follow this procedure for each of the remaining ideas from your brainstorming session. Look over your webs and decide which idea works best for reader's theater. Then develop the web you have chosen. Use it to help you organize your memories into a clear order—beginning, middle, and end.

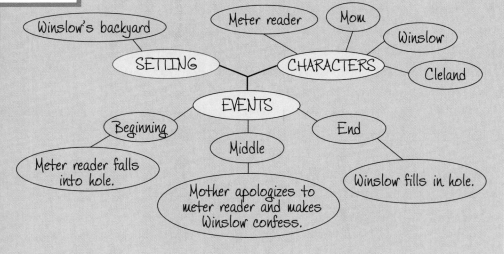

Getting the Details on Paper

Try visualizing to remember the details of the event you've chosen. What did people say? How did they say it? As you remember the details, jot them down quickly on paper as *key words* and phrases. Try to remember people's exact words to use in your script.

DRAFTING YOUR SCRIPT

You'll start your script by setting the scene–using the narrator to tell where and when the action is taking place. Most of your story will be told through dialogue– the words that people say to each other. You can use the narrator to help make your story clear to your listeners.

Setting the Scene

Your introduction should be brief but give enough infor- mation so that your audience can picture the setting of the play. Look at the introduction to "The Trap That Worked Too Well":

> **WORK IN PROGRESS**
>
> It's 8:45 A.M. on a sunny morning in spring as the meter reader enters the backyard of a house in Chicago and heads toward the back door.

This introduction establishes the setting and intro- duces one of the characters.

Writing Dialogue

There are many ways of writing dialogue. Here are some suggestions. You might use one or more of them, or you might add them to your own unique technique.

- Write the dialogue out as you hear it in your head.
- Say the dialogue aloud to yourself, as if you were each character. Then write down or tape record the dialogue.
- Work with a partner. Have your partner play the part of one character while you play the part of another. Then write down or tape record your dialogue.

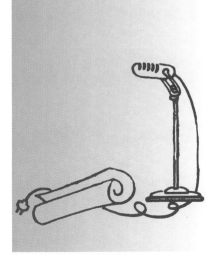

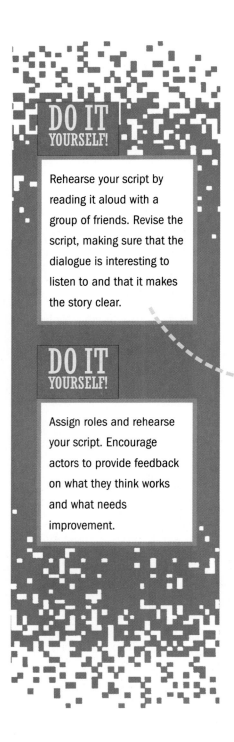

DO IT YOURSELF!

Rehearse your script by reading it aloud with a group of friends. Revise the script, making sure that the dialogue is interesting to listen to and that it makes the story clear.

DO IT YOURSELF!

Assign roles and rehearse your script. Encourage actors to provide feedback on what they think works and what needs improvement.

Choosing the Narrator

The narrator of a reader's theater play is like the announcer of a radio program. The narrator is not part of the action but plays the important role of describing scene changes or introducing new characters. Choose a narrator for your play.

REHEARSING AND REVISING YOUR SCRIPT

When you have the first draft of a script for your reader's theater, ask yourself the following questions:

- Is the action clear? Is it interesting and lively?
- Is each character's dialogue interesting? Is the dialogue realistic?
- Do the action and characters reveal the importance of the incident in your life?

APPLYING USAGE TO SCRIPT WRITING

Using Present Tense

When you revise your script, make sure that all narration is in the present tense. The present tense gives the listeners a sense of really being there as the story is happening. Notice how Anne Plummer revised to use the present tense in her script.

WORK IN PROGRESS

> NARRATOR: She falls forward. First, her right knee hits the ground, then her right elbow, and then her right ear.

For more information on using the present tense, see Chapter 15, Using Verbs.

The First Run-Through

One way to see whether your script is as good as it can be is to give it a trial run. Get together with several of your classmates and hear your script read for the first time. Follow these steps.

1. Select the **cast**. Choose the classmates who will play the characters in your script.
2. Provide each actor with a copy of the script. Let each actor highlight his or her own parts of the dialogue.
3. Set up chairs for the actors and narrator.
4. Encourage the actors to read loudly, clearly, and with expression.
5. Have your actors and your narrator read through your entire script, without interruption. It's important for everyone to hear the script before discussing the details.

Terms to Know

Cast is the name for the actors who will read the play. **Cues** are the signals that tell the actors when to speak. **Stage directions** are the directions that tell the actors how to move, speak, and behave. They usually appear in parentheses and italics beside the actors' lines.

Rehearsals

You'll want to have several rehearsals until you are satisfied with the finished product. As the director, you will have to pay careful attention to how the actors speak. If you decide to play your own character, don't be afraid to take advice from your fellow actors. Remind the actors to follow the dialogue closely as other actors are speaking, so that everyone will know his or her **cues**. Make sure everyone follows the **stage directions** and reads his or her lines in the appropriate tone of voice.

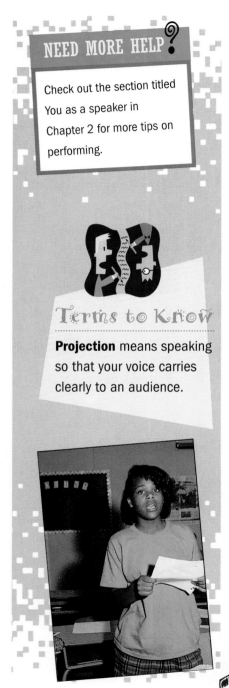

NEED MORE HELP?

Check out the section titled You as a speaker in Chapter 2 for more tips on performing.

Terms to Know

Projection means speaking so that your voice carries clearly to an audience.

Making Improvements

As your classmates read your script, take notes and make a record of words or scenes that you think could be improved. Immediately after the reading, ask your actors what *they* think should be changed. Then revise the sections that need improvement.

DELIVERY

In addition to tone of voice and expression, a good actor must be sure that the audience can hear his or her words clearly. Remember that you must speak loudly enough to be heard.

Speaking to Be Heard

Actors on a stage don't shout, but the audience can still hear their voices. This is because they use a technique called **projection**. An actor can project his or her voice by speaking clearly and forcefully, without shouting or straining. Practice projecting your voice until you can project with ease.

PERFORMING YOUR PLAY

By now you should feel confident enough to perform your reader's theater in front of an audience of your classmates. Relax and have fun, and your performance is sure to be a good one.

DO IT YOURSELF!

Perform your reader's theater script. Set up chairs at the front of the class-room and share your work with the class.

Evaluation

After each performance, jot down a comment or two about the perfor-mance itself, the script, or the actors. Tell the author and actors what you particularly liked about the performance. Then grade the performance according to the following guidelines.

Poor   Fair   Good   Excellent

- The actors spoke their lines at the appropriate time and with emotion.
- The dialogue went smoothly.
- The action and characters were lively and interesting.
- The performance was well organized and captivating.

3.3 Visual Project

Creating a Self-Portrait or a Collage

You'll create a self-portrait or a collage that will communicate something about yourself to your classmates.

Self Portrait Frida Kahlo

Artists often use art to communicate about themselves. Look at the painting to the left and talk with a few of your classmates about the feeling you get from it. Do you have any clues about what the artist was feeling?

Like music, art can communicate moods and feelings that language cannot express. Self-portraits and collages can sometimes convey more about the artist who creates them than do pages of the written word.

You, too, can use art to communicate about yourself. In this project you can choose to draw or paint a self-portrait or to make a collage. A collage is a form of art that is like a patchwork of images and materials arranged in a pleasing design. Before you get started, however, you might want to look at these two self-portraits by Chris Cloke, a 7th-grade student.

Comments by the Artist About His Self-Portraits

"I was trying to make them comical as well as realistic, and I think I got a pretty good mix. I gave myself big glasses and bananas for ears. I thought it would look like a creative way to do it without taking the assignment too literally. I really do wear glasses, but I don't think I have big ears. Some of the features are exaggerated, but it still looks like me."

STUDENT MODEL

VISUAL PROJECT

1. Look at some famous self-portraits in your local art museum or in an art history book. Try to imitate an old-fashioned style of art when you create your own self-portrait.

2. Create a self-portrait of yourself as the President of the United States, sitting in the oval office of the White House. What aspects of your personality would you emphasize or exaggerate?

SELF-PORTRAIT AND COLLAGE IDEAS

Would you like to do a self-portrait or a collage that reveals your identity? If you decide to do a self-portrait, think about what you want to express about yourself. Do you want to create a realistic portrait or one that expresses your feelings? Do you simply want to show a mood, or do you want to represent the complex nature of your personality? Could you communicate your personality through a facial expression? Finally, will you work from a photograph or a mirror?

What to Include

If you choose to make a collage, think about the images and materials that could express your personality. People make collages out of a variety of things: photographs, pictures, holiday cards—anything, in fact, that can be attached to a poster board. The following list will give you some idea of what you can include in a collage about yourself.

- family photographs and photographs of yourself
- pictures you drew or painted when you were younger
- magazine or newspaper photographs that show activities you like, such as sports or music
- stories or poems you have written
- glued materials that represent your interests—sand if you like the beach, leaves if you like hiking

The kinds of pictures and other items you need for your collage can be found in many places, such as newspapers, magazines, and catalogs. Most pictures that cannot be cut out can be copied by copying machines in your local library.

CHOOSING THE MEDIUM

For a Self-Portrait If you decide to paint your self-portrait, think about the medium, or the kind of paint you will use. Oils can give a heavy, rich effect, while pastels or watercolors can help create a lighter mood.

For a Collage If you are making a collage of materials as well as pictures, now is the time to collect these items. Then sort through all the pictures you've gathered for your collage and put them into piles or folders representing particular categories, such as sports, music, cooking, and so on. Go through each pile and make a first selection of items to use in your collage.

DRAFTING YOUR WORK

For a Self-Portrait Your self-portrait will require several drafts before it is finished, so don't be disappointed with your first rough sketch. If you are working from a mirror, position yourself for a profile, three-quarter (in which your head is turned slightly), or frontal view. Make several pencil sketches before you start painting.

For a Collage If you are making a collage, select and arrange one set of pictures. Keep trying different arrangements until you are satisfied.

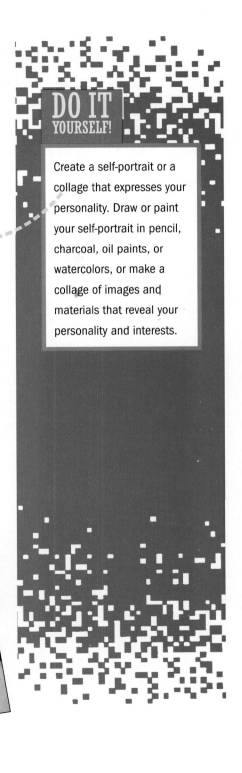

DO IT YOURSELF!

Create a self-portrait or a collage that expresses your personality. Draw or paint your self-portrait in pencil, charcoal, oil paints, or watercolors, or make a collage of images and materials that reveal your personality and interests.

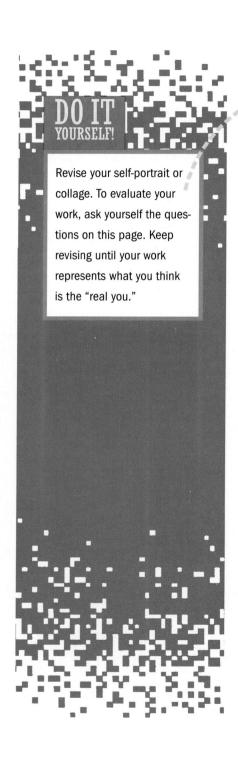

DO IT YOURSELF!

Revise your self-portrait or collage. To evaluate your work, ask yourself the questions on this page. Keep revising until your work represents what you think is the "real you."

REVISING YOUR WORK

Artwork, like writing, needs to be revised. After a few hours or days have passed, reassess your self-portrait or collage. Evaluate your work, keeping the following questions in mind:

- Does my self-portrait or collage represent my personality?
- If I've done a self-portrait, is it an honest expression of my personality?
- If I've done a collage, does it show the things that really matter to me? Is anything missing?
- Does my collage give too much emphasis to some things and not enough to others?

Let other people see your work. Ask them the same questions about your work that you asked yourself. Then make any necessary improvements.

EXHIBITING YOUR WORK

For a Self-Portrait Display your portrait on the classroom wall with your classmates' work.

For a Collage Exchange your collage with another student. Study his or her art and write a few sentences that tell what you think the work expresses about the artist's life, personality, interests, and so on. Return the collage to your partner and read what he or she has written about you. Then display your collage on the same wall as the self-portraits. Hold an "exhibition opening" with snacks and lemonade.

Evaluation

Based on your self-assessment and on what your classmates wrote, grade yourself in each of the following four categories:

Communication: Did I successfully communicate what I intended to say about myself?

Honesty: Did I present myself as I really am?

Thoroughness: If I did a collage, is it complete, or did I leave out something important?

Carefulness: If I did a collage, is it carefully and neatly arranged and pasted down?

Write a note to yourself, detailing what you did well and what changes you would still like to make.

Communicating
to Describe

You've observed the world around you from the moment you were born. Ever since you began to speak, you've been describing what you see, smell, touch, hear, and taste.

In the projects that follow, you'll have a chance to create a **description** of the world around you by writing a descriptive essay, making a speech, or creating a

photo essay. After you've finished any or all of these projects, not only will you have shared your observations, but you'll have learned more about yourself—

how you see the world. In addition, you'll have allowed others to see the world through your eyes.

Why Bother Observing and Describing?

Imagine that cousins have just returned from a visit to the Sonoran Desert in Arizona. You've dreamed of taking such a trip. You ask your cousins for a complete description. The only answer you're given is, "It was great" or "Too awesome for words." Chances are that you'd be frustrated. You'd want to share your cousins' experiences. Because of their response, you're shut out.

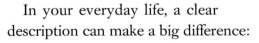

In your everyday life, a clear description can make a big difference:

- You witness an accident and must describe what happened for the police.
- You want to play soccer, but the field is damaged by spring floods. You take photographs so you can prove to the school board that the field needs repair.
- You plan a camping trip with your best friend and favorite cousin. You want them to hit it off, so before they meet, you describe each one to the other.
- You meet a homeless family and want to help them. To get community support, you write a letter to the editor of the local newspaper.

LOOKING AHEAD

TO THE PROJECTS

4.1 Writing Project
Write a description of a place or person in your community (pages 76-89).

4.2 Speaking Project
Give a speech about a person, place, or problem that is important to you (pages 90-95).

4.3 Visual Project
Create a photo essay about a place in your community (pages 96-101).

JOURNAL WRITING

Check out your powers of description! With a partner, go to a place such as a large room or a grassy section of a park. Blindfold your partner and then describe a specific detail of the surroundings. Switch roles. How well could each of you picture what the other described? After you've finished this exercise, write in your journal, describing what you observed. Draw on all five of your senses.

4.1 Writing Project

Describing a Community Place

Write about a special place that others may have overlooked–or a person who deserves recognition.

Nikki wants to be a landscape gardener. Every day she tends a small community flower garden. When Nikki learns of plans to make the garden a parking lot, she writes a description of the garden for the school newspaper. Others see why the beauty she sees should be preserved.

For his school's community service award, Eric nominates his friend Luis. His essay describing Luis's work entertaining children at the local hospital helps Luis receive the recognition he deserves.

Both Nikki and Eric know the value in being able to describe a place or a person. For this project, you'll write a description of a person or place in your community that's important to you. Your purpose is to share information or communicate your feelings about a person who deserves recognition or a place that matters to you.

Before you get started, read one student's description

of a diner in her town. Notice how she describes the diner's role as a social center, a friendly place where people gather to meet as well as to have a meal. Of course, when you begin your own writing, you'll want to select a topic that's important and meaningful to you.

The Tastee Diner

Deborah Truman, Grade 8

"Honey-child, this here diner has been here since 19 and 46," replies the cashier who is in the middle of a long conversation with an old man. The old man's name is Bill, and he always comes to the diner at about 6:15 every evening after his work shift at the metro station. Bill, like many of the customers sitting at the counter, is known as a regular diner customer. When they step into the diner, usually these few people immediately begin a conversation among themselves or with the waitresses about the day's news or their own experiences.

The waitresses at the Tastee Diner are best described as outgoing. They all have been there for years, and they always are willing to speak their minds. The waitresses wear casual clothes instead of uniforms and keep their hair in a ponytail. Most of them have Southern-sounding accents and call their customers "honey," "child," and "kitten."

To coin a word, the food at the diner is without a doubt *Tastee*. Maybe this is what makes people want to come back and eat here again and again. The menu has an assortment of all-time favorites, including hot cakes, eggs (both sunny-side up and scrambled), roast beef sandwiches, home fries, French fries, and the all-American burger.

The tasty food comes with a tiny price tag. For example, the T-bone steak dinner is only $8.95, and a big piece of pie is just a cheap dollar and a half. The varieties of pie resting inside a glass container behind the front counter are enough to make a young child sit and stare in wonder. Pies such as key lime, pecan, cherry, apple, rhubarb, lemon meringue, and chocolate peanut butter often are praised by customers for their great homemade taste.

The diner is decorated with bowling trophies, a juke box that plays oldies, rock, and rhythm and blues, a vending machine, and a wall of newspaper clippings. The subject of the newspaper articles is whether the Tastee Diner will be closed or moved to another location when downtown Silver Spring is remodeled. Many people are under the impression that the diner will be moved to the parking lot in back of its present location. The diner is likely to be moved rather than rebuilt because all of it, except for an extra section that was built 40 years ago, is portable.

By word of mouth, the reputation of the Tastee Diner for good-tasting, inexpensive food has lasted nearly 50 years. Male and female, young and old, wealthy and poor, all can come to the Tastee Diner and enjoy food, music, and good conversation.

IDEAS FOR YOUR

WRITING PROJECT

1. Describe your room in a letter to a friend who has moved away.

2. Write an article for the school paper about a person in your school who deserves recognition.

3. Enter a contest that asks you to write about "My Most Embarrassing Moment."

4. Write a description of a place in your community that is a "must see" and send it to a travel magazine.

PREWRITING

When you consider a subject to describe, let your feelings guide you. Strong feelings—either positive or negative—usually lead to strong writing. If you react strongly to certain people or places, consider them as subjects for a description.

Choosing What to Describe

Think about the people and places in your life. Who stands out? Which places are most likely to remain in your memory for a long time? Asking yourself the following questions may help to jog your memory.

Questions to Ask to Find a Descriptive Subject

People

- Who is my favorite teacher? Coach? Relative?
- Who has done me a favor that I'll never forget?
- Who among my friends, relatives, and acquaintances qualifies as a "real character"?
- Who is the bravest person I know? The most irritating? The most unselfish?
- What person do I associate with laughter?

Places

- What place qualifies as my favorite hangout?
- What is the most peculiar place I've ever been?
- What places or buildings do I see every day that are special?
- What places do I associate with certain smells or sounds?
- What place do I think of as comforting? Mysterious?

Purpose and Audience

When you write a description, your *purpose* is to share what you have seen or experienced with a particular *audience*. Your purpose and your audience are linked.

- If your purpose is to describe your experience at summer camp, your audience might be others who are interested in going to that camp—or your fellow campers who might enjoy sharing your memories.

- If your purpose is to describe a mural so others can appreciate its unique beauty, your audience might be your art class. On the other hand, if your purpose is to describe the mural as an eyesore, your audience will be those who have the power to remove the mural.

Identifying your audience helps you focus your description. Ask yourself the following questions to identify your audience.

Identifying an Audience and Its Needs

- Who is my audience? Does it include my teacher? Classmates? Family? Adults in the community?
- How well does my audience know my subject?
- Why will my audience *care* about my subject? What description can I give them that will make them care?
- What does my audience need to know so that they can visualize the person or place that I describe?

Seeing—Really Seeing—a Subject

To really see a subject, begin by looking at it with *all* your senses. Notice what your senses of sight, taste, touch, smell, and hearing perceive. Keep a notebook with you so you can jot down your observations.

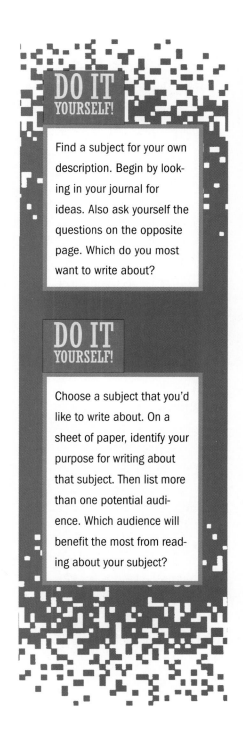

DO IT YOURSELF!

Find a subject for your own description. Begin by looking in your journal for ideas. Also ask yourself the questions on the opposite page. Which do you most want to write about?

DO IT YOURSELF!

Choose a subject that you'd like to write about. On a sheet of paper, identify your purpose for writing about that subject. Then list more than one potential audience. Which audience will benefit the most from reading about your subject?

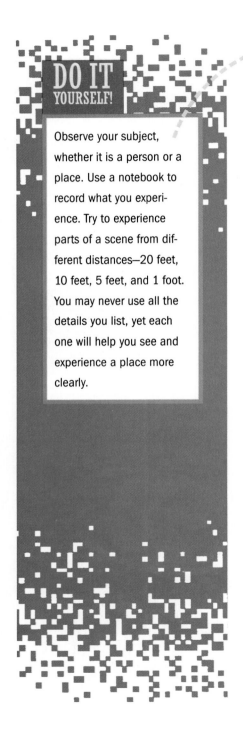

DO IT YOURSELF!

Observe your subject, whether it is a person or a place. Use a notebook to record what you experience. Try to experience parts of a scene from different distances—20 feet, 10 feet, 5 feet, and 1 foot. You may never use all the details you list, yet each one will help you see and experience a place more clearly.

How to "See" a Place

◎ Visit the place at different times of day—in the morning, the afternoon, the evening, or on a Saturday. Each time you visit, you'll notice different things. Use your notebook to record what each of your senses experiences.

◎ Visit outdoor places, such as parks, during all kinds of weather—when it's sunny, rainy, or cold. What does the sky look like? How do the trees smell after it rains? Are the birds chirping or playing tug-of-worm? How does the ground feel as you walk on it?

◎ Look at the people in a place. What are they doing? Reading? Talking? Eating? Playing? What do their voices sound like? Use your notebook to record what they say. What mood do the people create?

◎ Use your eyes like the lens of a camera. Focus on the whole scene, then move in and notice the up-close details.

WORK IN PROGRESS

The diner is decorated with bowling trophies, a juke box that plays oldies, rock, and R & B, a vending machine, and a wall of newspaper clippings.

If you're describing a person, let your readers see the *whole* person. Use your notebook to record how the person looks, speaks, and acts.

How to "See" a Person

◎ Note how a person looks from a distance—height, weight, and general build. Also note how a person looks up close—hair and eyes, smile, gestures.

◎ Look for what makes a person unique. It could be a hearty laugh, a bouncy walk, bizarre clothing, or something else. Ask yourself what would make this person come alive for you if you never had met him or her but were only reading a description.

◎ As you note a person's physical description, include clues to the person's personality. The speech of the waitresses at the Tastee Diner reveals their warm personalities.

◎ Include notes on a person's typical day or an observation of the person on the job.

WORK

IN PROGRESS

The waitresses wear casual clothes instead of uniforms and keep their hair in a ponytail. Most of them have an accent similar to a Southerner's and use such words as "honey," "baby," "child," and "kitten."

Organizing a Description

You can organize a description in many ways. If you're a visual person, you might begin by making a web of your notes. Deborah might have organized her notes by the categories they suggested.

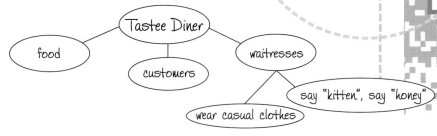

NEED MORE HELP?

For more suggestions on expanding your vision of a subject, see The Writing Process: Prewriting in Chapter 1.

DO IT YOURSELF!

Advertisements often appeal to all five senses in some way. Study a photograph in a magazine advertisement. Make a heading for each of the five senses: sight, sound, smell, taste, touch. Under each heading write as many words as you can think of to describe the images in the photograph.

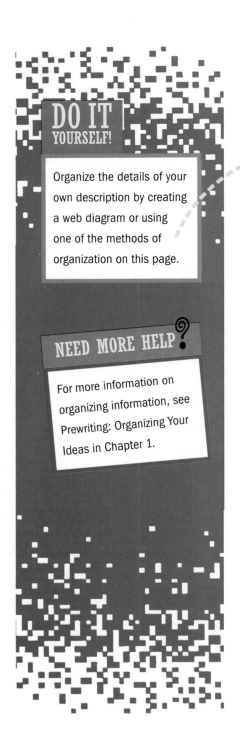

DO IT YOURSELF!

Organize the details of your own description by creating a web diagram or using one of the methods of organization on this page.

NEED MORE HELP?

For more information on organizing information, see Prewriting: Organizing Your Ideas in Chapter 1.

Methods of Organization

In Space Describe a sculpture from top to bottom. Describe your room by what you see as you slowly turn around. Describe a house room by room.

In Time Describe a process from beginning to end, or describe a person's accomplishments in the order in which they occurred.

By Impression The first thing you notice about Uncle Leon is his clothes—a pin-striped suit, a hat, and gold-topped walking cane. Then you notice his face and hear his voice. On the other hand, you might describe a desert scene by how it would look to someone if they walked into that scene. For example, first a person might notice the most obvious features, like a lot of sand and mountains in the distance. Then they might notice the scrub brush and a lizard darting by.

By Sensation Describe a garbage dump by what your senses perceive. First comes the smell—Wow! Then comes the sound of bulldozers climbing the mountains of garbage, and then you see individual objects.

By Function or Features Describe each ride at an amusement park separately. Notice how Deborah describes the Tastee Diner's features—a typical customer, the waitresses, the food, the decor.

DRAFTING

Many writers read through their notes before drafting and then use their notes only as reminders. Other writers refer to their notes repeatedly, even adding to them as they draft.

Getting It on Paper

When you draft, your purpose is to get words on paper. Don't try to find "the perfect word" just yet. You'll polish your work later.

Draft an Introduction An attention-grabbing sentence or two can make readers want to read every word. Deborah's description of the Tastee Diner intrigues the reader by starting off with a quotation, "Honey-child, this here diner has been here since 19 and 46." The quotation makes the description as friendly and inviting as the diner itself.

A good opening makes the reader say, "Why?" or "Tell me more." You might want to write your introduction first or last. Look at the ideas for introductions that follow.

- **A Surprising Statement** The quiet man who mows the grass on the soccer field is our state's most decorated war hero.
- **An Intriguing Question** Where can you go on a Saturday night that's fun and cheap—and that your parents will approve of?
- **An Important Point** When I went to the animal shelter to adopt a puppy, I was horrified to see rows and rows of whimpering, unwanted dogs.

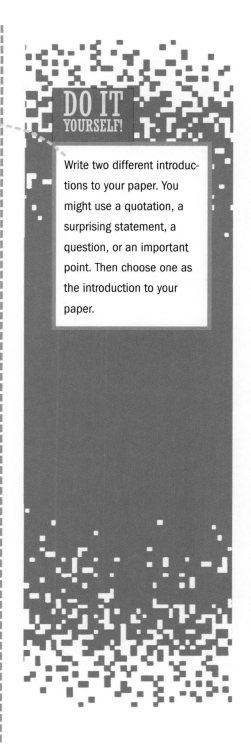

DO IT YOURSELF!

Write two different introductions to your paper. You might use a quotation, a surprising statement, a question, or an important point. Then choose one as the introduction to your paper.

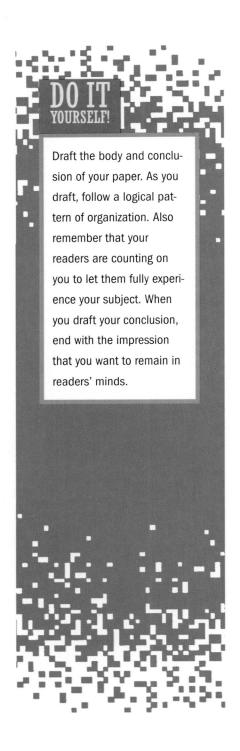

DO IT YOURSELF!

Draft the body and conclusion of your paper. As you draft, follow a logical pattern of organization. Also remember that your readers are counting on you to let them fully experience your subject. When you draft your conclusion, end with the impression that you want to remain in readers' minds.

Draft the Body When you draft the body of your work, use descriptive details that appeal to each of the five senses—sight, sound, smell, taste, and touch. Let readers experience what you experience. The more vivid your language, the more successful your writing will be.

WORK IN PROGRESS

The varieties of pie resting inside a glass container behind the front counter are enough to make a young child sit and stare in wonder. Pies such as key lime, pecan, cherry, apple, rhubarb, lemon meringue, and chocolate peanut butter often are praised by customers for their great home-made taste.

Draft a Conclusion Draft a conclusion that lets your reader know you're ending your description. Your final paragraph should leave a final, lasting impression of your subject with your reader.

WORK IN PROGRESS

Male and female, young and old, wealthy and poor, all can come to the Tastee Diner and enjoy food, music, and good conversation.

REVISING

When you revise a draft, look first at your overall organization. Would major chunks of description be more effective if they were in a different order? When you're satisfied with the overall organization, focus on the wording of individual descriptive details.

Improving Your Work

Read your draft with a reader's eye toward descriptive details and the effect that they create. Use the following checklist as you revise your draft.

Revising Descriptive Writing

- How well do descriptive details appeal to the senses of sight, taste, touch, smell, and hearing?
- Does the description include details that describe the subject from a distance and up close?
- Are descriptive details original? (See Chapter 11.1A, Clichés.)
- Where could **transitions** be added to help the reader move from one detail to another? When sentences and paragraphs are linked, readers clearly "see" the scene.

All writers work hard during the revision stage. No one gets it right the first time. If something doesn't sound right to you, erase it, and try again.

The revision process often is most successful when writers evaluate one another's work. Good feedback notes both what's right and what needs improvement.

Terms to Know

Transitions are words that link ideas and connect details in spatial order—*nearby, next to,* and *in front of*. For details to emphasize a person's traits, phrases such as *for example* or *in fact* are useful. To smooth the transition to a concluding paragraph, use transitional phrases such as *in summary* or *in conclusion*.

NEED MORE HELP

For more suggestions on how to use transitions, see Writing Transitional Sentences, Chapter 10.2C.

APPLYING LANGUAGE TO WRITING

Using Figurative Language

Figurative language—imaginative language that conveys a feeling or an idea—might compare two very different things or exaggerate some aspect of a thing or person. Some commonly used figures of speech follow:

- A **simile** compares two unlike things by using the words *like* or *as.* You might describe a person by writing, "When he leaves the bus, he bolts out like a race horse out of a chute."
- In a **metaphor,** a comparison says that one thing *is* another. A library's reading room, for example, could be "a cool, tranquil pond in the midst of the city's summer sizzle and noise."
- **Hyperbole** is exaggeration used for emphasis, as in "She has more running shoes than an athletic store." Exaggeration conveys the "feel" of something or someone, not the literal truth.

Using figurative language can be one of the most enjoyable parts of writing. Be careful, though, not to fall victim to a common mistake—mixed figures of speech, or mixed metaphors—as in the following sentence.

> Joe is a steam engine pulling his family through the mountainous waves of violence that beat against the people in his neighborhood.

To learn more about avoiding mixed metaphors, see Chapter 11.1B, Mixed Metaphors.

Don't Tell Me, Show Me Use figurative language and vivid adjectives and adverbs so you can *show* your subject to your reader. Showing is much more powerful than telling.

As you revise, replace descriptions that "tell about" with those that "show."

Telling: He has an odd laugh.
Showing: When he laughs, he sounds like a donkey with a corn chip caught in its esophagus, a sort of "Yee-huk—Yeehuk—Yeehuk . . . Gasp! Hiccup, Yeehuk—Yeehuk—Yeehuk."

Telling: The girls' locker room is run-down.
Showing: Entering the girls' locker room is like entering a subterranean cave. It's always dim because only a third of the light fixtures work. A leaking roof and constant high humidity have turned the walls, once a mint-green, to a mottled and streaked dark brown. Fuzzy gray mold thrives in the corners and around plumbing fixtures.

Telling: The Tastee Diner has a lot of different pies.
Showing: Pies such as key lime, pecan, cherry, apple, rhubarb, lemon meringue, and chocolate peanut butter often are praised by customers for their great homemade taste.

EDITING

To edit your writing, focus on eliminating errors—and on adding the finishing touches that can make a satisfactory description a great one.

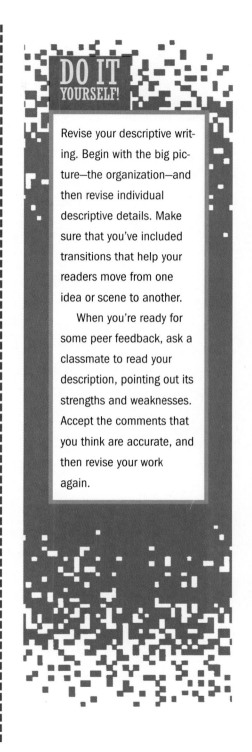

DO IT YOURSELF!

Revise your descriptive writing. Begin with the big picture—the organization—and then revise individual descriptive details. Make sure that you've included transitions that help your readers move from one idea or scene to another.

When you're ready for some peer feedback, ask a classmate to read your description, pointing out its strengths and weaknesses. Accept the comments that you think are accurate, and then revise your work again.

Making It Better

Don't try to edit your description by reading it once and making a few changes. Instead, read through your description several times, each time focusing on a different concern. Use the following checklist as a guide.

Editing Checklist

- Do all descriptive details make sense? Sometimes the sense of words gets jumbled in the revision process. For example, in the autumn, trees don't "spew" leaves.
- Are any details repeated so that they become boring or distracting? For example, if the grass is prickly, you only need to tell the reader once.
- Are words spelled correctly?
- Are grammar and usage correct?
- Is the description tight and concise? Avoid redundancy.
- Are adjectives and adverbs punctuated correctly? Look at your commas and hyphens.
- Is a new paragraph used each time the focus of the description changes? For example, if you describe how your room looks, use a new paragraph when you describe your mother's reaction when she enters.

APPLYING USAGE TO WRITING

Maintaining Verb Tense

As you revise, pay attention to verb tense. Whichever tense you use—past, present, or future—use it consistently. For example, Deborah's description is written in the present tense. She does shift tense, however, when she presents background information.

NEED MORE HELP?

Check out The Writing Process: Editing in Chapter 1 for more editing tips. Also see Chapter 11.1C, Redundancy, for suggestions on avoiding redundant words and phrases. Chapter 20.2, Commas, can help you with the punctuation of your description.

DO IT YOURSELF!

Edit your description, using the Editing Checklist. After you finish, exchange descriptions with a partner and use the checklist to evaluate each other's papers. Accept the suggestions that you feel are right, and make a final version of your paper.

WORK IN PROGRESS

The waitresses at the Tastee Diner are outgoing. They all have been there for years, and they always are willing to speak their minds. The waitresses wear ~~wore~~ casual clothes and keep their hair in a ponytail.

Refer to Chapter 15.2, Verb Tense, to learn more about avoiding shifts in tenses.

PUBLISHING

By publishing your description, you share it with others. Use the list that follows for publishing ideas.

Places to Publish Your Description

• Put your work in the school newspaper or magazine.
• Write a letter to the editor.
• Work with your classmates to create an anthology of descriptive writing.
• Include your work in your family's newsletter.

DO IT YOURSELF!

Submit your description for publication. You might begin by offering your description to some of the places listed on this page. Ask your teacher to suggest other places that might be interested in publishing your description.

Evaluation Activity

Book critics read and critique stories. Pretend you're a book critic for the school newspaper. Your assignment is to write a short review of your descriptive writing. Is it clear? Is it well written? Will your readers feel as if they've been to the place you described or made a new friend in the person you portrayed? Be a tough critic, but be fair to yourself! As a reviewer, would you suggest that a larger audience might appreciate your work?

4.2 Speaking Project
Writing and Giving a Descriptive Speech

You'll write and deliver a speech in which you describe someone or something so that listeners can see what you see when they close their eyes.

Terms to Know

A **descriptive speech** uses language that creates vivid images in listeners' minds. A descriptive speech usually employs sensory language—words that appeal to listeners' senses of sight, taste, touch, smell, and hearing.

Jeff loves giving speeches because he enjoys getting immediate feedback from his listeners. He didn't always feel this way, though.

When Jeff entered the county science fair, he knew that half of his score depended on an oral description of his experiment. With the help of his science teacher, Mr. Williams, Jeff was able to overcome his stage fright.

When Mr. Williams announced his retirement, Jeff helped to plan a school assembly honoring his favorite teacher. He even gave the opening speech!

What Is a Descriptive Speech?

A **descriptive speech** uses description to help listeners understand a subject in such a way that they will see, feel, and understand it. In this project, you'll prepare a speech that describes a person, a place, or a situation so that your audience can picture it in their minds as you do.

Read the following speech that a middle school student might have given to fifth grade students planning to enter her school. Because of the subject, most of the description appeals to listeners' sense of sight. When you draft your speech, of course, your description will be determined by your topic.

STUDENT MODEL

Express Yourself

by Carrie Larson, Grade 6

Being expressive is part of being a happy teenager. Colorful T-shirts are the easiest way to show your nosey friends who you are and who you wish you were.

Athletic guys in my grade usually wear their team shirts to school to show the world that they are needed, are included, and are important. These guys jostle along in groups, all wearing oversized, sagging white T-shirts with big bold numbers and the word "Wayland" draped across the back. Their shirts announce, "WE'RE ATHLETES."

Most girls in my grade are afraid to be original and stick out, so they will usually wear a plain colored shirt such as blue or red. These shirts are okay. I wear them. They're sort of like safety. People can't tease you, and you don't feel like people are staring at you. You blend in like crayons in a box. Everybody is a little different, but not too different. The best choices are real reds, like stop-sign red and rhubarb red, and real blues like sky blue and turquoise blue. These colors show you're a basically okay and confident sort of person. The only problem with these T-shirts is if someone else, someone with a great figure and perfect blond hair that falls naturally to her shoulders, happens to be wearing the exact T-shirt you're wearing.

To me, white shirts mean you feel free and open-minded. White T-shirts can go anywhere, with anything. You can wear them with jeans to go to the mall, or over a swimsuit at the beach.

If you wear stripes, I think of you as trapped or just wanting attention. People who wear a lot of stripes look like cotton-knit zebras.

Although plaid is a crazy mess of colors, usually it means you're laid back. A loose, wrinkled cotton plaid shirt, shirt-tails out, says, "Hey, nothing bothers me, bud."

Customized T-shirts really show everyone who you are. Any way you read them, the personal message is always the same. Take, for instance, the Save the Environment T-shirts. They show Earth as seen from space on a white background. Earth is blue with a few fluffy white clouds and is sprouting trees, cute animals, and people from different cultures who are arm in arm. The message is, "I'm committed. I care. I think."

Expressing your opinion is one of the most important things you will ever do. What you wear tells a lot about you and your personality.

IDEAS FOR YOUR SPEAKING PROJECT

1. Find a problem that needs fixing—roadside trash, a run-down community center, an overcrowded school cafeteria. In your speech, describe the problem and present a solution.

2. Choose a sporting event that will be televised. Gather information about the players and rules of the game. When the event is on television, turn off the sound. Then tape record yourself as a radio sports commentator describing the action.

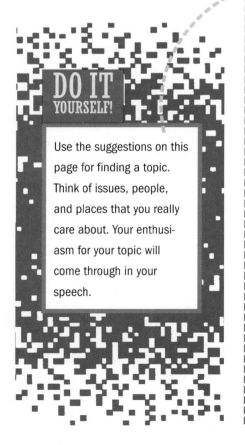

DO IT YOURSELF!

Use the suggestions on this page for finding a topic. Think of issues, people, and places that you really care about. Your enthusiasm for your topic will come through in your speech.

GETTING STARTED

When would you—or anyone—choose to make a speech describing something? The power of the spoken word lets you form a bond with your listeners. As they hear your words, they hear your feelings toward your subject. You also have their full attention. They can't skip a page or put you on "fast forward."

Determining Your Topic, Purpose, and Audience

When you choose a topic for a descriptive speech, be sure to choose one that works well as a speech.

How to Find a Topic

- Read your journal, looking for issues you care about.
- Think of activities that are best described orally, such as your adventures in babysitting.
- Think of situations in which you want others to see things your way. For example, if you're fund-raising, describe why the money is needed and how it will be used.

Once you have an idea for a topic, test it by asking yourself the following questions. Your answers will lead you to your purpose and audience.

Determining Purpose and Audience

- Why is this topic important to me?
- Why would this topic interest others?
- When I think of giving a speech on this topic, which group do I imagine as my audience? Why?

Gathering Your Material

For background material for your speech, you might use library resources, conduct interviews, or do on-sight observations. Take notes on what your learn.

When you finish gathering material, list the main points you'll make in your speech. After each point, note the information and description that supports it.

DRAFTING YOUR SPEECH

Draft your speech by one of two methods:

1. Make a complete written version of the speech.

2. Make note cards that are in outline form and list only main ideas and key supporting details.

Whichever method of drafting your speech you choose, the structure of your speech will be the same.

1. Open with a catchy introduction that introduces your topic.

2. Begin each section with one of your main points.

3. Support main points with facts, examples, or reasons.

4. Use descriptive details so listeners get a real sense of your topic. Notice that Carrie's speech appeals to her listeners' sense of sight. If your topic is a new cooperative restaurant, your description might appeal to listeners' senses of taste, smell, and sound.

WORK

IN PROGRESS

These guys jostle along in groups. They all wear oversized, sagging white T-shirts with big bold numbers and the word "Wayland" draped across the back.

5. Use **transitions** to move from idea to idea.

6. End with a conclusion that restates your purpose and leaves a lasting impression in listeners' minds.

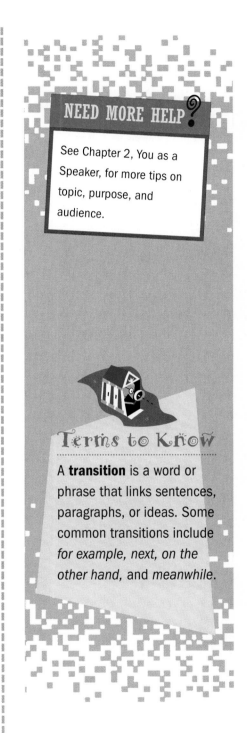

NEED MORE HELP

See Chapter 2, You as a Speaker, for more tips on topic, purpose, and audience.

Terms to Know

A **transition** is a word or phrase that links sentences, paragraphs, or ideas. Some common transitions include *for example, next, on the other hand,* and *meanwhile.*

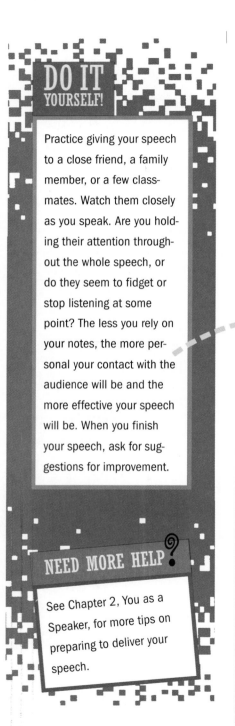

DO IT YOURSELF!

Practice giving your speech to a close friend, a family member, or a few class-mates. Watch them closely as you speak. Are you hold-ing their attention through-out the whole speech, or do they seem to fidget or stop listening at some point? The less you rely on your notes, the more per-sonal your contact with the audience will be and the more effective your speech will be. When you finish your speech, ask for sug-gestions for improvement.

NEED MORE HELP?

See Chapter 2, You as a Speaker, for more tips on preparing to deliver your speech.

REVISING AND EDITING YOUR SPEECH

Revise and edit your speech in stages. The first time that you revise, focus on organization and content.

- Will the opening grab the audience's attention?
- Are the subject and purpose clearly stated?
- How could main ideas be sequenced more effectively?
- Are main points supported by vivid details?
- Which portions of the speech might not appeal to the audience? Why?

The second time you revise and edit, focus on word choice, descriptive details, and effective transitions.

On the third pass through your speech, edit for errors in grammar and usage.

PRACTICING AND DELIVERING YOUR SPEECH

The delivery of your speech will be only as good as your preparation. Begin your preparations by making sure that you can read your note cards. If you are work-ing with a written version of your speech, you should know your speech well enough so that you only need to highlight key words to help you "remember" where you are. Don't try to memorize your speech, however, and don't plan on reading to your audience.

As you practice, time your speech. Know how long you'll be expected to speak and adjust your presentation to fit the time. If you'll be using a microphone to deliver your speech, practice using a microphone.

The Day of the Speech

Don't worry! The more relaxed you feel, the better your speech will be. Even if you don't *feel* confident, these tips will help you appear confident.

Tips for Delivering Your Speech

- Make eye contact. Pick a few friendly faces around the room and give your speech to those people.
- Don't sigh, laugh nervously, or cough. A microphone picks up every sound. Turn pages or cards quietly.
- Avoid adding meaningless words such as *like* or *um*.
- Speak clearly and slowly.
- Pause after each important point.
- Vary the tone of your voice. A monotone bores listeners.

DO IT YOURSELF!

Deliver your speech to an audience. Don't be afraid if you're a little nervous. A few "butterflies" will keep you alert and make you seem alive to your audience. Stand up straight and project your voice so that everyone in the room can hear you.

Evaluating Your Performance

Ask someone in the audience to record your speech. As you listen to it, ask yourself these questions.

1. Do I sound as if I'm speaking—or as if I'm reading?
2. Is the content of my speech interesting? Did I select vivid words and effective examples that sound good when spoken aloud?
3. Do I sound as if I'm interested in my topic?
4. Did I speak too quickly? Too loudly? Too softly? Did I pronounce each word clearly?
5. Did I make eye contact with the audience?

Did you give the speech you wanted the audience to hear? Be honest! Rate yourself on a scale from 1 to 10. A number 1 means you put your audience to sleep, and a number 10 means you woke them up!

4.3 Visual Project

You'll create a photo essay, using individual images that combine to present a powerful message.

Terms to Know

A **photo essay** consists of a series of photographs that show a particular point of view, make a point about a subject, or show how to do something. A photo essay might, for example, show daily life from the point of view of children in a war-torn country.

Creating a Photo Essay of a Community Place

Imagine that there's a special place—a park—in your neighborhood. You and your friends have been having fun there ever since you can remember. Now imagine that a community redevelopment project would turn that park into a municipal building. What can you do?

You could write an essay that describes the role of the park in the community. Or you could take photographs that show neighborhood residents enjoying the park.

When Words Aren't Enough

There are many instances when one image can convey an emotion or an idea that would take many words to describe. A **photo essay** presents an idea through a series of photographs. A photo essay can convey a point of view through the mood of the photos, or it can make a point by the subject matter that it focuses on.

For this project, you'll plan, execute, and present a photo essay about a place in your community. If you don't have a camera, you can create your essay with pictures from newspapers, brochures, or even your own drawings or paintings. You'll present your picture essay either as a slide show or an illustrated book.

Before you begin, look at this photo essay about a special place in one student's community.

STUDENT MODEL

Pinecrest Park
Kathleen Kennedy, Grade 8

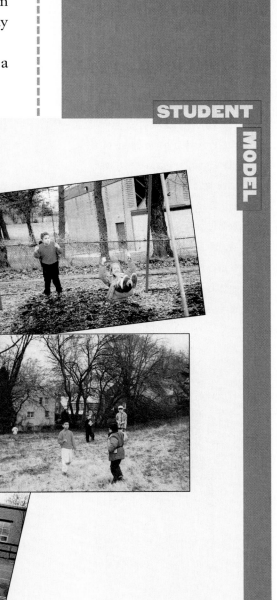

VISUAL PROJECT

1. Create a photo essay that describes a community event, such as a 4-H fair, a tractor pull, or a Founders' Day celebration.

2. Create a photo essay of a school performance, such as a play or concert. You should show what happens before, during, and after the performance.

3. Prepare a photo essay of a place most people haven't seen, such as a community recycling center. Your essay might show how the center processes materials.

4. Make a photo essay that saves a life. A photo essay of unwanted pets in a local animal shelter might move some families to adopt a pet.

PRE-VIEWING

Choose a topic that you think is best described visually. Your topic might be a favorite place, a place that needs improvement, or someone's lifestyle.

Audience and Purpose

As you develop your topic, consider your audience and your purpose. They go together, and both shape your work. If your purpose is to show how much fun people had at a concert, your audience might be your classmates. If your purpose is to show how safe the concert was, your audience might be adults concerned about rowdiness at concerts. Either way, your purpose and audience require different images.

Kathleen Kennedy's purpose was to record and share the unique nature of Pinecrest Park. To achieve her purpose, she chose images that revealed the diversity of people and activities in the park.

Using a Graphic Organizer

To plan a photo essay, you might use a sequence chain. On a piece of paper, connect a series of boxes with arrows. In the first box, tell the viewer what the subject of the essay will be. The pictures must present the subject in a clear and logical sequence.

DRAFTING, REVISING, AND EDITING YOUR PHOTO ESSAY

Drafting a photo essay means getting images, either with a camera or a sketchbook. Visit the location you'll show, and then collect images.

Collecting Images

1. Follow your sequence chain, or outline, of images. Remember to have one image that orients viewers to the subject by showing an overall view of the place.
2. Capture images of all sights that are *important* to your purpose. A beautiful picture that doesn't fit the subject is useless at best—at its worst, it will confuse viewers.
3. Get images of people who are important to the subject.
4. For a one-time event, gather more material than seems necessary. You can't go back to recreate an event.

Selecting and Arranging Materials

When you've finished all the photos or drawings, review them. On a large work surface, stack your slides, photos, or drawings in the order an audience should view them. Go through the images one by one. Remove any that don't fit the story. Ask yourself these questions as you study each image.

Questions for Revising a Photo Essay

- What idea or feeling does this image communicate?
- Does it help develop the intended mood or feeling?
- Is this image related to my purpose and audience?
- Does it add new details or information?
- Does it belong in the order in which it appears?

Number each visual in pencil—on the front of a slide, on the back of a photograph.

Putting on the Finishing Touches

When you have all the images in order for a photo essay, add a few finishing touches.

   ◎ Add a title that states the subject of your essay.

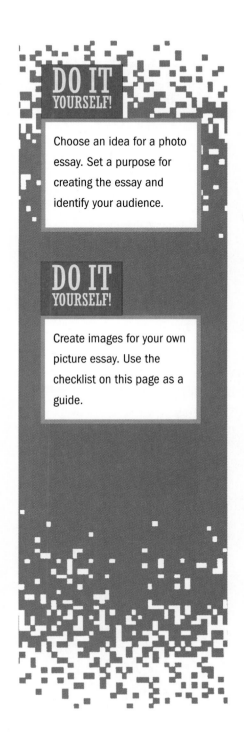

DO IT YOURSELF!

Choose an idea for a photo essay. Set a purpose for creating the essay and identify your audience.

DO IT YOURSELF!

Create images for your own picture essay. Use the checklist on this page as a guide.

DO IT YOURSELF!

If you think a visual presentation would benefit from music, spend an afternoon with your CD player and be your own disk jockey. Select different types of music to play while you look over a visual essay. Think about the mood each type of music creates. Then record music to accompany your presentation.

◎ If you wish, add captions that summarize the content of each photo.

◎ Depending on your topic and your presentation, you may wish to record selected music to accompany your presentation. For a slide show, you might want to tape record a narration with music in the background.

Now give your visual presentation a title and show your work to a few classmates, friends, or family members. Have them tell the story of your visual essay back to you. Are they seeing what you want them to see? If not, is everyone leaving out the same important idea or making the same mistake? If your audience isn't getting the message, go back and fill in the gaps by creating new art or reordering the photos.

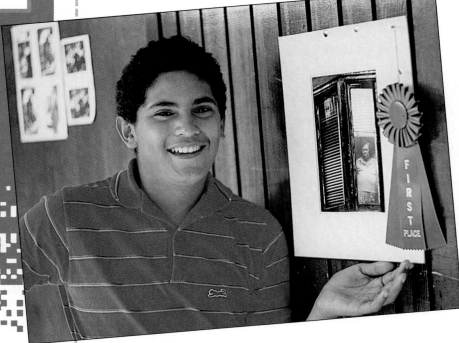

PRESENTING YOUR PHOTO ESSAY

When a photo essay has a title and a narrative or sound-track, it's time to present it to or display it for an audience. There are many ways you can share your work.

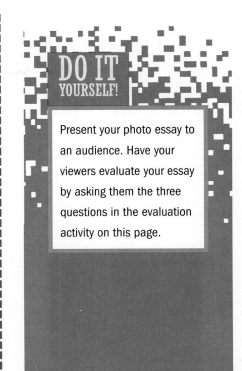

- **In class.** You might bring in your slides and perhaps provide musical accompaniment. Many schools have slide projectors and tape recorders.
- **In an after-school club.** A drama or photo club is a good place to present a photo essay.
- **At an assembly.** You can present a slide show at a school assembly and provide a narrative as the slides are shown.
- **In a library or community center.** If a visual project is made up of photographs or drawings, display it in a library or community center for others to enjoy.

DO IT YOURSELF!

Present your photo essay to an audience. Have your viewers evaluate your essay by asking them the three questions in the evaluation activity on this page.

Evaluation Activity

Evaluate your visual essay by asking your viewers to answer the following questions.

- What was the purpose of the essay?
- What message did the essay convey?
- What group or groups of people would be the ideal audience for this essay?

Review the answers to your questions. If your viewers didn't see your essay as you intended them to, follow up with more questions to find out why. Should you have gathered different material or organized your essay differently? By examining your viewers' comments, you'll be able to gauge your success.

CHAPTER 5

Communicating

to Tell a Story

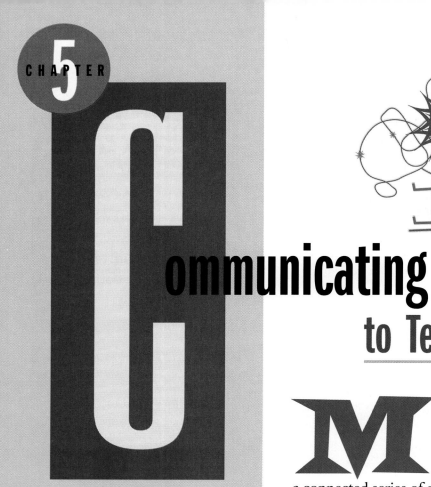

Terms to Know

A work of **fiction** is purely imaginary—the characters and events are not real but *might* be based on something that happened in real life. On the other hand, a work of **nonfiction** is factual. A newspaper story is one kind of nonfiction.

Most people enjoy reading, hearing, or seeing stories, either **fiction** or **nonfiction**. A story, as you know, is a narrative about a connected series of events. You probably have favorite kinds of stories—adventures or science fiction or mysteries, fairy tales or romances or true stories.

Do you think you could tell a story that others would enjoy? It's an exciting challenge. You may be surprised at how well you can meet it. Storytelling is more than words on paper. Long before writing was invented, people gathered around open fires at night to tell and listen to stories. Before television was invented, people clustered around the radio to listen to soap operas, police dramas, and mysteries.

You can also tell a story, or part of a story, with no words at all. "A picture is worth a thousand words" is a saying with a great deal of truth. Some of the most striking news photographs tell vivid stories.

Why Do People Tell Stories?

From cave dwellers' stories to those of modern film makers, two reasons for storytelling stand out.

- ◎ *To entertain.* Funny stories make us laugh. Suspense stories keep us on the edge of our seats. Science-fiction stories astonish us with a vision of the future.
- ◎ *To convey a message.* A storyteller often has deeply felt beliefs and creates a story to convey those beliefs imaginatively. For example, instead of simply stating, "Prejudice is wrong," a good storyteller shows why it's wrong through story events.

Developing any kind of story is a little like putting together a jigsaw puzzle. A story has a number of parts that must fit together to create the whole picture.

In this chapter you'll have a chance to practice your story-telling skills in three ways—in writing a **short story**, in orally telling a **tall tale**, and in drawing **storyboards**.

LOOKING AHEAD TO THE PROJECTS

5.1 Writing Project
Write a well-developed short story (pages 104–117).

5.2 Speaking Project
Tell a tall tale, using exaggeration and humor (pages 118–125).

5.3 Visual Project
Create a storyboard for a slide or videotape presentation (pages 126–133).

Terms to Know

A **short story** is a brief work of fiction, shorter than a novel. Most short stories include a character or characters who have a problem that they want to solve.

A **tall tale** is a story that exaggerates the deeds and abilities of its hero or heroine.

A **storyboard** is a visual outline of a narrative and is used to plan things like videos, commercials, or animated movies.

JOURNAL WRITING

Study the photograph. Then write three or four sentences that tell what you think is happening. If you were one of the people in the photograph, what do you think the ending of the story would be? Jot down your ideas in your journal in a sentence or two.

5.1 Writing Project

Writing a Short Story

You'll be writing to entertain or to convey a message.

Imagine a world without stories—without mysteries or tales of adventure or science fiction. In such a dull world there would be fewer books and magazines, nothing to see at the movies, and very little to watch on TV. Fortunately, our world is so full of stories that you don't have to look far to find them. Every day we hear or read stories in newspapers, on television shows, or simply through conversation with friends.

But no matter how many stories there are in the world, there are always new tales to tell. Think of a story that *you* might like to tell. The audience for your short story might be

- just one person;
- several readers, if, for example, it is posted on a classroom bulletin board;
- dozens of readers of a school literary magazine.

Before you begin your own story, you may find it helpful to read a short story written by a student your age. Of course, your own story will be entirely your own. Be prepared to use your imagination!

STUDENT MODEL

The Guard

Lauren Collogan, Grade 8

Loud breathing penetrated the crisp cold October air. We all stood in a circle, waiting for the captain's call on what to do on the next down. All around me, I could see the serious faces. The air of competition surrounded us like a cloud. We just <u>had</u> to win this game. We had beaten every team this year.

"Meredith." Liz's voice broke my train of thought. "Meredith, you guard."

"Okay." I always said okay. Every day, Liz, our captain, gave me the order to guard, and I always said okay, even though I never really wanted to. I could only imagine catching the pass, running into the goal line. I could only dream.

I sighed silently as I trotted over to the line of scrimmage, pushing up the sleeves of my blue Westing Middle School sweatshirt. I glanced up at the opposing team and into Alexis's fierce eyes. Ugh. Alexis.

I thought back to the day I met Alexis. Ms. Tanford had decided to let us vote on which sport we were going to do next. I love soccer, and we never played it. I planned to suggest it, and then for once in my life, I might actually have fun in P.E.

Just as Ms. Tanford was about to ask for sport suggestions, the gym door squeaked open, and in came Alexis. At first I thought that she was very pretty. Her raven-black hair flowed down her back, one strand

drooping lazily in her face. Her fair skin was spotted with freckles. Her white gym outfit accentuated her tall, thin figure. Ms. Tanford marked Alexis in the roll book and told her to take a seat. Alexis, unsmiling, strode over and sat next to me. I forgot all about my suggestion until Alexis's hand shot up.

"I think that we should do football. After all, it is autumn, and it's the perfect weather." Alexis's confident voice echoed throughout the gym. Football! Not football! I had waited days for soccer! Her cool stare challenged us to disagree. My classmates nodded in agreement. My heart sank.

Ever since that day, Alexis had ruled everything. She got to be captain of her team. She got to pick the field on which they played. She got to pick the color of their flags. She had made the class a dictatorship, and she was the dictator.

"17, 24, 11 . . . Hike!" All around me, people began to move. Everyone ran to their places, sweeping by me. I ran upfield to cover Liz when she got the ball. I turned around to see the play.

Jo had the ball, but Liz was on the other side of the field. I called to her.

"Jo, pass it to me!" She turned her head, and to my astonishment, she threw me the ball! The brown ball came spiraling toward me. It landed right in my outstretched hands. I brought the ball toward my body, and I ran to the goal. My legs seemed to stretch further and further until, finally, I crossed the goal line.

Continues ┈┈┈┈┈▶

I had done it!

I whirled around to see my teammates. Liz was running to me. Everyone was cheering. I could feel a smile on my face. I couldn't believe it! I had scored a touchdown. Liz came over and hugged me.

"That was great, Meredith! I can't believe it! You won the game." I was about to reply when a voice interrupted us.

"No, she didn't." I spun around. Alexis.

"What do you mean? She had the ball, and she crossed the goal line." Liz's voice, though calm, had an underlying layer of anger.

"She went out of bounds," said Alexis, sneering.

"Are you crazy? She didn't even go near the line," yelled Liz, her voice climbing.

"Yes, she did. I saw her myself." Alexis laughed cruelly. "After all, what makes you think that a wimp like her could ever score anything?"

"She scored the touchdown." Liz's face was right in Alexis's. My mind was spinning with hatred. How could she? She was the one who had suggested the sport, and now she couldn't even lose fairly. My jaw quivered in anger. All of the hatred, all of the madness boiled up inside of me. I turned around and ran up to Alexis.

"I never went near the line. You just . . ." My words were choked off by sobs. I turned around and raced to the other end of the field. Ms. Tanford was standing there getting ready to blow the whistle.

"What's wrong, Meredith?" Ms. Tanford had a questioning look in her dark eyes.

"Alexis lied. She said that I went out of bounds. I didn't." Tears spilled out of my eyes.

Ms. Tanford walked down to the other end of the field. I followed her.

"What happened?" she asked Liz.

"Alexis said that Meredith went out of bounds, but she really didn't." The rest of my teammates nodded in agreement.

"Alexis, is this true?" Ms. Tanford asked.

"No."

"All right. What did happen?" Ms. Tanford asked slowly. The bell rang then, and everyone ran toward the locker room.

The rest of the day passed quickly. I went home, did my homework, practiced piano, and ate dinner. I was just getting ready for bed when I heard my father's voice downstairs, "Meredith! Phone call!"

I ran downstairs and grabbed the phone from my father's hand.

"If you don't want to get beaten up before school tomorrow, stay home." Alexis's sneering voice shot in my ear. Then she hung up.

I slept surprisingly well, but my eyes slowly opened and then shut again when they saw the sunlight creeping in through my bedroom curtain. Oh, no. In one hour I would be at school. What would I do?

I showered and trudged off to school, my eyes on the sidewalk. Then I bumped into something. I focused and saw a pair of black Chucks. Alexis. I stood back and looked defiantly into her eyes.

"I thought I told you to stay home, tattle tale." Her voice was icy.

"Oh, shut up, Alexis." All around us, in a circle, people were beginning to gather.

Alexis pushed me to the ground. She pulled off my

leather jacket and threw it into a mud puddle. My leather jacket! I tried to stand up, but she punched me to the ground.

"I guess from now on, you won't mess with me, huh?" sneered Alexis. Then she pulled me to my feet and threw me down again into the mud. She turned and walked away. I sat in the mud, dazed, aching.

Most of the crowd drifted off toward the school. Some kids, though, including Liz, still remained.

I stood up slowly and walked over to my jacket. I bent over and picked it up. It was ruined. I had begged my parents for this jacket. "But," I said softly to myself, "I stood up to her."

PREWRITING

Some writers may just sit down and write, but that's rare, even among people who write for a living. Most writers need to do some up-front thinking and planning—in other words, some prewriting.

Freewriting—A Rich Source of Ideas

One way to get going is to start writing whatever comes into your head. This process is called freewriting. Your ideas may fall into some of these categories:

- **Personal Memories** A time when you were very sad or very frightened could be the basis for a story. Strong feelings can lead to strong stories.
- **Special Interests** Many good stories stem from a writer's interests. The phrase "Found a 1943 nickel" or "Made a super cherry pie," could lead to "The Five-Cent Mystery" or "Triumph in the Kitchen."
- **Friends' Experiences** Something in a friend's life might hold the germ of a story.
- **News of the Day** A news story might turn into a fantasy.

IDEAS FOR YOUR

WRITING PROJECT

1. An anecdote is a short, entertaining account of an event. Although an anecdote has some of the elements of a short story, it is often nonfiction. For your writing folder, write an anecdote about something you've experienced. Be prepared to read it in class and get others' reactions.

2. A short-short story is a complete but very brief fictional narrative. Write a 500-word (or less) short-short story with a surprise ending.

3. A narrative essay is a short piece of nonfiction that tells a true story, usually in chronological order. Write a short narrative essay about an event from your life.

Terms to Know

Plot is the sequence of actions in a story that keep the story moving.

Characters are the people, animals, robots, or other creatures who play an important part in a story.

Conflict is the problem in a story that the hero or heroine must resolve before the story ends.

DO IT YOURSELF!

With one or two other students, discuss your ideas for a story. Listen carefully to the ideas of others.

After you choose a plot for your story, map out a time line of the plot. Indicate a beginning, a middle, and an end. A time line doesn't need to provide all the action of a story, just the major events.

My Story Will Be About . . .

When Lauren planned her story, she began by thinking of a **plot**. Most stories have a plot that involves a main **character** who faces a problem. How the character tries to overcome the problem becomes the **conflict** in the story.

Lauren chose this problem: a girl faces a bully. The events that happen as the girl tries to resolve the conflict create the plot of the story.

To think of a plot and conflict for your own story, look at the ideas and freewriting notes in your writing folder.

Planning Your Plot

Once you have an idea for the conflict in a story and how it will be resolved, you have the basic plot. Mapping out a time line of events before you actually start writing helps you to create a beginning, a middle, and an end. Here's how Lauren mapped out her story, "The Guard."

WORK IN PROGRESS

BEGINNING

Meredith dislikes Alexis and hates playing football.

Meredith finally makes a touchdown.

MIDDLE

Alexis claims Meredith went out of bounds.

Meredith tells the gym teacher that Alexis lied.

Alexis threatens Meredith.

END

Meredith stands up to Alexis, gets beaten up, but feels proud of herself for standing up to a bully.

Planning Your Story

Before Lauren wrote "The Guard," she pictured the characters and the **setting** in her mind's eye. Then she jotted down notes on the details of what she imagined. For example, she noted, "Alexis—tall, thin, long black hair, strong, pushy, mean."

Put into words the details of what you see in your mind's eye.

MY SHORT STORY

Plot

    What is the conflict, the main problem, in my story?

    How is the conflict resolved?

Setting

    Where and when does my story take place?

    What are three important details about my story's setting?

        1

        2

        3

Characters

    Who is my main character?

    What are three important details about him or her?

        1

        2

        3

    Who is another important character?

    What are three important details about him or her?

        1

        2

        3

Terms to Know

The **setting** is the location and the time in which a story takes place. A story can be set in the present, the past, or the future, or even in an imaginary place and time.

NEED MORE HELP?

See the section called Developing Your Subject in Chapter 1 for additional tips on adding details. See the section called Organizing Your Ideas for more ideas on organizing your thoughts.

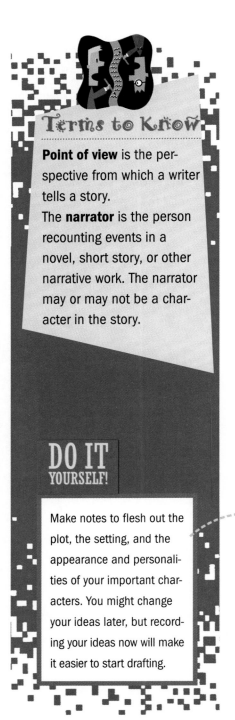

Terms to Know

Point of view is the perspective from which a writer tells a story.

The **narrator** is the person recounting events in a novel, short story, or other narrative work. The narrator may or may not be a character in the story.

DO IT YOURSELF!

Make notes to flesh out the plot, the setting, and the appearance and personalities of your important characters. You might change your ideas later, but recording your ideas now will make it easier to start drafting.

Choosing a Point of View

One more decision to make before drafting is the **point of view** of your story. Most stories are written from the first-person or third-person point of view. The pronoun *I* indicates first-person point of view. Lauren wrote "The Guard" in the first person. If you refer to all characters as *he, she,* and *they* or by name, and never use *I* or *we* to talk about the characters, then you're using third-person point of view—writing in the third person.

- *First person.* A character tells the story as he or she experiences it. First-person point of view reveals only what that one person (the *I*) sees, thinks, and feels. This **narrator** often makes the story seem more true to life. This first-person narrator, however, cannot give a complete view of the story because he or she can't directly reveal the thoughts and feelings of other characters.

- *Third person.* A third-person narrator uses pronouns like *he, she,* or *them* to refer to the characters. In a third-person limited point of view, the narrator sees the action through the eyes of one character. In an omniscient point of view, the narrator knows everything about all the characters. (The word *omniscient* means "knowing all things.")

DRAFTING YOUR STORY

After you've thought about and discussed the story you want to write, begin your first draft without worrying about making mistakes in spelling and usage—without even worrying about all the details of your story.

Professional writers sometimes say that all writing is rewriting. A first draft always needs work. Use your first draft to get your ideas on paper.

Hook 'Em Early

A good story starts with a hook—an opener that attracts interest and tempts the reader to continue. "The Guard" begins, "Loud breathing penetrated the crisp cold October air." When you read that, you immediately start wondering what's going on.

Creating Characters

The characters in your story should seem like real people. How do you make characters lifelike?

1. *Describe them.*

> **WORK**
> **IN PROGRESS**
>
> Alexis had pale skin spotted with freckles and perfect raven-black hair that hung down her back. She was tall, thin, confident, and unsmiling.

That Alexis is confident and unsmiling gives the reader a sense of her personality. Physical details also help the reader imagine what Alexis looks like.

2. *Have them act.*

> **WORK**
> **IN PROGRESS**
>
> Liz was running to me, and my teammates were cheering. I could feel myself smiling. A touchdown! Liz came over and hugged me.

The saying that actions speak louder than words applies to storytelling. Let characters reveal themselves by what they do.

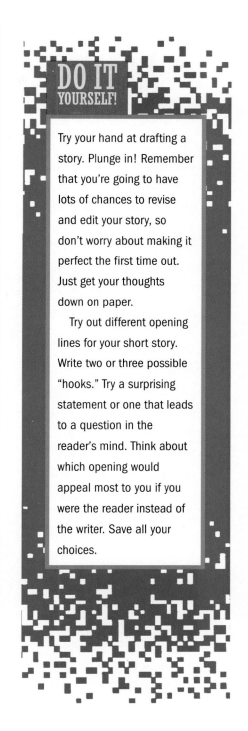

DO IT YOURSELF!

Try your hand at drafting a story. Plunge in! Remember that you're going to have lots of chances to revise and edit your story, so don't worry about making it perfect the first time out. Just get your thoughts down on paper.

Try out different opening lines for your short story. Write two or three possible "hooks." Try a surprising statement or one that leads to a question in the reader's mind. Think about which opening would appeal most to you if you were the reader instead of the writer. Save all your choices.

Terms to Know

Dialogue is the speech or conversation of characters in a story. A dialogue tag, such as *he said,* tells who spoke the words. Some dialogue tags tell how the words were spoken; for example, "Get your feet off that chair," he growled.
Concrete language employs nouns, adjectives, and adverbs to create vivid pictures in a reader's mind. These words appeal to a reader's sense of sight, hearing, taste, smell, and touch. When writers use concrete language, they focus on the specific rather than the general.

3. *Have them speak.*

"I guess from now on you won't mess with me—huh, wimp?" sneered Alexis.

Dialogue reveals character by portraying people through their own words or the words of others. Listen carefully to how people actually speak. Write distinctive dialogue that fits the character.

Developing Your Setting

Your story's setting may be familiar or unusual. It must, however, be consistent with the events that take place. To develop the details of your story's setting, consider the following elements.

Elements of a Setting

- physical location (towns, buildings, places)
- time of day
- weather and temperature
- people in the scene (what they say, wear, do)
- particular sights, sounds, and smells

To describe a setting and make it seem real for your readers, use **concrete language.** For example, if you're describing a nearly empty hallway at school, let readers see the rows of blue lockers and the gray walls. Let them hear the squeak of a pair of sneakers on the old linoleum and the vibrating *twang* of a locker door slamming shut.

Building Plot

Organize your plot according to how story events occur. You'll probably add or change events as you draft or revise your story. Your plot will change then. Sometimes the best stories seem to have a life of their own, surprising even the writer by the way they turn out.

Ways to Organize Your Plot

- You may find it easiest to write your story in straight chronological order. If this is your choice, you'll present events in the order in which they occur.
- You might, however, prefer to use **flashbacks**. A flashback in "The Guard" explains why the girls are playing football and why Meredith resents Alexis.

A good plot contains conflict—either **internal conflict** or **external conflict.** In Lauren's story, the conflict is external between Meredith and Alexis. The plot develops the conflict to a point where it must be resolved.

Ending Your Story

Your conclusion should be strong enough for your readers to remember. Some writers have their last sentence in mind before they write their first draft. They want the ending to be just right. Whenever you write it, try to make your conclusion a knockout.

Look at the endings of some stories you've liked. Reread the last sentence or last paragraph of each one. What did each writer do to wrap up the story? Consider using one of these techniques in your own writing.

Terms to Know

A **flashback** is a scene from another, earlier event. Flashbacks jump back in time to explain a character's feelings or memories or an event.
Internal conflict is within a character.
External conflict occurs between characters or between a character and nature or society.

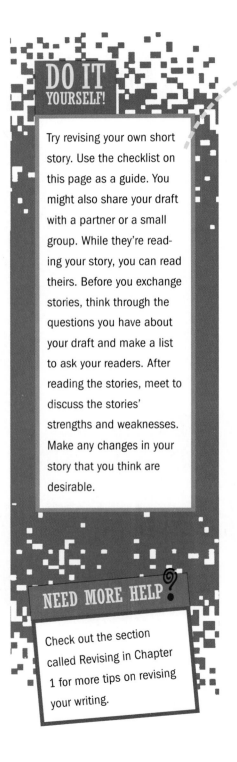

DO IT YOURSELF!

Try revising your own short story. Use the checklist on this page as a guide. You might also share your draft with a partner or a small group. While they're reading your story, you can read theirs. Before you exchange stories, think through the questions you have about your draft and make a list to ask your readers. After reading the stories, meet to discuss the stories' strengths and weaknesses. Make any changes in your story that you think are desirable.

NEED MORE HELP?

Check out the section called Revising in Chapter 1 for more tips on revising your writing.

REVISING

Before revising a draft of your story, let it rest for a few days. Then you'll be able to read your story as if someone else had written it. You'll see clearly the changes you want to make.

You may not want to show the first draft of your story to anyone. You may even hate it. Try not to be discouraged. Many writers have this first reaction to their own work, no matter how good it is. Remember that weak first drafts can become excellent short stories. Revision is the key.

Revision almost always requires more than just a few changes. You'll probably have to do some rewriting. You may have to add text or dialogue. You may have to get rid of parts that don't work or move sentences or even events from one place to another. Revision is essential if you want to produce the best story possible.

Checklist for Revising a Short Story

1. Does the hook catch the reader's interest?
2. Is my point of view clear?
3. Did I provide enough information?
4. Do details enable readers to picture characters clearly?
5. Is the time sequence clear?
6. Does the conflict start at the beginning of the story and last to the end?
7. Does the conflict seem important to the characters all the way through the story?
8. Does the story move clearly and logically from one event to the next?
9. Does the dialogue sound realistic?
10. Are any scenes or dialogue unnecessary?

APPLYING USAGE TO WRITING

Getting Rid of Clichés

A cliché is a boring, overworked expression. Try to eliminate such phrases as "red as a rose," "big as all outdoors," and "few and far between." One of the marks of good writing is the absence of clichés. For more on clichés, see Chapter 11.1A, Clichés.

EDITING

Editing means polishing. It means getting rid of errors in grammar, usage, spelling, and punctuation. To edit your story, ask yourself the following questions.

Checklist for Editing

1. Read your story through quickly for basic mistakes.
   - ◎ Have I repeated any details that don't need repeating? (Once you've mentioned that the villain has a menacing look, you probably won't need to tell the reader the same thing again.)
   - ◎ Have I contradicted myself? (You may catch yourself describing a hero whose eyes are blue on one page and brown a few pages later.)
   - ◎ Have I *told* the reader something I could have *shown* more effectively? (Instead of writing "Rosa was a genius," you might want to show Rosa solving a difficult math problem or creating an award-winning science project.)

2. Read each sentence slowly and carefully.
   - ◎ Is the meaning of the sentence clear?
   - ◎ Is the sentence grammatically correct?
   - ◎ Are any words misspelled?
   - ◎ Are any punctuation marks missing or wrong?
   - ◎ Does each sentence lead logically to the next?

DO IT YOURSELF!

Edit your short story, using a different color ink from the one you used for revising. You might also exchange stories with a classmate. Choose a different person from the one who read your story before. Accept the recommendations he or she makes if they seem valid. Make a final copy of your story.

Apply the ideas in the checklist to your own first draft.

NEED MORE HELP?

Check out the section called Editing in Chapter 1 for more tips on editing your writing.

Terms to Know

Proofreading is reading to catch errors in grammar, usage, mechanics, spelling, or typing.

NEED MORE HELP?

Check out these sections for more help in punctuating dialogue: 20.2F, Direct Address; and 20.5A, Direct Quotations.

DO IT YOURSELF!

Decide on a way to share your story with others. You might post it on a class bulletin board, arrange to read it aloud to other students, have it printed in a magazine or newspaper, or publish it as part of a class book of short stories. After you've published your work, ask yourself what you have learned from sharing your work that will affect the way you write your next short story.

APPLYING MECHANICS TO WRITING

Writing and Punctuating Dialogue

Keep the following points in mind when writing, revising, or **proofreading** dialogue.

1. Start a new paragraph when the speaker changes.

    "She went out of bounds," said Alexis, sneering.

    "Are you crazy? She didn't even go near the line," yelled Liz, her voice climbing.

2. Put quotation marks around the speaker's exact words. Don't use quotation marks for indirect quotations.

    EXACT WORDS: "What happened?" Ms. Tanford asked.

    INDIRECT: Ms. Tanford asked me what happened.

3. Don't use a dialogue tag when the identity of the speaker is clear without it.

    "Alexis lied. She said that I went out of bounds. I didn't." Tears spilled out of my eyes.

4. When a sentence is interrupted by a dialogue tag, don't capitalize the second half of the sentence. Put commas to the left of quotation marks.

    "Tomorrow," she said softly to herself, "we'll see what happens."

5. Vary your dialogue tags. It's more interesting for your reader. Don't always use *He said*, or *said Alexis*. Try using some of the following tags.

    - she shouted
    - he screamed
    - I whispered
    - he laughed
    - she chuckled
    - I giggled
    - she yelled
    - he gasped
    - I breathed

PUBLISHING

There are many ways to share a story besides having it printed in a book or magazine.

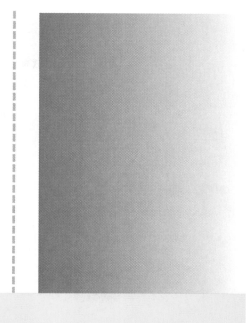

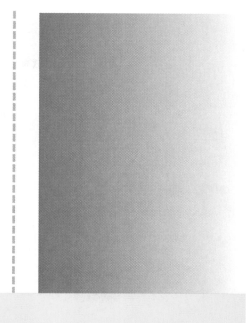 Read your story to a group of students from different classes and grade levels in an informal setting—at a library table or in the classroom with chairs arranged in a circle. If the response is positive, you might submit your story to the school newspaper—or even a literary magazine.

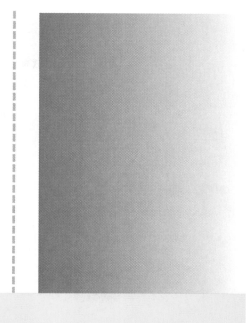 If you know a professional writer, ask that person to read and comment on your story. (Make sure your work is typewritten and double-spaced.)

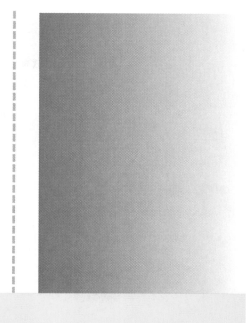 Magazines for students sponsor short-story contests. Find out who these sponsors are. Submit your story for consideration.

Evaluation Activity

To improve as a writer, you must be able to judge your own work. This checklist will help you assess and comment on your work and the work of your classmates.

Checklist for Evaluating Your Story

1. Does the story have a good title?
2. Do the events or dialogue in the story grab a reader's interest from the beginning?
3. Do the characters seem real and believable?
4. Is it clear where the events in the story take place?
5. Does the story move smoothly from sentence to sentence and from scene to scene?
6. Do holes in the plot lead readers to think, "It couldn't happen that way"?
7. Does the story slow down at any point?
8. Does the dialogue reflect the personality of each speaker, or do all speakers sound alike?
9. Is the ending strong and satisfying?
10. Is the story free from errors in grammar, usage, mechanics, and spelling?

Be frank with yourself. Your goal is to improve. Although criticism—even self-criticism—is often harder to accept than praise, it can be more valuable. Correct your weaknesses so that you can build on your strengths.

5.2 Speaking Project

Making up a Tall Tale

When you tell a tall tale, you can't exaggerate events too much!

Terms to Know

Hyperbole is the use of exaggeration to create humor or surprise. Hyperbole can be serious, for example, "She was so upset, she cried a river of tears." Hyperbole can also be fantastic, for example, "She was so upset, she cried a river of tears—and that river became a flood, and that flood lifted her house and floated it downstream, and didn't stop until it had deposited her in a new and beautiful land."

You may have read tales about Paul Bunyan, the giant lumberjack of the Great Lakes and the Pacific Northwest. According to the tales, he created the Grand Canyon and Puget Sound. His companion, Babe the Blue Ox, who measured 42 ax handles, shared in his adventures.

What Is a Tall Tale?

The stories about Paul Bunyan are tall tales—humorous stories that use exaggeration, a technique known as **hyperbole**.

Most tall tales were originally told aloud, not written down. Only later did someone put them down on paper. The purpose of a tall tale is always to entertain. As you read Mac Brodt's tale, look for hyperbole. You'll create your own exaggerations in your tall tale.

Paul the Dragon Tamer

Mac Brodt, Grade 8

There once was a boy who was respected and admired by all who knew him. His name was Paul Smith, and he has been hailed as the most famous roller coaster rider of all time. Throughout the land, there was not one roller coaster he could not conquer. Paul was brave and bold and never showed a bit of fear. He stood tall and proud with a hint of arrogance and a touch of majesty. He was (narrator pauses) invincible.

As the weeks turned into months and the months into years, Paul grew restless. He could not find a coaster that sparked even the most remote touch of interest in his young life, until one day.

An amusement park in Tampa, Florida, was advertising the unveiling of its newest masterpiece, the Dragon Slayer. It was an enormous roller coaster that stretched (narrator stretches arms up) like a rubber band 260 feet up into the air and whipped (narrator makes a whip movement with arm) across its tracks at speeds over 80 miles an hour. Its creators said that the Dragon Slayer's 12 loops and 85 degree turns would make jet pilots quake with fear. And indeed, the Dragon Slayer stole the courage of all who approached it. It was the fastest, it was the biggest, and it was the meanest roller coaster ever. It was exactly what Paul had been waiting for all his life.

When Paul heard of the roller coaster, he bellowed, "Grandma!" in his fifteen-year-old voice. "Get in the car! We're going to Florida!" and off they went.

They first saw the beast crouched like a colossal mountain across Tampa Bay. Its awesome stature and magnificent presence sent shivers up and down their spines. For a moment even Paul felt the sharp sting of fear, but only for a moment. When it passed, he was himself again—ambitious, determined, fearless. The sound of grinding metal rang in his ears as the Dragon shook the cars on its awful back, drowning all sounds with its own ferocious roar.

A dark cloud covered the sun as Paul Smith stepped into the first coaster car that fateful day. The car slowly chugged up and up. On the ground, people wrung their hands, held their breath, and closed their eyes so tight it was as if their lids had been stapled shut. If they'd had the courage to look, they would have seen Paul Smith, sitting nobly in that coaster car, his eyes glowing with a vibrant radiance and his arms (narrator raises arms) reaching straight up toward the heavens.

(narrator speeds up pace) The first turn snapped hard left like a firecracker. Then the roller coaster sped down the hill. One passenger was flung into the trees (narrator says "whoosh") and then landed with a thud (narrator stomps foot). The back half of the car leaped off the tracks and curled up until it bumped into the front car. People were ripped out of their seats and ended up landing on the seats behind them. Through all this, there was Paul, unmoved and firm.

When the ride ended, only one stepped out of the car, Paul Smith. He was the first, the first to survive the most dreaded roller coaster of all time, the Dragon Slayer.

SPEAKING PROJECT

IDEAS FOR YOUR

1. Prepare an oral presentation of a story about a humorous incident that happened to you. Although the story should be based on fact, exaggerate to make your story humorous.

2. A fable is a brief tale told to teach a lesson. Often the characters in fables are animals. Aesop is famous for his fables. Prepare an oral presentation of an original fable or one of Aesop's fables.

3. Prepare an oral presentation of a story or fairy tale that you think would appeal to young children. Present it to a group of preschool children.

DO IT YOURSELF!

Think of an idea for a tall tale and freewrite or web to flesh out the idea. Remember that tall tales thrive on exaggeration, so let your imagination run wild!

GETTING STARTED

To tell a tall tale, begin by thinking of a tale to tell. The tale that you tell should meet these criteria:

- The tale is one that lends itself to oral telling. Stories with lots of descriptive detail, a complex plot, and many characters aren't suitable for oral storytelling. Save those story ideas for written stories.
- *You* can tell the tale to listeners. That means that you, not your best friend and not a professional actor, feel comfortable telling the tale.
- The tale, from start to finish, takes only about five minutes to tell.

Webbing for Ideas

Webbing, or clustering, is one way to get and build on ideas for a tall tale. When you create a diagram of related ideas, one thought leads to another.

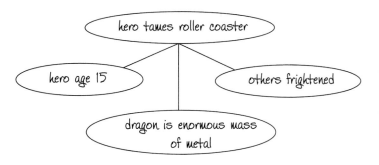

If you think your tall tale is getting too long and complicated, you may want to use only one branch of your web.

DRAFTING YOUR TALL TALE

After webbing or freewriting, develop your ideas in one of these two ways.

- Create a complete written version of your tall tale to flesh out details and ideas.
- Make **note cards**. Jot down key events. You can use your note cards when you tell your story aloud. (Be sure to number note cards so they don't get out of order.)

Mac Brodt started drafting "Paul the Dragon Tamer" by making these notes.

WORK IN PROGRESS

Introduction

Paul, age 15, loves roller coasters, is bold

— has ridden all roller coasters

— no more challenges

— is bored

— learns of the Dragon in Tampa, Florida

When you draft your tall tale, you must choose a point of view from which to tell it.

- *First-person point of view* includes the storyteller.

WORK IN PROGRESS

When my friend Jamail said to me, "Let's grow a Venus flytrap as big as a palm tree," I thought he was kidding. Then he showed me his laboratory.

Terms to Know

Note cards are usually 3" x 5" white cards. When you draft notes on note cards, print and use large letters. That way, you won't have to squint to read your writing when you're telling your tale. Also, don't try to cram too much information on one card. In fact, you might want to have one note card for each scene. You can revise your note cards as you revise your tall tale.

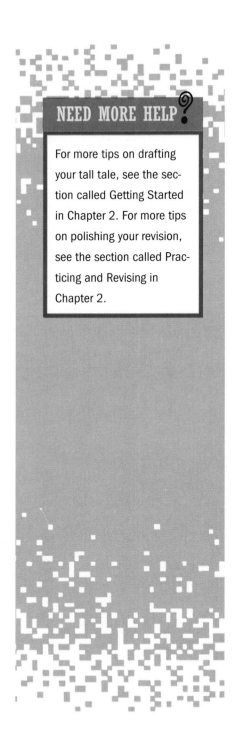

◎ *Third-person point of view* leaves out the storyteller.

WORK IN PROGRESS

When Paul heard of the roller coaster, he bellowed, "Grandma!" in his fifteen-year-old voice.

Don't change the point of view in the middle of a story. If you do, you'll confuse your listeners.

REHEARSING AND REVISING YOUR TALL TALE

A tall tale improves through revision–changing words, phrases, and ideas in the written-out story or on note cards. A tall tale also improves with rehearsing. You'll want your voice and gestures to make your tall tale as entertaining as it can be.

Making It Better

Check your draft or notes to see how you can add life to your tall tale. When you feel comfortable with the revised version of your tale, rehearse with someone. What did he or she like most? Least? Keep what works. Change what doesn't.

Revising for an Audience

◎ Jump right into the story. Don't say, "I'm going to tell you about—"

◎ Remove excess wording. Avoid repeating the same idea or incident, unless you're doing it for effect.

- Make sure you've got some great dialogue. Exaggeration in dialogue enhances the story: "Hand me that sliver of wood," the giant said, pointing to a telephone pole. "I need a toothpick."
- Use your voice to create character. (Speak the words, "I won't go" as a hostile giant, a frightened child, and a peevish old woman. Your voice can create character even more effectively than a description.)
- Use your voice to add to the mood of the story. Speak quickly to speed up the action. Whisper to add to the suspense.
- Make sure the conclusion is satisfying—like the punch line of a joke.

EDITING

To edit an oral presentation, first ask yourself, "Can the listeners easily follow the story?" Remember, they can't go back and reread a passage.

Checklist for Editing a Tall Tale

- Are the sentences too long and complicated?
- Does my delivery sound relaxed and natural?
- Did words slur together? Was the pace too fast?
- Are there places to pause, slow down, or use emphasis to make ideas clear?

To use these or other suggestions, note the points lightly in pencil on your draft or note cards.

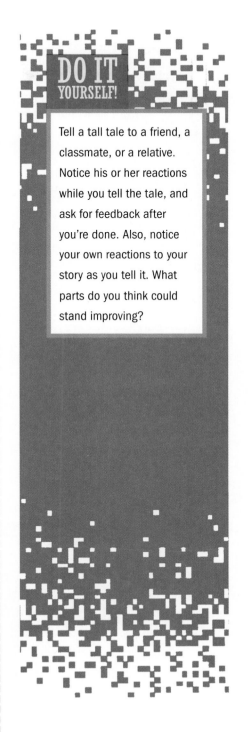

DO IT YOURSELF!

Tell a tall tale to a friend, a classmate, or a relative. Notice his or her reactions while you tell the tale, and ask for feedback after you're done. Also, notice your own reactions to your story as you tell it. What parts do you think could stand improving?

NEED MORE HELP ?

For more tips on delivering your tall tale, see the section called Delivering in Chapter 2.

DO IT YOURSELF!

Find an audience that wants to hear your tall tale—your classmates or a group of younger children. Tell your listeners your tall tale. Be prepared to enjoy sharing your work, and you'll find that your audience enjoys hearing it too!

DELIVERING YOUR TALL TALE

Time spent rehearsing is never wasted. A tall tale improves with an excellent delivery. When you're ready to deliver your tall tale, use the checklist below as a guide.

Speaker's Tips

◎ Look at the people in the audience. Really look at their faces. Listeners give hints about their reactions. If they're straining to hear, speak louder.

◎ Stand tall, shoulders square, head up. Don't slouch. Posture is an important part of any oral presentation.

◎ Use gestures for emphasis. A tall tale benefits from gestures. To exaggerate the size of something, it's natural to hold your arms wide for emphasis.

◎ Vary tone of voice to suit the content of the story. If a story is exciting, volume increases as excitement builds.

◎ Use different voices to speak as various characters. A character might have a high squeaky voice, a low, booming voice, or a nasal voice. Selecting voices for characters makes them come alive—and it makes it easy for listeners to follow what is happening.

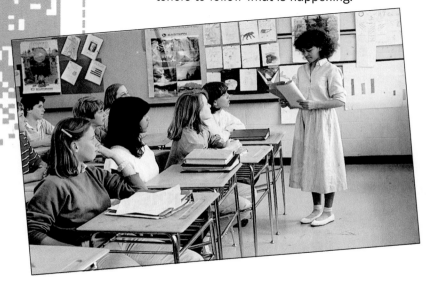

Another Way of Telling a Tall Tale

If you have access to a tape recorder, make a tape of your story. You might want to experiment with adding background music or sound effects.

What Did You Think?

Here are two ways of evaluating a tall tale.

◎ *Peer evaluation.* Ask three to five students to be peer evaluators. The rest of the class should sit back and enjoy your tall tale. Peer evaluators will

—find one or more positive comments to make.

—ask questions about any parts that are unclear.

—suggest ways to improve the story.

◎ *Self-evaluation.* Accurate self-evaluation isn't easy. Here's one way to proceed.

—Write out a list of questions about your performance: "Did I speak clearly?" "Did the audience pay attention?" "How many students were smiling or laughing?"

—Compare your written answers with those of your teacher or peer evaluators.

To evaluate a tall tale, use the following checklist.

Eight Questions About Tall Tales

- Does exaggeration create a funny situation?
- Is the tale interesting from the very beginning?
- Does the tale have coherence—does it move smoothly from one incident to the next?
- Does the speaker's voice help make the story funny and entertaining?
- Are the details clear and specific?
- Does the tale keep moving from start to finish?
- Does the tale contain some conversation?
- Does the tale have a strong, interesting ending?

5.3 Visual Project

Developing a Storyboard

You don't need to be a great artist to create a storyboard.

Terms to Know

A **storyboard** is a series of pictures, like a cartoon strip without the words, that tell a story.

Captions are descriptive statements under illustrations. Photographs in newspapers and magazines often have captions. The purpose of a caption is to tell something about the illustration that the viewer may not know simply by looking at it.

What do comic books, ballets, paintings, and photographs have in common? You guessed it—they all tell stories visually. Images can tell a story, or they can help to plan a story. For example, people who make movies, music videos, and television programs plan their work with a device called a **storyboard**—a series of pictures that shows the shots that they want to get.

Why Use a Storyboard?

A storyboard for any visual piece of work tells the order of the pictures. A storyboard does not necessarily have a plot and characters, but it does show a progression.

In this chapter, your goal is to create a storyboard for the purpose of entertaining your audience—your classmates or a group of younger children. You may or may not produce the program, but a storyboard gives you the plan.

Mike Vidmar created a storyboard for a short movie about two students—one big and strong, the other smaller and weaker. When challenged to a wrestling match, the smaller student practices and then beats the bigger student. **Captions** sometimes appear on a story-board. Mike's frames include captions. Key pieces of dialogue for a scene help viewers understand what is planned for the final product.

The Match

Mike Vidmar, Grade 8

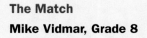

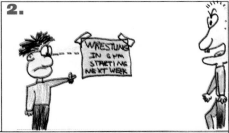

1. The MATCH

2.

Noviski (thinking) Uh-oh! Wrestling. And look, there's Mutzo!
Mutzo: Hey, Wimpto Noviski!

3.

4.

Noviski (thinking): I hate wrestling so much. I better not say anything to Mutzo, though!

Mutzo: Hey, Noviski! It's time for wrestling! Fun!
Noviski: Not really. I think wrestling is for gorillas on steroids—OOPS!

Continues ························▶

5.

Mutzo: What was that you said, Noviski?
Noviski: Mmmmph! Mmmph! Hey! Lemme go, brute!

6.

Mutzo: I'll get you back for saying that, Noviski!

7.

Mutzo: Hey, Coach! How about letting me and my buddy Noviski wrestle on Monday?
Coach Linguini: Sure!

8.

Noviski (thinking): Well, I have to wrestle Mutzo. I had better get a plan!

9.

Noviski (thinking): I'll really have to learn about wrestling before Monday.

10.

11.

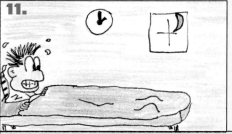

Noviski (thinking): I wonder what Mutzo is going to do to prepare?

12.

Mutzo: Ha-ha! Ha-ha-HA!

IDEAS FOR YOUR

WRITING PROJECT

1. Find photographs taken by your family and create a story around them. Make a storyboard.

2. Decide on a story you would like to re-create. Then make puppets for the characters in the story and a puppet theater on which your puppets will perform. Present your story in a puppet show for young children.

3. Make a mural showing different scenes that depict a story of your choice.

DO IT YOURSELF!

Choose a story to present visually. Name the story and tell why you chose it. Then name the kind of project you have in mind and tell why you made that decision. Keep your notes and your ideas for these projects in your writing folder.

PRE-VIEWING

Before you make a storyboard, you need to decide what you're going to do and how you're going to do it.

What's the Story?

A storyboard outlines what you expect to include in the slide show or videotape. It can never show all the scenes you hope to include in the final product.

Planning a Storyboard

1. Choose a story. It can be your favorite published short story or a story or tall tale you've written.

2. Consider your audience—or audiences. You may have one audience that views your storyboard panels and another audience that views the final product, such as a film, that your storyboard helped you plan.

3. Plan what the story will include, such as the events that make up the story's plot. Also plan the characters and what they look like.

4. Decide on the final product. You might choose to make a slide show, a videotape, or a flip book.

5. Determine how you'll create the storyboard. You might draw a series of sketches or take original photographs.

But I Can't Draw!

Although most storyboards have hand-drawn pictures—sketches or stick figures—it's also possible to create a storyboard without any pictures. You might describe, in words, a picture rather than sketching or photographing it. You tell about the pictures that will appear in the finished production without showing them.

DRAFTING YOUR STORYBOARD PANELS

Often the person who does a storyboard is comfortable with drawing or photography. Because some people don't like to draw or take pictures, though, you may create a storyboard as a group project. In this case, one person can do the drawing or photography while the others act as "creative consultants" (a movie and TV term you may have seen in on-screen credits). The consultants suggest

—the number of panels needed for the storyboard.
—ideas for individual panels.
—the best order in which to arrange the panels.
—the elements needed in each panel to make the story clear.

Whether you take the next steps individually or as part of a group, the steps are the same.

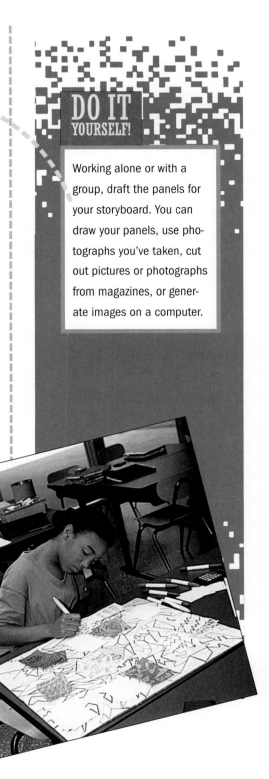

DO IT YOURSELF!

Working alone or with a group, draft the panels for your storyboard. You can draw your panels, use photographs you've taken, cut out pictures or photographs from magazines, or generate images on a computer.

Steps for Drafting a Storyboard

1. Begin by drawing, on scrap paper, ten to twenty boxes. These should be large enough to hold your sketches, photographs, or descriptions.

2. Prepare a rough sketch for each of these boxes. If you are using photographs or descriptions, prepare them and decide which one will go in each box.

3. Put each sketch, photograph, or description in the appropriate box. Then you will have a first look at your panels.

4. Draft the captions for the storyboard panels.

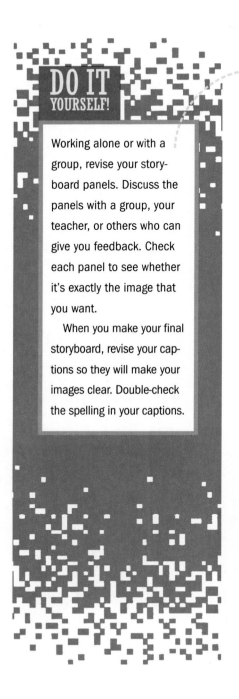

REVISING YOUR STORYBOARD PANELS

No matter how well you've planned, your rough sketches and draft captions will probably need revision. Here's how to go about revising.

- Discuss the proposed panels with your group, your teacher, or someone else who can suggest possible improvements.
- Revise your panels on the same or different scrap pages, using the following guidelines:
    - —Make sure each main event in the story is included.
    - —Check that each panel adequately presents the idea you want to convey.
    - —Eliminate any panels that are unnecessary to present the story.
- Go over each panel carefully. Grammar and spelling are not important at this point. The scrap paper will not be part of your final presentation. Your focus is on your choice of pictures, not on your choice of words.
- Obtain a fairly large piece of white cardboard or oak tag to use for your finished storyboard.

Completing Your Storyboard

To create the final storyboard, use a large piece of cardboard or oak tag to draw the panels needed. You might have drawn the sketches out of sequence, but you'll need to draw them in the correct sequence now.

Add captions to make the panels clear. Use the captions you've already drafted on scrap paper. Since the captions are part of the final presentation, grammar and spelling should be correct.

APPLYING SPELLING TO STORYBOARD CAPTIONS

Spelling

Make sure that the words in your captions are spelled correctly. Some words, such as *success* and *occur*, may even look right when misspelled. To make sure you've spelled the "tricky" words right, review Chapter 24.2, One Hundred Most Frequently Misspelled Words.

DISPLAYING YOUR STORYBOARD

When a storyboard is complete, a film maker or advertising executive presents it at a meeting of producers or company executives. You can present your storyboard to your class or to another audience.

Although a storyboard is more or less self-explanatory, it's still necessary to go over the ideas it shows. Summarize the content and discuss the overall idea panel by panel.

DO IT YOURSELF!

Present your work to your classmates, talking your way through the images you've chosen. Then find a way to display your storyboard to share it with others. You might post it in your classroom, put it on display in the school library, or show it to other classes. If possible, make a slide show or videotape from your storyboard to bring your work to life.

Self-Evaluation

You've been evaluating your storyboard ever since you wrote the first notes about it. To judge it now as a finished work, consider the following questions.

1. Does my storyboard clearly outline my story?
2. Does my storyboard provide details of the story's setting, characters, and events?
3. Is my storyboard carefully prepared, with useful artwork or descriptions as well as useful captions?
4. Does my audience understand my storyboard?

Communicating to Explain

"What is it?" Juan asked.

"It's a gerbil," beamed Aunt Renee as she handed the squirming little animal to him. It was another birthday gift from Juan's favorite aunt.

"Gee, thanks, Auntie," Juan said, adding, "What am I supposed to do with it?"

"Just follow the instructions in that little book," said Aunt Renee, pointing to a small book on top of the animal's cage.

That evening, Juan read the book, which told how to care for a gerbil. He learned that a gerbil is a furry, mouselike animal that jumps like a tiny kangaroo. Juan was looking forward to having fun with his new pet.

Have you ever received a gift and needed an explanation of what to do with it? Like Juan, maybe you got your information by reading. You may also have had a verbal explanation. Perhaps you have even found instructions on a chart or another kind of visual.

Why Explain?

When you communicate to explain, you're using exposition, which can be written, spoken, or even presented visually.

Expository writing increases a reader's understanding. For example, a cookbook author tells how to cook certain foods. You might write a note to a friend explaining how to get to your home. Think back over the past few days. When did you explain something to someone else?

People also explain or inform by speaking. Some speaking is informal, such as information you share with your teachers, your parents, your friends, and your classmates. A more formal speech is called a **demonstration speech** because it explains an idea or tells how to do a task.

To inform others graphically, you might use a diagram, a map, or a chart—all of which are usually easier to understand than a written or verbal report.

In the pages that follow, you'll have an opportunity to write an essay, give a speech, and design a chart to explain and inform. After completing any one or all three of these projects, you'll know better how to communicate information that others can understand.

LOOKING AHEAD

TO THE PROJECTS

6.1 Writing Project
Write an expository essay about a matter that's important to you or that's a problem (pages 136–149).

6.2 Speaking Project
Prepare a speech in which you demonstrate how you solve a problem or carry out a task (pages 150–159).

6.3 Visual Project
Create an explanatory chart about a special interest of yours (pages 160–167).

Terms to Know

Expository writing is writing that informs. Exposition explains concepts, gives information, explores ideas, or gives directions.
A **demonstration speech** is a speech that explains to an audience how to do a task or how a machine or some other object works.

6.1 Writing Project

You'll write an expository essay about a problem or another matter that's important to you.

Writing an Expository Essay

Whenever Eli's mom looks into his room, she's horrified at the mess. She constantly begs him to clean up his room or at least make it look neat. One day, Eli's mom reached the end of her rope.

She stormed upstairs and shouted, "I don't understand why you can't at least be neat. Your room is an eyesore. Don't you feel ashamed to have your friends see it? I wish you could explain to me why you can't tidy up!" Eli looked at his mom. Then he said, "Okay. I'll try." His mom said, "I can't even talk to you about it now, I'm so angry. But, Eli, I'd really like you to make a plan for cleaning your room. Do me a favor, write down on paper some ways you could improve your room. I'm trying to understand you better." Eli shrugged and replied, "I'll try to do it, Mom, if it will help us get along better."

How do you explain messiness to someone? Eli realized his explanation would take some thought, planning, and maybe even some research, but he began to look forward to the challenge.

To help you get started on your own expository essay, read Eli Wilson's essay. While he was planning what to write to his mom, he came up with a way to explain himself to his middle school friends. Of course, your essay will be entirely your own. Be prepared to use your own ideas.

STUDENT MODEL

How to Clean Your Room
Eli Wilson, Grade 7

I'm a slob. My entire family is made up of slobs, with the exception of my mother, who seems to enjoy cleaning. If it weren't for her, our house would be a dump. She expects us always to have a clean house, including my room, which she assumes I will clean. She constantly reminds me that if I would spend a few minutes on it every day, it wouldn't get out of control. She's right, but somehow I can't ever keep anything neat for very long. Like many other kids, I trash my room on a regular basis. Unfortunately, with the trashing comes the responsibility of cleaning the room again.

I have developed a system for cleaning my room that will probably work for almost any room that has not already been condemned by the health department. The first basic step is to scout out any dirty clothes that are in the room. These clothes may be found on chairs, on top of the dresser, or on the floor, even under the bed! Clothes take up a lot of room, so this will make a big difference right away. Having a hamper in your room where you can put dirty clothes as you take them off should prevent the clothes ending up on your floor, but it has never worked for me. Occasionally some clean clothes may get mixed up with the dirty ones. This mixup is caused by a failure to put clean laundry away promptly. But it may be better to wash these clothes again than to try to figure out which are which.

If there are clean clothes to be put away, they should be put in dresser drawers or the closet. Make sure that you don't mistake dirty clothes for clean ones. While washing clean clothes may be okay, wearing dirty ones definitely is not! Some clothes will need to be hung on hangers, so if you see any hangers lying around on the floor, pick them up now and use them.

The next essential step is to look on the floor and pick up any large objects like books or magazines. These objects also take up a lot of space on your floor. Clearing the big stuff off the floor makes it look like you're making progress.

Now look for small items on your floor. Usually you can find small scraps of paper and candy wrappers. These items should be placed in a trash bag or waste basket to be emptied later into an outside garbage can. Sweeping might increase the speed and quality of this process.

There will probably be some things that need to be put away. Video games, shoes, and pencils are some examples. Don't even pick them up until you know where you will put them. Just moving things around

Continues ⋯⋯⋯⋯▶

wastes time. Try to collect the items that belong in other rooms so only a few trips will be necessary. Empty glasses and plates should go back to the kitchen. If these have been in your room too long, they may need to be soaked for a while. But don't forget about them and leave them in the sink. If your mother is like mine, she will hold you responsible for your mess, even after you have taken it out of your room.

As soon as the bed is empty of junk, it should be made up. Don't bother asking why you should make up a bed. Everyone knows you are just going to mess it up again, but for some reason, this argument never works on mothers. This may be a good time to change the sheets. Putting clean sheets on the bed occasionally is a good idea. In fact, some families insist that sheets be changed regularly—as often as once a week!

By now the room should be looking pretty good. Depending on how thoroughly your parents inspect, some things may be passed over. Some parents will overlook messy drawers or closets. Some may not look under beds. But just in case you have a picky mom like I do, you'll need to do everything, even dust dressers and clean windows and mirrors. The easiest way to dust cabinets and tables is to take everything off them, dust the surfaces, then dust and replace each item one by one. Glass can be cleaned with a window cleaner spray and paper towels or a sponge. Check the label to see if you can use the same stuff to wash fingerprints off the woodwork. Of course, if you don't ever touch the woodwork, there won't be any fingerprints.

The final step is to use the vacuum cleaner to suck up any bits and pieces of stuff that you left behind. Make sure to get into all the little nooks and crannies. If your vacuum cleaner has a dusting brush, you can use it to dust table tops and window sills and this will shorten your dusting time immensely. But be careful not to suck up anything you want to keep. It's no fun searching through the dust and dirt for things lost in the vacuum cleaner bag.

Even though I don't really like cleaning up my room, at least with this system, it doesn't seem to take too long. It stops my mother's complaining for a while. And in only a few days, it is exactly as it was before—wrecked, just the way I like it.

Terms to Know

Brainstorming means thinking about ideas and writing them down in the form of a list without stopping. Brainstorming helps you discover all the possible ideas you might have.

PREWRITING

You don't normally sit down, pen in hand or computer keyboard in front of you, and start writing an expository essay. You need to do prewriting–thinking and jotting down ideas. The more ideas you think of and jot down in any order at all, the easier it will be for you to decide what to write about.

How do you begin writing an expository essay? The logical way is to think of a topic—what you'll explain to your audience. Believe it or not, you're an expert in many things. For example, you can probably give information about some historical place in your own town. You may be able to give information about a sport or another activity or give helpful advice on doing homework.

When you explore possible topics for an expository essay, just keep in mind that a good place to start is with a subject you're familiar with or interested in. You may also start with a broad topic. You'll have a chance to narrow your topic later in the process. Below is a list that should help you think of ideas of your own. Remember, you're listing subjects that you might want to inform others about.

Subjects for an Expository Essay

- Why friends are so important
- How to improve in soccer
- Picking out a vacation spot you like
- Picking out a computer that suits your needs
- Important messages in rock music
- How to become a math whiz
- How to improve the community environment

Brainstorming: Listing Your Interests

One technique for discovering a topic to write about is **brainstorming**. Quickly list all the topics or subjects you're interested in. Don't worry about how much you know about the subject. Don't stop to think. Just brainstorm and jot down your ideas in a list!

IDEAS FOR YOUR

WRITING PROJECT

1. Write about your favorite subject—literature, math, sports, music, you name it—for students in a lower grade. Talk with teachers of younger students about topics that you might be able to help them with. Keep in mind the age of your audience.

2. Write directions on how to do a job or task, such as how a friend should feed your pet when you're away for a weekend.

3. Write a letter to someone you don't see very often, explaining a favorite activity.

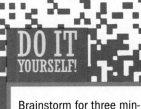

DO IT YOURSELF!

Brainstorm for three minutes to get ideas for topics for an expository essay. Examine your list and then circle three or four topics you think you would like to inform others about. When you finish your list, store your ideas in your writing folder.

Narrowing Your Topic

After you explore possible topics, choose one and narrow it down for your expository essay. If you've made lists or clusters to get ideas, see whether any one topic comes up more than others. Once you decide, jot down your favorite topic.

Narrowing down means making your topic specific. If your subject is too broad, you may not be able to include interesting details about it. For example, if your topic is basketball, narrow the topic down to writing about a specific player, a specific game, or a specific court. Then you can give details and interesting information about the subject.

Purpose and Audience

When narrowing your topic, keep in mind your expository purpose for writing. For example, Eli's purpose in "How to Clean Your Room" is to inform and give directions.

Also, keep in mind those who'll read your work. You may be writing your essay for your parents or a teacher or a younger person or for a friend who knows nothing about your topic. Deciding who your audience is will determine what information you write about and what words you use.

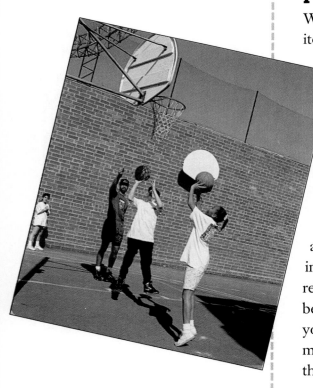

To help organize your essay and decide who your audience will be, write the field or subject of your topic in your writing folder. List a number of specific topics related to your main topic and what audience would be interested in these topics. For example, if you decide you want to write about the topic of school, there are many specific topics and audiences you might list. See the next page for an example of one way to organize an essay about school.

SCHOOL

Specific Topic	Audience
•A guide for the first day of middle school	A new student
•How to do well in Mr. Martin's algebra class	A student in Mr. Martin's class
•The history of our school	All students
•How the student government works	Students interested in becoming involved in student government
•How the local school board works	Parents and students

Gathering Information

The next step in the process is gathering information. You might wonder, "Where will I get the information I need?" The answer depends on your topic. In most cases, there are three main sources: your own knowledge and experience, other people's knowledge and experience, and written information. The chart on this page shows how these sources work.

NEED MORE HELP?

For more information on reference sources, see Chapter 27, Test, Study, and Research Skills.

Topic	Source
How to do well in algebra class	Self—use own experience
	Friends—ask about their experience
How the school board makes decisions	President of board, board members—ask for information
How to use a word-processing program or a computer	Books, pamphlets—read and take notes

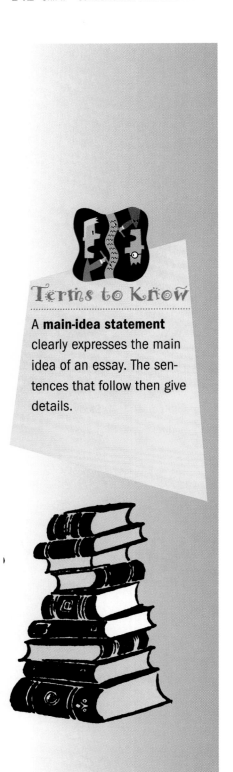

Terms to Know

A **main-idea statement** clearly expresses the main idea of an essay. The sentences that follow then give details.

Developing an Expository Topic

How do you go about developing an expository topic? The list that follows suggests different kinds of information for developing your topic. As you read the list, think about the source of each kind of information; there may be more than one source for some of the information.

Ideas for Developing Expository Topics

- Specific facts, such as dates, places, events, times, and so forth
- Examples of what you're telling about
- Anecdotes, or personal stories related to the topic
- Steps in a process
- Quotations from people who have given you information
- Reasons or explanations
- Causes and effects
- Similarities and differences

Also, jot down a **main-idea statement**—a sentence that expresses the main idea of your essay. You may want to change some of the wording of this sentence later on, but it's a good idea to write out such a sentence while prewriting. It can help keep you on track.

Organizing Your Information

If you're using books or maps for your information, make sure you've read them carefully and that you've conducted your planned interviews with experts. Once you have the information, you're ready to organize it.

Using 3 x 5-inch note cards is a good system for gathering and organizing your information. Use a separate card for each piece of information and write your information as phrases, sentences, or paragraphs.

Don't worry about the order in which you record your information. And don't decide now whether it's information you really want to use. You can decide that later. Use all the sources you've decided on for your topic. Be sure to record just one idea on each card.

Making an Informal Outline

An informal outline is one that organizes your information by main ideas and supporting details. Look at the cards in each pile. Decide on the order in which you want the information to appear in your writing. The order will depend on your information, of course. You may want to arrange your information by **order of importance**. You might also want to order your material by the **steps in the process** that you're explaining, as in "How to clean a room" in the following informal outline for Eli's essay. You'll notice that there are no numbers or letters. Eli just indented the supporting details under the two main ideas.

WORK IN PROGRESS

Problems with cleaning room
    Inherited sloppiness
    Mom's neatness

How to clean room
    Get rid of dirty clothes
    Put clean clothes away
    Pick up stuff from floor
    Make bed
    Dust and vacuum

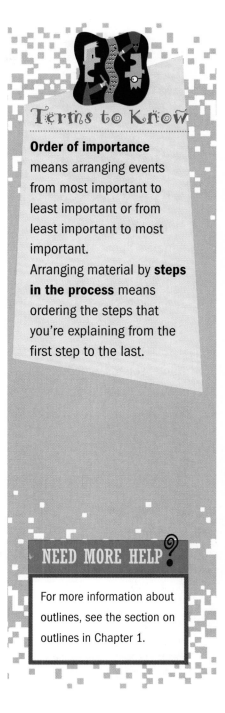

Terms to Know

Order of importance means arranging events from most important to least important or from least important to most important.
Arranging material by **steps in the process** means ordering the steps that you're explaining from the first step to the last.

NEED MORE HELP?

For more information about outlines, see the section on outlines in Chapter 1.

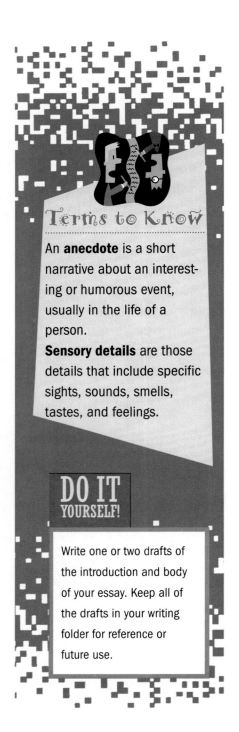

DRAFTING

When you've found all the information you need, go back through your prewriting notes and cards. You may have written some good sentences and paragraphs already. Gather this material and begin your draft.

Drafting the Introduction of Your Essay

Although you can begin writing your essay at any point, you may want to start with the introduction. There are many ways to write an interesting introduction. Below are several possible ways to begin.

Drafting Your Introduction

- Use a startling statement, as Eli does when he begins his essay with "I'm a slob."
- Use an **anecdote**. Relate an incident about yourself, a family member, or a friend.
- Ask questions to make your reader feel part of your essay.
- Use strong **sensory details** to make your reader care about your topic and want to know more about it. Eli's description of his room gives his readers a vivid picture.

Drafting the Body of Your Essay

Keep in mind that an expository essay is written to increase your reader's understanding of your topic. Stick to the point. Get rid of unnecessary information.

As you draft the body of your essay—the place where you do most of your explaining—be guided by your note cards, your outline, and any other prewriting that you've done, but don't be afraid to include new ideas that come to you. Make sure each paragraph has enough supporting information to explain that part of the topic fully. Your goal is to inform your readers thoroughly.

Use the following clues for drafting the body.

Drafting Clues	
What to Do	How to Do It
Use specific details.	Tell the reader to be prepared with paper, pencil, compass, ruler, and protractor for Mr. Martin's algebra class.
Use transitional words.	Time: after, when, first, second, third, last, next, soon, before Addition: and, furthermore, in addition to, also, another, as well Contrast: but, however, nevertheless, instead, even so

Drafting the Conclusion of Your Essay

Your conclusion should summarize or reflect your ideas about the most important point in your essay, leaving your readers with a clear understanding of what you want them to know. In Eli's essay, "How to Clean Your Room," the last paragraph shows that having a system makes the task faster and easier. If you're writing about how to do well in algebra class, conclude with a paragraph that shows how you've succeeded.

REVISING

Revising involves reading your essay carefully. Read it to see whether it's clear and consistent, whether your ideas are in a logical order, and whether it will grab your audience's attention.

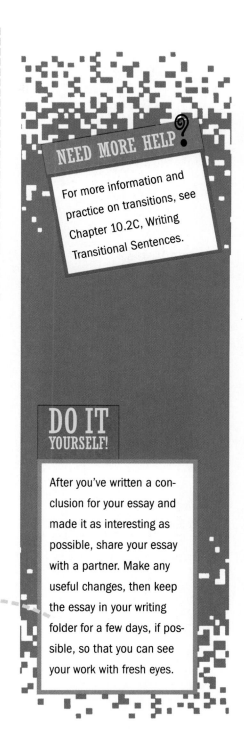

NEED MORE HELP?

For more information and practice on transitions, see Chapter 10.2C, Writing Transitional Sentences.

DO IT YOURSELF!

After you've written a conclusion for your essay and made it as interesting as possible, share your essay with a partner. Make any useful changes, then keep the essay in your writing folder for a few days, if possible, so that you can see your work with fresh eyes.

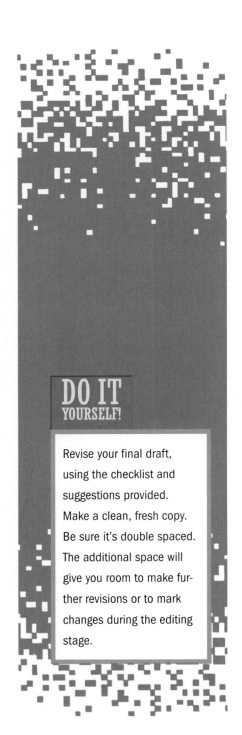

Making Your Work Better

During the revision process, review your writing and decide how you can improve it. Revision is the time to make your writing the very best it can be. Using a checklist for revising like the following one will help you look for places to make your expository essay better. Ask a classmate to help you answer the questions.

Checklist for Revising an Expository Essay

- Does my introduction "grab" my readers?
- Is my topic focused?
- Do I provide enough information to support my topic sentence?
- Will readers have a clear understanding of my topic?
- Is the information I provide interesting and provocative?
- Is the organization logical?
- Are my transitions effective?
- Does my conclusion leave my readers with a clear understanding of my main idea?

Strategies for Revising an Expository Essay

Look at the following list to get some revising ideas.

Revising Strategies

- As you read your essay, you may notice sentences or paragraphs that need to be moved or changed. Rather than rewriting, cut out the sections of your paper and tape them on a new sheet of paper in the new order. If you have a word processor, use cut and paste.
- Create a response group with a small group of peers. Share your writing and provide feedback.
- Find the best sentence in your essay. Rewrite everything in the paragraph except this one sentence. You may find that you can express your ideas in a new and stronger way.

APPLYING LANGUAGE RESOURCES TO WRITING

Concluding Sentences

Your conclusion should draw all your information together and give your reader a clear explanation of the main idea of your essay. For example, Eli concludes his essay by saying that, although he doesn't like cleaning his room, his system works—even if only in a temporary way. He realizes that his conclusion isn't the place for coming up with new ideas. For more information about conclusions, see Chapter 10.2D, Writing Concluding Sentences.

EDITING

When you edit your essay, pay attention to the appearance of your work. Look for spelling errors and errors in grammar and usage. You want to be certain that your readers won't be put off by messiness or errors. The best essay in the world can be spoiled by careless errors.

When you have a final draft of your essay, proofread it to find any errors in spelling, grammar, mechanics, and usage. Also, ask a partner to proofread your paper. Sometimes a second pair of eyes can be helpful. Even though you're not editing for ideas at this stage and are concerned mainly with spelling, grammar, mechanics, and usage problems, you may find a section of your essay that isn't quite right. If so, go back and edit that part. Then proof it again. The following proofreader's list can be your guide.

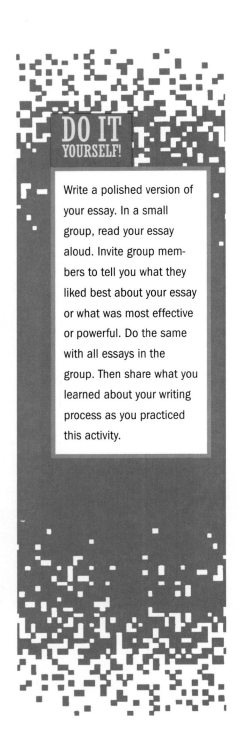

DO IT YOURSELF!

Write a polished version of your essay. In a small group, read your essay aloud. Invite group members to tell you what they liked best about your essay or what was most effective or powerful. Do the same with all essays in the group. Then share what you learned about your writing process as you practiced this activity.

Checking Your Proofreading

- Are my paragraphs indented?
- Are all my sentences complete?
- Did I eliminate all run-on sentences?
- Did I begin all sentences with a capital letter?
- Did I punctuate all sentences correctly?
- Are all the words spelled correctly?
- Did I use commas correctly?
- Do all subjects and verbs, pronouns and antecedents agree?

APPLYING MECHANICS TO WRITING

Avoiding Run-On Sentences

As you draft your essay, make sure you avoid run-on sentences. A run-on sentence is two or more sentences that are written as one sentence and are separated by a comma or even by no punctuation. If Eli were to say in his essay, for example, "I'm a slob, my entire family is made up of slobs," he would have written a run-on sentence. To correct such a run-on sentence, either turn it into two sentences or make a compound or compound-complex sentence. Eli's run-on sentence would become, "I'm a slob. My entire family is made up of slobs," or "I'm a slob, and my entire family is made up of slobs." For more help, see Chapter 14.4B, Run-On Sentences.

PUBLISHING

Publishing gives you the chance to share your ideas with an audience. There are lots of ways: through your class bulletin board, your school or community library, your school newspaper, or even your local paper.

Publication is important. You want others to read what you've written and to think about your ideas. Here are a number of possible ways for sharing your writing.

Opportunities for Publishing Your Expository Essay

- Create your own class newspaper or magazine with a student editorial board to select and edit the best papers submitted for publication.
- Send photocopies of student writing to other classes and grade levels that might be interested in them.
- Create a bulletin board in the hallway to showcase essays that other students in your school might want to read.
- Submit your essay to a local magazine or newspaper.
- Start an exchange with another school in your district or in another city in the United States. If you have a modem hook-up for a computer in your school, you can send essays through your modem to other schools with similar equipment.

Evaluation Activity

When you complete an essay, evaluate it to see whether or not you've fulfilled your purpose and reached your audience. Ask yourself whether you've accomplished your goal. Give your essay to one or two people to read. Then ask them questions like the ones that follow.

Evaluation Form

- Does my introduction make you want to continue reading?
- Is my purpose clear?
- Have I included all necessary steps? Can you follow them?
- Does my conclusion tie everything together?

6.2 Speaking Project

You'll write a speech to demonstrate how to carry out a task.

Giving a Demonstration Speech

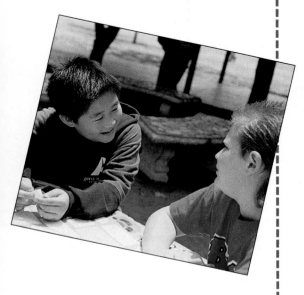

Martin and Kip grew up in the same neighborhood and went through elementary school together. They had similar interests, but they were also very different. Martin was athletic, while Kip was artistic. In seventh grade, both boys tried out for soccer and both made the team. Then Kip and Martin were chosen to play the position of goalie—Martin first string, Kip second. Kip was glad to have Martin to practice with. He admired Martin's natural talent and asked him to demonstrate the skills a goalie needs.

Have you ever, like Kip, had difficulty doing a task and asked someone to show you how, or have you been an expert, like Martin? Maybe you've demonstrated how to use a new computer, how to protect the goal while playing soccer, or given an informative speech on how something works. For this project, you'll write and deliver a clear, accurate, organized, and detailed demonstration speech to show your audience how to do a task or how something works.

Before you begin your own speech, you may find it helpful to read a demonstration speech written by middle school student Amanda Bicknell. Of course, your own speech will be entirely your own. Be prepared to use your own ideas.

STUDENT MODEL

How to Study for a Test
Amanda Bicknell, Grade 8

Today I am going to talk to you about how to study for a test. Tests are sometimes a pain, but we have to take them. So here is the situation: You're getting ready to do your homework, when you suddenly remember that you have a history test on Friday. Oh, no!!! Before you go into a total panic, there are a few things you should know to help you do as well as you can on the test.

When you come to school the next day, be sure to bring paper and pencils for good note taking. Some of your teachers won't give reviews, but most of them will. When you take notes, be sure to write down only the main idea. And abbreviate! If your teacher says, "George Washington was the first President of the United States of America," you write down, "G. Washington, 1st Pres. of USA." This way it will take you less time to write and you will get more of the material your teacher is covering.

Another good idea is to tape record the teacher's review. If you don't have a tape recorder at home, you can get a little hand-held one at your local drugstore for only a few dollars. But don't use it as a substitute for regular note-taking!

Now let's move on to studying your notes. Okay, so you took great notes in class. You may be asking yourself, "What's next?" Most notes you have to just plain memorize. Reading them over and over again works well, especially since you can read them anytime. Carry them in your pocket or backpack. Then you can practice while you're waiting for the bus, while you're sitting in the dugout during baseball practice, or while you're baby-sitting. I know that no one likes to do it, but writing the notes over and over and over helps, too.

Whether or not you took notes, always go over the material in your textbook. If you don't have time to reread it all, then at least skim and scan it to pull out the important things.

After you finish studying, be sure to test yourself on the information in your notes. Do this by having someone else ask you questions. Siblings and parents work great for this, but if you don't have any or if you don't want to admit you need help, don't worry. There is hope for you yet. This is another time your tape recorder will come in handy. Record yourself as you ask the questions from the notes you took. Then, as you play your tape back, write the answers to the questions on a piece of paper. Check your answers with your notes.

If you use these steps, and add some of your own, you should have no problem getting that "A." If you work hard and give it your best effort, nothing will hold you back.

IDEAS FOR YOUR

SPEAKING PROJECT

1. Imagine that you developed a method for studying for a test and wrote a handbook for fellow students. You're being interviewed for your school paper. Get a friend to play the role of the reporter who asks you questions about the handbook and wants you to explain how your method of taking a test works. Rehearse your interview together. Then perform it for the entertainment of the whole class.

2. Pretend you're a famous chef who has a TV show. Think of a wonderful dish you know how to prepare and explain how to prepare it. If possible, do a demonstration along with your explanation.

3. Work with several classmates to explain a card game. Take turns explaining your game to the other members of your group. Then play the game to see how successful you were with your explanation.

GETTING STARTED

What do I talk about? That's probably your first question, so start by thinking of a topic for your speech. Do some brainstorming or clustering to help you find ideas.

Choosing a Topic

How do you choose a topic? When you give a demonstration speech, it's best to choose a topic that you know about or are interested in. If you're giving a demonstration speech that tells how something is done, brainstorm for ideas to find a topic or skill that you can easily demonstrate to others. If no topic or skill comes to mind, notice things around you. Carry a small notebook with you and jot down your observations. Then, when you see an interesting topic, give it a twist. Look at the following list for help in getting started.

How to Find a Topic

- Observe family members or friends.
- Listen to the radio or television news, or look at the headlines in the newspaper.
- Watch a favorite sport.
- Think about a favorite hobby.
- Go to a mall or a park and observe people or animals or plants.

Purpose and Audience

Part of your decision about a topic for your speech involves who your audience will be. If your listeners are already interested in the topic and want to know more, you can add to what they already know. If you're trying to make the topic interesting to an audience that knows nothing about it, you'll go into details, using questions and anecdotes. Your audience is a very important factor in the formula for a successful speech. With your audience in mind, decide on your topic and include it in your writing folder.

DRAFTING AND PRACTICING YOUR SPEECH

Even when you give a speech, you need to draft what you plan to say. You also need to practice your speech—to check on the way you'll speak, stand, and keep the attention of your audience.

Organizing Your Information

Decide on a topic for your speech and write down your steps. You might begin by performing. For example, if you're demonstrating how to make peanut butter sandwiches, actually make the sandwiches. As you do, keep a notepad handy and write down each step in the process. By performing your skill or task for yourself, you'll notice all the necessary small steps that you might have overlooked if you were writing from memory. People who are especially good at certain skills or tasks often fail to mention all the little steps that are part of the process.

NEED MORE HELP?

For more information about purpose and audience, see Chapter 28.13, Purpose and Audience.

DO IT YOURSELF!

Make a list of topics for your demonstration speech, using the ideas on finding a topic on page 152. Choose one topic and write it down. Then decide on your audience and write down who it will be.

Adding Visuals

Look at all your steps and details. Ask yourself whether there are any visual aids that will add to your listeners' understanding of the information you're demonstrating. See the examples that follow.

Topic	What to Do
How to make a peanut butter sandwich	Make sandwiches and offer them to the audience
Martial arts moves	Wear appropriate clothing and demonstrate
Tricks with a yo-yo	Perform for audience

Making Note Cards

When you decide how to present your speech and what visual aids you need, write your information on note cards. The best way to deliver a speech is by using large 5 x 7-inch note cards instead of reading from sheets of paper. When you use note cards, your speech shouldn't be completely written out.

Drafting an Introduction for Your Speech

The goal of your introduction is to capture your audience's attention and introduce your subject. Look at the following hints for planning an introduction.

DO IT YOURSELF!

Draft an introduction to your speech, but don't worry if it's not perfect. Your goal is just to get your ideas down. You'll get a chance later to revise what you've written. You may want to review the section called Drafting in Chapter 1.

Planning Your Introduction

- Tell the audience what your demonstration is about. If your topic isn't familiar to your listeners, start with a definition. For example, if you're demonstrating how to make salsa, you'll want first to define what salsa is. If you're demonstrating karate, you might begin your speech by describing it and telling a little about its history.

- Provide factual information—especially exciting or unexpected facts that your listeners don't know about. For example, if you're demonstrating how to play a simple tune on the violin, you might start by saying, "Did you know that playing the violin includes using items like tree sap and horse hair?" (The bow is made of horse hair, and resin, or tree sap, is rubbed on the bow.)

- Tell an anecdote or story. If you're telling how to make peanut butter sandwiches, you might include the fact that your little sister eats the same sandwich for lunch nearly every day, all year long.

Making It Your Own

There's no one type of language that's right for every speech. The type of language you choose depends on your topic and audience. If your speech topic is formal and you aren't familiar with your audience, you probably want to use formal language. But if your topic is how to make peanut butter sandwiches, you might choose to use **colloquial language**. Why? The topic is less formal and may even be considered humorous.

No matter what type of language you use, you can make it your own by using one of the several techniques listed on the next page.

Terms to Know

Colloquial language is informal conversational language that isn't appropriate in formal writing.

Techniques for an Effective Speech

◎ Use personal examples throughout your speech. The examples will help your audience feel more comfortable with you.

◎ Use local or personal expressions, if they fit. For example, during the 1988 Democratic National Convention, Ann Richards of Texas delivered the keynote address. She grew up in Texas and used many expressions that were unique to that part of the country. As a result, she sounded down-to-earth. The audience felt they were listening to a Texas woman and not a politician.

◎ After writing the first draft, tell your speech rather than read it. When telling it, listen to the way you construct your sentences and any additions you make when explaining concepts. Telling your speech will help you sound more like yourself.

Drafting the Body and Conclusion of Your Speech

Begin by writing out your introduction on one card. Then go on to the body of your speech and write each step on a separate card. Write a brief statement covering what you want to say or do. Don't write your speech out word-for-word. If you do, you might end up reading directly from your cards, and you'll sound unnatural. Write your conclusion on the final card.

Once you have your note cards written, practice giving your speech in front of a mirror. As you demonstrate or explain each step in your speech, remember to include the details and specific information you decided on when you drafted your ideas.

APPLYING USAGE TO WRITING A SPEECH

Colloquialism Versus Formal Diction

Use colloquial words in giving an informal speech—that is, one for friends or family. Be yourself, but use formal diction if you don't really know your audience well. You wouldn't use slang, for example, if you were giving an explanation of your science project at a school assembly. For more information, see Chapter 11.3B, Formality and Informality

REVISING YOUR SPEECH

Once your speech has been drafted, revise it and decide whether you'll need to make any changes. Revision gives you the chance to work on different ideas and different ways to present your information. You may decide that you need to change certain parts or add more information. Perhaps you need to change the order. Maybe the wording seems confusing. If so, revise.

Deliver your speech to a partner; then ask him or her to use the following checklist to help you revise.

Checklist for Revising a Speech

- Does my introduction make you want to know more?
- Does my introduction clearly show what the rest of the speech is about?
- Are there enough details and information to help you understand my topic?
- Do my sentences flow and sound natural?
- Is the language clear and specific?
- Do my visual aids help make my information clear?
- Does my conclusion summarize the information and leave you with a strong impression?

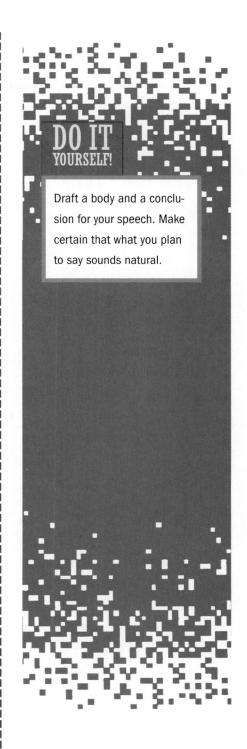

DO IT YOURSELF!

Draft a body and a conclusion for your speech. Make certain that what you plan to say sounds natural.

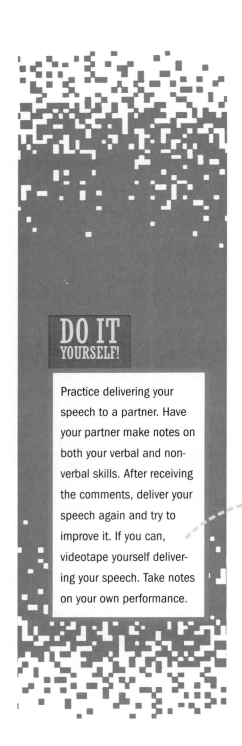

DO IT YOURSELF!

Practice delivering your speech to a partner. Have your partner make notes on both your verbal and nonverbal skills. After receiving the comments, deliver your speech again and try to improve it. If you can, videotape yourself delivering your speech. Take notes on your own performance.

APPLYING GRAMMAR TO SPEECH WRITING

Sentence Combining

You don't want to sound as if you're reading when you give your speech. Try combining short sentences so that what you say will have a natural sound and flow. For more about sentence combining, see Chapter 14.5D, Sentence Combining.

EDITING YOUR SPEECH

When you're preparing a speech, you need to be concerned about a spoken product rather than a written product. Your grammar and usage during your delivery, though, must be correct. One way to check to see whether you're using any incorrect grammar or usage is to record your speech and then listen for any mistakes. You can also ask someone else to listen for mistakes. If you notice any errors, make sure to check the correct form and use it in your delivery. Read the following list to check for mistakes in grammar and usage.

Checking Grammar and Usage in Your Speech

- Are all my sentences complete?
- Do all subjects, verbs, and pronouns agree in kind and number?
- Do I use the appropriate language—formal or informal—for my topic and audience?
- Am I using adverbs and adjectives correctly?

DELIVERING YOUR SPEECH

Be aware of both verbal and nonverbal aspects of your delivery. The following are some tips for good delivery of your speech.

Tips for Delivering Your Speech

- Speak clearly and at a normal speed.
- Be enthusiastic, but don't exaggerate.
- Be careful of *ums* and too many *ands*.
- Stand naturally and look directly at your listeners or over their heads.
- Don't look at your notes for too long.
- Speak loudly enough so that everyone can hear you.
- Watch people on television give a speech. Notice the way they speak—making good eye contact, keeping a relaxed stance, having good volume and speed in their delivery.

Evaluation Activity

It's difficult to evaluate how well you deliver your speech because you can't see yourself. If you can, make a videotape of your speech as a method of self-evaluation. As you view the tape, think about the questions that follow. If you can't make a videotape, ask someone in your audience whose judgment you trust to answer the questions for you.

Checklist to Evaluate a Speech

- Did I know my topic well enough?
- Was my purpose clear?
- Were my ideas organized?
- Did I present facts to support the main idea?
- Was my voice loud enough?
- Did I speak clearly and slowly enough?
- Did I give an energetic delivery?
- Did I have good posture?
- Did I make good eye contact?
- Did I control my hand movements?

6.3

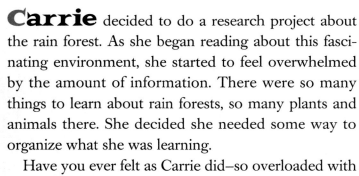

You'll create an explanatory chart about a special interest.

Visual Project

Creating an Explanatory Chart

Carrie decided to do a research project about the rain forest. As she began reading about this fascinating environment, she started to feel overwhelmed by the amount of information. There were so many things to learn about rain forests, so many plants and animals there. She decided she needed some way to organize what she was learning.

Have you ever felt as Carrie did–so overloaded with information about some topic that you felt your brain was all tied up in knots? Sometimes you have to keep track of so much information that it's hard to keep it straight. A chart, a graph, or a map are ways to organize information and help you understand these relationships.

In this visual project, you'll design a chart to organize factual information. You might want to chart the metamorphosis of the milkweed worm into a monarch butterfly or the way a club you belong to is organized. Your chart will help your audience see the entire picture.

Before you get started, you might find it helpful to see the chart middle school student Blair Borders created to show the steps in a space-shuttle flight. As you study the chart, notice how easy it is to see all the information and understand the process of spaceflights. Of course, your chart will be entirely your own. Be prepared to use your own ideas.

STUDENT MODEL

Space Shuttle Mission
Blair Borders, Grade 8

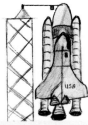

1. The space shuttle awaits the countdown on the launch pad.

2. The space shuttle blasts off on the back of its huge fuel tank, powered by the two long booster rockets on either side as well as by the main engines. The shuttle is a reusable spacecraft.

3. At a height of about 27 miles, the boosters are empty and parachute back into the ocean for recovery.

4. Once the shuttle has reached orbit under its own power, the large empty fuel tank is detached.

5. In orbit, the shuttle's payload bay doors are opened for releasing or retrieving a satellite.

6. By firing two engines that reduce its speed, the shuttle enters into the earth's atmosphere, glides back to the ground, and lands.

IDEAS FOR YOUR VISUAL PROJECT

1. Create a flexible chart that includes all the people you know, organized according to how you know them. Are they relatives, school friends, neighbors, friends you met in different situations, friends of friends?

2. How would you give someone directions from school to your house, using pictures instead of words? On your way home today, look at what you see, and think about what visual clues show you the way. Then make a picture map to show someone the route.

Why Use a Chart?

Charts are useful when you want to convey a great deal of information in a few words. Charts also help to make difficult ideas easier to understand by presenting them graphically with symbols and pictures. For example, you might use a family tree to help explain how someone is related to you. You could use a chart in the form of a map to explain the migration patterns of birds or butterflies. Charts also give an overview of information about clubs and other organizations.

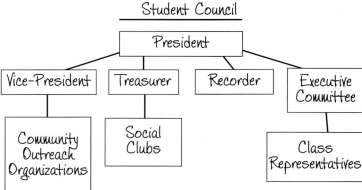

PRE-VIEWING YOUR CHART

You can begin thinking about a topic for your chart by identifying all the organizations in which you are involved, such as your school, a club, your church or temple, your local government, or the nearest YMCA or YWCA. Then think of school subjects that interest you. Within those subjects, think of specific topics you would like to learn about. For example, you might enjoy learning about Native Americans, astronomy, or the environment. Then think of favorite hobbies or sports, such as football, track, or chess. These interests can be a good place to start when deciding on a topic for your chart. Be sure that what you choose works on a chart.

Start by freewriting a list of your ideas. Look at the following for some ideas about what to include on your list.

Ideas for Making a List

- Your school's organizational structure
- The three branches of the United States government
- The organizational structure of your city or state government
- The organization and sequence of a tournament or championship play-offs
- Teams in the NFL or NBA, players on each team, and their positions
- Makes and models of major automobiles
- Types of trees
- Food chains
- Some fictional characters and their relationships

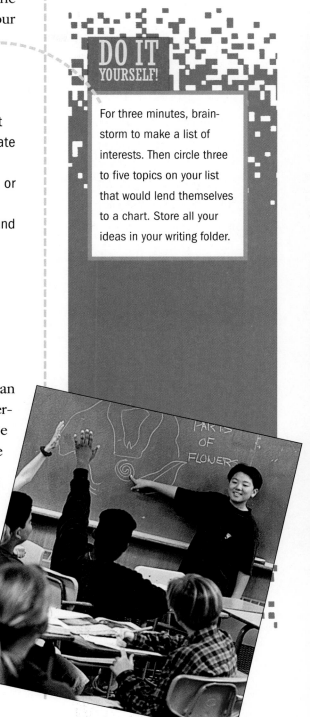

DO IT YOURSELF!

For three minutes, brainstorm to make a list of interests. Then circle three to five topics on your list that would lend themselves to a chart. Store all your ideas in your writing folder.

Making a Decision

Choose a topic that you're interested in, that you can present clearly, and that you think people would understand well if presented on a chart. Your topic should be one that has related parts, such as soccer plays or the organization of your state and federal governments. It shouldn't be a topic that needs to be described.

Purpose and Audience

Make a chart to show your audience the relationships within a body of information. The relationships should be clear so that the audience can see them at a glance. Make the information factual and brief.

Gathering Information

Use 3 x 5 note cards to gather and organize the information you'll include in your chart. Record only one piece of information on each card. For example, if you're making a family tree, you'll put each family member's name on a separate card. If you're charting the plants and animals of a rain forest, write the name of each plant or animal on a separate card. If you're charting a process, put each step in the process on a different card.

DRAFTING AND DESIGNING YOUR OWN CHART

Your note cards are great tools for organizing your chart. Find a big space where you can work—on the floor or a tabletop. You're about to put together a big puzzle. Start by putting the card with the broadest category at the top. Then put down the cards that go at the next level. Continue until you've placed all your cards. Write any missing information on new cards and put them in the correct place.

You can also organize information by arranging it from left to right. This works if you're showing sequences or order of importance.

Organizing Your Information

Look at the blank charts that follow to see how you can organize your information from left to right or from top to bottom. If you wish, copy one of these charts on a separate piece of paper or design a chart of your own.

The Rain Forest	
Plants	Animals

How to Save the Rain Forest	
Problems	Solutions

REVISING YOUR CHART

Revise your chart while it's still in this movable form on note cards. Experiment with the placement of cards. Ask yourself whether you've included enough information. Check the order and see whether all equal items are placed at the same level. When you're satisfied with your chart, copy it onto paper.

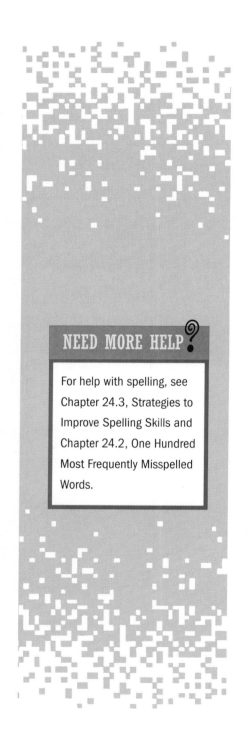

NEED MORE HELP?

For help with spelling, see Chapter 24.3, Strategies to Improve Spelling Skills and Chapter 24.2, One Hundred Most Frequently Misspelled Words.

Create boxes on your paper for each piece of information. These boxes take the place of the note cards. Write each piece of information in a separate box. Then draw lines joining the boxes to show the relationships. You only need lines to connect related items. Put numbers on the boxes only if you're showing a step-by-step process.

Now ask a partner to look at your chart. Ask him or her questions about the relationships. For example, if you're creating a family tree, ask your partner who someone's daughter is. For a movie chart, ask who starred in what film. See if your partner finds the information easily on your chart.

EDITING YOUR CHART

Check your chart for neatness and clarity. Be sure that people will be able to see it from a distance. Check also for any errors in mechanics, spelling, grammar, or usage. You'll probably be mostly concerned with spelling, because most charts use only a few words for each box. Look at the following strategies for editing your chart.

Strategies for Editing a Chart

- Is my chart neat and readable? Is it attractive?
- Is my chart complete?
- Is my chart large enough that my audience can see it easily?
- Have I used the correct words? Would a synonym be better or more effective?
- Have I spelled all words correctly, especially those in a content area such as science?

DISPLAYING YOUR CHART

Think about your audience when deciding how to display your chart. Will they be young children, a large group of parents, fellow students, or an unknown group of people? The audience will help determine the type of display you choose.

Ideas for Displaying Your Chart

- Make a window display of charts in your classroom.
- Ask permission to display your charts in the school corridors.
- Place your chart on a library or classroom bulletin board. If possible, include pictures or photographs in this display.
- If you've created a chart for an organizational structure, ask the organization to display your chart on one of its bulletin boards or in its newsletter.

Evaluation Activity

Was creating your chart a real chore, or was it easy? How effective is the chart? Whenever you finish a visual project, it's good to evaluate the activity so you can apply what you've learned to the next visual activity. Ask others to comment on your chart. Then ask yourself the following questions:

Checklist for Evaluating a Chart

- Was my chart effective? Could people look at it and answer questions about the relationships?
- Did I show items in an organized manner, or was my information scattered?
- Was creating a chart an enjoyable experience?
- Would I use a chart again for presenting material? Why, or why not?
- How can I improve my next visual project?

CHAPTER 7

Communicating

to Give
Your
Opinion

- How much homework do you think middle school students should do each night?
- Should CD's, tapes, and music videos be rated the same way movies are?
- Is it a good idea for cities and towns to enforce curfews—times after which teenagers must be off the streets?

N o matter how you answer the questions above, you're expressing an **opinion**, a personal judgment or your own thoughts and feelings. If you plan to share your opinion with others, you need to give **facts** and reasons in order to communicate convincingly to others.

Terms to Know

An **opinion** is a personal view that can be based on facts but can't be proved right or wrong.

A **fact** is information that can be proved.

Editorials are magazine or newspaper articles communicating opinions with facts and reasons to support the opinions.

Why Give Your Opinion?

It's a useful skill to be able to communicate your opinion clearly and convincingly. If you can express your thoughts effectively, you might be able to help someone else understand an issue better or to influence the kind of action another person takes. It's useful also to understand how other people's opinions affect the way they communicate.

You find out the opinions of others in many ways. For example, friends might tell you about a sports team or rock group they think is good or bad. You might read opinions of a politician or about a community issue in your daily newspaper. Advertisements, reviews, and TV talk shows all offer various forms of opinions.

Occasionally people offer their opinions simply to let the world know what they think. But a person offering an opinion is probably using persuasion—the intent to influence people to think or do as you suggest—to get a listener or a reader to agree and to accept that opinion as correct. See the examples of opinion that follow.

It's Just an Opinion

- People write letters to newspapers giving their opinions, trying to convince readers of the letters-to-the-editor page that their opinions are correct.
- Newspaper **editorials** communicate a wide variety of opinions about public issues and events.
- On television news programs, reporters interview people who try to convince the viewer that their interpretation of events is the most valid one.
- Advertisers use ads or posters to persuade people to buy a certain product.

LOOKING AHEAD TO THE PROJECTS

7.1 Writing Project
Write an editorial presenting your opinion on an issue you care about (pages 170–185).

7.2 Speaking Project
Prepare and give a persuasive speech offering your opinion (pages 186–197).

7.3 Visual Project
Design and create a public service poster (pages 198–205).

JOURNAL WRITING

Over the next two or three days, copy or clip at least three interesting editorials from your daily newspaper, listen and make notes on three news broadcasts, clip three ads from a publication, or copy a poster you like. In your journal, write a few sentences summarizing the opinions offered in the material you found. Add a brief note stating whether you found good support for the opinions and whether you were persuaded to agree.

7.1 Writing Project

Writing an Editorial

You'll be writing an editorial that gives your opinion on an issue that's important to you.

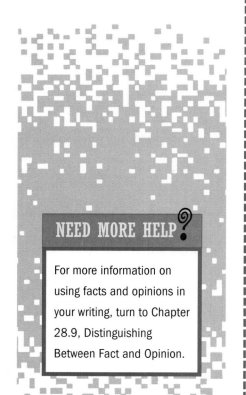

NEED MORE HELP?

For more information on using facts and opinions in your writing, turn to Chapter 28.9, Distinguishing Between Fact and Opinion.

When middle school student Kris Kendall returned to school in the fall, she was shocked to find out that one of her favorite books had been banned from the school curriculum. She investigated to find out what kind of people would ban books—and why.

While researching, she found several reasons for the banning, but she saw that the reasons were mainly based on the personal opinions of the book banners.

Kris decided to do something. She chose to write an editorial for her school paper in which she stated the problem, gave her opinion, listed facts, and tried to convince her readers that banning books for personal reasons interferes with students' learning about important facts and ideas.

Writing about something that means a great deal to you, communicating your opinion effectively, and supporting it with facts can be a way of affecting how other people think or act.

Before you get started on your editorial, you might find it helpful to read Kris Kendall's editorial that appeared in her school newspaper. You'll use your own ideas in your editorial, of course, but Kris's paper may help you get started.

STUDENT MODEL

Banning Books: A Real Necessity?

Kris Kendall, Grade 8

Each summer, while kids relax in the glow of another year of school completed, some members of the community are hard at work changing what kids will be reading when they return to school in the fall. These community members argue with the school board, write letters, sign petitions, and do anything to get their point across and their message out. They are the book banners, the people who protest other people's writing and try to keep it from being read in school. They are the ones who, year after year, try to get all types of books banned, from literary works to an English-language dictionary. I think that these community members, instead of spending time banning books, could help students learn important lessons from some of these books.

The book banners' reasons are varied. Some find evidence of racism in a particular book, while others object to vulgarity. Still others believe the subject is not appropriate for students. Whatever the reason, their message is clear: If they think a book is unsuitable for them, it is unsuitable for everyone. There is no probation for a book; once it's labeled inappropriate, it can be gone forever.

Take, for instance, Good Ol' Boy, a memoir by Willie Morris. Taking place in the 1930s and 1940s, this book is different from books set in current times. Events that were commonplace then would be considered inappropriate and vulgar now. However, the book tells readers a great deal about how people lived at that particular time in history. I read this book in seventh grade, and I learned a great deal about the period. However, I have heard recently that this book has been taken out of the seventh-grade curriculum and no longer is read in class. Why? Several people found indications of racism in it and the book was banned in the classroom. No questions asked. No opinions taken from supporters of the book. It simply was banned. Another proud accomplishment for the book banners.

People were really shocked--teachers and students alike. Taking a realistic, well-written book that teaches history out of the curriculum? It is an outrage. When we, as people, cannot look back upon past mistakes and learn from them, how can we learn at all? Because a book has the word Nazi in it does not mean that it celebrates Hitler. It simply is trying to teach us about history, something that we must learn.

Good Ol' Boy was one of the lucky ones, however. Although it was removed from the curriculum, curious readers still can find it in the school library. Other books have not been so lucky. Book banners have gone so far as to have them banned from school libraries so that no one can read them, regardless of

Continues ································▶

opinion. It is truly an outrage when we students cannot have access to books we can learn from.

Although there are some books that are inappropriate for some age groups, the list of books that have been banned for one reason or another has shocked many people. For example, "Cinderella" was taken out of several libraries because parents and school board members believed it showed "unhealthy family relationships." Mark Twain's immortal Huckleberry Finn was taken out because of profanity and perceived racism. The American Heritage Dictionary was removed because some definitions did not quite satisfy some people. The list goes on and on.

We live in a country plagued by a failing educational system and a budget too tight to do anything about it. And now, on top of all the problems this country has, people are banning the very materials from which we learn. This is truly an outrage. Book banners should stop trying to think of ways to ban books and start trying to come up with ways to help us learn from them.

NEED MORE HELP?

To help you get ideas for prewriting, look at Prewriting in Chapter 1.

DO IT YOURSELF!

Make a cluster to help you get ideas for topics. Then, based on your cluster, jot down three possible topics for an editorial. For more information about clustering, see Prewriting in Chapter 1.

PREWRITING

When you get started on your writing, you don't just write everything all at once and it's over with. You need to do prewriting—writing or thinking that gets you started. Use any device you can think of to get the words flowing from your brain down to your pen or your word processor. Cluster, brainstorm, make lists, or do whatever helps you to start the writing process.

Opinions and Facts

Giving your opinion is great, but be sure to include facts to back up your opinion. At the same time, write about something that you care about. Otherwise, you won't reach your audience.

How do you know what your opinions are? You could start by reading articles on a favorite topic to see what opinions come to mind as you read. Ask yourself whether the article turned out to be what you expected. Were there enough facts? Did you agree with the writer's opinion? Whatever answer you get, you've learned more about what interests you and what your opinions are.

Choosing a Topic

Brainstorm to find a topic that's important to you and that you have strong opinions about. Use the hints below.

Ways to Select a Topic

- Make a list of all the places you've been in the last twenty-four hours and visualize what you did, what you saw, and anyone you talked to.
- Write notes about any recent occurrence that made you angry, sad, glad, proud, or concerned.
- Clip three important stories from today's newspaper. Listen to the radio and watch television news programs and take note of the stories that interest you.
- Now ask yourself why you cared about these stories. If you find that you've clipped more than one article on the same subject, that's a strong hint that you care about it very much.
- Ask yourself why you chose any of the above and write down your reasons.

Thinking About Your Purpose and Your Audience

Decide on a purpose before you begin writing. Your introduction and conclusion should point your audience toward your purpose. See the following list to find different purposes.

Purposes

- Expressing your opinion
- Persuading your readers
- Calling for action

IDEAS FOR YOUR

WRITING PROJECT

1. Write a letter to the editor of a newspaper or magazine you read regularly. Give your opinion about an article.

2. Write a letter to a public figure or someone in the news—a government official, a victim or a hero in a news story, a writer whose book you've read, an entertainer, and so forth. Express your opinion about whatever it was that brought this person to your attention.

3. Write an editorial expressing your opinion about some classroom or schoolwide policy. Ask your teacher's permission to post your editorial on the bulletin board in your classroom.

The evidence you present in the body of your work will also vary depending on your purpose.

Your audience is the particular group of readers to whom you're addressing your editorial. The following tips may help you decide who your audience will be.

What You Need to Know About Your Audience

- Know your audience's interests, education, experience, and shared beliefs. Then you can plan your argument and choose the right words.
- Imagine the vocabulary and arguments you'd use to persuade an audience of middle school students to join a recycling program. Now think of how different your words would be if you wanted to persuade the local school board to abolish the school dress code.

As you write, always keep your audience in mind, imagining what they might say, think, and feel in response to your arguments. That will help you choose just the right words and style to reach them.

Focusing Your Topic

When you've found a topic that you care about, write down your opinion about it. Suppose the topic that inspired you was world peace. What would your opinion be? That world peace is a good thing? That we all should work to achieve it? That's pretty broad. It would be better if you had one specific idea about what world leaders could do to achieve world peace that you could explain or defend.

It would be the same if your topic were the environment. It might be your opinion that we need to do more to protect the environment, but you'll be able to write a much stronger editorial if you focus the topic and

suggest one thing people in your town can do to conserve energy or reduce waste.

Student writer Kris Kendall's topic is book banning. Her editorial states her opinion that banning books is a bad thing because it denies students access to books they could learn from and therefore limits what they can learn.

Testing Your Opinion

Maybe this is the first time you've expressed this particular opinion clearly, even to yourself. You need to see just how firmly you hold your opinion before you offer it to others. Ask yourself, "Can I imagine any situation in which I would *not* hold this opinion?" Look at the arguments against your opinion and ask, "Is there even one situation in which these would be true?" If the answer to either question is *yes*, you might need to revise or qualify your opinion until you can stand behind it fully.

Finding the Facts You Need

You have an opinion, but do you have enough facts to support it? Your library or media center is the place to begin. Encyclopedias, almanacs, and other standard references might supply the information you need for some topics. Other topics might call for reading books on a particular subject or using the *Readers' Guide to Periodical Literature* for magazine articles. Don't forget to take advantage of your library's on-line services too.

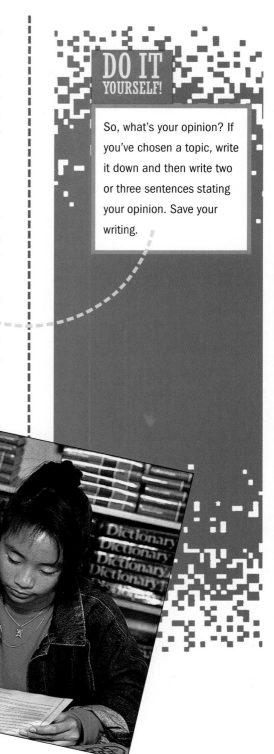

DO IT YOURSELF!

So, what's your opinion? If you've chosen a topic, write it down and then write two or three sentences stating your opinion. Save your writing.

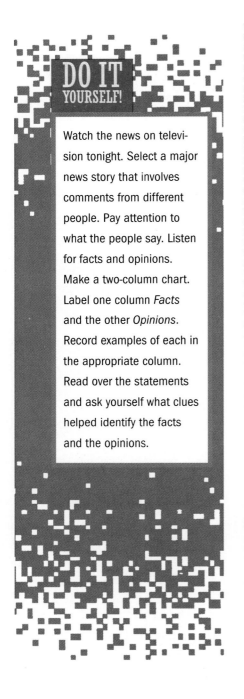

DO IT YOURSELF!

Watch the news on television tonight. Select a major news story that involves comments from different people. Pay attention to what the people say. Listen for facts and opinions. Make a two-column chart. Label one column *Facts* and the other *Opinions*. Record examples of each in the appropriate column. Read over the statements and ask yourself what clues helped identify the facts and the opinions.

While you're searching for facts to support your opinion, also be on the lookout for facts that oppose your views. If you encounter negative information, keep revising your opinion until you've taken full account of all the facts.

One of the most common mistakes a writer can make is to present all the necessary facts but not to explain why or how they support an opinion. As the writer, *you* know what is important about the facts you're presenting, but you must make sure that your readers understand your thought processes as well as your facts. For example, if you want your town to build a new quarter-mile track, be sure your editorial tells why you feel strongly about the issue.

Using Graphic Organizers

As you conduct your research into the topic you've chosen, you'll need to organize the information you collect. The following is a graphic organizer that shows how you might organize your main ideas before writing an editorial on building a new town track.

Topic: New town track
Opinion: Our town badly needs a new quarter-mile track.

Reasons for having a new track
good health
place for runners to practice
place for after-school games

Who would use the track?
students
athletes
senior citizens

Conclusion: a new town track will contribute to the health and enjoyment of town members of all ages.

DRAFTING

When you reach the drafting stage, it's time to put your prewriting to use and even to see what new material you can come up with. Read on for hints that can help you put your editorial together.

Parts of an Editorial

All good editorials have a strong introduction and a clear concluding statement to help the reader understand the writer's opinion. The body of the editorial presents facts and reasons.

Look at the list that follows to see how to put together an editorial.

How to Put Together an Editorial

- Write an introduction containing a clear, brief statement that gives only what your belief or judgment is, without explaining why.
- Save your facts and reasoning for the body of your editorial.
- Construct your editorial's conclusion to get the readers to agree with what they've read—and perhaps to act on it.

Drafting a Main-Idea Statement

A **main-idea statement** is a sentence or two in the introduction that presents your main idea and your opinion briefly and clearly. It's important to keep your main-idea statement in mind throughout the writing process. It will keep you focused so that you'll be less likely to lose track of your argument or get bogged down in irrelevant or unimportant side issues. Look at the following list to see the important functions of a main-idea statement.

Terms to Know

A **main-idea statement** (also called a thesis statement) clearly presents the main idea of a piece of writing.

What a Main-Idea Statement Does

◎ It narrows your topic to the single idea that you want readers to grasp from your editorial.

◎ It states two things about the topic: your opinion and your purpose.

◎ It also might give a very brief preview of how you'll arrange the ideas in your argument.

Below are several versions of student writer Kris Kendall's main-idea statement.

> 1. How do the book banners expect us to learn anything when they throw out so many books that will help us to become well-informed people?
>
> 2. People who ban books should think about the education of kids and stop interfering with the learning process.
>
> 3. I suggest that these community members, instead of spending time banning books, could help students learn important lessons from some of these books.

As you can see, each time Kris wrote more about her main idea, she expressed what she wanted to say more clearly and precisely. She began with her feelings of anger against the book banners. Her second try sharpened the focus: book banners should consider the importance of education. She used this idea later in her editorial. Her third version became her main-idea statement, stating her opinion—community members could help kids learn lessons from some of these books.

Drafting an Introduction

When you're ready to draft your introduction, go back to your prewriting to see what you want to use. The list that follows can help you decide what belongs in your introduction.

Writing the Introduction

1. Decide what your main idea will be.

2. Jot down your main idea as a statement.

3. Begin your introduction with this statement of your idea.

4. Alternatively, begin with an example or an illustration of your subject and then give your main idea statement.

Kris has chosen to place her main idea statement at the end of her introduction. She could have started her writing with a different main idea statement and then given a brief description of the problem of censoring books. Then her introduction might have looked like the following.

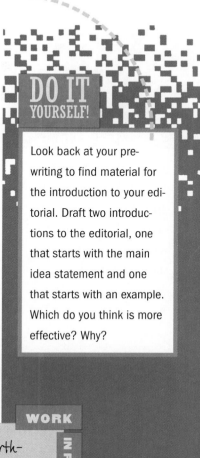

DO IT YOURSELF!

Look back at your prewriting to find material for the introduction to your editorial. Draft two introductions to the editorial, one that starts with the main idea statement and one that starts with an example. Which do you think is more effective? Why?

WORK IN PROGRESS

In my opinion <u>Good Ol' Boy</u>, a memoir by Willie Morris, is a worth-while book for students to read. I read it last year in seventh-grade English. The book tells readers a great deal about the 1930s and 1940s, about some events that were commonplace then that would be considered inappropriate and vulgar now. I learned a great deal from reading this book. Recently, however, I learned that this book has been taken out of the curriculum and is no longer read in class. Why? Some people found indications of racism, and the book was banned in the classroom.

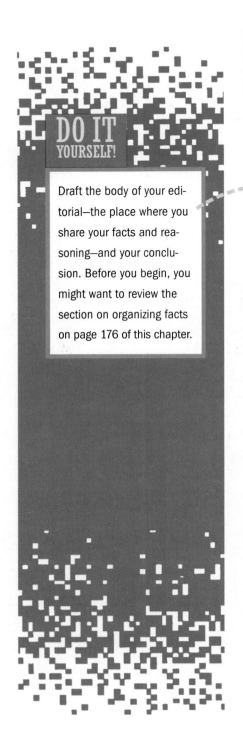

DO IT YOURSELF!

Draft the body of your editorial—the place where you share your facts and reasoning—and your conclusion. Before you begin, you might want to review the section on organizing facts on page 176 of this chapter.

Look at the following list to see what to save for the body of your editorial.

What to Save for the Body of Your Editorial

- Your reasons for holding your opinion
- Your reasons for wanting readers to adopt your opinion
- Your reasons for wanting readers to act on your opinion

Don't try to pack your entire argument into the first paragraph. Save your reasoning and your facts for the body.

Drafting the Body of Your Editorial

An old folk saying states, "You can catch more flies with honey than you can with vinegar." You can't persuade someone of anything if the person is angry or hurt by what you write. Even if a reader isn't personally offended, he or she might still be put off if it appears that you're attacking other people unfairly.

Look at the following thoughts for drafting the body of your editorial.

Thoughts for Drafting the Body

- Try Kris's approach. Her editorial talks about what *we* should do. By writing as though she and her readers are already on the same side, she is more likely to reach them.
- Avoid using extreme words or exaggeration. If you say something is *the worst* or *the best*, a reader is likely to think, "There's probably something worse" or "I bet there's something better."
- Avoid overstating what will happen if your opinion is or isn't followed. Readers tend to be skeptical about threats and promises—unless you can back them up with solid facts.

◎ Think about what your readers want to hear. If you're writing about the rain forests, you might focus on the opinion that saving the rain forests also saves planet Earth. Find a way to relate your topic to your readers, showing them specifically why adopting your opinion would be to their advantage.

Drafting Your Conclusion

When you're ready to begin drafting your conclusion, check out the next group of ideas.

Ideas for Drafting Your Conclusion

◎ Sum up in a few short sentences the facts you've presented and how they support your opinion.

◎ Restate your opinion in words slightly different from the words you've used before.

◎ Offer your audience some alternative ways to fulfill your purpose. If you're arguing for trash barrels at city inter-sections, for example, you might want to conclude with a suggestion that the city begin by placing barrels at a half dozen major intersections. Then it might add them at more intersections as funds become available.

REVISING

You probably have many versions of your editorial and you may not be completely sure how and what you want to include in the final product. Revising is a vital step in getting your editorial ready for someone else to read. If you don't put your writing into a clear and logical order, your readers will give up at their first look. Read on for some ideas for revising your editorial.

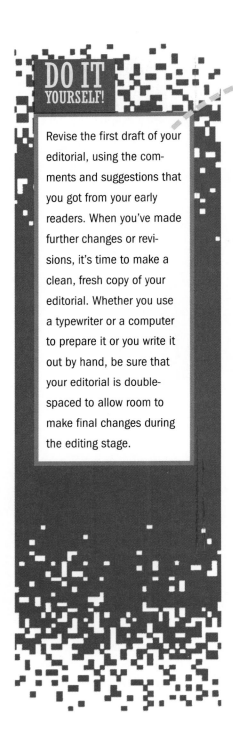

DO IT YOURSELF!

Revise the first draft of your editorial, using the comments and suggestions that you got from your early readers. When you've made further changes or revisions, it's time to make a clean, fresh copy of your editorial. Whether you use a typewriter or a computer to prepare it or you write it out by hand, be sure that your editorial is double-spaced to allow room to make final changes during the editing stage.

Strategies for Revising

Choose one or two of the following strategies to evaluate and revise your writing–or invent a strategy of your own.

How to Evaluate and Revise Your Writing

- If possible, ask someone who represents your intended audience to read your work and respond honestly to it.
- Exchange papers with a classmate. Read one another's editorials with the questions in the following revision checklist in mind. Make notes on points where you think your partner's editorial might be improved. Then try to fix the weaknesses that your partner has pointed out in your editorial.
- Read your editorial aloud to several people. Ask your audience to tell you what they liked and what needs more work.

After revising your editorial based on the strategies list, you may find that you still have some polishing to do. Use the checklist that follows for further revising help.

Checklist for Revising an Editorial

- Does my introduction clearly state my opinion?
- Do the facts in the body support my opinion?
- Can I think of any additional facts or arguments to support my opinion?
- Are there any unnecessary facts or arguments?
- Might any parts confuse or bore my audience?
- Does my conclusion clearly restate my opinion and summarize my support for it? Is it clear what I want my readers to do?
- Does my editorial address the arguments that someone who disagrees with my opinion might offer? Can I revise my editorial to respond to these objections?

APPLYING GRAMMAR TO WRITING

Varying Your Sentence Structure

Good writers vary the length and complexity of their sentences in order to keep the reader interested and to focus attention on important points. When you edit your editorial, check for variety in the length and structure of your sentences. Don't use short sentences all the time. Combine some of them and even turn some declarative sentences into questions. For information on simple, compound, complex, and compound-complex sentences, see Chapter 14.2, Types of Sentences. Look also at 14.5, Effective Sentences.

EDITING

At the editing stage, you start getting your paper ready for others to see. When you edit, concentrate mainly on matters other than content.

Making It Better

You give your paper a final polish at the editing stage. The content of your editorial should be fairly well set, but make any content changes that seem necessary. Your main attention at this stage should be directed toward correcting errors in grammar, usage, and mechanics. You don't want your reader's attention to be interrupted by such mistakes. The following procedure will help you review your editorial for errors.

Suggestions for Editing Your Editorial

- Read each sentence slowly and carefully, silently or aloud. Make sure that each sentence makes sense.
- Check all punctuation marks.
- Use a dictionary or the spell checker on a computer for any doubtful spelling.

◎ Look for clear transitional words and phrases.

◎ Read the editorial from the last sentence to the first, focusing on grammar, usage, and mechanics, rather than on content.

APPLYING USAGE TO WRITING

Making Good Transitions

One way to help the reader understand the reasoning of your editorial is through the use of good transitions that make a clear connection between what has come before and what follows. Use words such as *first, next, finally, also, while,* and so forth. For suggestions on how to use transitions effectively, see Chapter 10.2C, Writing Transitional Sentences.

PUBLISHING

Publishing is the payoff for the time and care you've invested in prewriting, drafting, revising, and editing your editorial: it is the chance to communicate your opinion to an audience of readers. Of course, you can always save work that you're especially proud of in your writing folder. But you might also want to share your editorial with others.

Where you publish your editorial will depend on the audience you choose to write for. Here are some suggestions, but don't stop here! You might be able to think of an even better way to share your work with others.

Ideas for Publishing Your Editorial

◎ If you've chosen the readers of a particular magazine or newspaper as your audience, send your editorial to that publication's editor. Include a cover letter explaining why you've written this editorial and asking that your letter be published.

◎ Send photocopies of your editorial to friends, family, neighbors, or others who might be interested in your topic. Enclose a note asking readers to write back to you with their comments. Ask also whether they agree with your opinion, what part of the work they found most or least persuasive, or whether they know of any facts that support or undermine your opinion.

◎ If your local newspaper invites readers to send articles to appear on a reader's page, submit your editorial for that page.

◎ If your editorial involves some school or community activity, ask to read your editorial aloud at a meeting or ask to have the group's leader read it.

Evaluation Activity

Now that you've finished creating and sharing your work, sit back and evaluate it. How did you do? Copy and use the following self evaluation form. It can help you assess your work.

Self Evaluation Form

Type and purpose of writing: _____

1. What do I like most about my editorial?
2. What do I like least about my editorial?
3. What could I improve on that I can apply to my next writing assignment?
4. Did I support my opinion with facts?
5. What skills in grammar, usage, or mechanics would I like to improve?
6. I feel _____ about this paper because _____ .

7.2 Speaking Project

You'll prepare and give a persuasive speech presenting your opinion about an important issue.

Presenting a Persuasive Speech

What was the last persuasive speech you heard? You might say it's been a while, especially if you're thinking only of a formal speech with someone standing in front of a listening audience. But if you think for a moment, you'll realize that you hear persuasive speeches all the time. Look at the following list.

What's Persuasion?

- A coach getting a team fired up before the game
- The school principal explaining a new school policy
- A politician on television asking for votes
- A radio or television advertiser selling a product
- Your friend trying to persuade you to go to a movie
- Yourself trying to convince your parents to let you stay out an hour later than usual

As the list shows, making and hearing persuasive speeches is part of your life! In this project you'll learn more about how to prepare and deliver a persuasive speech.

What Is a Persuasive Speech?

Persuasion, whether written or spoken, is based either on appeals to reason or appeals to emotions. Appeals to reason ask the listener to think or reason about something. Appeals to emotions ask the listener to feel a certain way.

Both appeals to reason and appeals to emotions have their proper place in persuasive speaking. But watch out for false reasoning–reasoning that seems logical but in fact is not. Also, be careful not to use emotions to persuade your listeners to agree with something that more careful reasoning would tell them is false or wrong.

Here is a speech prepared and delivered by middle school student Laura Sheedy for an audience of students and teachers. The speech you give will be your own, but you may get some good ideas from Laura's speech.

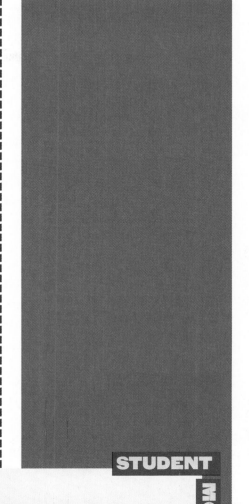

STUDENT MODEL

Crime

Laura Sheedy, Grade 7

Crime has gotten out of control in the United States. A recent poll indicated that crime is the problem Americans are most concerned about today. Our country has the highest crime rate of any industrialized nation, and although nobody is happy about crime, nobody seems to be able to come up with a solution either.

When people talk about crime and the causes of crime, the causes most people talk about are drugs, unemployment, lack of education, and gangs. If you think about these four things, you can see that there are some connections. All these things separate people from the way the rest of society lives. People do drugs because they think it will make them feel better. They want to escape from their regular life. When people are unemployed, they really are outside the whole system of working and earning money and

Continues ·············▶

buying things that most people are part of. Lack of education is usually the reason people can't get a job or can't find a new job if they become unemployed. For people who think they are not a part of society or can't be successful playing by the rules, gangs are a way to get status and be successful.

I think we all have to start paying more attention to the people in this country. We have to do what we can so that kids can grow up believing that they really do have a chance for a good life in regular society. If you believe in your own future, you're less likely to mess yourself up with drugs or to get involved with a gang.

We need to make a real effort to fix the economy so that there are jobs for people. Even people who want to play by the rules can get angry and frustrated when they don't have any money and they don't have a job and they can't see any way to make their lives better.

We also have to help people get the education and the training they need to get a job by improving the public education

system and making it work better for the kids it's supposed to serve.

All that, however, has to do with preventing crime and preventing people from becoming criminals. What about people—teenagers and grownups—who already have committed crimes? For teenagers, I think we need to try to counsel and rehabilitate them so that they don't become grown-up criminals. Grown-up criminals should be locked up for longer periods of time so that they don't get let out just to go back and repeat their crime.

One of the reasons criminals are released from jail too soon is that we can't afford to keep them there. My solution for that would be to make criminals work in prison at making things that could be sold. The profit would go to pay back the rest of society or the people they hurt.

Crime threatens everybody. Everybody is afraid of becoming a victim of crime. I think we all have to try to think of ways we can help prevent crime by helping to eliminate some of the causes of crime.

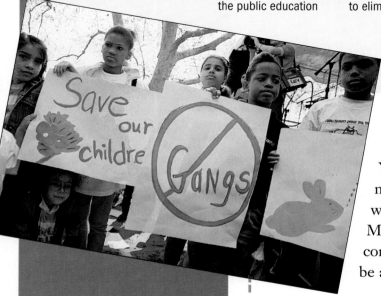

GETTING STARTED

You probably have an opinion that means a great deal to you. Maybe you want to save the whales or the rain forest. Maybe you want your school to buy more computers. Maybe you think you should be able to stay out later at night than you can now. All of these are valid subjects for a persuasive speech. Dig out those important opinons of yours, add some facts to support them, and prepare a speech that will convince the world that you're right.

Choosing Your Subject, Audience, and Purpose

Your first step in preparing your speech is to choose a subject, an audience, and a purpose. If you don't already have a subject in mind, here are three strategies to help you find one.

Strategies for Choosing a Subject Read the following strategies and jot down notes to yourself when you think about ideas. Make a list of your ideas.

Getting Ideas	Problems	Solutions
Look around in your community	Local park dirty	Clean it up
	Garbage not picked up	Talk to officials
	Street repair needed	
	Food needed	Contact local business for help
	Library closes early	Try to change hours
Watch local news on TV	Does some local problem make you sad, happy, angry?	Contact local officials
Think about friends	Need jobs, sports, arts, safe place to hang out	Help organize activities

IDEAS FOR YOUR

SPEAKING PROJECT

1. Record your persuasive speech on audio cassette or videotape for distribution.

2. Volunteer to make a nominating speech for a friend who wants to run for office in an organization you both belong to.

3. Telephone a local radio talk show and offer your opinion on a topic that interests or concerns you.

DO IT YOURSELF!

Jot down three possible topics for your persuasive speech. Use your notes or new ideas you get as you do this activity. Can you think of a focus or an angle for each topic? Who will your audience be? What do you want them to think or do as a result of hearing your speech?

NEED MORE HELP?

For more information on taking notes, see Chapter 27.2, Taking Notes.

Audience and Purpose Once you have a subject in mind, think about your audience and your purpose. If you've decided, for example, to give a speech about the need for a bicycle path in your community, your audience might be the mayor and the city council or a citizens' group.

Set some realistic limits on your choice of a topic for your speech. Laura Sheedy chose a very broad and difficult topic, but she found a way to focus her speech by defining the causes of crime and seeing what those causes had in common. If you choose a really broad topic, such as air pollution, for example, keep the focus narrow and specific, such as curbing air pollution from a local factory or dump. Narrowing your topic helps you see possible audiences—local business leaders, the chamber of commerce, an environmental action group, or a civic group.

Taking Notes

Whatever subject you've chosen for your persuasive speech, you'll need to gather facts to support your opinion. As you do your research for your speech, record each fact that you uncover on a separate note card. Write your notes on only one side of each card, so that later you can spread out all the cards and rearrange them, keeping all the facts before your eyes. On the next page, see three note cards Laura might have used for her speech on crime.

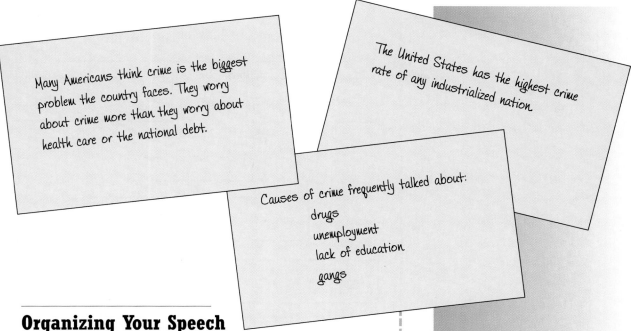

Many Americans think crime is the biggest problem the country faces. They worry about crime more than they worry about health care or the national debt.

The United States has the highest crime rate of any industrialized nation

Causes of crime frequently talked about:
drugs
unemployment
lack of education
gangs

Organizing Your Speech

When you've completed your research, read over all of your note cards carefully. Spread the cards out on a table and then make piles of cards that seem to go together. Keep moving the cards around until you have all the cards in the piles where they seem to belong. How you'll select these piles depends upon your subject. For example, Laura might have sorted her cards with facts about the causes of crime in one pile and ideas about solving the problem of crime in another pile.

Using a Graphic Organizer

To organize your speech, it sometimes helps to draw a graphic showing how the main ideas relate to one another.

Each of the boxes in the chart on the following page represents one set of note cards. The arrows show how these main topics relate to one another. When Laura wrote her draft, she decided which point should come first, second, and so on.

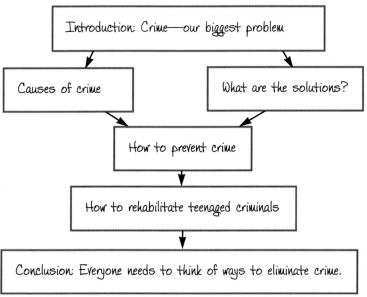

Introduction: Crime—our biggest problem

Causes of crime

What are the solutions?

How to prevent crime

How to rehabilitate teenaged criminals

Conclusion: Everyone needs to think of ways to eliminate crime.

DRAFTING YOUR SPEECH

Draft a speech as you would a written document—with an introduction, a body, and a conclusion. Using your organized note cards and any other notes you've jotted down, begin deciding what you want to say.

To help draft your speech, you can prepare an outline or you might prefer writing out exactly what you're going to say.

When it comes time to prepare to give your speech, use your outline as your speaking notes or transfer the outline to note cards—one card for each main point, with additional cards containing facts and arguments relating to that point.

The Speaker's Option

It's not necessary to draft your speech in the order in which you will actually give it. You might find it easier to begin with the body or even the conclusion and then draft your introduction.

All good speakers use a three-part strategy that can be summed up in the following sentence: "Tell them what you're going to say, say it, and then tell them what you said." Since most people don't absorb information as well or as quickly when they hear it as when they read it, a good speech needs to make its points more simply and more frequently than a piece of writing does.

A Strong Introduction

An effective way to begin a speech is with a question, a startling fact, or an interesting anecdote that will grab the listeners' attention. If your listeners' minds begin to wander, it can be hard to win them back—so grab their attention and hold on! Here are several suggestions for a strong beginning.

Getting Off to a Strong Start

Starter	Example
Ask a question and answer it.	What's an inexpensive, safe, and healthy way for people of all ages to exercise and enjoy our beautiful countryside at the same time? How about a community bike path?
Relate an anecdote.	A fun thing happened to me last weekend when I decided to dust off my old ten-speed bicycle and get some exercise.
State a fact or statistic.	Last year both of the sporting goods stores in town sold three times as many bicycles as they ever had before.

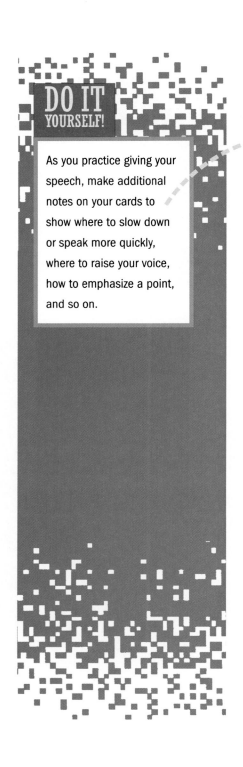

An Easy-to-Follow Body

Because your audience is listening to you rather than reading your writing, they can't go back over points they don't understand. So, when you draft, keep your sentences simple and present only one fact or concept at a time. You can restate points if you think your listeners might not understand or remember what you said. It's also a good idea to summarize occasionally so that listeners keep the big picture in mind while you fill in additional details.

A Powerful Conclusion

Your conclusion should be even stronger and simpler than your introduction. Your conclusion should restate your opinion, summarize your supporting arguments, and then close with a clear statement of exactly what you want your audience to do or think.

REVISING AND PRACTICING YOUR SPEECH

Revising the draft of a speech is a little different from revising a written draft. To revise your speech effectively, you must work not only on paper but also aloud. Using your cards, give your speech to a friend, a family member, or a writing partner, or possibly only to yourself. Think about the following questions while you're practicing your speech.

What to Think About While You Practice Your Speech

- Are any words, phrases, or sentences awkward to say aloud? How can I change them?
- Do I sound natural when I speak?
- Do I talk slowly enough and smile when appropriate?
- How long does it take to give my speech? Does it seem too short or too long? How could I cut or extend it?

- How much variety is there in my speech? Do I need to add more anecdotes, examples, or summarizing sentences?

If you're giving your speech a trial run in front of several listeners, ask them the questions listed here.

What a Practice Audience Thinks

- Does the introduction grab your attention? Can you tell what my purpose is?
- Are there parts you didn't understand or that you have questions about?
- Is there anything that doesn't seem related to the main purpose?
- How was my voice and delivery? Was I easy and pleasant to listen to? How might I improve?

Listen carefully to your listeners' comments and revise your speech and delivery to respond to their feedback.

EDITING YOUR SPEECH

Because your speech is an oral project, the editing stage calls for different strategies from the ones you would use for a written product. Look at what comes next for two possible strategies for editing your speech.

Clarity

Slowly deliver your speech aloud to yourself. Ask the following questions and then fix anything that needs changing.

- Are my pronoun antecedents clear?
- Have I made clear transitions?
- Have I summarized occasionally?

NEED MORE HELP?

For more information on subject-verb agreement, active and passive voice, clichés and slang, and the connotation of words, see Unit III, Language Resources.

Terms to Know

A **cliché** is an overused expression that is trite rather than meaningful. **Slang** expressions are nonstandard expressions developed and used by particular groups.

Word Choice

As you practice your speech, ask yourself these questions.

- Do my verbs agree in number with their subjects?
- Am I using the active rather than the passive voice?
- Am I pronouncing each word correctly?
- Am I avoiding **clichés** and **slang**?

APPLYING USAGE TO WRITING

Pronoun Antecedents

In your writing, pay attention to pronoun antecedents—the nouns that pronouns refer to or replace. You can throw your listeners off if they aren't certain about the pronouns you use. For example, if you were speaking about your school hockey team, you wouldn't say, "Kim Wong is the best goalie I've ever seen. *They* all love him." Your listeners might guess that *they* refers to the fans at a hockey game, but don't make them guess. If using a pronoun takes away the clarity of what you're saying, use a noun instead. For more information about antecedents, see Chapter 16.2, Pronouns and Antecedents.

DELIVERING YOUR SPEECH

Ideally, you should deliver your speech to the audience for whom you prepared it. If that's impossible, ask the members of your class or your family to be your audience. Ask them to respond and evaluate your speech the way they imagine the intended audience would.

Evaluation Activity

Peer-Evaluation Scale On a separate sheet of paper, copy the following scale to evaluate your classmates' persuasive speeches. Use *5* to indicate a rating of *superior.* Use *1* to indicate an area in need of improvement.

5 4 3 2 1 The speaker made eye contact with the audience.

5 4 3 2 1 The speaker spoke clearly.

5 4 3 2 1 The speaker varied tone and volume.

5 4 3 2 1 The speaker spoke smoothly and without hesitation.

5 4 3 2 1 The introduction captured my attention.

5 4 3 2 1 The speaker's persuasive purpose was clear.

5 4 3 2 1 The speaker occasionally summarized.

5 4 3 2 1 The evidence was easy to understand.

5 4 3 2 1 The evidence clearly supported the speaker's opinions.

5 4 3 2 1 The speaker used anecdotes and examples well.

5 4 3 2 1 The conclusion clearly stated what the listeners were supposed to think or do.

5 4 3 2 1 The conclusion was well supported by the evidence and the reasoning in the speech.

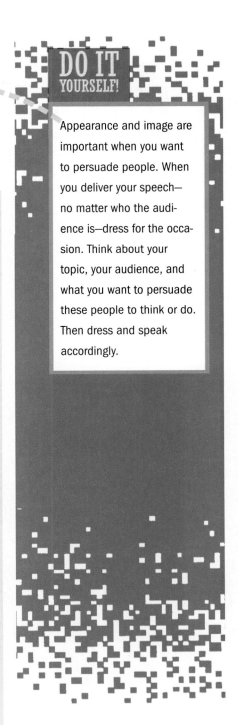

DO IT YOURSELF!

Appearance and image are important when you want to persuade people. When you deliver your speech—no matter who the audience is—dress for the occasion. Think about your topic, your audience, and what you want to persuade these people to think or do. Then dress and speak accordingly.

7.3 Visual Project

You'll design and make a public service poster about an issue that's important to you.

Creating a Public Service Poster

Rachel Wiley and her middle school classmates were worried about the effects of drugs on other students in their school. They realized that being worried wouldn't help. They had to do something.

They decided that the best way to reach students, parents, and teachers would be by making public service posters. For several weeks, the students made posters, some on their own, others in groups. They then met to decide which posters should be displayed in the community and where they should be displayed. Some posters went to their school and other schools in the community, some went to the library, others went into public buildings and stores.

Is there an issue that concerns you? Perhaps you can do something about it with a poster that reaches many people. You may even be able to help your community.

Pictured here is the poster that middle school student Rachel Wiley created for a school-wide campaign against drugs. You'll do your own special poster, of course, but looking at Rachel's poster may help you get some ideas.

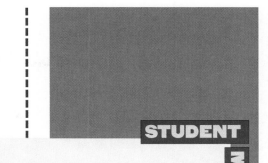

STUDENT MODEL

Is It Worth It?
Rachel Wiley, Grade 8

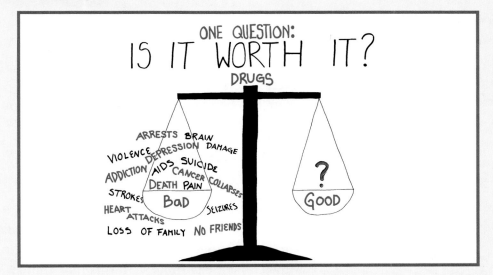

ONE QUESTION:
IS IT WORTH IT?
DRUGS

ARRESTS BRAIN DAMAGE
VIOLENCE DEPRESSION
ADDICTION AIDS SUICIDE
CANCER COLLAPSES
DEATH PAIN
STROKES BaD
HEART ATTACKS SEIZURES
LOSS OF FAMILY NO FRIENDS

? GOOD

What Is a Public Service Poster?

Businesses frequently use posters as part of a **campaign** to advertise their products or services. During election years you have probably seen posters describing the issues the candidates think are important and making campaign promises. There's a third kind of poster that's quite common: a public service poster. Public service posters provide information to the public. Private and public health organizations, libraries, zoos, and museums present posters to acquaint the public with what they have to offer.

Terms to Know

A **campaign** is a series of activities undertaken to reach a particular goal, such as electing a candidate, raising money for a cause, or taking a specified action.

VISUAL PROJECT

1. Work with a partner to create a poster for a real or imaginary political candidate. You can both brainstorm for ideas. Then one of you can be the designer who does the art work. The other can be the copywriter who writes, edits, and proofreads the words on the poster.

2. With one or two partners, pretend you're an ad agency, with a contract to make an ad for a newspaper or magazine. Advertise a new movie, music video, or rock group. Work together to plan and create your ad.

3. Magazine ads often feature posters. Select a real or imaginary product or service and create a persuasive magazine poster.

YOUR OWN CAMPAIGN

One visual way to communicate an opinion is to create a poster for a public service campaign. In this activity, you'll have the chance to choose an issue that you care about and to promote it with a poster.

To prepare for your poster, you'll go from choosing a topic to choosing an audience. Whom do you want to reach with your poster? Your audience should be people who will see your poster, so choose an issue that is either local or has a local connection. A campaign to help the fishing industry, for example, wouldn't be suitable if you live in a farming community far from the ocean or fresh water.

For this activity, you'll create a poster about three feet tall by two feet wide.

PRE-VIEWING YOUR POSTER

Think about what your want to do for your public service poster. What do you care most about? Helping the homeless and the hungry? Protecting animals? Recycling? Promoting the importance of sports? Before you even think about a poster, jot down some notes about your favorite cause and what you could do to get others interested in it.

Choosing a Subject, Audience, and Purpose

If you could influence the students in your school or the people in the community to take just one action, what would it be? The first step in planning your public service campaign is to choose a subject. Most public service campaigns try to make people aware of problems or dangers or to inform them of assistance or resources that are available to them. The following chart shows some organizations that regularly conduct public service campaigns, along with some of the specific campaigns they conduct. Does this list give you any ideas for your own campaign?

Ideas for Your Campaign

Organizations	Campaigns
Highway Department	Traffic Safety Pedestrian Safety
Red Cross	Blood Drive Emergency/Disaster Plans
Hospitals	AIDS Awareness Prenatal Care Emergency Poison Treatments Lead Paint Poison Warnings
Police Department	Protection against Burglary Neighborhood Crime Watch
Fire Department	Home Fire Safety
Other Organizations	Drug Abuse Prevention Literacy and Adult Ed Classes Food Banks Homeless Shelters Free Health Clinics Recycling Plans

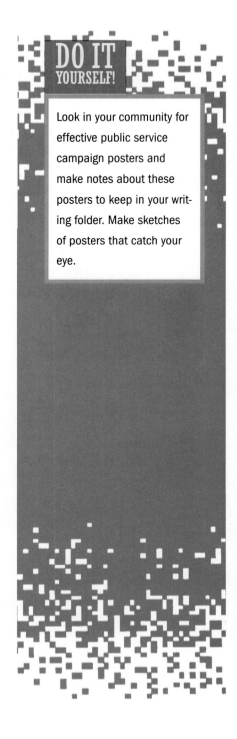

DO IT YOURSELF!

Look in your community for effective public service campaign posters and make notes about these posters to keep in your writing folder. Make sketches of posters that catch your eye.

DO IT YOURSELF!

As you conduct your research, take careful notes on what you learn. Make special note of the most interesting facts or statistics; they'll make great eye-catchers for your poster.

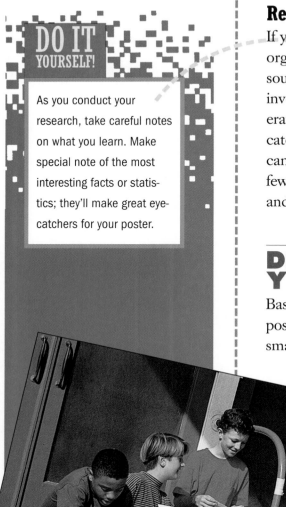

Researching Your Subject

If you choose to do a campaign poster for a particular organization, the organization itself will be your best source of information. You'll need to interview people involved with the group and read the organization's literature in order to know what needs to be communicated to the public. If you're planning an independent campaign, you might want to try out your idea on a few friends or classmates. See what questions they have and tailor your questions accordingly.

DRAFTING AND DESIGNING YOUR POSTER

Based on your notes, plan the physical layout of your poster. You might want to make preliminary sketches on smaller sheets of paper cut to the same proportions as your finished poster, or your imagination might work better with a piece of paper the same size as the final product.

Begin by making some very general decisions about where art and writing will appear on your poster. Lightly sketch your ideas in pencil or cut out illustrations and place them where you think they should go. You might need to experiment for quite a while, moving things around, adding and subtracting pictures and words, until you find the arrangement that you think is most effective.

Strategies for Designing Your Poster

◎ To make your main image stand out more, don't use many words. Boil your key point down to a few words and do the rest visually.

◎ Use colors to draw viewers to the poster and to its most important part.

◎ Make the words and images on your poster large enough to be seen clearly from several feet away.

REVISING YOUR POSTER

Revise your poster so that it will grab the attention of viewers. When you've completed a rough layout of your poster, get ready to test it out on other people.

For help in revising your poster, ask classmates, friends, or family members to give you their reactions. Ask them to be kind but honest. Be prepared to take some but not all of their advice. If your practice audience has good ideas, use them. If some of their suggestions don't make sense to you or don't apply to your poster's purpose, don't make the changes. As long as your message is clear, you're on the right track.

Strategies for Revising Your Poster

◎ Ask the viewer to stand three or four feet away from the poster.

◎ Show the poster for about one minute or so and then put it away.

◎ Ask viewers what they remember.

   1. What was the first thing they saw?

   2. What were they looking at or reading when you put the poster away?

   3. Was there something they didn't understand?

◎ Jot down your viewers' answers to help you decide what parts of your poster need revision.

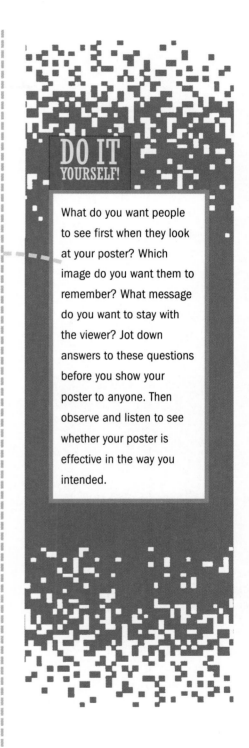

DO IT YOURSELF!

What do you want people to see first when they look at your poster? Which image do you want them to remember? What message do you want to stay with the viewer? Jot down answers to these questions before you show your poster to anyone. Then observe and listen to see whether your poster is effective in the way you intended.

DO IT YOURSELF!

When you're creating the finished product for your poster, sketch out the poster with a soft-lead art pencil before you paint or use markers. Put into position whatever you plan to glue on. Then stand back and take a final look to be sure everything is the right size for the space and everything is exactly where you want it.

EDITING YOUR POSTER

In the editing stage, check any writing on your poster for correct grammar and usage. Be especially careful about spelling. Make sure that the art work is appropriate and neatly done.

Transfer the draft version of your poster to a clean piece of stiff poster board. Make the drawing and lettering your best efforts. Fasten down, neatly and precisely, illustrations clipped from other sources.

APPLYING SPELLING TO WRITING ON A POSTER

Spelling Clues

Since posters usually have very few words, one small spelling error can be a disaster. Posters are also in public for all to see. Always check the spelling of each word, even the easiest one. For more help in spelling, see Chapter 24, Spelling.

DISPLAYING YOUR POSTER

Get ready to show your poster to your audience. The following are some ideas for displaying your poster.

Show It Off

- Volunteer to let the organization for whom you made the poster use your material.
- If you know someone who works in public relations, invite him or her to visit your class to comment on your posters.
- Think of some other appropriate public place to display your poster: a bus or train station, the lobby of an office building or theater, a restaurant or hotel lobby, a senior citizens center, a museum, a public park, the zoo, a grocery or department store, the YMCA, YWCA, or Boys Club.
- Display your poster in your classroom, in a hall in your school, or in the school library.

DO IT YOURSELF!

Sometimes public service posters achieve the status of art. With the permission of the principal, you and your classmates can exhibit your posters at the entrance to your school or in the hallway—someplace where adult visitors to your school will see them. Put a notebook near the exhibit with a sign asking visitors to look at the posters and write their comments about the ones they found particularly effective.

Evaluation Activity

On a separate sheet of paper, write out the answers to each of the following questions. Your responses will help you to decide how effectively your poster promotes your public service campaign.

- What's the first thing on your poster that catches the viewer's eye? Is this what you want the viewer to notice?
- What could be done to improve the art or the lettering on your poster?
- What part of your poster will make even the most casual viewer look at it closely?

8

Communicating
to Evaluate

Terms to Know

To **evaluate** something is to make a judgment about it. You don't just express an opinion; you also give reasons for that opinion.

isten to the people around you as you leave a movie, play, or concert. What do you hear?

"The whole thing was awesome!"

"Absolutely great–NOT!"

"What about that opening song? Excellent!"

"But the drummer was way off."

These people are expressing their opinions about what they just saw. That's the natural thing to do after a performance. In fact, producers often plant "spies" outside a theater to listen and take notes. It's a good way to pick up hints about the strengths and weaknesses of a show and to get an idea about whether it's going to be a hit.

Everybody's a Critic

You don't have to be a paid professional to be a critic or reviewer. All you have to do is see a movie or show, read a book, use a product, or observe a sunset and then tell someone what you thought of it. That's what a reviewer does–**evaluate**, or judge, something and then communicate that judgment to someone else.

Like everybody else, you evaluate, or judge, things all the time. You've probably written a book review for class. Maybe you liked a certain story so much that you want your best friend to read it. Or maybe you've had so many problems with a brand of sneakers that you want to talk your brother out of buying the same kind. Or maybe you feel so strongly about a photo you've seen that you want to learn to be a photographer. Whatever the reason or form, you communicate judgments to others just about every day.

In this unit, you'll have the chance to evaluate books and a movie. You can present a written review or a spoken review or use art to convey your impression of a piece of literature.

After completing one or more of these projects, you'll not only be better at communicating your opinions, but you'll also know more about yourself–about what you like and don't like and why.

LOOKING AHEAD
TO THE PROJECTS

8.1 Writing Project
Write a review of a book (pages 208-225).

8.2 Speaking Project
Prepare and deliver a spoken review of a movie (pages 226-239).

8.3 Visual Project
Create a book jacket for a book, another piece of literature, or a piece of your own writing (pages 240-247).

JOURNAL WRITING

Look at the photo on this page of a piece of sculpture. Actually, don't just look at it. Observe it closely for several minutes. What does it make you think of? How do you feel about it? In your journal, write answers to these questions.

1. What thoughts come to mind when you look at the sculpture?

2. What do you like most about the sculpture? Why?

3. What do you like least about the sculpture? Why?

Writing Project

Writing a Book Review

You'll be writing a review of a book you've read.

Cliff wants to be a newspaper journalist. His dream is to begin as a reporter and end up as a star columnist. As a start, he's joined the staff of his school newspaper.

When the faculty advisor, Ms. Jackson, gives Cliff his first assignment—a book review—he's confused and disappointed. "A book review? That's not reporting!" protests Cliff.

In answer, Ms. Jackson shows Cliff some newspapers and magazines, pointing out the many reviews of books, movies, TV programs, plays, recordings, art exhibits, and so forth. Ms. Jackson continues, "People are so busy today that they rely on reviews to save them time. A review gives readers important information about what's going on, so it *is* a kind of reporting."

Ms. Jackson convinces Cliff when she says. "If you want to be a columnist, writing a book review gives you practice in making judgments, supporting them, and then communicating them to your reader. That's exactly what good columnists do."

Now you, like Cliff, are going to write a book review to share with others–to read to your classmates, perhaps, or to submit to the school paper.

Before you start, take a look at a book review by middle school student Erik Reed. You may want to write your own review differently. Still, there may be some things you notice in this review that will help you.

STUDENT MODEL

Anne Frank: The Diary of a Young Girl
Erik Reed, Grade 7

Can you imagine having to hide in an attic with seven other people for two years? Every day brings the danger that you might be caught and sent to an almost certain death! Staying alive becomes your daily goal.

That is how a Dutch Jewish girl, Anne Frank, had to live during World War II to keep from being captured by the Nazis, who were rounding up all Jews. In Anne Frank: The Diary of a Young Girl, her actual diary, Anne movingly describes her fears and her deep frustrations at having to stay hidden away in an attic, unable to do the things that fourteen- or fifteen-year-old kids normally do.

Anne Frank conveys a sense of what it was like to live in hiding for over two years. She describes each incident in vivid detail. For example, she makes the reader feel her fright when burglars seem to be breaking into the Secret Annexe. She describes her terrible fears about what may happen to her, her family, and the others in the attic if they are caught. Then she makes the reader feel her relief when the "burglar" turns out to be a friend who was struggling to open a stuck door. She also writes about her experiences with Paul, a boy who was also hiding in the "Secret Annexe."

Anne Frank's diary is real. Reading it made me feel anger, pity, and sorrow for her and for every other person who had to hide or who was sent away to a concentration camp during World War II. And it made me realize how lucky I am and how grateful I should be for the freedom I enjoy. I also learned to appreciate the everyday things that Anne could not do, such as just walking in the park. Finally, her experiences helped me understand what some people must go through to survive and what they are still going through in certain places in the world today.

My only criticism is that some of the passages seemed long and repetitive and did not add much. However, those passages were not enough to spoil the effect of the book.

Anne Frank: The Diary of a Young Girl is an important, interesting, and very moving book. I recommend it to everyone, especially to young people. Maybe if young people read it, they will try to create a world where no one has to hide because of who they are.

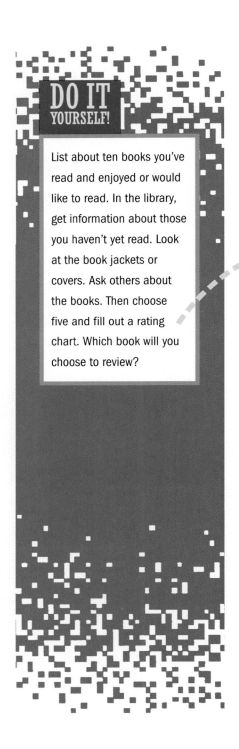

DO IT YOURSELF!

List about ten books you've read and enjoyed or would like to read. In the library, get information about those you haven't yet read. Look at the book jackets or covers. Ask others about the books. Then choose five and fill out a rating chart. Which book will you choose to review?

PREWRITING

How do you prepare to write a book review? If you want to say something worth saying, you have to put some thought into what you're going to read, how you're going to read it, and what you're going to say about it.

Choose a Book

Just like a professional reviewer, you'll sometimes be assigned a book to review and other times be able to choose your own. When you have a choice, look for a book that interests you—one you might want to share with others. Here are some strategies to help you.

Strategies to Help You Choose a Book to Review

- List books you've read recently.
- List books you want to read.
- List authors you like or think you would like.
- List the kinds of books you enjoy—mysteries or adventures or biographies, for instance.
- List subjects you enjoy or are curious about.
- Look at books you haven't read. Read the jackets. Read the openings. Skim.

Jot down the best possibilities. For each one, ask yourself whether you're likely to understand the book well enough to write about it. Will you need background information on the book or the topic, and if so, is it easy to get? Most important, are you likely to care enough about the book to share your opinion of it with others?

To help you select a book, try making a chart like the one Erik might have made before he decided to review Anne Frank's diary. The rating is based on a scale of one to five.

Rating Books to Review

	Understand the Book	Can Get Background	Care About It
Call of the Wild	3	3	3
The Contender	3	2	3
Fantastic Voyage	2	1	2
Diary of Anne Frank	4	5	4+
I Am the Cheese	3	2	3
Hoops	3	3	3+
My Side of the Mountain	4	5	4

Rating books in a chart makes it easier to see which books are the best candidates for your review. You don't have to base your decision entirely on the numbers in the chart, but they will help make your choice clearer.

Why You're Writing and for Whom

Your main purpose in writing a book review is to communicate your opinion of a book—to explain to others what you liked and didn't like about it. In the process, you'll be helping your readers decide whether or not they might want to read the book too.

Who are your readers? Classmates? Parents? Young children? You need to know who your audience is and what they are like in order to know what to say and how to say it. These questions will help you.

Know Your Audience

- Are readers likely to know the book?
- Are they likely to be interested in it?
- How much will they know about the topic? The background? The author?

IDEAS FOR YOUR

WRITING PROJECT

1. Write a report card for something that isn't normally evaluated that way—a movie or song or book, for example. Decide what subject areas to grade and what grading system to use.

2. Write a review of a product or a service. Use your school or local library to find examples of such reviews in consumer magazines.

3. Performance evaluations are usually written by supervisors in business situations. They discuss and evaluate an employee's job performance in detail. Write a performance evaluation of a brother, sister, or friend, judging how effective they are in their role.

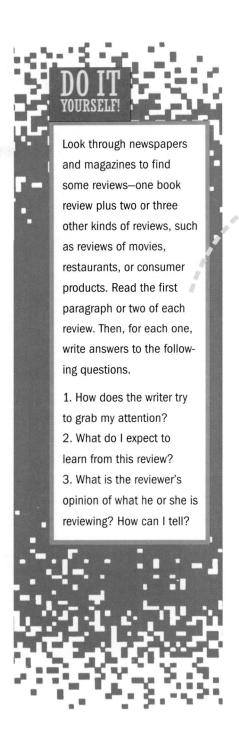

DO IT YOURSELF!

Look through newspapers and magazines to find some reviews—one book review plus two or three other kinds of reviews, such as reviews of movies, restaurants, or consumer products. Read the first paragraph or two of each review. Then, for each one, write answers to the following questions.

1. How does the writer try to grab my attention?
2. What do I expect to learn from this review?
3. What is the reviewer's opinion of what he or she is reviewing? How can I tell?

Read with a Critic's Eye

Even though you've chosen a book, you're still not ready to begin reading. You need to do some thinking and planning first. You might also want to get some background information about the author, the subject, or the time and place.

Decide How to Evaluate You wouldn't evaluate a sweater and sneakers the same way. They're both clothing, but they're designed to do different things. For the same reason, you don't evaluate a mystery and a biography the same way either.

Your first step is to decide the purpose of the book you're reviewing. Is the purpose to relate an adventure? Make you laugh? Keep you in suspense? Convey information? Once you've decided on the book's purpose, you can go on to judge how well it does what it's supposed to do. Look at the following steps. Erik Reed may have used them to evaluate *Anne Frank: The Diary of a Young Girl* before he read the book. Adapt the steps for your own book. Pay special attention to the questions under step 2.

WORK IN PROGRESS

To Evaluate a Book
1. Decide the purpose
    To relate events during a period of the
        writer's life
2. List the important elements for that purpose
    How well does the reader get to know Anne?
    How well are the events described?
    How real does Anne seem?
    How real do the events seem?

The elements in step 2 and the questions about them will be different for different kinds of books. If Erik Reed had read a work of fiction, for example, he would have listed and asked questions about **setting, characters, plot,** and **theme**. Then his questions might have included those shown below.

WORK

IN PROGRESS

To Evaluate Fiction

Setting

    Is the setting realistic and interesting?

    How does the setting add to the plot?

Characters

    Which characters are most interesting? Least
        interesting? Why?

    Do the characters change? If so, how?

    Do the main characters seem real? Why or why
        not?

Plot

    Do the events make sense?

    Do I keep turning the pages to see what
        happens?

    What's the turning point? Does it fit the story?

Theme

    Why did the author write the book? What did he
        or she want to say?

    Does the book teach me something new or help
        me see something in a new way?

Other elements to think about and perhaps include in your list are the author's **style** and **tone.**

Terms to Know

Setting is the time and place in which a piece of literature takes place.

The **characters** are the people who are part of the action of a piece of literature.

The **plot** is the sequence of actions and events in a work of fiction or drama.

The **theme** is the main idea of a work of literature.

Style refers to the special way an author composes a work of literature in written or spoken language.

The **tone** is the attitude that a work of literature expresses through its style.

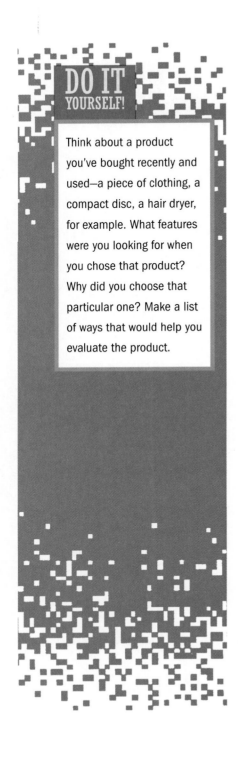

Think about a product you've bought recently and used—a piece of clothing, a compact disc, a hair dryer, for example. What features were you looking for when you chose that product? Why did you choose that particular one? Make a list of ways that would help you evaluate the product.

Read with Care Don't start to read until you've thought about and listed some of the things you'll be looking for. Since you're going to be judging the book, you need to keep your eyes and mind focused and alert. If you've already read the book, read it again. If you're reading it for the first time, read it carefully again. Concentrate. Reflect. Respond.

Respond as Yourself Put yourself into your review. Your readers want to know about more than just the contents and the author. How does the book make you feel? Why? What does it bring to mind? As you read, be aware of how you respond, and let your reader know about it.

Note What You Notice

Think about the questions you want to answer about your book, answer them, and take notes on the answers. Here are some additional questions for you to answer.

More Questions to Answer

- Does a passage make you curious? Excited? Giggly? Teary? Does your heart start thumping? Do you smile or laugh out loud? Note the passage.
- Is there a word, a sentence, or a description that strikes you in some way? Write it down.
- Does something remind you of a person, place, or experience in your own life? Write down some notes about it.

There are several ways you can mark passages and reactions you want to remember.

Noting What You Read

- Take notes on index cards. At the top of the card, write

the page number and the key point. Use quotation marks around words or passages you copy directly.

- Use stick-on notes in the book to mark special parts and make notations.
- Keep a Reader's Log as you read. Note page numbers, passages, and your reactions.

Here are some of the kinds of passages you might decide to mark.

Passages to Mark

- Reactions to characters
- Reactions to events
- Reactions to the theme
- Passages that surprise you
- Passages that bother you
- Passages that dazzle you
- Passages that make you curious
- Questions that come to mind
- Descriptions you can picture vividly
- High points and low points

DO IT YOURSELF!

Get some index cards or stick-on notes or both. As you read, use them to note passages that attract your attention, feelings and questions that arise, and anything else that comes to mind that might be useful in writing a review.

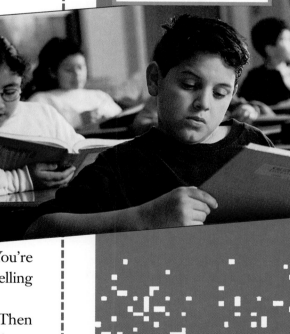

Make a Judgment

Making a judgment is what a review is all about. You're not just telling your readers about a book; you're telling them what you thought of the book and why.

When you finish reading, reflect for a while. Then look at your notes and reflect some more. How did you react to the book? Why? What did you like? What didn't you like? Would you recommend the book? Why or why not?

Remember Erik Reed and the two steps in the Work in Progress on page 212? After reading *Anne Frank: The*

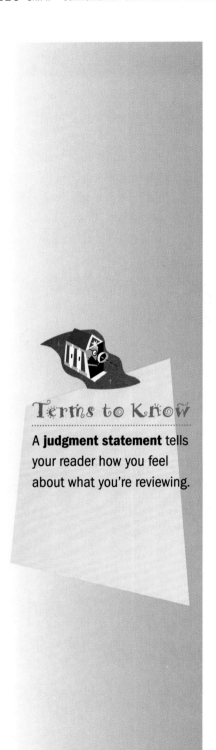

Terms to Know

A **judgment statement** tells your reader how you feel about what you're reviewing.

Diary of a Young Girl, he could have added a third step with answers to the questions in step 2. Look at the following three steps.

WORK IN PROGRESS

To Evaluate a Book

1. Decide the purpose

   To relate events during a period of the writer's life

2. List the important elements for that purpose

   How well does the reader get to know Anne?

   How well are the events described?

   How real does Anne seem?

   How real do the events seem?

3. Judge each element

   Feel as if I know Anne well

   Events are described vividly and in detail

   Can identify with Anne's feelings

   Events are frighteningly real

Once you've done your evaluating, as Erik did, try writing some statements that capture your opinion. Keep writing until you get a **judgment statement** that accurately sums up how you feel. Your evaluation doesn't have to be all good or all bad. "The book left me with mixed feelings" is an evaluation, too, as long as you explain it.

Finally, look back at your notes. See whether you have evidence to back up your opinion—examples from the book itself. If not, look for some. If you can't find enough evidence, then change your judgment statement to one you can support. An opinion is only as convincing as the evidence that backs it up.

Plan It Out

If you have a plan, your writing will be easier. You'll have a sense of where you are and where you're going.

Look at the general plan for a review that follows. Copy the plan and then fill in the details for your book.

> ### Review Plan
>
> Introduction
> Name the book and the author.
> Tell something about the book.
> In a judgment statement, say what you think of the book.
>
> Body
> Evaluate the most important elements, one by one.
> Arrange the elements in order of importance—from most to least important or from least to most important.
>
> Conclusion
> Include your judgment statement and make a conclusion about the value of the book.

In the body of the review, choose just a few elements–those that stood out in some way. Perhaps the setting was especially vivid or dull. Perhaps the humor was really sharp or really silly. Or perhaps, as in Erik Reed's review of *Anne Frank: The Diary of a Young Girl,* the feelings aroused were very strong.

DRAFTING

After you've read the book, taken notes, and made an outline, write a draft. Follow your plan to give yourself a sense of direction. Feel free, though, to change that direction as you write and revise.

For Openers

Use the opening paragraphs of your introduction to present the book to your readers and get them interested in reading what you have to say about it. The first paragraph or two should include the following.

Introducing a Review

- Hook your readers with a question, a quotation, or an anecdote from the book.
- Name the book and the author.
- Offer some background information.
- Express your general opinion or slant.
- Tell something about the book or summarize it, but don't tell everything.

Here's a possible first draft of Erik Reed's opening.

WORK IN PROGRESS

A Dutch Jewish girl, Anne Frank, had to hide in an attic for two years during World War II. That is how she and her family kept from being captured by the Nazis who were rounding up all Jews. In _Anne Frank: The Diary of a Young Girl,_ Anne describes her fears and her deep frustrations at having to stay hidden away in an attic.

Erik decided he needed a more exciting opening. In his revision he added a section that addressed readers directly, asking them to imagine themselves in Anne's place. Here are other openings he might have chosen.

WORK IN PROGRESS

Some Ways to Hook the Reader

Ask a question.

Can you imagine having to hide in an attic with seven people for two years?

State your opinion.

Anne Frank: The Diary of a Young Girl can move you to tears.

Start with a quotation.

"In spite of everything I still believe that people are really good at heart," wrote Anne Frank in her diary.

Tell something about the book.

During her two years in hiding in an attic in Holland, Anne Frank kept a diary.

Tell something about the author.

Anne Frank was only thirteen years old when she had to go into hiding to escape the Nazis.

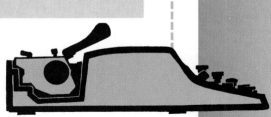

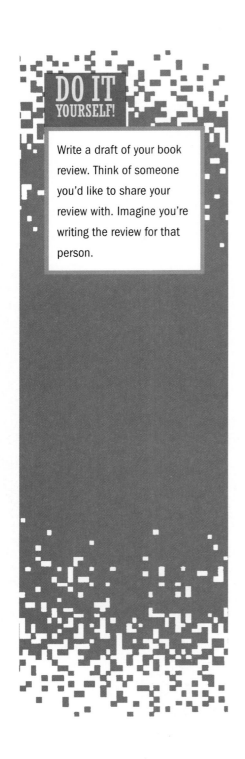

DO IT YOURSELF!

Write a draft of your book review. Think of someone you'd like to share your review with. Imagine you're writing the review for that person.

Back Up Your Opinions

Remember, your purpose in a review is to offer readers your opinion on the value of a book and to support that opinion. Without evidence, your readers will have no reason to take seriously what you say. Here is how Erik Reed might have drafted his support in his review.

WORK IN PROGRESS

Supporting Your Opinion

1. State your opinion or evaluation.

Anne Frank conveys a sense of what it was like to live in hiding for over two years.

2. Support your opinion with examples from the book.

For example, she makes the reader feel her fright when it seems that burglars are trying to break into the "Secret Annexe."

In the drafting stage you can make full use of your notes. The passages you marked can provide the evidence you need to back up your main points.

You may want to create a new paragraph for each important point. Each paragraph, then, will state an opinion and reaction, give the reasons for your statement, and offer one or more examples from the book—an event, some dialogue, a quotation, a description, or background information, for example.

When you state your opinion, avoid weak words such as *good, great, poor, bad.* They tell the reader very little. Instead, use strong words such as *gripping, monotonous, exciting, lifeless, believable.* And explain exactly *why* those words apply, giving illustrations from the book.

Talk to Your Reader

As you write your draft, picture a reader, and write for that person. What do you want to say to him or her? What parts of the book will be especially meaningful? What will he or she find convincing or interesting or funny or moving? What's the best way of expressing yourself to that reader? Give enough information to allow the reader to decide whether to read the book, but not so much that you spoil it for her or him.

Sum It Up

Write a conclusion that sums up your personal reaction and makes a recommendation. Do you think others will enjoy the book? Why or why not? Who might enjoy it most? Least? Don't just fade away with a statement such as "You'll enjoy reading the book." Explain why. End with a statement that leaves the reader with something to think about and remember.

REVISING

A draft isn't a finished piece of writing. It needs to be read, reread, thought about, talked about, and revised until you're happy with it.

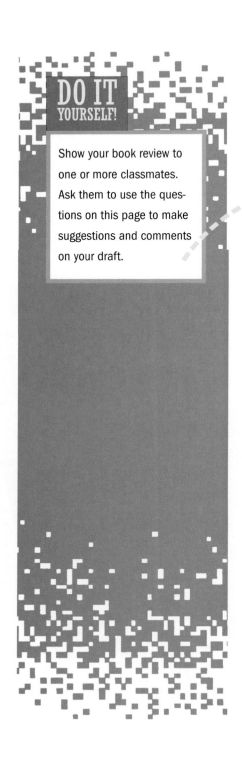

DO IT YOURSELF!

Show your book review to one or more classmates. Ask them to use the questions on this page to make suggestions and comments on your draft.

Review Your Review

A good way to begin reviewing your review is to share it with someone—a family member, classmates, a neighbor, a friend, for example. Ask your reader for an honest response, using questions like those that follow.

Questions for Reviewing the Review

- Does the opening grab you?
- Are the title and author stated at the beginning?
- Is there enough background information?
- Does the review contain a clear judgment statement about the book?
- Does it provide a clear picture of the book?
- Is each opinion supported with enough examples from the book?
- Does the organization make sense?
- Does the review include personal responses?
- Does it close with a clear judgment statement and a recommendation?
- What are the strengths of the review?
- What are the weaknesses? What could be improved?

When you've collected some responses from others, go over the review yourself. Try to forget you're the writer and read it as if you were an editor. Think about your readers' comments. Then make any and all changes that you think will improve the review.

APPLYING USAGE TO WRITING

Comparing with Adjectives

When you're evaluating, you often need to use adjectives that compare things. For example, you may want to say why one chapter of a book is more gripping than another or why one book is the most absorbing one you've ever read. For more on adjectives in comparisons, see Chapter 18.1, Comparison of Adjectives and Adverbs.

EDITING

Reviewers normally use the present tense to refer to events in a book. Look back at Erik's paper and see that he uses the present tense and the present progressive tense. For example, he says, "She **makes** the reader feel her fright when it **seems** that burglars **are breaking** into the Secret Annexe."

Check to see that you've used the present tense consistently in such sentences. Then go over your review again, paying close attention to other matters of usage, grammar, mechanics, and spelling. Check the spelling of names and the accuracy of quotations. Small errors can make readers doubt the big things you have to say.

APPLYING USAGE TO WRITING

The Present Tense

Use the present tense when you write a review, especially when you're writing about a piece of literature. Your reader will experience the book that much better. It's also important to be consistent in your use of tense. Use the present tense throughout as long as it makes sense. For more about the present tense, see Chapter 15, Using Verbs.

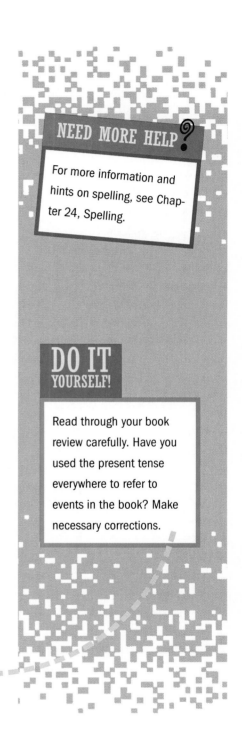

NEED MORE HELP?

For more information and hints on spelling, see Chapter 24, Spelling.

DO IT YOURSELF!

Read through your book review carefully. Have you used the present tense everywhere to refer to events in the book? Make necessary corrections.

NEED MORE HELP?

For more information about publishing, see Chapter 27, Test, Study, and Research Skills.

DO IT YOURSELF!

With your teacher's permission, get together with three or four classmates to conduct a book talk. Sit in a circle and take turns reading your book reviews aloud while the others take notes. After each review, use your notes to discuss the points made in the reviews. Do you think you would follow the reader's recommendation? Why or why not?

Formatting the Publishing Information

Although each newspaper and magazine may have its own specific format, book reviews almost always provide the following information: the book title, author, publisher, number of pages, and price. Sometimes the publishing date is included as well, as in the example that follows.

> My Side of the Mountain
> Jean C. George
> E. P. Dutton, 1988
> 177 pp. $7.98

PUBLISHING

Take a look at the following ideas for publishing your book review.

Publishing Your Book Review

- Bind your class's reviews together to create a book-review magazine.
- Conduct a book talk in which one reviewer reads the review aloud and others in the group react to it.
- Submit your review to a newspaper or magazine.
- Exchange book reviews with a pen pal.
- Add illustrations and background information and create a book poster around your review.
- Post your review on the library bulletin board.
- Help organize a Book Day at your school. Take turns with classmates in reading your reviews aloud.

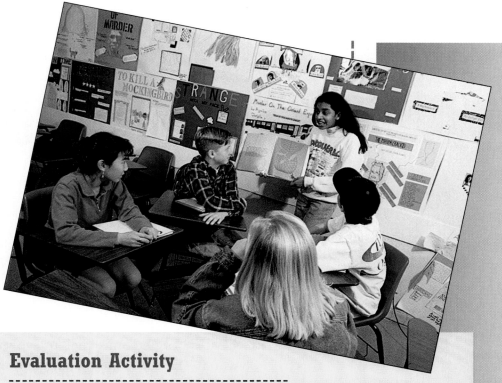

Evaluation Activity

The goal of a book review, like every other kind of writing, is to communicate—in this case, to communicate something about a book. Have you met this goal? Give your review to one or more people to read. Then ask questions like the following.

Reader Evaluation

1. What is the book about?
2. What kind of book is it?
3. Who is the main character or person? What is he or she like?
4. What is the point or theme of the book?
5. What judgment is made about the book? Why?
6. What do you remember most about the review?
7. Would you want to read the book? Why or why not?

The closer readers come to what you are trying to say, the better you have succeeded at communicating.

8.2 Speaking Project

Giving a Spoken Movie Review

You'll prepare a speech in which you give your opinion of a movie.

It's a dream come true! You've won a trip to Hollywood! There you are, visiting movie studios, cheering the Los Angeles Lakers, viewing screenings of movies, and going to tapings of TV shows. This afternoon you're sitting in the front row of a TV talk show. Before the taping starts, you're chatting with the famous host about the movie screenings that you've just seen.

The show begins. Out come the movie reviewers. After some chitchat, the host announces, "And now a special reviewer will join our regular reviewers." Suddenly both the host and the camera turn to you, and you find yourself escorted to the stage!

What will you say? You've got some opinions about movies, but how well can you express them? Can you back them up? Millions of people are watching and listening to YOU!

Although you're not likely to find yourself in this situation, you may sometimes *feel* as if millions are watching when you give a speech or defend an opinion.

The trick is to practice and be prepared. This chapter's speaking project—a movie review for your class or another group—will help you do just that.

Here's an example of a spoken theater review that middle school student Deborah Gail Bernstein wrote out. She rehearsed and rehearsed it until she was comfortable speaking from notes alone. Your speech will be your own, of course. But Deborah's speech may help you with yours.

STUDENT MODEL

The Movie *Hook*
Deborah Gail Bernstein, Grade 6

As a child I used to like listening to and reading the story of Peter Pan, and I watched the animated movie too. I looked forward to seeing the movie Hook, a Steven Spielberg film starring Robin Williams and Dustin Hoffman, because it's a modern version of Peter Pan. I wasn't disappointed.

While Peter Panning, played by Robin Williams, is visiting England, his kids are kidnapped by the cruel Captain Hook. Tinkerbell shows up and tries to convince Peter he is really Peter Pan, but he doesn't believe her. She takes him to NeverNever Land, and there the Lost Boys finally help Peter remember his adventures as a young boy. The climax comes when Peter, trying to save his children, has to duel with his old enemy Captain Hook.

The step-by-step transformation of Peter Panning into Peter Pan really works. First the Lost Boys don't believe he is Peter Pan and have to be convinced by Tinkerbell. Next they have to convince Panning. They do this by playing games that help him remember how to fly and how to use his imagination. This gradual transformation makes the movie more believable and more interesting.

The theme of love holding a family together kept me interested too. The family has realistic problems. The dad is so busy that he is rarely around, and the kids resent it. When the dad goes after the kids to save them, they realize how much they care for and need one another. The family's love brings it together.

The special effects were awesome, especially the flying. I liked Tinkerbell's glow and pixie dust too, for they made her look like a pixie.

The acting and directing were excellent, and all the actors seemed to become their characters. Robin Williams, especially, has always been one of my favorites, and he didn't disappoint me in Hook. Steven Spielberg, who has made films like Jaws, E.T., and Close Encounters of the Third Kind, kept the action moving and the camera work interesting.

I really enjoyed this movie. I liked the story, the theme, the special effects, the acting, and the directing. Go see it, find out how it ends, and decide whether you enjoy it too. I hope you do!

SPEAKING PROJECT

1. Evaluate the architecture of a building or part of a building. Prepare by looking through reviews in an architectural magazine in the library. In your evaluation, you might lead your audience on a "tour" of the building.

2. Review a musical performance, live or recorded. If possible, play sample selections on a CD player or tape recorder during your spoken review.

GETTING STARTED

As a movie viewer, your opinion is important. To prepare your movie review, you need to do some thinking and planning, and that begins long before you see the movie.

Telling Versus the TelePrompTer

Have you ever watched someone on TV give a speech that sounded stiff and a little too perfect? They were probably reading their speech from a TelePrompTer—a machine out of camera range that displays the text of the speech.

Reading a speech means that you can't forget anything and that you can stick to a certain time limit. But you sacrifice naturalness and a close connection with your audience.

To sound more natural, you can use notes. Instead of writing a speech out word for word, you write key words to cue you on what you want to say.

There's a compromise approach, too. You can write out a speech and then practice, practice, practice it until you know it almost by heart.

Again, the trick is to work at speech making. The more you do it, the more comfortable you'll be using notes—and the better you'll be as a speaker.

Pick a Flick

When you have a choice about what movie to review, you can use the following questions to guide your selection.

Guidelines for Choosing a Movie to Review

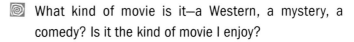 What kind of movie is it—a Western, a mystery, a comedy? Is it the kind of movie I enjoy?

◎ Am I likely to understand it well enough to write a review about it?

◎ Is the subject one I know about or would like to learn about?

You may also want to choose between viewing a movie in a theater or on videotape. (Try to avoid movies on TV that are heavily edited and broken up by commercials.) Each has advantages and disadvantages, as you can see from the information that follows.

Movie Theater or Video?

◎ A movie in a theater offers a live audience as well as a large screen. It's always more exciting and revealing to watch with other people and sense their reactions.

◎ A videotape offers the ability to control your viewing. You can pause, replay, and watch as many times as you like. You can stop to take notes, and you can leave a light on, which makes note-taking easier.

Of course, this choice might be out of your hands. The film might be too new to appear on video or too old to be playing in a theater.

Fill in the Background

Try to get some background information about the movie. You'll make a better viewer and reviewer if you know something about what you're seeing. Look back at Deborah Gail Bernstein's review of *Hook* and notice how she included information about the Peter Pan story, Robin Williams, and Steven Spielberg.

For recent releases, professional reviewers receive press kits containing information about the making of the movie, the people involved, and other related topics.

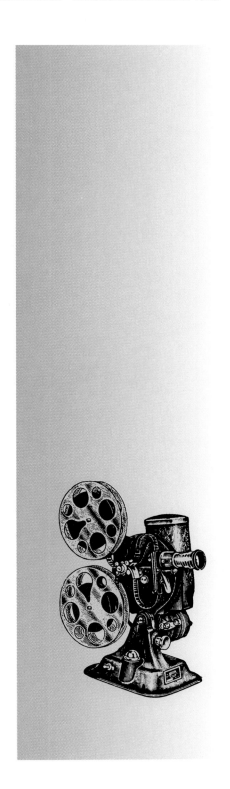

If you can find out what film company produced the movie, you can get their address from the library and write or call their public relations department, asking for a press kit. Otherwise, your library can probably provide some information.

You may want to rent videos of movies with the same actors or director to get an idea of the range and abilities of the people involved.

What to Watch For

When you go to the movies with friends, you probably just sit back, relax, and let the film roll by you. When you go to the movies as a critic, you need to keep your eyes and mind working. That doesn't mean you can't enjoy the movie. In fact you may end up enjoying it more because you become more aware of the reasons it works–or doesn't work.

Here are some things you can do to become a more thoughtful viewer.

To Watch like a Critic

Before You Watch

- Get some background information about the movie.
- Don't make any judgments about it before you see it.
- Make a list to remind yourself of the elements to think about: the acting, directing, script, music, camera work, special effects, and so on.
- Take a large note pad and some pencils with you.

While You Watch

◎ Watch and listen actively. Keep your mind going. Notice things.

◎ Keep the list of elements in mind.

◎ Take notes on things you observe and think. Just jot down key words and phrases as cues.

◎ Pay attention to the opening and closing credits. There may be names you want to mention.

After You Watch

◎ As soon as possible, write down your reactions while they are fresh in your mind.

◎ Expand on your notes before you forget what the cues stand for.

What Do You Think and Why Do You Think It?

"What did you think of that movie?" Rita asks.

"Yucko!" says Kyle.

"Why?" Rita wants to know.

"I don't know," he replies. "I just hated it."

If Rita trusts what Kyle says, she just might miss a terrific movie. Without reasons–good reasons–there's no way to know whether his judgment is appropriate or not.

So how do you evaluate a movie–or anything else? You follow three basic steps.

How to Evaluate

1. Set up standards.
2. Measure how well what you're evaluating meets the standards.
3. Make a judgment based on those measurements.

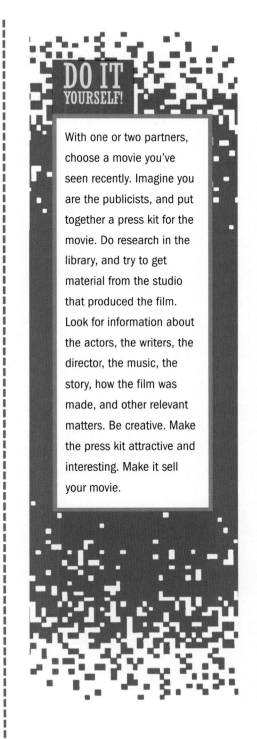

DO IT YOURSELF!

With one or two partners, choose a movie you've seen recently. Imagine you are the publicists, and put together a press kit for the movie. Do research in the library, and try to get material from the studio that produced the film. Look for information about the actors, the writers, the director, the music, the story, how the film was made, and other relevant matters. Be creative. Make the press kit attractive and interesting. Make it sell your movie.

To set up your standards, think about the elements of the movie. Then make a list of questions based on those elements. Below are a few examples for a comedy. For a book or for a different kind of movie, the questions would be different.

Setting up Standards

Script:	Did the story make sense?
	Did the plot hold my attention?
	Did I laugh? When?
Acting:	Were the actors believable and natural?
	Were they funny?
Music:	Did the music suit the events?
	Did it heighten the effect?

These questions then function as the standards by which you judge the movie. Some other elements you might ask questions about include the directing, camera work, special effects, costumes, setting, and theme.

Write the answers to your questions as soon as possible after you see the movie, while your reactions are still vivid. Then give examples from the movie to support each answer. Those examples will provide the *why*–the evidence you need to back up your judgments.

Remember your personal responses, too. Did you laugh? Cry? Shudder? Yawn? Your readers will want to know how the movie made you feel.

Put Your Thoughts Together

The next step is to develop an outline. Get all your notes together and review them.

Which elements were the most important in this movie? The acting? The script? The special effects? The costumes? The music? Use them as the body of your outline, point by point. Organize them from most to least or from least to most important. Include your evidence too.

Here's Deborah's outline for her review of *Hook*.

WORK IN PROGRESS

I. Introduction: Background, statement of
    judgment
II. Plot summary
III. Elements
    A. Script: Believable transformation from Peter
        Panning to Peter Pan
    B. Interesting theme: Love holding family
        together
    C. Special effects awesome
        1. Flying
        2. Tinkerbell
    D. Acting, directing excellent
        1. Robin Williams
        2. Steven Spielberg
IV. Conclusion
    A. Liked movie
    B. Go see it

DRAFTING AND PRACTICING YOUR SPOKEN REVIEW

If you decide to write out your speech, your first draft can be your outline. Make note cards based on the outline. Write key words or phrases that will remind you of

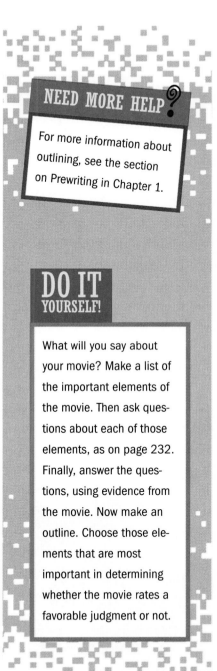

NEED MORE HELP?

For more information about outlining, see the section on Prewriting in Chapter 1.

DO IT YOURSELF!

What will you say about your movie? Make a list of the important elements of the movie. Then ask questions about each of those elements, as on page 232. Finally, answer the questions, using evidence from the movie. Now make an outline. Choose those elements that are most important in determining whether the movie rates a favorable judgment or not.

exactly what you want to say when. Make your writing or printing large so that you can use your cards as cues when you speak.

The following is a note card that Deborah Gail Bernstein might have prepared for her spoken review of *Hook*.

WORK

IN PROGRESS

3

TRANSFORMATION of Panning to Pan

LOST BOYS convinced by Tinkerbell

Play GAMES with P.

P. FLIES

Uses IMAGINATION

Don't write out your review yet. First try delivering it from your notes, several times. Don't expect to get it right at first. Remember, seasoned reviewers have years of experience behind them. Write out the speech only if you really, honestly feel you can't do without a script.

Sound like Yourself

The best reason to speak from note cards rather than a script is that you're likely to sound more natural. When people read speeches, they may sound stiff and artificial. Listeners tend to turn off. Using just cues from note cards, you'll find it easier to sound like yourself and to connect with your audience–and keep them awake.

If you really feel you need a script, try writing it as you speak it to make it "sound" like you.

APPLYING USAGE TO SPEECH WRITING

Slang

Slang is a form of language that's different from standard usage. It's informal and can be quite colorful and expressive. The problem with slang is that not everyone understands it, and the expressions appear and disappear in no time. For more about slang, see Chapter 11.3B, Formality and Informality.

REVISING YOUR SPOKEN REVIEW

Start revising a spoken review by talking it through to see how it sounds. After you've practiced several times, ask a few people to listen and comment. Here are some questions they should keep in mind.

Questions to Ask Listeners

- Does the beginning grab your attention?
- Is the statement of judgment clear?
- Do the basic points seem important and clear?
- Is the evidence strong enough?
- Do I need more examples? If so, where?
- Do my personal responses seem genuine?
- Would you follow my recommendation? Why or why not?
- What, if anything, don't you understand?
- What, if anything, should I add or leave out?
- Was the speech too long or too short?
- Was my delivery too slow? Fast? Soft? Loud? Dull?

After you've gotten comments from others, try listening to yourself. That isn't easy. A tape recorder, video camera, or mirror can help. Also, use a watch to time yourself. Try not to sound too stiff or formal, and vary

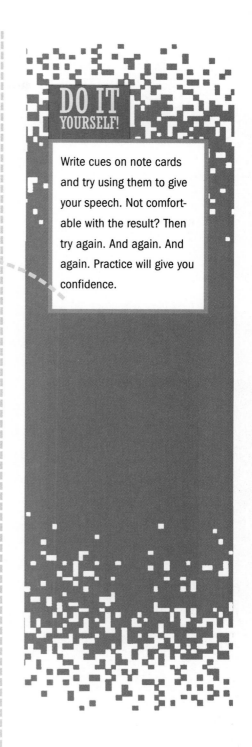

DO IT YOURSELF!

Write cues on note cards and try using them to give your speech. Not comfortable with the result? Then try again. And again. And again. Practice will give you confidence.

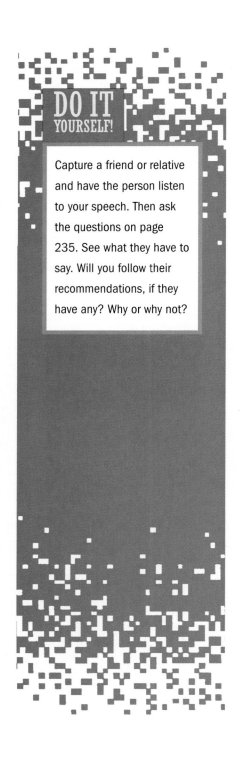

DO IT YOURSELF!

Capture a friend or relative and have the person listen to your speech. Then ask the questions on page 235. See what they have to say. Will you follow their recommendations, if they have any? Why or why not?

your expression. Picture a friend and imagine you're talking to him or her. Smile, try to look relaxed, and experiment with different gestures. See how you look; listen to how you sound.

To make revisions, just revise your note cards. Also make notes to remind you about gestures and expression. Write cues such as *Smile!* or *Slow!* Add symbols to cue you about when to speed up or slow down. Keep practicing until you're satisfied with both the content of your talk and the way you deliver it.

Here's how Deborah Gail Bernstein might have revised one of her note cards as she was preparing her talk about the movie *Hook*.

> **WORK IN PROGRESS**
>
> 3
>
> TRANSFORMATION of Panning to Pan
>   LOST BOYS convinced by Tinkerbell
>   Play GAMES with P.
>   P. FLIES
>   Uses IMAGINATION
> GRADUAL = believable, interesting

APPLYING GRAMMAR TO SPEECH WRITING

Prepositions

In your movie review, when you talk about how ideas, objects, and people are related, you'll use prepositions—words that show relationships, such as *at, by, in, over, with, near, like*. For more information, see Chapter 12.6, Prepositions.

EDITING YOUR SPOKEN REVIEW

Although you're speaking your review instead of writing it, you still have to edit it. You don't have to worry about spelling, of course, but there are matters of grammar and usage that will need your attention.

In general, speaking is less formal than writing. Still, grammar and usage need to be correct. Your audience can't go back and reread to be sure they understand you.

Tape-record your speech if possible, then play it back, listening for errors. Otherwise, ask someone else to listen to you and note any slips for you to correct.

DELIVERING YOUR SPOKEN REVIEW

Whether you present your review to a friend or classmate or tape it as part of a TV show, there are certain guidelines you should follow.

Guidelines for Presenting a Spoken Review

- Don't just blurt out the beginning. Pause, take a deep breath, smile, and begin.
- Speak slowly and clearly. Be sure your audience can hear you, but don't shout.
- Glance at your notes, but look at your audience as much as you can. Make eye contact.
- Keep your voice lively and expressive. Vary your tone.
- Keep your expression pleasant. Smile sometimes.
- Use gestures appropriately.

DO IT YOURSELF!

Working with a partner, choose the same movie to review. Evaluate it separately and then get together and give a joint review. One of you will introduce the review. Then you'll take turns reviewing the movie. Do you agree with one another? Why or why not? Finally, one of you will conclude, summarizing the two reviews.

There are different ways to present your spoken review. Here are a few.

How to Present Your Spoken Review

◎ Deliver your review to the class.

◎ Work with a partner to review the movie. One of you can introduce and sum up the movie. Each of you can make different points about it, to which the other can respond, agreeing or disagreeing.

◎ Hold a round-table discussion with others who have seen the same movie. Take turns offering two- or three-minute reviews as the others take notes. Use the notes as the basis for a follow-up discussion.

◎ Put your review on tape. Combine it with others to create a Show of Reviews.

◎ Call your local cable TV station. Offer to present the review on a show for young people.

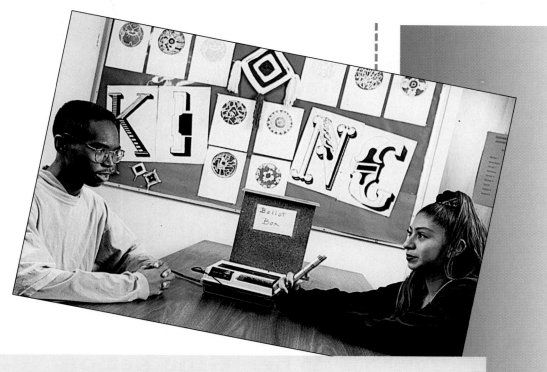

Evaluation Activity

After you've presented your review, think about how well you think you did.
Try to evaluate yourself fairly and honestly, without being too harsh.

Self-Evaluation Form

- Did I hook my audience in the beginning?
- Did they seem to remain interested?
- Did I have appropriate and convincing evidence to back up my judgment?
- Did I state my judgment clearly?
- Did I include personal responses?
- Did I use my voice expressively?
- Did I add gestures appropriately?
- Was I able to follow my notes?
- Did I say everything I wanted to say?
- Did I make eye contact with the audience?

8.3 Visual Project

Creating a Book Jacket

You'll design and create a book jacket that will sell a book to potential readers.

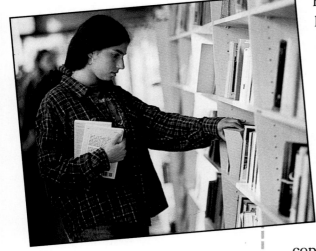

When Gina set out to buy her cousin Patrick a gift, she knew exactly what he liked–books. He loved to read, especially exotic stuff like adventures, fantasies, and myths. All she had to do was look around the bookstore.

When Gina reached the bookstore, she wandered, just looking. She picked up anything with an exciting picture on the jacket and read the flap copy to see whether the story, subject, and author were ones that Patrick might like.

She finally spotted a jacket design with swordsmen and creatures and medieval costumes. The title was *Prelude to a War.* When she read the flap copy, she saw that the story had everything Patrick liked–an exotic setting, mythical beings, and lots of action. Satisfied, she bought the book and went home smiling as she pictured Patrick opening his gift.

Have you, like Gina, ever gone shopping for a book and been sold on one by reading the book jacket? For this activity, you'll design a book jacket of your own with convincing art and flap copy that will capture potential readers.

Below is a sample of a student's jacket design and flap copy for *Prelude to a War*. Examining it may give you ideas for a book jacket of your own. Of course, your book jacket will reflect you. Make it your own.

Prelude to a War
Julie Huang, Grade 7

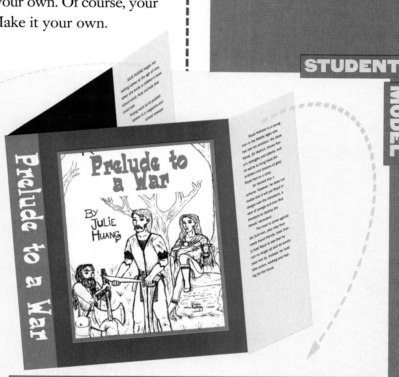

JULIE HUANG began her writing career at the age of nine, when she wrote a children's book about small, furry animals that could talk.

Huang went on to publish stories in a magazine and school newspapers.

When she was ten, she became fascinated with medieval stories, and that interest continues.

Ms. Huang was born in Taiwan, where she lived till she was three. Now she lives in Rockville, Maryland, with her parents and her older brother.

Royal Webster is a young man in the Middle Ages who has lost his ambition. His close friend, Sir Hedrick, knows Royal's strengths and talents, and he wants to bring back the ambition and dreams of glory Royal had as a child.

Sir Hedrick has a scheme. However, he does not realize that it will put Royal in danger with the mino-taurs, a race of savage bull-men that threatens to destroy the friends' homeland.

The need to strike against the bull-men, plus help from newly found friends, does finally lead Royal to see that he can no longer sit and let events pass him by. Instead, he must take action, working and hoping for the future.

Terms to Know

A **book jacket** is the cover that wraps around a hardcover book. (Paperback books ordinarily don't have separate jackets.)

The **spine** of a book is the narrow part where the front and back come together. The book title and author's name are always printed on the spine so that the book can be identified when placed vertically on a shelf.

The **flaps** are the parts of the jacket that fold around inside the front and back covers.

The **flap copy** is the information that is printed on the flaps.

What's on the Jacket?

In a bookstore, where do you get information about a book's contents and authors? You do what Gina did. You look at the **book jacket**.

Probably the first thing you look at is the cover illustration, which should tell you something about the flavor of the book. On the cover and on the book's **spine** you'll find the book title and the author's name. Next you open the cover, look at the **flaps**, and read the **flap copy**. That should tell you about the contents of the book and about its author. If the flap copy is written well, it just might persuade you that this is the book for you.

FIRST THINGS FIRST

Book jackets probably started as a way to protect the books they covered, but today they offer much more than protection. Publishers take book jackets very seriously, for they know that a good jacket can help sell a book. Before you put together a book jacket of your own, you need to do some thinking and planning.

Choose a Book

For what book would you like to design a jacket? You can choose any kind of book you like. Just be sure to choose a piece of writing you care about and understand. Here are some options to consider.

What Book?

- Create a book jacket for a favorite book.
- Create a new, improved book jacket for a book with a jacket you don't like.
- Create a book jacket for a piece of your own writing.

Choose an Effect

Is your book an adventure story? A romantic story? A fantasy? Science fiction? A biography? Is it aimed at children? Young people? Adults? The design of the book jacket should suit the book. It should tell the reader what the contents are like and who the audience is. If the jacket doesn't have the same effect as the book, then it will mislead rather than help the reader.

Look at book jackets in the library and bookstores. What impression do they make? Notice the designs, the use of color, the way things are drawn and written.

Decide what effect the book has, and plan for the jacket to have the same effect. Look at these questions.

What's the Effect?

- What really stands out about the piece of literature?
- What key image can represent the book?
- What is the mood of the piece of literature?
- What is special about the setting?
- Does it make the reader laugh? Cry? Smile? Frown?

Choose a Medium

The most obvious way to create the illustration for a book jacket is to draw or paint a picture. That's not the only way, however. Here are other options to consider.

Some Ways to Illustrate a Book Jacket

- Create an abstract design—one that uses various shapes, forms, and colors.
- Make a collage by cutting up construction paper, magazines, newspapers, or other materials.
- Create a design on a computer.
- Use a photograph or a magazine illustration.
- Create a statue or sculpture and then photograph it.

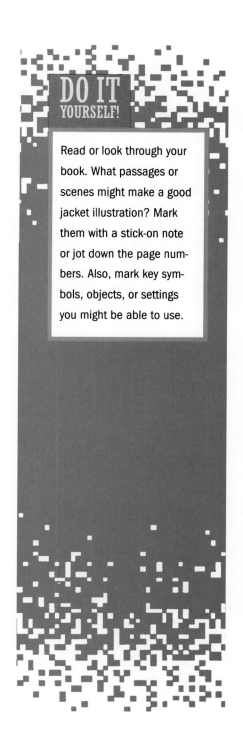

DO IT YOURSELF!

Read or look through your book. What passages or scenes might make a good jacket illustration? Mark them with a stick-on note or jot down the page numbers. Also, mark key symbols, objects, or settings you might be able to use.

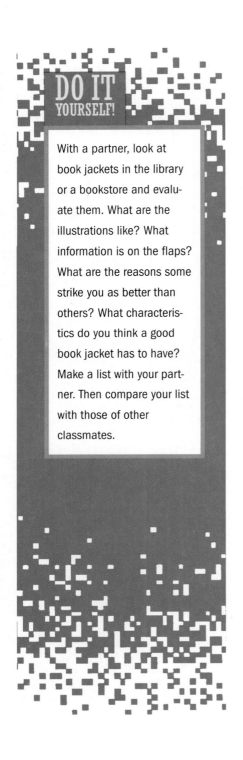

With a partner, look at book jackets in the library or a bookstore and evaluate them. What are the illustrations like? What information is on the flaps? What are the reasons some strike you as better than others? What characteristics do you think a good book jacket has to have? Make a list with your partner. Then compare your list with those of other classmates.

Look through art books in your school or public library and see the many different ways artists express their ideas. Choose a medium that seems right for you and for the book.

Sketch It Out

Keep in mind that the jacket illustration is probably the first thing people notice when they pick up a book. It can make them want either to look further or to put the book down. So take the design seriously. The following questions suggest some issues to think about.

Deciding on a Jacket Illustration

- What colors would best represent the mood of the book?
- Who should be pictured? What should they look like? What should they be doing?
- How should the setting be pictured?
- Would an abstract illustration be suitable?
- Where should the title and author's name appear? How should they be printed?

Start by making some rough sketches. These can be full size, or they can be small sketches. Don't be afraid to try out twelve or twenty or even more. When you come up with two or three you really like, work on them more carefully. Then decide which suits the book best and will grab the reader most forcefully.

Get Your Facts Together

Once you've decided on a design, turn your attention to the flap copy. (Actually, you can do things the other way around too. It really doesn't matter.) Here's what to include in the flap copy.

Summary of book

◎ Begins on front flap; can continue onto back flap

◎ Tells part of the story but not all

◎ Ends with a teaser—a hint at exciting event or climax—to make reader want to read book

Author information

✕ Date and place of birth (and death)

✕ Additional works, if any

✕ Personal information

✕ Quotations, if available

You can obtain information about the author from biographical dictionaries in the library.

FASHIONING YOUR BOOK JACKET

Use a paper bag to make a mock book jacket. Fold it around the book and cut it to size. Then make a sample illustration and tape it to the jacket.

The Flap Copy

Use your outline and notes to draft your copy for the flaps. As you write a draft of the summary, think about what attracted you to the piece of literature or, if it's your own writing, what made you want to write it. Try to incorporate that into your draft. Also, remember to tease the reader. Leave the reader with something to think about, be curious about, or be excited about.

You may want to copy your draft onto a narrow sheet of paper and paste or tape it onto the flaps. This will give you an idea of how well it will fit and what the jacket will look like.

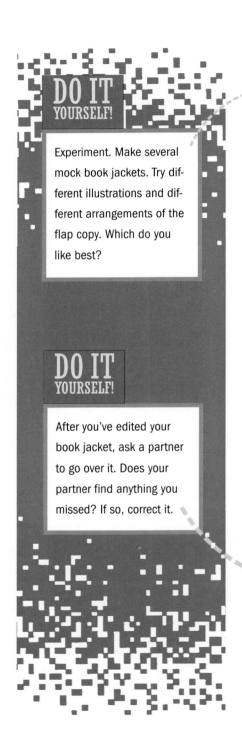

DO IT YOURSELF!

Experiment. Make several mock book jackets. Try different illustrations and different arrangements of the flap copy. Which do you like best?

DO IT YOURSELF!

After you've edited your book jacket, ask a partner to go over it. Does your partner find anything you missed? If so, correct it.

REVISING YOUR BOOK JACKET

Show your jacket to friends, classmates, and family members and see what they think. Ask the questions in the following list.

What Do You Think?

- Would you pick this book up in a bookstore? Why or why not?
- Does the illustration grab you? If not, why not?
- What mood does the design set? What kind of book does the illustration represent?
- Does the summary tell you enough? Too little? Too much?
- Do you want to read the book? Why or why not?

Review the jacket yourself, trying to see it as someone else might. Make changes you think will improve it. Once you're satisfied with it, make your final version.

EDITING YOUR BOOK JACKET

An error on a book jacket is going to drive potential readers away. As your last step, read and reread the flap copy carefully to check grammar, usage, spelling, and mechanics. Don't forget to check the title and author's name too, both on the cover and on the spine. You certainly wouldn't want any errors there.

APPLYING SPELLING TO WRITING

Spelling Strategies

Use your dictionary to check any words that you're not certain about. If you have a computer, use the spell-check function.

You can also keep a list of problem words. Concentrate on the spelling of these words, and, when you want to use them, check your own list. For more help with spelling, see Chapter 24.3, Strategies to Improve Spelling Skills.

DISPLAYING YOUR BOOK JACKET

Here are some ideas for displaying your work so that others can enjoy the jacket, and perhaps the book too.

To Display Your Book Jacket

◎ Display your book jacket in the classroom, arranged on a table, the bulletin board, or around the walls.

◎ Create a window display of book jackets. Visit a bookstore for ideas on various kinds of displays.

◎ Create a video library tour. Videotape your class jackets. Zoom in on the illustration, then pull back to show the title and author as someone reads the flap copy.

◎ Create a Read Me display in the library.

DO IT YOURSELF!

With two or three partners, contact the librarian in your school or public library. Ask for permission to use your book jackets to create a Read Me display in the library.

Evaluation Activity

Think about the book jacket you made. Did you enjoy doing it? Do you think you did a good job? Evaluate your work. Try to be fair and honest.

Self-Evaluation Form

• Does my jacket design attract people to the book?

• Does the design give an accurate impression of what the book is like?

• Does the summary on the flap tell enough but not too much? Does it make people want to read the book?

• Is the book jacket attractive and accurate? Does it sell the book?

Communicating to Report

Research is a search for information—facts and experts' opinions—from reliable sources.

You're munching a homemade quesadilla at your new friend's house. Since the Esparza family moved to the neighborhood, you've never eaten so well. Between bites, your friend asks when your family moved to the community. "I don't know," you reply. "My parents probably came on the first covered wagon." The two of you have a good laugh, but you begin wondering—where *did* all the people in your community come from? And when?

The next day you're passing by a library, and you decide to pop in and find the answer to your question. You browse through a few books on community history and are totally amazed by what you read.

You tell classmates of your findings. A teacher hears of your interest and suggests that you do a **research paper** on community history. You do, and it's a winner.

Classmates tell their parents about your fascinating research findings and then the whole thing snowballs.

You're invited to give a report on a local public radio station. Then one of the local cable TV stations invites you to do a videotaped special feature on your research. For one frantic week, you race around town with a video camera. You tape interviews with senior citizens, photograph historical documents, and make charts.

Whew! You didn't expect everyone to be *that* interested in what you had to say!

The Need for Reports

During your lifetime, you'll prepare many reports for many people. Sometimes you'll need information before making a decision, like which new sound system to buy.

Then you'll be reporting to yourself. You'll also be asked to prepare research papers and reports for your classes. When you have a job, you may need to prepare reports on your department and about the people you supervise.

One specific kind of report is a news report. What distinguishes a news report from other kinds of reports is that it is almost always about a current topic and is aimed at a general public audience. Another kind of report is a videotape demonstration that combines words and images to show viewers how or why something works.

All reports—written, spoken, and visual—have the same purpose: to help the reader, listener, or viewer understand more about the subject of the report.

LOOKING AHEAD

TO THE PROJECTS

9.1 Writing Project
Do library research about a topic that fascinates you and then write a research paper that presents your findings (pages 250–269).

9.2 Speaking Project
Write a news report to present on the air (pages 270–277).

9.3 Visual Project
Create a videotape presentation (pages 278–285).

JOURNAL WRITING

In your journal, complete one of the following sentences. Then continue writing to develop your ideas.

1. I wish I knew why _____ .

2. If I could spend my time doing anything that I wanted to do, I'd _____ .

3. One thing that really bothers me is _____ .

4. I'd like to show people _____ .

9.1 Writing Project

Writing a Research Paper

You'll do library research to gather information about a topic that you really care about. Then you'll share your findings with others.

Terms to Know

A **research paper** is a written report that contains facts and experts' opinions that the writer has gathered from library sources. The purpose of a research report is to provide readers with information. The sources of information are named in the body of the paper and at its conclusion.

You're a wizard on a skateboard. In fact, in local competition, you're the best there is. So it comes as no surprise when the wealthy grandfather of one of your fans calls and asks for your expert advice on skateboards. He wants to buy his granddaughter the best skateboard on the market—but he wants to make sure she'll be safe. Here's the deal: You give him a fact-filled report on brands of skateboards plus information on safety equipment and skateboard injuries. In return, he'll give you a new skateboard of your choice. Okay, skateboards and safety equipment you know, but you'll have to do some library research to find out about injuries. (You're so good, you don't fall down.)

Even if you're not an expert on skateboards, there's something you'd probably like to learn more about. Writing a **research paper** gives you an opportunity to become the class expert on something that interests *you*. In the portion of the research paper that follows, a student explored his interest in dinosaurs.

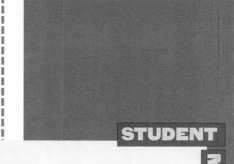

STUDENT MODEL

How Did the Dinosaurs Die?

Laliev Ben Avraham, Grade 7

Why don't dinosaurs roam the earth as they once did? What animal—or force—could have been so powerful that it exterminated a world full of the largest and strongest animals that the world has ever known? In 1980, Walter and Luis Alvarez proposed an answer. They believe that dinosaurs may have become extinct when a huge asteroid crashed into the earth, changing the climate (Dietz 32).

It may have happened this way: An asteroid hurtling through space is on a collision course with Earth. It tears through Earth's atmosphere, a ten-kilometer-wide fireball hurtling downward at about 15 kilometers per second. It slams into the earth, "blasting a crater 150 to 200 miles across" (Dietz 32). Then, "With a thousand times the power of all the world's nuclear arsenals, it . . . shot thousands of cubic miles of debris skyward, casting the entire planet into darkness for months or possibly years to come" (Dane 96).

The asteroid theory links several pieces of evidence. First, dinosaurs' bones are found in rocks from the Cretaceous Period, a geological time from 140 million years ago to 65 million years ago (Horner 38-39). No dinosaur bones, however, are found in rocks from the Tertiary Period following the Cretaceous Period (Dane 96).

Second, a thin layer of clay separates the Cretaceous Period and the Tertiary Period. Scientists call this layer the K-T (Cretaceous-Tertiary) boundary layer. The Alvarezes analyzed the clay in the K-T boundary layer and discovered that it contained a lot of a rare element, a metal called iridium (Dane 96). Iridium is, however, "thousands of times more abundant in primitive meteorites than in terrestrial rocks" (Dietz 32).

Third, in 1991 when the Alvarezes investigated an ancient meteorite crater in the Caribbean near the Yucatan peninsula, they found that the age of the crater matched "the age of the impact debris scattered over Earth at the geologic moment of the mass extinction. The ages are indistinguishable . . . " (Kerr 160). That geologic moment is the K-T boundary layer. Walter Alvarez said, "It looks to me like this is the smoking gun" (Kerr 878).

One way to examine the soundness of the asteroid theory is to look at each piece of evidence in turn. First, consider the fact that there are no dinosaur bones in Tertiary rocks. How can scientists tell the difference between Cretaceous and Tertiary rocks? Easy. Scientists determine geological time periods by looking at layers of rocks and the fossils within each layer. The layers of rocks are put down one on top of another, as space dust falls, as volcanoes go off, and

Continues ┈┈┈┈┈┈┈┈┈┈┈┈┈┈┈┈┈┈┈▶

so on. The older layers are the deepest within the earth. The newer layers are more toward the surface. When forces beneath the earth shift, the older layers are thrust up. [Research paper continues.]

Works Cited

Dane, Abe. "Why the Dinosaurs Died." Popular Mechanics. Aug. 1991: 96–97.

Dietz, Robert S. "Demise of the Dinosaurs—A Mystery Solved?" Astronomy. July 1991: 30–37.

Kerr, Richard A. "Extinction by a One-Two Comet Punch?" Science. 10 Jan. 1992: 160–161.

———. "Huge Impact Tied to Mass Extinction." Science. 14 Aug. 1992: 878–880.

Horner, John R., and James Gorman. Digging Dinosaurs. New York: Workman, 1988.

PREWRITING

Choosing a good topic is the first—and maybe the most difficult—part of your job when you write a research paper. Part of the problem might be that there are too many choices. Even if your teacher assigns you a broad general subject, such as *Conflict*, you still need to choose a topic. A topic is one small part of a big subject.

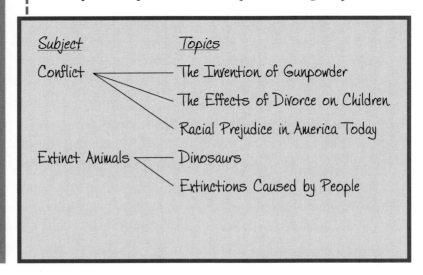

Subject	Topics
Conflict	The Invention of Gunpowder
	The Effects of Divorce on Children
	Racial Prejudice in America Today
Extinct Animals	Dinosaurs
	Extinctions Caused by People

You and Your Interests: The Adventure Starts Here

Begin looking for a topic by looking at yourself and what interests you. Read through your recent journal entries. Which ideas spark your interest? Circle them as possible choices.

Now take some time to write in your journal. What is it about each of your circled choices that interests you? What other interesting ideas does each choice suggest? Jot down a few notes about each possible choice.

Brainstorming for Topics

The ideas in your journal will not be a complete list of everything you're interested in. Get some topic ideas bubbling by looking at the world—or your general subject—from a variety of angles.

Angles to Think About

- Current topics in the news
- Places that are significant in some way
- Nature (weird nature, hostile nature, animals)
- Things that worry you (the environment, endangered species, homeless people)
- Things that anger you (racial prejudice, garbage dumps, abandoned animals)
- Things you're curious about (sports medicine, spider webs, prison conditions)
- Theories or terms you don't fully understand (biological warfare, cloning)
- Famous people (the good, the bad, and the odd)
- How things change over time (technology, attitudes)

When you finish brainstorming, choose one topic idea that gives your curiosity the strongest tug. In your journal, write about *why* that topic interests you.

IDEAS FOR YOUR

WRITING PROJECT

1. Investigate a controversial topic, such as rights of endangered species versus rights of people, gun control, or prison reform. Be sure to present both sides.

2. Do research about a career field that interests you.

3. Investigate a history-changing event or invention.

NEED MORE HELP?

For more ideas on how to generate topic ideas, try some of the strategies in the section called Prewriting in Chapter 1. To make sure you've got a good grip on your purpose and audience, take a look at Chapter 28.13, Purpose and Audience.

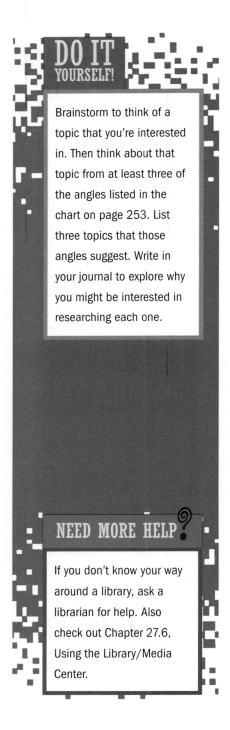

Who's Your Audience?

Make sure that you provide your audience with information that is new and interesting.

Questions to Evaluate an Audience

- Who is my audience? Identify your audience as specifically as possible. Then you'll be better able to target their needs and interests.
- What does my audience already know about my topic?
- What might my audience want to know about my topic? Your audience will be most likely to care about your topic if you consider their interests.

Narrowing Your Topic

Now it's time to do a little reading *before* you begin researching. Go to a library and look up your topic in the resources that follow.

Places to Begin Your Reading

- an encyclopedia for a general overview
- the computer catalog or card catalog for book sources
- *Readers' Guide to Periodical Literature* for magazine sources

Questions to Evaluate Your Topic

1. **What's the Big Picture?** Think of what larger category your topic fits in, and look it up in an encyclopedia. For example, *Automobile Exhaust* is a part of the larger category, *Pollution*. An encyclopedia will show how your topic fits into the big picture.

2. **Is the Topic Too Broad?** If the encyclopedia article on your topic has subcategories, your topic is probably too broad. If the card catalog lists more than two complete books written on your topic, it's probably too broad. A

topic is too broad when there's so much information on it that you can't cover it in depth. For example, if you try to cover the main ideas in a broad topic, such as *African Americans*, you'll end up telling your readers what they already know. Borrrring! A more narrow topic, such as *African American Cowboys,* will let you explore in depth and provide new information to your readers.

3. **Is the Topic Too Narrow?** On the other hand, if you can't find any references in card catalogs or the *Readers' Guide*, your topic might be too narrow. Make sure that you can find at least four sources of information.

Focusing Your Topic

You now have a topic, the "what" of your research paper. Next, you need to focus on the "what about it"– your approach to your topic. For example, if your topic is the *Underground Railroad,* do you want to focus on slavery conditions that led to its origin? Underground hero Harriet Tubman? The lives of fugitives after they fled to the North? To find a focus for your topic, ask *Who? What? When? Where? Why?* and *How?*

Here are some questions that the writer of "How Did the Dinosaurs Die?" wrote at this stage.

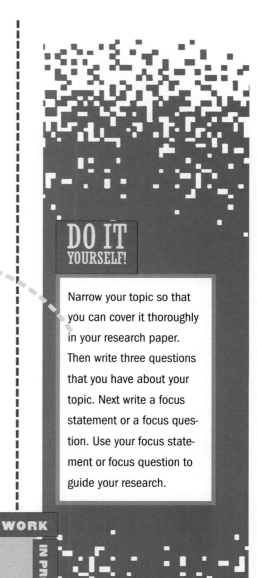

DO IT YOURSELF!

Narrow your topic so that you can cover it thoroughly in your research paper. Then write three questions that you have about your topic. Next write a focus statement or a focus question. Use your focus statement or focus question to guide your research.

WORK IN PROGRESS

Did the Ice Age kill the dinosaurs? Animals are supposed to be able to adapt to their environment, so why didn't the dinosaurs adapt to the colder weather? Or why didn't they go somewhere else? Did the dinosaurs die off everywhere at once?

Terms to Know

A **focus statement** is a sentence that states the purpose of a writer's research. Instead of a focus statement, some writers prefer to use a focus question. An example of a focus question is "Why did the dinosaurs die out?" The point of the writer's research is to gather enough information to answer the focus question.

NEED MORE HELP?

See Chapter 23.3, Research the Modern Way, for tips on how to use computer card catalogs. Consult Chapter 27.6, Using the Library/Media Center, for library help.

State the Point of Your Research When you've finished listing questions, read them over. Then complete this **focus statement**:

The point of my research is to _____ .

This focus statement and your questions about your topic will guide your research. Laliev completed the statement by writing, *"The point of my research is to find out why the Ice Age killed the dinosaurs."*

As you do research, you may discover facts that change your focus statement. For example, Laliev discovered that the dinosaurs died out about 64 million years before the Ice Age occurred. This discovery didn't cause Laliev to drop the topic—but it did change his focus statement and his search for information.

Doing Library Research

To write a good research paper, you must find good information. Make sure that you know how to use library resources to find books, magazines, and other sources of information. Before taking notes from a source, ask yourself the following questions.

Questions for Evaluating a Source

- Is the information related to the point of my research or does it answer one of my questions?
- Can I understand what is written?
- Is the source up to date? Check when a book or magazine was published. If your topic is about a current problem, you'll want the most recent information. Use a dated source only if you want to do a then-and-now comparison.
- Is the source one that I can rely on for the truth? Most library sources are dependable. Supermarket tabloids, on the other hand, are not dependable sources.

You can take notes from a source in one of three ways: **direct quotation**, **paraphrase**, or **summary**.

Taking Notes from Sources

- Record your notes on 3 x 5 cards or on notebook paper.
- Identify the number of the page or pages where you found the information. (See page 258.)
- Make a separate card that identifies the source's full publication information. (See page 259.) You'll identify your sources of information within the body of your paper and at its end.

When you take notes from sources, you must make clear which words and ideas are yours and which are borrowed. You must also *always name the source of all information that you borrow.*

Reasons for Identifying Sources

- Naming experts as your sources of information will make your paper more believable.
- Identifying sources lets readers know where they can find the ideas, facts, and information in your paper.
- Naming your sources lets readers know which words and ideas are yours.
- Naming a source lets you avoid **plagiarism.** Always put quotation marks around direct quotations. When you paraphrase, use your own words *and* credit the source of the information.

Terms to Know

A **direct quotation** is the author's own words, *exactly copied and put in quotation marks*.

A **paraphrase** is a restatement of ideas in your own words. Merely changing a few of the author's words and inserting your own isn't a paraphrase. A paraphrase means your own words—all your own words.

A **summary** is a brief recap of a long passage—or even whole pages—in a few words.

Plagiarism is claiming someone else's words and ideas as your own. Plagiarism is stealing.

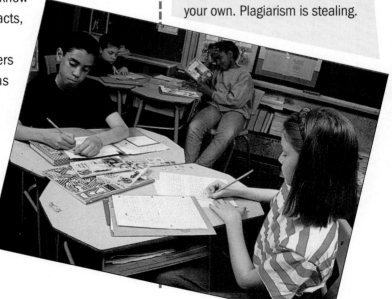

Original Source
At least 99 percent of all species that ever lived are now extinct.

Is it plagiarism?

Note from Original Source
About ninety-nine percent of all creatures that ever lived are now extinct.
page 213 bib #4

NEED MORE HELP?

Check out Chapter 27.2, Taking Notes, for more help in paraphrasing and summarizing.

Yes, this is plagiarism! The source is credited *but* the note is not a paraphrase—too many of the original author's words are used. How can a researcher avoid such plagiarism? Either copy the author's words exactly and put them in quotation marks—or use your own words to paraphrase the passage.

Below are two note cards. One note card is a direct quotation taken from a source. The other note card is a paraphrase of that same information. Notice that the paraphrase uses the student's own words.

Note Card: Direct Quotation
"The Chicxulub feature is in the right place, of the right size, and apparently of the right structural style, with the right rocks, and of the right age to satisfy the constraints of evidence."
page 37, bib. # 1

Note Card: Paraphrase
The Chicxulub crater matches scientists' idea of the crater that a dinosaur-killing asteroid should have made.
page 37, bib. #1

The page number at the bottom of each note card identifies the page number from which the information was taken. The "bib. #" on the note cards refers to a separate **bibliography card** on which the student has written all of the necessary information to identify the source.

The bibliography card below identifies the source of information on the note cards on page 258. The source is a one-page article. On a bibliography card, always give the *span of pages* of an article, for example, 45–49, for articles longer than one page.

> Bibliography Card #1
> Zimmer, Carl. "The Smoking
> Crater." <u>Discover</u> Jan.
> 1992: 37.

What to Write on Bibliography Cards

- **Encyclopedias:** author of article (if there is one), title of article, name of encyclopedia, year of edition
- **Books:** author, title, name of the editor (if there is one), volume number (if the book is part of a multivolume work), city or place of publication, name of the publisher, and date of publication
- **Magazines and newspapers:** author, title, name of the periodical, date of publication (abbreviate the month), and the span of page numbers of the article. (Remember, use your note cards to record the specific page number from which you take information.)

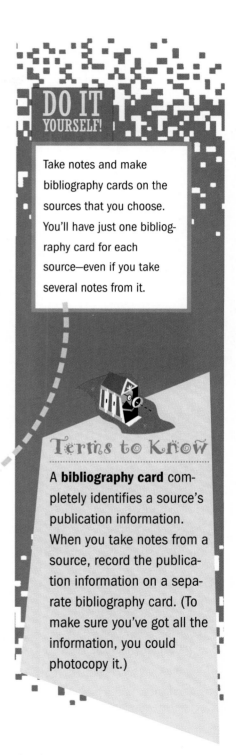

DO IT YOURSELF!

Take notes and make bibliography cards on the sources that you choose. You'll have just one bibliography card for each source—even if you take several notes from it.

Terms to Know

A **bibliography card** completely identifies a source's publication information. When you take notes from a source, record the publication information on a separate bibliography card. (To make sure you've got all the information, you could photocopy it.)

Magazine title

Date of publication

Title of article

MAGAZINE MASTHEAD

Author of article

Beginning page number of article

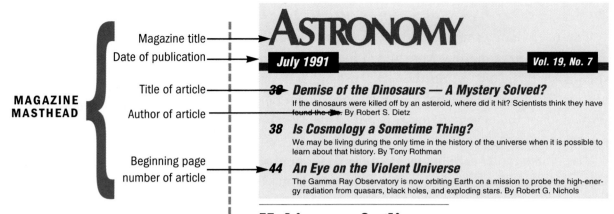

ASTRONOMY

July 1991　　　　　　　　　　　　**Vol. 19, No. 7**

38 Demise of the Dinosaurs — A Mystery Solved?
If the dinosaurs were killed off by an asteroid, where did it hit? Scientists think they have found the one. By Robert S. Dietz

38 Is Cosmology a Sometime Thing?
We may be living during the only time in the history of the universe when it is possible to learn about that history. By Tony Rothman

44 An Eye on the Violent Universe
The Gamma Ray Observatory is now orbiting Earth on a mission to probe the high-energy radiation from quasars, black holes, and exploding stars. By Robert G. Nichols

Making an Outline

To help organize all the information you've collected, you'll prepare an outline. Begin by thinking about your focus statement and what your research revealed. Then reread your notes and sort them into piles of similar information. *Your goal is to develop a pattern of organization for your ideas.*

If you're not sure how to organize your ideas, imagine that you're telling your audience about what you've learned about your topic. Imagine the questions they might ask if you were speaking, and then organize your ideas as a series of answers.

A formal outline uses Roman numerals to indicate main ideas, capital letters to indicate subtopics of those main ideas, and numerals to indicate supporting information. Look at the portion of Laliev's outline on the next page.

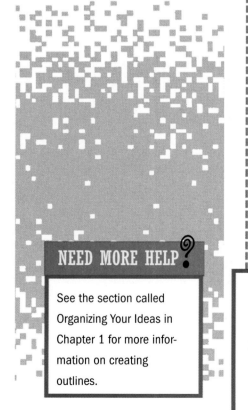

NEED MORE HELP?

See the section called Organizing Your Ideas in Chapter 1 for more information on creating outlines.

Possible Patterns of Organization

Historical	Cause and Effect
Introduction	Introduction
Background	Causes of the Situation—1, 2, 3
What Happened	Effects of the Situation—1, 2, 3
Why It Happened	Possible Solutions
Why It's Important	Conclusion
Conclusion	

WORK IN PROGRESS

I. Introduction

II. Asteroid Theory

   A. Theory Origins

   B. Theory Links Evidence

      1. No Dinosaur Bones in Tertiary Rocks

      2. Iridium Found in Boundary Layer

      3. Yucatan Crater Matches Expectations

   C. Examining the Evidence

      1. K-T rocks

      2. Other Sources of Iridium

      3. Craters

III. Other Theories

Terms to Know

An **introduction** identifies your topic and summarizes the point that your paper will make. An introduction is the first one or two paragraphs of a paper.

The **body** of a research paper contains paragraphs that support your main idea.

A **conclusion** should tie everything together. It usually contains a restatement of the main idea.

As you sort your note cards, look for an interesting quotation that will whet your readers' appetite for your topic. You might use that quotation when you write your **introduction.** Also look for a quotation that sums up research about your topic. On the other hand, you might use that quotation when you write your **conclusion**.

The remainder of your note cards will form the **body** of your outline and your research paper. Which note cards suggest main ideas? Which note cards suggest facts or details to support those main ideas?

Terms to Know

A **main-idea statement**, also called a *thesis statement,* states the main idea conveyed by your research paper. Just as your focus statement guided your research, a main-idea statement will guide your writing.

You'll present your main-idea statement in the *introduction* to your paper, the first one or two paragraphs. Then, in the *body* of your paper, you'll give evidence that supports that statement. In your paper's *conclusion,* you'll rephrase your main idea in a way that makes it memorable.

DRAFTING

As you write your first draft, use your outline and your note cards as guides.

Writing the Draft

Follow your outline to write your first draft. Remember, however, that your outline is only a tool. As you draft, you may discover a better method of organization. If so, revise your outline.

As you draft your introduction, concentrate on getting the reader's attention and give the main idea of your paper.

How to Grab Your Audience's Attention

- Begin with an interesting fact.
- Begin with a quotation.
- Begin with a curiosity-tickling question or statement.

However you begin your introduction, include a **main-idea statement** that captures your topic *and* reveals the main idea of your paper. Try to sum up your research findings in one sentence—as you did when you wrote your focus statement.

WORK IN PROGRESS

Interest-grabbing introduction:

Why don't dinosaurs roam the earth as they once did? What could have been so powerful that it exterminated a world full of the largest and strongest animals that the world has ever known?

Main-idea statement:

Dinosaurs may have become extinct when a huge asteroid crashed into Earth, changing the climate.

Drafting from an Outline

- Drop information that doesn't support your main-idea statement.
- As you draft, make each outline subtopic (*A, B,* and so on) a new paragraph.
- Go back to the library to fill gaps in information.

Identify Your Sources as You Draft. You'll need to **cite**, or identify, your sources. After each piece of borrowed information, refer to your bibliography cards and note cards to get the *author's name* and the *page number or numbers* of the source from which the information came.

Citing Sources

- Put the author's last name and page number in parentheses, as near as possible to the borrowed information. For example,

WORK IN PROGRESS

Iridium is, however, "thousands of times more abundant in primitive meteorites than in terrestrial rocks" (Dietz 32).

"Dietz" is the author's last name. The information was take from page 32 of the source.
- Place citations before periods.
- If you're using borrowed information in just part of your sentence, place the citation after the part you borrow and before a comma, if there is one. (See Work in Progress, page 265.)
- If one of your paragraphs is a paraphrase or summary, place the citation at the end of the last sentence in the paragraph.

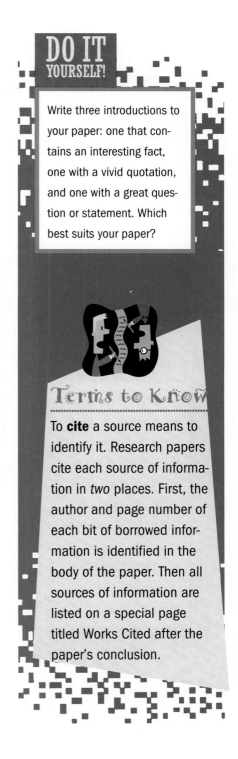

DO IT YOURSELF!

Write three introductions to your paper: one that contains an interesting fact, one with a vivid quotation, and one with a great question or statement. Which best suits your paper?

Terms to Know

To **cite** a source means to identify it. Research papers cite each source of information in *two* places. First, the author and page number of each bit of borrowed information is identified in the body of the paper. Then all sources of information are listed on a special page titled Works Cited after the paper's conclusion.

DO IT YOURSELF!

Write the body for your paper, adding parenthetical citations. Then write a conclusion. Make sure that your conclusion restates your main idea.

NEED MORE HELP?

If you need more help writing your draft, the section called Drafting in Chapter 1 can help you. If you're not sure whether to use some of the information you've gathered, check Chapter 28.7, Evaluating Information, and Chapter 28.9, Distinguishing Between Fact and Opinion.

In the final part of your paper, the conclusion, bring your paper to a fitting end. Here are some tips for writing a good conclusion.

Tie Information Together in the Conclusion

- Provide a brief summary of important points.
- Restate the main idea so that it is clear in your audience's mind.
- Use an especially good quotation if you can find one.

WORK IN PROGRESS

In conclusion, no one knows for sure why dinosaurs became extinct. However, when scientists consider the possibilities—volcanic activity, a giant asteroid, or poisonous pollens—the asteroid theory remains the strongest possible explanation.

REVISING

When you revise your research paper, look at the overall organization first and then examine the details. Use the checklist that follows as you revise your draft.

Revision Checklist

- Does the introduction include a main-idea statement that accurately summarizes the point of the paper?
- Do all paragraphs support the main-idea statement?
- Does the organization of main ideas seem logical?
- Do all facts and details support the main ideas?
- Is all borrowed information cited?

- Are all direct quotations enclosed within quotation marks? (You may need to look back at your notes.)
- Have you defined terms that might be unfamiliar to readers? (Don't forget that you've learned a lot! Try to remember what you *didn't* know before your research.)
- Have you used the word "I" or "my" to refer to yourself or your opinions? Remember, this a research paper, not an opinion piece. Don't use first-person pronouns.

APPLYING MECHANICS TO WRITING

Using Quotation Marks Correctly

Look at how Laliev used quotation marks to set off direct quotations in his research paper. Note also how he included parenthetical citations. Make sure to put quotation marks around sentences *and phrases* that you quote.

WORK IN PROGRESS

As a result of the impact, airborne dust "could turn day into night for several years" (Wilford 226), or, more optimistically, for months (Dodson 218). At any rate, this darkness would cause a chain reaction. "The lack of plant growth killed off many of the plant-eating dinosaurs. As the plant-eaters died, so also did the meat-eating dinosaurs that fed on them" (Dodson 218).

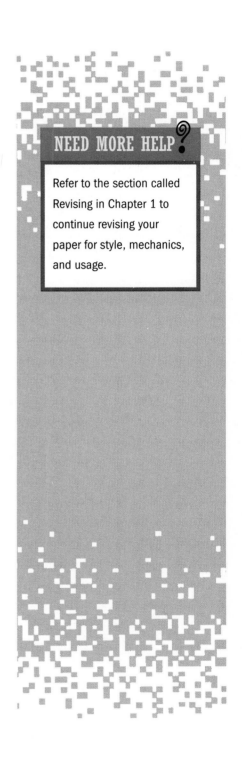

NEED MORE HELP?

Refer to the section called Revising in Chapter 1 to continue revising your paper for style, mechanics, and usage.

NEED MORE HELP?

To prepare your Works Cited page, check out the formats in Chapter 27.5, Bibliographical Forms.

DO IT YOURSELF!

Revise your research paper and make a Works Cited page. Use the checklist on this page to check your own research paper. Then trade research papers with a partner to double-check for errors.

The Works Cited Page

The last page of your paper will be a **Works Cited** page. This page lists and completely identifies each source.

WORK IN PROGRESS

```
                Works Cited
Dietz, Robert S.   "Demise of the
     Dinosaurs—A Mystery Solved?"
     Astronomy July 1991: 30-37.
Dodson, Peter. "Dinosaurs."  World
     Book Encyclopedia. 1992 ed.
Wilford, John Noble. The Riddle of
     the Dinosaurs. New York: Knopf,
     1985.
```

Formats for a Works Cited Page

- Present the publication information for each source. Use the order listed under "Doing Library Research."
- Alphabetize the sources by the authors' last names. If a source has no author listed, use the title of the source, excluding the words *A*, *An*, and *The*.
- Underline book titles and magazine titles. Put article titles in quotation marks. Abbreviate publishers' names. For example, the word *Knopf* is an abbreviation of the publisher's full name, *Alfred A. Knopf, Inc.*
- For an article, include the page numbers for the whole article—not just the page numbers from which you took information. (Put the exact page number of the borrowed information within the body of the paper.)

EDITING

You'll edit your research paper to make it as correct as possible. Try reading your draft aloud to catch errors in usage and punctuation. Sometimes "hearing" a usage error will make you spot it faster than reading it. Also, if you find yourself pausing where there is no punctuation, that may be a clue that you need a comma or a period. Use the following checklist as you edit your research paper.

Editing Checklist

- Are the citations and the Works Cited page correct?
- Are any words left out?
- Have all errors in grammar and usage been eliminated?
- Is punctuation correct?
- Are all direct quotations in quotation marks?
- Are all words spelled correctly?
- Are proper nouns capitalized?

APPLYING MECHANICS TO WRITING

Using Capitalization Correctly

Look at how Laliev corrected capitalization in his paper. Because job titles are not proper nouns, the word *paleontologists* is not capitalized. However, the names of geologic periods, such as *Cretaceous* and *Tertiary,* are proper nouns and are capitalized.

WORK IN PROGRESS

Geologists and paleontologists study the composition of layers of rocks and fossils within the rocks. That's how scientists can tell the difference between the **C**retaceous and **T**ertiary--by comparing the kinds of rocks and the fossils within them.

For more information on capitalization, see Chapter 21.

NEED MORE HELP?

Use the guidelines in the section called Editing in Chapter 1 as you edit to catch errors in grammar, usage, and mechanics.

DO IT YOURSELF!

Try reading your paper aloud to catch errors in grammar and punctuation. If you feel silly reading to yourself, try to get a family member to serve as an audience. (In a pinch, even the dog is better than nothing.)

PUBLISHING

Make your research paper as appealing as possible by assembling it with your reader in mind.

Assemble Your Research Paper

1. A cover sheet with your name, the date, and the title of your paper goes on top.

2. The research paper and any illustrations come next.

3. A Works Cited page ends your research paper.

Give your research paper to your intended audience. You might, at this point, also consider other audiences for your paper. For example, Laliev's topic might be of interest to other students in his community who like to read about or look for dinosaur bones.

Ideas for Expanding Your Audience

◎ Share your paper with other students who have written on the same subject.

◎ Do a "research paper exchange" with students in other schools. You'll learn about their interests and perhaps even make new friends!

◎ Bind your research paper and those of your classmates into a classroom anthology. Students in future classes can use your research papers as models.

◎ Send your paper to a special-interest group who might be interested in your work. Consider clubs, hobbyists, historical societies, and the PTA.

How Did the Dinosaurs Die?

by
Laliev Ben Avraham

May 18, 19--

DO IT YOURSELF!

Take the plunge and look for an additional audience for your paper. Be brave! Remember that you've got something interesting to share.

Evaluation Activity: Write a Survey

One of the best ways to measure the success of your research paper is to survey your audience. You'll want to find out what they liked and didn't like—and why.

Begin by drawing up a list of check-the-box items and short-answer questions like the ones below. The actual questions that you use will depend on the topic of your research paper.

Examples of check-the-box items

1. The content of the research paper was
   - ☐ too easy—I already knew the information.
   - ☐ easy to understand.
   - ☐ difficult to understand in some places.
   - ☐ over my head.
2. My interest in the topic
   - ☐ increased after reading the paper.
   - ☐ remained about the same as before I read the paper.
   - ☐ decreased after reading the paper.

Examples of short-answer questions

1. What's the most interesting fact or idea that you learned from reading the research paper?
2. What did you want to know about the topic that the writer didn't tell you?

Give the survey to people who have read your paper. Include your teacher. Collect the surveys and read the results. Based on your readers' reactions, what grade would you give yourself?

9.2

You'll share local news with an audience of local listeners.

Speaking Project
Giving a News Report

Terms to Know

A **news report** is a factual report of a recent event. A reporter's opinions won't be revealed in the news report.

Melissa and her friend Molly go to two different middle schools, but that doesn't stop them from being friends—and comparing notes about what's new.

On Tuesday night, Melissa had some extraordinary news for Molly. One of Melissa's classmates, Andrea, had just received a call from their school's principal. He told Andrea that she and two other students from their school had been chosen to speak to the President the following day. Using a satellite hook-up, they would speak to him "live." Each student could ask him one question. A cable news service would film the interview.

Melissa knew that her classmates' interview with the President of the United States would interest many people. So, on the day of the interview, Melissa prepared a **news report** of the event. Her report, recorded on audiotape, could be broadcast over local radio stations and on school public address systems.

It's Define Time

What makes news *news*? Your aunt's new puppy may be news to you, but it's not news in a public sense.

What News Is

- News is true—as true as can be known.
- News is about something that the public has a *right* to know, a *need* to know, and an *interest* in knowing. (Thus, family events aren't news, and neither is gossip.)
- News is objective. When a reporter's opinions enter into the news, the report lacks believability.

In the following pages, you'll find suggestions for how to prepare and deliver a spoken news report about an event or issue in your school or community.

Here's the script for a spoken news report presented by middle school student Melissa Hiibel.

IDEAS FOR YOUR

SPEAKING PROJECT

1. Interview someone at your school—a coach, a music teacher, a librarian. Ask for any information about upcoming events or possible changes in school policy that they might know about.

2. Do a "personality profile" interview. Consider as subjects a person with special needs, a visiting celebrity, or someone with a unique hobby.

STUDENT MODEL

Students in Boise Talk to President Clinton

by Melissa Hiibel

Something remarkable happened in Boise this afternoon. Three students from Les Bois Junior High School interviewed President Clinton.

The three students were Andrea Broyels, John Hale, and Natalie Morris. They spoke to the President live, via satellite hook-up from Channel 7.

The President wanted to know what was on students' minds, and that's just what he found out. Andrea Broyels asked the President this question: How are students supposed to pay for college when it's so expensive?

After the interview, Natalie Morris said, and I quote, "I never dreamed that I would be talking to the President of the United States. This is the best thing that's ever happened to me."

The students found out last night that they would speak to the President. Earlier yesterday, Les Bois principal, Gary Slee, got a call saying that three students would be able to ask President Clinton one question. Slee then asked history teachers to choose the three lucky students.

So why did the President choose Les Bois? No one knows for sure. The students of Les Bois, however, are glad that he did.

It just goes to show, you never know when the President might be calling you.

This is Melissa Hiibel, reporting for Les Bois Junior High School.

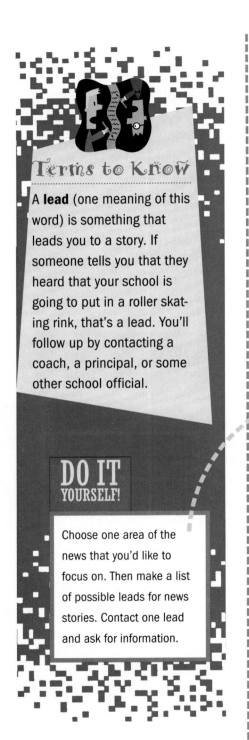

DO IT YOURSELF!

Choose one area of the news that you'd like to focus on. Then make a list of possible leads for news stories. Contact one lead and ask for information.

GATHERING INFORMATION

You'll prepare a better report if your subject is one that you really care about. So take a minute to think about what kinds of news you'll enjoy reporting. Chances are that it will be the same kind of news you enjoy reading.

Kinds of Local News

- *Sports* (school sports, local sports, Special Olympics)
- *Meetings* (Student Council, School Board, school clubs)
- *Events* (planned and accidental)
- *Upcoming Events* (dances, guest speakers)
- *Special Features* (controversies, surveys, interviews of people who are interesting or who do unusual things)
- *Reviews* (of school plays, concerts, videos)

Looking for a Lead

If you're interested in a certain kind of news, such as sports news, you'll look for story ideas in that area. You'll need to look for a **lead**, someone or some item of information that can lead you to a story.

How to Find Leads

- List everything you've heard about this week that relates to your area of interest.
- Talk to people who are involved in or know about your area of interest.
- Read what has been written about recent events and then contact the people and places mentioned to see whether there are any new developments.

Preparing for Interviews

When you interview a **source** of news, avoid asking questions that can be answered with a *yes* or *no*. Ask questions beginning with the words *Who, What, Where, When, Why,* and *How.* Prepare a list of questions to ask.

Kinds of Questions to Ask

- Who is involved? What happened? When did it happen? How did it happen? Why did it happen?
- How are you involved in what happened?
- Why is what happened important?
- When is the situation likely to change?

Taking Notes

A reporter must take good notes in order to write a good news report.

Tips for Taking Good Notes

- Take notes for each interview on a separate sheet of paper. Identify the date, time, and source's name. If you have a tape recorder, tape-record the interview.
- Spell the source's name and other words important to the story correctly.
- Get the source's phone number so that you can follow up later if you need to.
- If the source says something particularly well, try to write it down exactly.
- As the source answers your prepared questions, *listen to the source's answers* and follow up with questions based on the answers.
- Don't interrupt the source.
- Be alert to whether your source is giving you facts or expressing an opinion.
- Ask your source for leads to other sources.

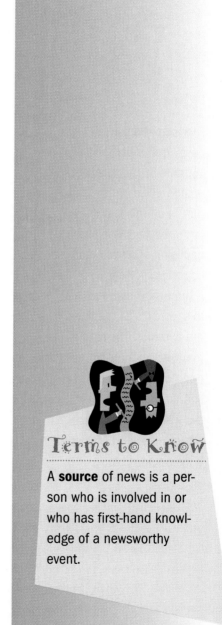

Terms to Know

A **source** of news is a person who is involved in or who has first-hand knowledge of a newsworthy event.

Terms to Know

The **inverted pyramid** of a news story describes a pyramid that is turned upside down, so the broad part is on the top. Information is presented in declining order of importance.

A **lead** (one meaning for this word) is at the top of the pyramid. The lead summarizes the most important point of the report. A lead should answer as many of the *who, what, when, where, why,* and *how* questions as possible.

DRAFTING

Remember that your news report is a *spoken* report. Your goal is to make it sound as close to natural speech as possible.

Notes or a Script?

You have three options for delivering your report:

1. Memorize the report. Memorizing a report is not a good idea. You'll sound like a machine. Also, you run the risk of getting stage fright and forgetting your report.
2. Read from a script—a written version of the report. A script gives a reporter the security of having all the words in hand. On the negative side, it's difficult to read and it sounds as if you're reading. Also, when you read to a "live" audience, you lose eye contact with them—and their interest.
3. Speak from notes. Instead of writing out a word-for-word script, you write just key phrases, quotations, and facts. Speaking from notes lets a reporter use the natural rhythms of speech.

The Inverted Pyramid

News reports, whether in the form of notes or a script, follow a form called the **inverted pyramid**.

A **lead** summarizes the most important point of the report. Melissa's lead is, "Something remarkable happened in Boise this afternoon. Three students from Les Bois Junior High School interviewed President Clinton." Her lead answers the *who, what, when,* and *where.*

lead

other important information

background information

Follow with information that adds to the explanation. Melissa answers the *how* and *why* in subsequent paragraphs.

Background information, which is interesting but not essential, is at the most narrow point of the pyramid.

As you draft, remember that you'll be speaking and your audience will be listening.

Drafting a Spoken Report

- Use short sentences so you don't run out of breath.
- Use short paragraphs. Don't throw too many complex ideas at your listeners. They won't be able to go back and reread information that confuses them. In a spoken report, confusion is forever.
- Use quotations that let your listeners understand how people who are involved in the event feel.

REVISING, REHEARSING, AND EDITING

Revise your script or notes until you have a tight, well-organized report. You should answer the *who, what, when, where, why,* and *how* early in your report.

Practice Speaking to an Audience

As you practice delivering your report, remember that you're speaking to people.

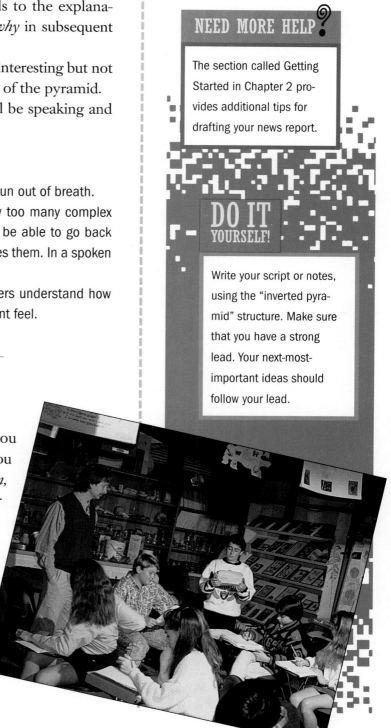

NEED MORE HELP

The section called Getting Started in Chapter 2 provides additional tips for drafting your news report.

DO IT YOURSELF!

Write your script or notes, using the "inverted pyramid" structure. Make sure that you have a strong lead. Your next-most-important ideas should follow your lead.

DO IT YOURSELF!

Speaking from a script means you must *practice* to sound natural as you read. Sounding natural is a challenge even for professional broadcasters. Try practicing delivering your report, both by reading from a script and speaking from notes. Which works better for you?

NEED MORE HELP?

For other tips on revising and editing the written portion of your report for clarity, see the section called Practicing and Revising in Chapter 2.

Tips for Speaking to an Audience

- Speak loudly, clearly, and distinctly.
- Don't reveal your own feelings about your subject by tone of voice or gesture. Reporters are impartial.
- If you speak to an audience who can see you, practice speaking in front of a mirror. Keep gestures and facial expressions to a minimum—they're distracting. Look alive but not frantic. Maintain as much eye contact as possible with your audience.

Because listeners won't see the quotation marks in your script or notes, listeners won't know which words are yours and which are an interview subject's words. You must use words *to tell* listeners when direct quotations begin and end.

Here's a section of a script. As you read it aloud, notice that you can tell where the direct quotation begins and ends.

WORK IN PROGRESS

Natalie Morris said, and I quote, "I never dreamed that I would be talking to the President of the United States. This is the best thing that's ever happened to me." End quote.

You can also quote a source indirectly.

WORK IN PROGRESS

Natalie Morris said that she never dreamed that she would be talking to the President of the United States.

DELIVERING YOUR NEWS REPORT

At this point, you may have some decisions to make about how you're going to deliver your report.

Ways to Deliver Your Report

- Give your report over the school public address system.
- Give your report "live" at a school assembly, student council meeting, or PTA meeting.
- If your report concerns your whole community, video-tape or tape-record your report. Send it to a local TV station or a local radio station.
- Tape-record your report and exchange it for reports from students in other schools.

Go For It! Does the thought of speaking to a live audience strike terror in your heart? Look at it this way. Each person in the audience is probably someone with whom you could comfortably talk one-on-one. They just happen to be sitting together.

Before you begin speaking, take a deep breath. Imagine that you're speaking to just one person. Then go for it!

DO IT YOURSELF!

Are your listeners getting the point you're trying to make? If possible, have someone listen to you and offer feedback. What does your listener think is the main point of your report? Can your listener tell when a direction quotation begins and ends?

EVALUATION ACTIVITY: Listener Response

After you've presented your news report, ask your listeners to rate your news report on a scale of 1 to 10, ten being the highest. A score of 10, for example, means the report was of professional newscaster quality. A score of 5 means the report covered the bases. A score of 1 means the report was confusing or left questions unanswered.

If you broadcast your report from a local radio station, ask listeners to call in or mail in their comments. If you broadcast your report over the school PA system, listeners can drop off their responses in a special box in the school's office.

When you receive all your listeners' responses, add up all the scores and divide by the number of responses. So, how did you do?

Visual Project

9.3

A videotape report lets you combine words and images to share information.

Preparing a Videotape

Terms to Know

A **camcorder** is a video camera that shoots moving pictures and records sound on 8 mm film. The word *camcorder* is a combination of the words *camera* and *recorder*.

Picture this: Science whiz that you are, you've been invited to do "show and tell" demonstrations of science experiments for grade school students. You're in such demand, however, that you can't accept all the invitations you receive and continue your career as a student. (Stardom has its drawbacks.)

One of your sidekicks has the answer. He suggests that you make videos of your demonstrations. Then you can stay in school and send your videos on the road. Hmmm.

You borrow a **camcorder** and begin to plan your first videotaped demonstration.

Why Use Media?

If a major disaster happened, would you rather read about it in a newspaper–or *see and hear* what happened on television? If you're like most people, you'd click on the TV.

The medium of video is powerful because it can combine live action, spoken words, printed words, still pictures, graphs, tables, sound effects, and music. Video can give viewers a sense of being on the scene, of sharing an experience, that printed words can't.

This section will show you how to prepare a videotape report.

What follows is a script for a videotaped presentation of a science experiment. (You'll see some still pictures from the video too.) The intended audience is students in elementary schools.

IDEAS FOR YOUR

VISUAL PROJECT

1. Prepare a videotape report of your favorite sport. You'll show people playing the sport and provide examples of good form and penalty actions.
2. Make a video report of a problem in your community—litter, stray pets, lack of crosswalks, and so on.

STUDENT MODEL

A Videotape Presentation of a Science Experiment

Script by Matt Petersen and Giordana Segneri, Grade 8

H: Hello, I'm Hocus

P: and I'm Pocus.

H: Today in our amazing

P: and mystifying science show,

H: we'll learn how to use simple household goods to create a fascinating experiment.

P: Remember that, like us, you should always have a supervisor when doing any experiment that might be dangerous, like today's experiment that uses fire.

H: First you need to gather a hard-boiled egg, a glass bottle or jar with a mouth small enough that the egg can sit on it but big enough that the egg can almost fit through it, a piece of paper, tongs, and matches—though we're using an alcohol burner.

P: Remember, you should always have a parent or supervisor who can help you light the matches.

H: The first thing you have to do before you start the experiment is peel off the shell of the hard-boiled egg. Also, if your bottle or jar is not clean, you should clean it. Then crumble a piece of paper, and have your supervisor light it with a match—or in

Continues ·····························➤

this case, the alcohol burner.

P: Now this is the hard part. You have to do this very quickly. Stick the paper into the jar and grab the egg and put it on top. WOW! How did the egg fit through the mouth of the jar?

H: Actually, this is quite simple. When air is heated, it expands. The air in the jar expanded so much that it pushed past the egg and caused it to dance. Once the fire went out, the air cooled and contracted and took up less space in the bottle. This left an empty space. The air on the outside of

the bottle pressed in to fill the space, but it couldn't because the egg was in the way. It pushed the egg out of its way and into the bottle so it could fill the empty space.

P: WOW! That is so easy to set up. All you need is the bottle, the egg, the paper, and the matches.

H: That's it!

P: This has been another exciting edition of Hocus Pocus, the Incredible Science Show.

H and P: So long!

PLANNING A VIDEOTAPE

If you're planning on making a videotape, you've probably got a subject you want to show visually. Before you begin planning a videotape, however, make sure that you have a camcorder, 8 mm video film cassettes, a **VCR**, and **VHS tape**. Next *learn how the equipment works.* Feel comfortable using the equipment.

Focus on What You Want to Accomplish

Perhaps the most important part of planning is to define and limit your goals. You'll want to cover your subject thoroughly in the time that you have. For example, you can't give an in-depth report on a major social problem in ten minutes—but you can show overcrowded conditions in your school's cafeteria. Ask the following questions.

- **Time:** How much time do I have? How many minutes do I want my video to run?
- **Subject:** What is my subject? Can I cover it in the time I have?
- **Audience:** Who are they? What are their interests? What do they already know about my subject?
- **Purpose:** What is the main thing I want to show and tell my audience? Focus on that idea and on presenting it as clearly and as vividly as you can.

When evaluating an audience, consider the kind of presentation that will appeal to them. The students who videotaped the science experiment with the egg used the format of a magic show. The humorous format really got the viewers' attention. The simple explanations suited viewers' level of understanding and need for information.

As you prepare your presentation, pretend that your audience is looking over your shoulder as you gather information, do experiments, or make observations. Imagine the questions your audience might ask.

Terms to Know

A **VCR** (Video Cassette Recorder) hooks into a TV and plays back images directly from a camcorder. (You'll need special jacks for the connection.) Use blank **VHS tape** cassettes in the VCR to revise and edit your 8 mm tape. You'll copy portions of 8 mm cassettes onto the VHS tape, adding narration and music to your final product.

DO IT YOURSELF!

Before you turn on your camcorder, complete the following:
1. My finished video will run _____ minutes.
2. My subject is _____ .
3. My videotape report will interest my audience because _____.
4. The main thing that I want my audience to remember is _____.

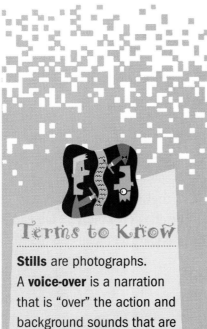

Terms to Know

Stills are photographs.
A **voice-over** is a narration that is "over" the action and background sounds that are being recorded on camera. Most (not all) VCR equipment lets you do voice-overs by plugging in a microphone into the "mic" jack and then speaking.

NEED MORE HELP?

As part of your drafting, you may wish to prepare a storyboard. See Chapter 5.3 for suggestions on how to prepare a storyboard.

What to Show? What to Tell?

Which elements of your subject might be best explained by words? By images? By music? By a combination of words and images? For example, suppose you are preparing a videotape report on "The British Rock Invasion of the 1960s." You'll certainly want your audience *to hear* the music of those times, *to see* how the hit groups looked and dressed and performed, and *to learn* how the invasion came to be.

Ways to Explain

Words	Visuals	Sound Effects
narration	action scenes	background
interviews	close-ups of	sounds
conversations	people	added sound
	locations and	effects
	scenes	music
	stills of	
	documents, art,	
	photos	

DRAFTING AND FILMING

For some videotape reports, you'll need to draft twice, once for the audio and once for the video. Use a script when you need to time your words *exactly* to match up with the video and sound effects.

On the other hand, you can't provide a script for something like a football game because you don't know what will happen next. You might, however, go back afterward and provide a **voice-over** commentary. (Use the film counter on your camcorder so you know when action is about to happen and how long it lasts.)

Matching the Words and Pictures

Refer to the following chart as you plan and create your videotape.

Introduction

Words: Identify the subject for the audience.

Images: Film a typewritten page with the title of your videotape. You might also shoot a panorama or wide-angle shot that establishes the scene (football stadium, classroom).

Interview

Words: Identify the interview subject. Ask one question at a time and let the interview subject speak uninterrupted.

Images: Film the speaker to establish identity. (When you edit, you can cut away to a scene showing the speaker's subject. Avoid a video with nothing but "talking heads.")

Demonstration/Explanation

Words: Explain what is going on and why, but make sure that the narration doesn't distract from what is being shown.

Images: Visuals should be easy to see, easy to understand. Remember that the camera's eye becomes the viewer's eye.

Locations, Action Scenes

Words: Don't point out what viewers can obviously see for themselves, for example, "He's running with the football!" You don't need to fill every second with chatter. Natural sound effects can be effective.

Images: To show a location, vary the *focal length,* the distance that the subject appears to be from the camera—in other words, what fills a frame. (Viewers naturally want to look around and peer closer.) Combine shots of whole scenes with those of a few people doing something and close-ups of people's faces. To follow fast action, hold the camera steady. If you jerk the camera, there may be a lag time as it refocuses.

Transitions From Scene to Scene

Words: Use the transitions that you use in speech—words and phrases like "next," "meanwhile," "back at the gym."

Images: You can use your camera's zoom and fade-in/fade-out features to move from one scene to another. If you overdo these features, however, viewers will feel seasick. Look for visual "bridges," scenes with the same light level and focal length, that will seem natural.

DO IT YOURSELF!

Decide what portions of your explanation should be presented as words, as visuals, or as sound effects. Then make a storyboard, prepare a chart, or write a description of how you will tie them all together. If you're using a script, draft it now. Your script will guide your filming.

After you finish shooting, make a list of difficulties that you have run into. Next to each, write a sentence or two evaluating the need for that part of your presentation. If the information is necessary, answer this question, "Would it be possible to give the information in a simpler way?"

REVISING/EDITING

The amount of revising and editing that you can do depends on the technology you're using. Check your video for the elements that follow.

Revising and Editing a Videotape

- Does the video as a whole follow a logical pattern of organization and have an obvious purpose?
- Do the words work with the images?
- Does the narration sound like natural speech?
- Are transitions—both visual and verbal—from scene to scene and from shot to shot smooth?
- Are the shots well lighted and in focus?
- Does the video contain a variety of focal lengths?
- Are special effects such as zooms, oddly tilted camera angles, and fade-in/fade-outs at a minimum? Do they distract from the point of the video?

The best way to solve any problems that you might encounter is to use common sense. For technical difficulties, think *simple is better*. Every technical "bell and whistle" that you add to your presentation multiplies your chances for difficulties.

PRESENTING YOUR VIDEOTAPE

How you present your videotape may depend on whether or not you are present when it's shown. You may want to give a brief introduction to present it—either in person or on tape. You may also want to include **credits** at the end of the tape. Whatever your method of presentation, take a bow!

Evaluation Activity: Audience Interviews

After your audience has seen your videotape, you'll want to know how well you communicated your information. One method is to interview your audience on camera after they've watched your video.

Ask your viewers questions that will reveal how well you got your point across. For example, you might ask "Why do you—or don't you—agree with the point that the video makes about _____ ?" Also ask questions that will give you specific feedback about what you did wrong and what you did right. Try using some of the following questions.

- What did you like best about the video?
- What did you like least about the video?
- How would you rate the quality of the filming?
- How would you rate the quality of the narration?
- What questions did the video leave unanswered?
- Who would be the ideal audience for this video?

When you finish your interviews, you can watch the tape and evaluate the comments. (Weed out the less-than-serious comments.) What do the comments suggest are your video's strongest points? Your weakest points? If you had the videotape to do over again, what would you do differently?

DO IT YOURSELF!

Evaluate your videotape, using the checklist on the opposite page.

Terms to Know

Film **credits** mention people who were interviewed or spoke on camera—or who helped you in some way (such as librarians who helped with research). Also credit the sources of borrowed information, such as music, artwork, photographs, film clips, and documents.

Unit III

Language Resources

Even though communicating comes naturally to most people, everyone needs a little help once in a while. Maybe you're not certain where to start a new paragraph in an essay, or you want to make sure your antecedents are clear when you're giving a speech. Even a poster requires careful spelling, punctuation, and capitalization. When you want to be sure your use of the English language is correct–for written, spoken, or visual projects–you'll find explanations and examples in this unit.

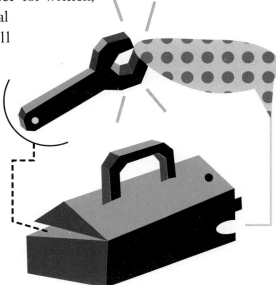

CONTENTS

BUILDING BLOCKS OF WRITING
CHAPTER 10 Paragraphs 288
CHAPTER 11 Writing Style 294
GRAMMAR
CHAPTER 12 Parts of Speech 299
CHAPTER 13 Phrases and Clauses 314
CHAPTER 14 Sentences 322
USAGE
CHAPTER 15 Using Verbs 337
CHAPTER 16 Using Pronouns 345
CHAPTER 17 Subject-Verb Agreement 352
CHAPTER 18 Using Adjectives and Adverbs 356
CHAPTER 19 Glossary of Usage 360
MECHANICS
CHAPTER 20 Punctuation 366
CHAPTER 21 Capitalization 381
CHAPTER 22 Italics, Numbers, and Abbreviations 388

Chapter 10 Paragraphs

Just as words are the building blocks of sentences, so sentences are the building blocks of larger units of writing called paragraphs. The easiest way to recognize a paragraph is to know that the first line usually is indented, or set in, from the margin. But that visual clue tells you only what a paragraph looks like in your writing. It's much more important to know what role a paragraph plays. A **paragraph** is a group of related sentences that express and develop a thought.

Paragraphs are used to develop the ideas in your writing. Just as you write each sentence to state a complete thought, you tie together the sentences in a paragraph to develop your thoughts and ideas.

A **paragraph** is a group of related sentences that express and develop one main idea.

10.1 TYPES OF PARAGRAPHS

Paragraphs may be categorized by the purpose for which the writer uses them in presenting his or her ideas. Some paragraphs, for example, are written to persuade the reader of a certain viewpoint. Some paragraphs describe a scene or a person.

Other paragraphs narrate a sequence of events or explain a topic or give information about it. Your writing may sometimes combine these different kinds of elements in order to engage the reader's interest. Which kind of paragraph—or which combination of paragraph types—you decide to use will depend on your purpose in writing.

▪▪ 10.1A PERSUASIVE PARAGRAPHS

Persuasive paragraphs express an opinion or a viewpoint. You use these kinds of paragraphs to persuade your readers and convince them that the views and arguments you set forth favoring certain actions or ideas make sense. Read the following example of a persuasive paragraph.

The Olympic Games should stop the practice of inviting athletes to compete as members of national teams. Instead of promoting international unity, this policy increases rivalries among nations. It also strengthens a feeling of nationalism that undermines the internationalism the games are supposed to promote. As a result, the Olympic Games divide nations rather than bring them closer together.

10.1B DESCRIPTIVE PARAGRAPHS

Descriptive paragraphs paint a vivid, precise picture of a person, place, or thing. You use these kinds of paragraphs to help your reader see, hear, and feel what you may have experienced or wish to describe. In writing descriptive paragraphs, avoid vague terms and make your language as specific and vivid as possible. For example, compare the following pairs of sentences.

E X A M P L E S

The flower was pretty.
The tall sturdy green stem supported a crown of yellow petals that glowed in the sunlight.

Phoebe held the pencil in her hand.
Phoebe grasped the red pencil so firmly that her fingers hurt.

The first sentence in each pair gives the reader a general description. The second sentence in each pair fills in the details of color, size, and feeling, and therefore makes the picture come alive for the reader. A writer can use vivid description to enrich a paragraph. For example, read the following descriptive paragraph of a dog by its owner.

Sometimes I look at my dog and wonder what he's thinking and feeling. This task is easier with Webster than it is with some other dogs because his face is amazingly expressive. Like many

English springer spaniels, he has droopy eyes with a gaze that switches between a wisdom and a sadness that destroy my defenses when I'm heartless enough to

consider refusing him table scraps. But Webster's human qualities, though clearest in the eyes, seem to come from somewhere else as well: his boxy snout, with its moist, floppy jowls, suggests both sincerity and patience like a helpful doctor's smile; his long, soft ears, covered with thickly waved fur, remind me of pictures of early Americans wearing elaborately styled wigs. Like an actor whose facial features arouse feelings in us that words cannot, Webster speaks a language that often puts our poor human tongue to shame.

Notice the use of vivid adjectives (*droopy, heartless, boxy, floppy*); adverbs (*amazingly, thickly, elaborately*); verbs (*wonder, switches, suggest, arouse*); and nouns (*wisdom, sadness, defenses, tongue*). Note also the use of figures of speech–comparisons between unlike things–(*like a helpful doctor's smile, remind me of pictures,* and *puts our poor human tongue to shame*).

■■ 10.1C NARRATIVE PARAGRAPHS

While descriptive paragraphs give a picture of things in space, **narrative paragraphs** convey a sequence of events in time. Narration is an essential element in telling a story–in letting the reader know *what happened*. Read this descriptive paragraph, by Sir Arthur Conan Doyle, about an intruder entering a bank vault where the detective

Sherlock Holmes waits silently, ready to arrest the robber.

With a rending, tearing sound, one of the broad, white stones turned over upon its side, and left a square, gaping hole, through which streamed the light of a lantern. Over the edge there peeped a clean-cut, boyish face, which looked keenly about it, and then, with a hand on either side of the aperture, drew itself shoulder-high and waist-high, until one knee rested upon the edge. In another instant he stood at the side of the hole, and was hauling after him a companion, lithe and small like himself, with a pale face and a shock of very red hair.

Sir Arthur Conan Doyle,
"The Red-Headed League"

Notice how Doyle stretches out the tension of the moment by lingering over important details. The paragraph clearly shows how good narration uses elements of description in order to hold the reader's interest.

■■ 10.1D EXPOSITORY PARAGRAPHS

Expository paragraphs explain or convey facts. A good expository paragraph contains specific examples and definitions in order to give the reader a clear picture of the matter being explained. The following paragraph is adapted from a student's essay on bees.

> The Austrian scientist and Nobel laureate Karl von Frisch spent fifty years studying the hive. He saw that bees communicate by vibrating in the hive. In this way they tell other bees in what direction and how far to fly to reach a flower; they use the sun and gravity as reference points. Von Frisch discovered that even those few dunces who fly off at the wrong angles benefit the hive, since they find new sources of flowers and communicate these discoveries back to the hive.

Thoroughness and attention to detail allow the reader to follow the writer's account easily. In expository paragraphs, thoroughness is a very important factor. Always keep in mind that your reader probably knows a great deal less about the topic than you do.

10.2 PARTS OF PARAGRAPHS

Paragraphs are made up of several basic elements. The topic sentence presents the paragraph's main idea. Supporting sentences explain the topic sentence. Transitional sentences help expand the topic sentence and provide links between ideas. Concluding sentences restate the main idea and end the paragraph on a strong note.

■■ 10.2A WRITING TOPIC SENTENCES

One of the best ways to make your meaning clear is to begin a paragraph with a sentence that states the paragraph's main idea. Such a sentence is called the **topic sentence**. It may come at the beginning of a paragraph or someplace else in the paragraph.

Note how a topic sentence gains the reader's attention at the beginning of the paragraph in the following example.

> The Olympic Games should stop the practice of inviting athletes to compete as members of national teams. The Olympic Games are held to promote international unity among nations. Yet every four years, the world's finest athletes compete as representatives of national teams, with the goal of promoting their own country above all others.

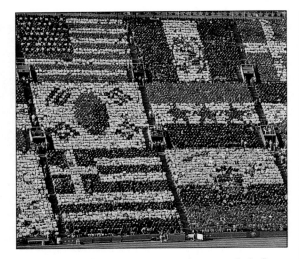

This strengthens nationalism and defeats the very spirit of cooperation that the games claim to encourage. The Olympics must return to the goal of creating harmony among nations.

The **topic sentence** states the main subject or topic of a paragraph.

■■ 10.2B WRITING SUPPORTING SENTENCES

The sentences that follow or precede your topic sentence in the paragraph have the job of supporting and explaining your main idea. These sentences are known as supporting sentences. **Supporting sentences** expand the topic by adding details and examples that make the paragraph more interesting and believable. For instance, in an expository paragraph the topic sentence may make a statement. The supporting

sentences would explain the statement by defining terms or providing examples.

Supporting sentences expand and explain the topic sentence.

■■ 10.2C WRITING TRANSITIONAL SENTENCES

The sentences in the paragraphs you write can expand on your topic. They can also provide effective transitions between your thoughts. By using words and phrases that link one sentence with another, you can create smooth **transitional sentences**. The following paragraph contains several sentences that include transitional words and phrases in italics.

Cold weather is particularly difficult for older people. *For one thing*, the icy streets make walking hazardous. Some older people may already have trouble

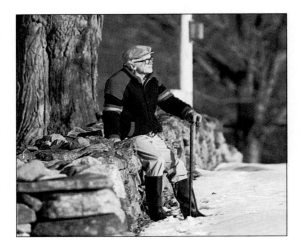

getting about, and broken bones often heal less quickly in the elderly than in the young. *In addition*, the elderly are much more likely to suffer from illnesses like the flu, especially in the winter. The cold weather's effects on senior citizens, *however*, often can be psychological as well as physical. *In fact*, one of the worst problems an older person may face is a feeling of being isolated. During severe winter storms, some of them may not be able to leave their homes for several days. This picture, though, is not necessarily all bleak. Younger friends and family members can often brighten up an older person's day by visiting or making phone calls.

Transitional sentences can give your readers a clue about the way your thoughts are linked. Note some of the words and phrases used in the paragraph on older people: *for one thing, in addition, in fact, though*. Such words show how the writer's thoughts are connected. In addition, pronouns such as *this* or *it* refer the reader to a key term in the previous sentence.

Transitional words can serve a variety of purposes: illustration (*for example, as we can see, for instance*); emphasis (*in fact, moreover*); further development (*in addition, besides*); comparison or contrast (*but, however, yet, nevertheless, although*); or conclusions (*thus, hence, therefore*). Correlative conjunctions are especially effective in providing bridges from one sentence to another or between paragraphs (*just as . . . so; not only . . . but also; either . . . or; neither . . . nor*).

Transitional sentences help expand the topic sentence and provide links between ideas.

■■ 10.2D WRITING CONCLUDING SENTENCES

The **concluding sentence** restates the main idea of a paragraph and adds a strong ending to it. It adds weight to the topic you have presented and shows your audience exactly what your purpose is.

You can use several strategies to write your concluding sentence. You might want to repeat the main idea by restating your topic sentence in different words. You might use the concluding sentence to summarize the paragraph. You might tell the reader how you feel about the subject. (The paragraph on older people ends with such a sentence.) Or you might add a new insight about the subject that will capture your reader's attention. A memorable sentence that ends a paragraph is called a clincher.

A **concluding sentence** restates the main idea of a paragraph and adds a strong ending to it.

Chapter 11 Writing Style

When you write, you can develop a **style**, which is simply the way you express yourself in language. Sometimes it may be helpful to imitate the style of authors you admire, but it's important to find your *own* style. You can create a style of your own just by putting words on paper. Look at this chapter for some hints.

11.1 STYLE

Style is easy to recognize but difficult to define. It might be called the personality of writing. Some aspects of style are positive, such as coherence and sentence variety (see Chapter 14). Style also involves avoiding constructions that detract from the effectiveness of your writing. These writing flaws are like weeds in a garden. They need to be removed.

■■ 11.1A CLICHÉS

A cliché is an overworked expression. "Red as a rose" is a cliché. So is "wise as an owl." Clichés were once effective expressions–imaginative similes or metaphors–but now they are worn out. Here are a few clichés to erase from your writing. (Don't worry about clichés in ordinary conversation.

You're sure to use them. In fact, it would be hard to carry on a conversation without them.)

EXAMPLES

Marie was as *pale as a ghost*.
The trees stood *like silent sentinels*.
Senator Doe really *hit the nail on the head*.
The recording was *selling like hot cakes*.
It was raining *cats and dogs*.

You can probably think of many more such overworked expressions. They're as thick as flies in August. Oops!

11.1B MIXED METAPHORS

A **metaphor** is a figurative expression that expresses a comparison without using the word *like* or *as* (used in a simile). If you were to write "The trees were silent sentinels," you would be using a metaphor (as well as repeating a cliché). "Hitting the nail on the head" is a metaphor for making a statement that is exactly right. (It, too, is a cliché.)

Metaphors should either stand alone or work effectively together. They should not conflict with one another. If they do, they are **mixed metaphors**. Although unintended mixed metaphors can be amusing, they suggest poor writing and thinking skills. You'll want to keep them out of the papers you write.

EXAMPLES

Life is like a football game; three strikes and you're out.
Our one ray of hope has been shattered on the rocks.

11.1C REDUNDANCY

Redundancy occurs when you repeat an idea unnecessarily.

EXAMPLES

Today's modern executive wears a dark suit. (It's unnecessary to include both *today's* and *modern*, which have the same meaning. See the following corrected sentences.
Today's executive wears a dark suit.
The **modern** executive wears a dark suit.

Redundancy can also occur from sentence to sentence.

EXAMPLE

Dr. Agarwal told her patient to speak more loudly. "Talk more loudly," Dr. Agarwal said. (Use only one of these sentences.)

Occasionally repetition is intentional and effective. Knowing when to use and when to avoid repetition is one mark of a good writer.

11.1D POINT OF VIEW

A writer always has a point of view. This isn't quite the same thing as a viewpoint. A *viewpoint* is an opinion. A **point of view** is the relation of the writer to the action described.

There are two basic points of view: **first person** and **third person**. Each one has certain usage requirements.

First-Person Point of View

Prose or poetry written in the first person or spoken aloud uses the words *I, me, we, my, our, us.* A writer who chooses the first person creates a narrator or a speaker who reports only what he or she personally experiences.

A first-person narrator wouldn't write, "I was excited when the ball cleared the fence. The outfielder who watched it go over thought, 'Is that kid lucky, or what?'" See the example for the correct version.

> EXAMPLE
>
> I was excited when the ball cleared the fence. I saw the outfielder watch it go. His face wore an expression of disbelief. I'm sure he thought I was just lucky.

Third-Person Point of View

The writer who uses third-person point of view has a narrator who steps back and leaves himself or herself out of the picture entirely. Third-person point of view may be *limited* or *omniscient*. A **limited** point of view means that the narrator is an observer who reports what is going on. An **omniscient** point of view means that the narrator knows everything that's going on, including what the characters think and feel. The narrator even knows what's happening in two places at the same time.

> EXAMPLE
>
> The batter was excited when the ball cleared the fence. The outfielder watched it, totally unable to believe what he was seeing. Everybody figured it was just a lucky hit. (Omniscient third-person point of view)

Point of view means the writer's relation to what he or she writes.

11.2 DICTION

Diction has two meanings. In speaking, it means "manner of speech, or enunciation." In writing, it means "word choice." Word choice is crucial in writing, but it is an extremely broad topic. The choice of words includes every aspect of usage. Pronoun choice, decisions about verb tenses, subject-verb agreement—all these and more are involved in word choice.

In writing, **diction** has to do with choosing exactly the right word to convey the intended meaning. Mark Twain once said, "The difference between the right word and the almost-right word is the difference between lightning and the lightning bug." That is the essence of diction—choosing the precise word you need.

When your friend enters a room, does she simply *walk* in, or does she *strut, amble, stride, shuffle, lurch, glide, stroll, waddle, slink,* or *saunter?* All of these verbs have a somewhat similar **denotation** but quite different **connotations**.

In writing, you should think about the word choices you make. If the denotation is right, be sure the connotation is right, too.

If your friend *glides* into the room, she is likely to attract favorable attention. If she *shuffles* in, she probably won't. Whenever you choose words, especially nouns and verbs, you make decisions about diction. Pay close attention to the connotations of the words you choose. Do the words convey exactly the meanings you want? If you choose carefully and well, you'll get the reaction you expect from your readers.

The **denotation** of a word is its dictionary meaning. The **connotation** of a word is everything the word suggests—all its attached emotional meanings.

11.3 TONE

The **tone** of a piece of writing is the attitude the writer takes toward his or her subject. Tone can often be described by a single adjective. This adjective might be *serious, breezy, sarcastic,* or *brisk*. What creates tone in writing? There are a number of elements.

11.3A WORD CHOICE

If you were to use mostly one- and two-syllable words in your writing, your tone might seem plain or even boring. If, on the other hand, you were to fill your paper with words of many syllables (the "multitudinous seas incarnadine" of Shakespeare), your tone might seem pretentious or maybe even very difficult to understand.

11.3B FORMALITY AND INFORMALITY

Another distinction in tone is between formal and informal wording. Formal English is language for serious compositions, such as essay answers to examination questions. Informal English is the language of ordinary conversation and is suitable for most writing except the most serious.

Formal English creates one tone, while informal wording or slang creates another.

For example, if you choose the word *cuisine* instead of *grub*, you are probably writing in a formal tone. The tone of the "cuisine" paper might be serious, the tone of the "grub" piece, casual.

Chapter 12 Parts of Speech

Every word in a sentence has a special function that relates it to some other word or words in the sentence. You might think of each sentence as a jigsaw puzzle in which each word has a special shape that interlocks perfectly with the shapes of the words around it. This distinctive shape or function of each word is called a **part of speech**. The parts of speech are *nouns, pronouns, verbs, adjectives, adverbs, prepositions,* and *interjections.*

12.1 NOUNS

When you see or think of a person, place, thing, or idea, you probably identify it by its name: *Juanita, desk, flower, happiness, town.* Each of these italicized words is a **noun**.

EXAMPLES

Rani, Japan, tomato, umbrella, loyalty, beauty

A **noun** is a word that names a person, place, thing, or idea.

12.1A PROPER AND COMMON NOUNS

You may have noticed that some nouns, such as *Chan, Idaho,* and *Saturn,* are always capitalized. Nouns of this kind name a particular person, place, thing, or idea. They are called **proper nouns**.

EXAMPLES

Michael Jordan (person), Nairobi (place), the Mona Lisa (thing)

A **proper noun** names a particular person, place, thing, or idea and is always capitalized.

Other nouns aren't capitalized and name any one of a group of people, places, things, or ideas. These are called **common nouns**.

EXAMPLES

classmate (person), ballroom (place), shoelace (thing)

A **common noun** names any person, place, thing, or idea and is not capitalized.

▪▪ 12.1B CONCRETE AND ABSTRACT NOUNS

Different kinds of nouns name different kinds of things. Some nouns, called **concrete nouns**, name things you can see or touch: *pen, book, VCR.*

EXAMPLES

tree, dog, lamp, apple, newspaper

A **concrete noun** names something you can see or touch.

Other nouns, called **abstract nouns**, name things you cannot see or touch: *happiness, fear, joy.*

EXAMPLES

justice, happiness, intelligence, humor

An **abstract noun** names something you cannot see or touch.

▪▪ 12.1C COMPOUND AND COLLECTIVE NOUNS

Nouns that are made up of more than one word are called **compound nouns**. The words might be combined into one word, such as *notebook*, or the words might be separate, as in *post office*. Sometimes the parts of a compound noun are connected by hyphens, as in *brother-in-law*.

A **compound noun** is a noun that is made up of two or more words.

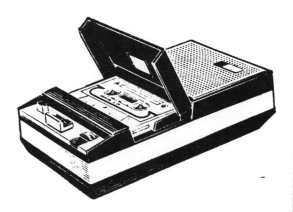

Nouns that name a group of persons or things, such as *audience* and *class,* are called **collective nouns**. Collective nouns are singular in form, but can be either singular or plural in meaning. A collective noun takes a singular verb when it refers to the group acting as a whole: *Our softball team wins every game.* It takes a plural verb when it refers to each member of the group acting individually: *The team have their bats in their lockers.* Some common collective nouns are *team, family, jury, faculty,* and *audience.*

A **collective noun** is a noun that names a group of persons or things. It is singular in form, but may be either singular or plural in meaning.

12.2 PRONOUNS

Think about what a noun is. Then it will be easy to identify another part of speech, called a pronoun. A **pronoun** is a word that takes the place of a noun.

The word that a pronoun stands for is called the **antecedent** of the pronoun.

In the previous example, the noun *Tariq* is the antecedent of the pronoun *He*, and the noun *medal* is the antecedent of the pronoun *it*.

Sometimes the antecedent of a pronoun is not stated.

EXAMPLE

You are a good friend.

There is no antecedent stated for the pronoun *you* in this sentence.

A **pronoun** is a word that takes the place of one or more nouns.

▰▰ 12.2A PERSONAL PRONOUNS

Personal pronouns refer to the one speaking (called *first person*), the one spoken to (*second person*), or the one spoken about (*third person*). They have singular and plural forms. Personal pronouns are the most frequently used pronouns.

EXAMPLES

Jesse looked at the **elephants**.
He waved to **them**.

In the second sentence, *He*, referring to *Jesse*, and *them*, referring to *elephants*, are personal pronouns.

Personal Pronouns		
	Singular	Plural
First person	I me my mine	we us our ours
Second person	you your yours	you your yours
Third person	he him his she her hers it its	they them their theirs

▰▰ 12.2B REFLEXIVE PRONOUNS

Some personal pronouns end in *-self* or *-selves*, for example, *yourself* and *themselves*. They are called **reflexive pronouns**. Reflexive pronouns refer to the subject of a sentence and direct the action of the verb back to the subject.

Reflexive Pronouns		
	Singular	Plural
First person	myself	ourselves
Second person	yourself	yourselves
Third person	himself herself itself	themselves

▰▰ 12.2C POSSESSIVE PRONOUNS

Another type of pronoun is one that shows possession, or ownership. This pronoun is called a **possessive pronoun**. Possessive pronouns often act as adjectives.

Possessive Pronouns		
	Singular	Plural
First person	my mine	our ours
Second person	your yours	your yours
Third person	her hers his its	their theirs

E X A M P L E S

Tom swung **his** racket.

The jacket is **mine**.

In the first sentence, the pronoun *his* shows that the racket belongs to Tom. Notice that *his* acts as an adjective, modifying *racket*. In the second sentence, the pronoun *mine* shows that the jacket belongs to *me*.

▊▊ 12.2D DEMONSTRATIVE PRONOUNS

A **demonstrative pronoun** points out a specific person, place, thing, or idea.

Demonstrative Pronouns			
this	that	these	those

Demonstrative pronouns can also be adjectives. When demonstrative pronouns tell *which one(s)* about a noun, they are **demonstrative adjectives**. (See Adjectives, 12.4.)

E X A M P L E S

PRONOUN: **This** is an excellent song.

ADJECTIVE: **This** song is excellent.

In the first example, *this* is a demonstrative pronoun; in the second example, *this* modifies the word *song* and tells which song.

▊▊ 12.2E INDEFINITE PRONOUNS

An **indefinite pronoun** refers to a person, place, thing, or idea that is not specific.

Common Indefinite Pronouns			
all	each	more	one
any	either	much	other
anybody	everybody	neither	several
anyone	everyone	nobody	some
anything	few	none	somebody
both	many	no one	something

E X A M P L E S

None of us thought it would rain today.

Everyone except me saw it was a surprise party.

▚ 12.2F INTERROGATIVE PRONOUNS

An **interrogative pronoun** asks a question.

Common Interrogative Pronouns
what   which   who   whose

EXAMPLES

Who is Noam's teacher?
What did Ms. Rodriguez want?

Some interrogative pronouns can also be adjectives. When these words ask *which one(s)* about a noun, they are **interrogative adjectives**.

EXAMPLES

PRONOUN: **Which** is Candice's book?
ADJECTIVE: **Which** book is Candice's?

12.3 VERBS

A sentence is a group of words that expresses a complete thought. To do so, a sentence must have a word that expresses action or a state of being. This kind of word is called a **verb**.

EXAMPLES

I usually **go** to the park each week. (The verb *go* expresses an action.)
I **am** happy there. (The verb *am* expresses a state of being.)

A **verb** is a word that expresses action or a state of being. A sentence needs a verb to make it complete.

▚ 12.3A ACTION VERBS

An **action verb** expresses action by telling what someone or something does. The actions expressed can be either physical actions (*run, sit, speak, buy*) or mental actions (*think, intend, love, deny*).

EXAMPLES

Christina **serves** dinner. (physical)
Micaela **forgot** her father's birthday. (mental)

Have, has, and *had* are often used as action verbs that show possession.

EXAMPLES

Carmine **has** a new cat.
Elena and Patrice **have** a younger brother.
Ahmed **had** a tough day.

An **action verb** tells what action the subject is performing. The actions can be either physical or mental.

▦ 12.3B LINKING VERBS

Verbs express not only physical and mental actions but also states of being. They do so by linking the subject of the sentence with another word that identifies the subject or describes it in some way. Such verbs are called **linking verbs**. The most common linking verb is **be.** See the chart on this page for a list of other linking verbs.

EXAMPLES

Ravi **is** handsome. (Notice that the linking verb *is* connects, or links, the subject, *Ravi*, to a word, *handsome*, that tells about the subject.)
Barry **is** a plumber.
Tatiana **seems** healthy.

A **linking verb** links, or connects, the subject of a sentence with a word in the predicate that describes or explains the subject.

Common Forms of *Be*		
be	has been	would be
is	have been	should be
am	will be	could be
are	may be	
was	can be	
were	might be	

Other Common Linking Verbs		
become	stay	look
feel	appear	smell
seem	taste	grow
sound	remain	

EXAMPLES

Francesca **remains** content.
Chou **looks** well.
Leroy **feels** seasick.

Some of these linking verbs are also used as action verbs.

EXAMPLES

I **smell** the pizza. (action)
The pizza **smells** good. (linking)
The plant **grows** in the garden. (action)
Wesley **grows** restless during home-room. (linking)

▪▪ 12.3C VERB PHRASES

A verb sometimes consists of more than one word. Such a verb is called a **verb phrase**. A verb phrase always has one main verb and at least one helping verb. In each of the following sentences, the verb phrase is underlined once, and the helping verb is underlined twice.

> **EXAMPLES**
>
> Jaclyn <u>will</u> be late.
> Toby <u>has</u> pitched twice.
> Franz <u>should have</u> gone to the game.

▪▪ 12.3D TRANSITIVE AND INTRANSITIVE VERBS

An action verb often has a direct object—a noun or pronoun that receives the action of the active verb.

> **EXAMPLE**
>
> Pamela drives a yellow **convertible**.

If we ask, "Drives whom or what?" we realize that *convertible* is the direct object of the verb. Verbs that have direct objects are called **transitive verbs**.

Sometimes an action verb doesn't have a direct object.

> **EXAMPLE**
>
> Pamela walks swiftly.

If we ask, "Walks whom or what?" we realize that there is no direct object in this sentence. *Swiftly* is an adverb and therefore cannot answer these questions. Verbs that don't take direct objects are called **intransitive verbs.** Verbs that do take direct objects are called transitive verbs. Some verbs, like *walk* and *stand*, are always intransitive.

> **EXAMPLES**
>
> Everyone, stand.
> Walk tall.

We cannot ask, "Stand whom or what?" Other verbs, like *leave*, are intransitive in some cases and transitive in others.

> ### E X A M P L E
> The children **left** yesterday. (intransitive)
> Sharon **left** the room. (transitive)

12.4 ADJECTIVES

Remember that words that name persons, places, or things are nouns, and words that take the place of nouns are pronouns.

A person, place, or thing has qualities: size, shape, color, weight, and other features. You can describe the person, place, or thing in various ways: *large* or *small*, *light* or *dark*, *red* or *green*, and so on. Each italicized word in the last sentence is an **adjective**, a word that describes (or modifies) a person, place, or thing. Adjectives tell what nouns and pronouns are like. For example, notice how adding adjectives to the following sentence tells us more about each noun.

> ### E X A M P L E S
> The girl walked her dog.
> The **tall, cheerful** girl walked her **scruffy little** dog.

In the example above, the adjectives *tall* and *cheerful* tell more about the noun *girl*, and the adjectives *scruffy* and *little* tell more about the noun *dog*.

Adjectives usually answer one of three kinds of questions about nouns: What kind? (a *brown* bag) How many? (*seven* apples) Which one? (*that* window). Can you tell which questions the adjectives answer in the following sentences?

> ### E X A M P L E S
> The **yellow** taxi picked up **two** passengers on **this** street. (what kind? *yellow* taxi; how many? *two* passengers; which one? *this* street)
> The **long, green** grass waved in the **strong** wind. (The adjectives *long* and *green* modify the noun *grass;* the adjective *strong* modifies the noun *wind*.)

An **adjective** is a word that describes, or modifies, a noun or pronoun.

12.4A ARTICLES

The words *a*, *an*, and *the* are special adjectives called **articles**. *A* and *an* are **indefinite articles**; they don't identify a noun as a particular person, place, or thing.

EXAMPLES

a shoe
an ocean

The is a **definite article**; it identifies a noun as a particular, or definite, person, place, or thing.

EXAMPLES

the bandleader
the Riviera

An **article** is a special kind of adjective that helps identify a noun in either a definite or an indefinite way.

12.4B POSITION OF ADJECTIVES

In the examples you have seen so far, the adjective comes before the word it modifies. Sometimes, however, the adjective comes after it.

EXAMPLE

The **beautiful** park, **peaceful** and **calm** during the week, now bustled with **weekend** visitors.

In the preceding sentence, the adjectives *beautiful* and *weekend* precede the nouns they modify (*park, visitors*). But two other adjectives, *peaceful* and *calm*, also modify the noun *park* even though they come after it.

12.4C NOUNS AS ADJECTIVES

Nouns can also act as adjectives. The word *weekend*, which acts as an adjective in the preceding example, is usually a noun.

EXAMPLES

a joyful **weekend**
a **weekend** adventure

In the first example, *weekend* is a noun modified by the adjective *joyful*. In the second example, *weekend* is an adjective that modifies the noun *adventure*. Many nouns can also function as adjectives.

EXAMPLES

train station, **soup** bowl, **television** monitor, **United States** government

When a noun is used in this way, it is treated as a true adjective.

■■ 12.4D PROPER ADJECTIVES

Perhaps you recognize that the adjective *United States* in the last example is capitalized. It is a **proper adjective**, an adjective formed from a proper noun. Proper adjectives are always capitalized. Unlike *United States*, most proper adjectives have endings different from those of the related proper nouns.

EXAMPLES

Proper Nouns	**Proper Adjectives**
Africa	African
China	Chinese
Spain	Spanish

The following boldfaced words are all proper adjectives.

EXAMPLES

Pacific Ocean, **Rocky** Mountains, **Long Island** Rail Road, **International Date** Line

12.5 ADVERBS

Just as adjectives modify nouns, **adverbs** modify verbs, adjectives, and other adverbs.

EXAMPLES

Sasha plays the piano.
Sasha plays the piano **beautifully.**

Beautifully tells more about *how* Sasha *plays*. It fills out the picture of the verb *plays*.

An adverb may also modify, or tell more about, an adjective.

EXAMPLES

That piano solo was beautiful.
That piano solo was **very** beautiful.

The adverb *very* tells more about the adjective *beautiful*.

An adverb may also modify another adverb.

EXAMPLES

Sasha plays the piano beautifully.
Sasha plays the piano **quite** beautifully. (The adverb *quite* tells *how* beautifully Sasha played.)
The actors memorized that **incredibly** difficult script **rather quickly**. (The adverb *incredibly* modifies the adjective *difficult*; the adverb *rather* modifies the adverb *quickly*; and the adverb *quickly* modifies the verb *memorized*.)

Adverbs answer the questions *How? When? Where?* and *To what extent?* Consider these examples.

> E X A M P L E S
> ....
>
> The police drove **rapidly** to the scene.
> (*How* did the police drive?)
> The letter arrived **yesterday**.
> (*When* did the letter arrive?)
> We stayed **inside**. (*Where* did we stay?)
> The water is **too** cold. (*To what extent* is the water cold?)

An **adverb** is a word that modifies a verb, an adjective, or another adverb.

▓▓ 12.5A INTERROGATIVE ADVERBS

Some adverbs ask questions. These are interrogative adverbs.

> E X A M P L E S
> ....
>
> **Where** is the theater?
> **When** will the plane take off?
> **How** do lasers work?
> **Why** are you avoiding me?

An **interrogative adverb** is used to ask a question. *Where, when, how,* and *why* are some interrogative adverbs.

▓▓ 12.5B NEGATIVE ADVERBS

Negative adverbs are another group of adverbs. The word *not* and its contraction, *-n't,* are the most common examples of this group, but there are others as well.

> E X A M P L E S
> ....
>
> Your joke is **not** funny.
> (*Not* modifies *funny.*)
> We **can't** rent a car.
> (The contraction *n't* modifies *can rent.*)
> Kareem is **quite** late.
> (*Quite* modifies *late.*)
> We could **scarcely** believe his story.
> (*Scarcely* modifies *could believe.*)
> He **no longer** expected an answer.
> (*No longer* modifies *expected.*)

Keep in mind that *no* can sometimes be an adjective too.

> E X A M P L E S
> ....
>
> There are **no** pencils in that box.
> (*No* modifies the noun *pencils.*)

A **negative adverb** is used to express a negative. *No, not, -n't, no longer, scarcely, hardly,* and *never* are some negative adverbs.

12.6 PREPOSITIONS

A word that shows the relationship of a noun or pronoun to some other word in a sentence is a **preposition**. Prepositions often tell something about direction or position.

> E X A M P L E
>
> Malcolm put the ring **on** the table.

The preposition *on* shows the relationship between the *ring* and the *table*. *Table* is the object of the preposition. A different preposition would create a different relationship.

> E X A M P L E S
>
> Malcolm put the ring **under** the table.
> Malcolm put the ring **behind** the table.
> Malcolm put the ring **beside** the table.
> The girl **on** the corner is my sister's friend. (The preposition *on* shows a relationship between the nouns *girl* and *corner*.)

A **preposition** shows the relationship of a noun or pronoun to some other word in a sentence.

The Most Commonly Used Prepositions			
aboard	below	in	throughout
about	beneath	into	to
above	beside	like	toward
across	between	near	under
after	but (meaning	of	underneath
against	*except*)	off	until
along	by	on	unto
amid	down	onto	up
among	during	over	upon
around	except	past	with
at	for	since	within
before	from	through	without
behind			

12.6A COMPOUND PREPOSITIONS

Sometimes prepositions consist of more than one word. These are called **compound prepositions**.

Compound Prepositions		
according to	because of	instead of
along with	in addition to	next to
apart from	in front of	on top of
aside from	in spite of	out of

12.6B ADVERBS OR PREPOSITIONS

Be careful! Some words can be either adverbs or prepositions, depending on how they are used.

> E X A M P L E S
>
> Pearl looked **around**, smiling curiously. (adverb)
> Pearl looked **around** the room, smiling curiously. (preposition)

In the first sentence of the preceding example on page 311, *around* is an adverb that tells *where* Pearl looked. In the second sentence, *around* is a preposition and *room* is its object.

12.7 CONJUNCTIONS

When you need to connect words in a sentence, you often use words like *and, but, or,* and *for.* Such connecting words are called **conjunctions**.

There are three main types of conjunctions: coordinating, correlative, and subordinating.

▓ 12.7A COORDINATING CONJUNCTIONS

Coordinating conjunctions join words or groups of words of equal importance in a sentence. *And, but, or, nor, for,* and *yet* are coordinating conjunctions.

EXAMPLES
....

The infant waved **and** giggled. (joins words)

The test was difficult, **but** I think I passed. (joins groups of words)

Two horses **and** three dogs scampered across the meadow. (joins groups of words)

▓ 12.7B CORRELATIVE CONJUNCTIONS

Correlative conjunctions are pairs of conjunctions such as *both . . . and, either . . . or,* and *neither . . . nor* that are used together.

EXAMPLES
....

Both Yoko **and** I will be there.

Either Ms. Fong **or** Dr. Alvarez will go with you.

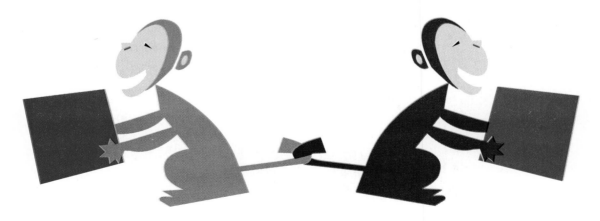

▦ 12.7C SUBORDINATING CONJUNCTIONS

Subordinating conjunctions are used in complex sentences. (See also Subordinating Conjunctions, 13.2F.)

EXAMPLES

Alejandro **and** I love chess.
The store sells shoes **but** not socks.

A **conjunction** is a word that joins words or groups of words in a sentence.

12.8 INTERJECTIONS

An **interjection** expresses strong feeling or emotion. Note that interjections are often followed by exclamation points and sometimes by commas.

EXAMPLES

My, how you've grown!
Oh! What a catch he made!
Phew! That unpleasant job is now completed.
My goodness! I can't decide what to order.
Hey! Wait for me!

An **interjection** is a word or phrase that expresses strong feeling. An interjection is not related grammatically to any other word in the sentence.

Chapter 13 Phrases and Clauses

Groups of words that have special functions in sentences are called **phrases** and **clauses.** Think of a phrase as a part of speech. In fact, a phrase can be used as a noun, an adjective, or an adverb. A clause can also be a noun, an adjective, or an adverb. Read on to learn about and to see the differences between phrases and clauses.

13.1 PHRASES

As you know, individual words function as various parts of speech. Groups of words can also act as parts of speech. **Phrases** are groups of words that have no subject and no verb. Phrases can act as nouns, adjectives, or adverbs. (See Verb Phrases, 12.3C.)

A **phrase** is a group of words that doesn't have both a subject and a verb and that can act as a noun, adjective, or adverb.

■■ 13.1A PREPOSITIONAL PHRASES

One kind of phrase is the prepositional phrase. **Prepositional phrases** always begin with a preposition and end with a noun or a pronoun called the object of the preposition. See the next column for examples of these phrases.

EXAMPLES

After the game, the coach thanked the team.
Jeff has made great progress **in mathematics**.
The runner headed **toward third base**.
Chita is the best **of the runners**.

Each of the boldfaced phrases above is a prepositional phrase.

A **prepositional phrase** is a phrase that begins with a preposition and ends with a noun or pronoun that is the object of the preposition. (See Prepositions, 12.6.)

Adjective and Adverb Phrases

Prepositional phrases can act as adjectives or adverbs. An **adjective phrase** is a prepositional phrase that acts as an adjective. Like an adjective, an adjective phrase modifies a noun or a pronoun.

> **EXAMPLES**
>
> The car **at the corner** has stalled.
> Please meet my cousin **from Puerto Rico**.
> Most **of my friends** play basketball.

When a prepositional phrase modifies a verb, an adjective, or an adverb, it acts as an adverb and is called an **adverb phrase**. The following adverb phrases modify verbs.

> **EXAMPLES**
>
> Rosario hurried **to the classroom**. (where)
> George exercises **after school**. (when)
> The temperature rose **above ninety degrees**. (to what extent)
> Rhoda sang **with expression**. (how)
> Shelley stayed **for the speech**. (why)

In the first example below, the adverb phrase modifies an adjective. In the second example, the adverb phrase modifies an adverb.

> **EXAMPLES**
>
> Risa is the best **in the class**. (modifies the adjective *best*)
> Tommy stayed away **from the dog**. (modifies the adverb *away*)

13.1B VERBALS AND VERBAL PHRASES

Verbals are words that come from verbs but act as nouns or modifiers. **Verbal phrases** are phrases containing verbals. There are three kinds of verbals: **participles,** which act as adjectives; **gerunds**, which act as nouns; and **infinitives**, which can act as nouns, adjectives, or adverbs.

Participles

Verbals that act as adjectives are called **participles**. See the examples that follow.

> **EXAMPLES**
>
> Look at the **faded** photograph.
> We heard the **chiming** bells.

Notice that four of the words in the example sentences look like verbs. The words that express action in the sentences are *look* and *heard*. What about the other two words? Both come from verbs—*fade*

and *chime*–but both act as modifiers. Notice *faded*: it tells what kind of photograph, and so *faded* functions as an adjective that modifies the noun *photograph*. *Chiming* tells you what kind of bells are heard. Thus, *chiming* functions as an adjective that modifies the noun *bells*.

A **participle** is a verb form that acts as an adjective.

Participle or Verb?

Participles also function as parts of verb phrases. **Present participles** and **past participles** are two of the principal parts of verbs. (See Parts of Verbs, 15.1.) Many verb phrases are made up of one or more helping verbs and a present or past participle.

EXAMPLES
....

The telephone **was ringing** all day. (The participle *ringing* follows the helping verb *was*.)
Ekkehard **has exaggerated** the size of his house. (The past participle *exaggerated* follows the helping verb *has*.)

Don't confuse a participle acting as an adjective (as in a *ringing telephone* or an *exaggerated remark*) with one acting as part of a verb phrase.

Participial Phrases

Participles can have complements (for instance, direct objects) and modifiers. A participle and its complements and modifiers form a **participial phrase**.

EXAMPLES
....

Racing madly, Marie just made the bus.
Tasting the soup, Michio felt satisfied with the result.
Filled with hope, Perry peeked at his test score.

In the first example, the adverb *madly* modifies the participle *racing*, which modifies the noun *Marie*. In the second example, *soup* is the direct object of the participle *tasting*, which modifies the noun

Michio. In the third example, the prepositional phrase *with hope* modifies the past participle *filled*, which modifies the noun *Perry*.

A **participial phrase** consists of a participle and its objects and modifiers.

Gerunds and Gerund Phrases

Verb forms ending in *-ing* can act as nouns. Such words are **gerunds**. Gerunds can play the same roles that regular nouns do, including subject, direct object, object of a preposition, or predicate nominative.

E X A M P L E S

Parking is difficult on this crowded street. (subject)
Paula does not enjoy **flying**. (direct object)
What's the use of **complaining**? (object of preposition)
My favorite form of exercise is **jogging**. (predicate nominative)

A **gerund** is a verb form ending in *-ing* that acts as a noun.

Like participles, gerunds can have modifiers and objects. A gerund and its modifiers and objects form a **gerund phrase**.

E X A M P L E S

Parking a car is difficult on this crowded street.
Paula does not enjoy **flying at night**.
What's the use of **complaining about it**?
My favorite form of exercise is **jogging vigorously**.

In the first example, the noun *car* is the direct object of the gerund *parking*. The gerund phrase *parking a car* is the subject of the verb *is*. In the second example, the prepositional phrase *at night* modifies the gerund *flying*. The gerund phrase *flying at night* is the direct object of the verb *enjoy*. In the third example, *about it* is a prepositional phrase that modifies the gerund *complaining*. The gerund phrase *complaining about it* is the object of the preposition *of*. In the fourth example, the adverb *vigorously* modifies the gerund *jogging*. The gerund

phrase *jogging vigorously* is a predicate nominative that identifies the subject of the sentence, *form*.

A **gerund phrase** consists of a gerund and its complements and modifiers.

Infinitives and Infinitive Phrases

When the word *to* comes before a verb, the resulting phrase is another kind of verbal called an **infinitive**. Infinitives can act as nouns, adjectives, and adverbs.

EXAMPLES

My aunt loves **to knit**. (*To knit* acts as a noun and is the direct object of the verb *loves*.)
To forgive is a virtue. (*To forgive* acts as a noun and is the subject of the sentence.)
Andre has the ability **to succeed**. (*To succeed* is an adjective modifying the noun *ability*.)
It is important **to try**. (*To try* acts as an adverb modifying the adjective *important*.)

An **infinitive** is a verb form that usually begins with the word *to* and acts as a noun, adjective, or adverb.

Just like participles and gerunds, infinitives can have modifiers and objects. When you add a modifier or an object to an infinitive, the result is an **infinitive phrase**.

EXAMPLES

My aunt loves **to knit sweaters**.
To forgive your enemies is a virtue.
Andre has the ability **to succeed in medicine**.
It is important **to try harder**.

In the first example, *sweaters* is the direct object of the infinitive *to knit*. The infinitive phrase *to knit sweaters* is the direct object of the verb *loves*. In the second example, *enemies* is the direct object of the infinitive *to forgive*. The infinitive phrase *to forgive your enemies* is the subject of the verb *is*. In the third example, *in medicine* is a prepositional phrase modifying the infinitive *to succeed*. The infinitive phrase *to succeed in medicine* is an adjective modifying the noun *ability*. In the fourth example, *harder* is an adverb modifying the infinitive *to try*. The infinitive phrase *to try harder* is an adverb modifying the adjective *important*.

An **infinitive phrase** consists of an infinitive and any complements and modifiers it may have.

13.2 CLAUSES

A phrase never contains a subject and a verb. There is another kind of word group that does, though. A group of words that contains a subject and a verb is called a **clause**.

Notice the difference between the bold-faced groups of words in the following sentences.

> E X A M P L E S
>
> I arrived at the post office **after closing time**. (phrase)
> I arrived at the post office **after it had closed.** (clause)

The first example contains a prepositional phrase that has no verb and no subject. The second example contains the verb phrase *had closed*. The subject of this verb is the pronoun *it*.

A **clause** is a group of words that contains a subject and a verb.

13.2A SUBORDINATE CLAUSES

Although a clause like *after it had closed* contains a subject and a verb, it cannot stand alone as a sentence. It doesn't express a complete thought. Clauses that cannot stand alone as sentences are called **subordinate clauses** (or **dependent clauses**).

A **subordinate clause** is a group of words that contains a subject and a verb but cannot stand alone as a sentence.

13.2B INDEPENDENT CLAUSES

In order for a subordinate clause to work in a sentence, it must be joined to a clause that contains a subject and a verb and can stand alone as a sentence. A clause that can stand alone as a sentence is called an **independent clause** (or **main clause**). Any complete sentence must have at least one independent clause, although it may also have one or more subordinate clauses.

> E X A M P L E S
>
> Sophia set the alarm clock.
> Sophia set the alarm clock **that she bought yesterday**.

Both sentences contain the subject *Sophia* and the verb *set*. Both sentences express a complete thought. But the second sentence also contains the subordinate clause *that she bought yesterday*. The clause has a subject (*she*) and a verb (*bought*) but cannot stand alone as a sentence. Clearly, a subordinate clause can work in a sentence only when it is joined to an independent clause.

An **independent clause** is a group of words that contains a subject and a verb and can stand alone as a complete sentence.

▪️▪️ 13.2C ADJECTIVE CLAUSES

An independent clause does not function as a part of speech in a sentence. A subordinate clause, though, can act as an adjective, adverb, or noun. Look again at the example in this sentence.

E X A M P L E

Sophia set the alarm clock **that she bought yesterday**.

You can ask, "Which alarm clock?" and find the answer: *that she bought yesterday.* The subordinate clause functions as an adjective in this sentence.

Most adjective clauses begin with the relative pronouns *who, whom, whose, which,* or *that.*

E X A M P L E S

This is the day **that I have dreamed about**. (The subordinate clause *that I have dreamed about* modifies the noun *day.*)
She is the candidate **who favors term limits**. (The subordinate clause *who favors term limits* modifies the noun *candidate.*)
I went to the doctor **whose office is around the corner**. (The subordinate clause *whose office is around the corner* modifies the noun *doctor.*)

An **adjective clause** is a subordinate clause that modifies a noun or pronoun.

▪️▪️ 13.2D RELATIVE PRONOUNS

Most adjective clauses begin with a relative pronoun such as *who, whom, whose, which,* or *that.*

E X A M P L E

Everyone **who** checks out a library book must return it. (The relative pronoun *who* relates the clause *checks out a library book* to the pronoun *everyone.*)

A **relative pronoun** relates an adjective clause to the noun or pronoun the clause modifies.

▪▪ 13.2E ADVERB CLAUSES

Subordinate clauses may also function as adverbs. When a subordinate clause modifies a verb, an adjective, or an adverb, it is an **adverb clause**.

> E X A M P L E S
>
> Chris stayed home **because he was ill**. (The subordinate clause *because he was ill* modifies the verb *stayed* by telling *why.*)
> Juanita is stronger **than I am**. (The subordinate clause *than I am* modifies the adjective *stronger.*)
> Renata runs faster **than Tracy does**. (The subordinate clause *than Tracy does* modifies the adverb *faster.*)

An **adverb clause** is a subordinate clause that modifies a verb, an adjective, or an adverb.

▪▪ 13.2F SUBORDINATING CONJUNCTIONS

Adverb clauses always begin with **subordinating conjunctions**. See the following list of subordinating conjunctions.

Subordinating Conjunctions		
after	as though	than
although	because	though
as	before	unless
as far as	if	until
as if	in as much as	when
as long as	in order that	whenever
as soon as	since	while
	so that	

▪▪ 13.2G NOUN CLAUSES

A subordinate clause that acts as a noun can play the role of subject, direct object, object of a preposition, or predicate nominative. This kind of clause is a **noun clause**.

> E X A M P L E S
>
> **What we need** is a full investigation. (subject)
> My little sister always wants **whatever I have**. (direct object)
> Please return it **to whoever gave it to you**. (object of a preposition)
> Mystery stories are **what interest me most**. (predicate nominative)

A **noun clause** is a subordinate clause that functions as a noun.

Chapter 14 Sentences

Every word has a meaning that gives voice to your thoughts. These thoughts, though, remain incomplete–like unconnected links in a chain–until you connect them with other words to form complete thoughts. Look at the difference between these two thoughts: *Diego, good,* and *friend,* and *Diego is my good friend.* The first word group leaves the links unconnected. The second word group connects the links to form a complete chain of thought called a **sentence**. Sentences are the basic units of all meaningful writing and speaking.

14.1 PARTS OF A SENTENCE

Every word expresses a thought. A group of words that expresses a complete thought is a **sentence**. How can you tell if a group of words is expressing a complete thought?

EXAMPLES

Across the table.
Amiri passed the plate across the table.

The first example is a partial thought that leaves you hanging–it begs for completion. You might wonder what went across the table. The second example leaves no unanswered question. It expresses a complete thought.

14.1A SUBJECTS AND PREDICATES

Subject

Each of the words in a sentence plays a role in helping the sentence express a complete thought. Some words tell what a sentence is about. When a word (or group of words) plays this role, it acts as the subject of the sentence. Every sentence has a simple subject and a complete subject. The **simple subject** is the key noun or pronoun the sentence is about.

EXAMPLES

The distant **star** twinkled faintly. (*Star* is the simple subject.)

The **line** of ticket holders included many teenagers. (*Line* is the simple subject.)

The **simple subject** of a sentence is the key noun or pronoun the sentence is about.

The **complete subject** consists of all the words that tell who or what the sentence is about. Sometimes the complete subject consists of only one word, as in this sentence, "Water seeks its level." In this case, *Water* is both the simple subject and the complete subject of the sentence. At other times, the complete subject contains several words. In the previous example, *line* is the simple subject. *The line of ticket holders* is the complete subject.

EXAMPLES

The Grand Canyon is a magnificent sight. (*The Grand Canyon* is the complete subject.)

Millions of tourists visit it each year. (*Millions of tourists* is the complete subject.)

The **complete subject** of a sentence consists of all the words that tell who or what the sentence is about.

Predicate

In order to express a complete thought, a sentence must have more than just a subject. It must have a predicate, which contains a verb. Consider the sentence "Water seeks its level." The subject, *Water*, doesn't express a complete thought by itself. The rest of the words in the sentence tell what the subject does—*seeks its level*. The words that tell what the subject does make up the predicate. Just as there is a simple subject and a complete subject, there is also a simple predicate and a complete predicate. Look at the example sentence, "Water seeks its level." The **simple predicate** is the verb *seeks*. The verb and its object—*seeks its level*—is the complete predicate.

EXAMPLES

Trees and other plants **bloom** in the spring. (The verb *bloom* is the simple predicate.)

The traffic **is moving** slowly. (The verb phrase *is moving* is the simple predicate.)

The earth **revolves** around the sun. (The verb *revolves* is the simple predicate.)

The **simple predicate** of a sentence is a verb or verb phrase that is the main word in the complete predicate.

The **complete predicate** consists of all the words that tell what the subject is or does. Look again at the last example. The verb *revolves* is the main word in the complete predicate, *revolves around the sun.*

EXAMPLES

The sun **set slowly**. (*Set slowly* is the complete predicate.)
The sky **was pink and yellow**. (*Was pink and yellow* is the complete predicate.)

The **complete predicate** consists of all the words in a sentence that tell what the subject is or does.

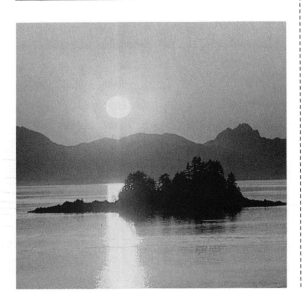

Compound Subjects and Compound Predicates

Some sentences have more than one simple subject. Take another look at the sentence "Trees and other plants bloom in the spring." The verb *bloom* tells about both *trees* and other *plants*. In other words, the sentence has two subjects, which form a **compound subject**. Notice that the two subjects are connected by the conjunction *and* and have the same verb, *bloom*.

EXAMPLES

Iman and **Frieda** gave the best speeches. (The compound subject, *Iman* and *Frieda*, is made up of two subjects connected by the conjunction *and* with the same verb, *gave*.)
Stan or **Elaine** will hold the camera. (The compound subject, *Stan* and *Elaine*, is made up of two subjects connected by the conjunction *or* with the same verb phrase, *will hold*.)

A **compound subject** consists of at least two subjects that are connected by a conjunction and have the same verb or verb phrase.

A sentence may also have a compound predicate. Consider the sentence "The surprised intruder turned and ran." The subject of the sentence, *intruder*, did two things: *turned* and *ran*. The two predicates have the same subject and are joined by the conjunction *and*. Two or more predicates joined by a conjunction make up a **compound predicate**.

E X A M P L E S

Sheila **folded the chair** and **put it away.**

Ms. Cantrow **has taught for many years** and **is now retiring.**

This doll **walks, talks,** and **cries.**

A **compound predicate** consists of two or more predicates that have the same subject and are joined by a conjunction.

Position of Subjects

Usually the subject of a sentence is not hard to find. First you locate the verb and ask *who* or *what* performs the action of the verb. In the sentence "I run," for instance, you can pick out *run* as the verb and ask, "Who or what runs?" The answer is *I*–the subject of the sentence. But a sentence such as the following may prove a bit trickier.

E X A M P L E

On my birthday, **we** are going out to dinner.

Many students make the error of looking for the first noun in the sentence–in this case, *birthday*. They assume that the first noun is the subject. However, the subject may actually be a noun that comes later in the sentence. This is why you should always find the verb first and then ask *who* or *what* about the verb. In the sentence above, the verb is *are going*. Who or what are going? *We* are going. The subject of the sentence is *we*.

Sentences that are questions may present another problem.

E X A M P L E

When are **you** going to the dentist?

If you look carefully for the main verb, you will see that it is the verb phrase *are going*. If you then ask who or what is going, you'll realize that the subject is the pronoun *you*.

Sentences that begin with the words *here* or *there* can also mislead students. Look at the examples on page 326.

EXAMPLES

Here comes my **friend.**

There are many fascinating
ruins in Mexico.

Keep in mind that the words *here* and *there* are never the subject of a sentence. When you look for the subject, follow the usual method of finding the verb first. In the first example above, ask, "Who or what comes?" You can then see that *friend* is the subject of the sentence. In the second example, the verb is *are*. Who or what are? *Ruins*. The subject of the sentence is *ruins*. (Perhaps you noticed that in sentences beginning with *here* or *there*, the subject comes after the verb.)

■■ 14.1B DIRECT OBJECTS AND INDIRECT OBJECTS

Sentences must have a subject and a verb. Many sentences need a third element—a completer, or *complement*—to make sense. There are several types of complements, including **direct object** and **indirect object.**

Direct Object

Read the example to find the direct object.

EXAMPLE

Sandra is training her dog.

You can find the subject of the sentence by first locating the verb—in this case the verb phrase *is training*—and asking, "Who or what *is training*?" The answer tells you that *Sandra* is the subject of the sentence. You can then ask another question: "*Sandra is training* whom or what?" The answer to this question is *dog*. Unlike the subject of the sentence, which performs the action of the verb, *dog* receives the action of the verb directly, and is therefore called the **direct object** of the verb. In the following example, notice how the direct object completes, or complements, the meaning of the verb in receiving its action.

EXAMPLE

Pamela drives her **car** to school. (Pamela drives what? Her **car**. *Car* is the direct object of the action verb *drives*.)

The **direct object** is a noun or pronoun that receives the action of an action verb. It answers the question *whom* or *what* about the verb.

Indirect Object

A noun or pronoun that follows an action verb can also answer the question *to whom* or *for whom* or *to what* or *for what.* Such a noun or pronoun is an **indirect object**. Indirect objects follow such verbs as *give, send, tell,* and *lend.* An indirect object always comes before a direct object in a sentence.

San Francisco

E X A M P L E S

Sally sent her **friend** a card. (Sally sent a card to whom? To her **friend.** *Friend* is the indirect object of the verb *sent.*)
Tino gave the **dog** its dinner. (Tino gave dinner to what? To the **dog.** *Dog* is the indirect object of the verb *gave.*)

An **indirect object** is a noun or pronoun that anwers the question *to whom, for whom,* or *to what, for what,* about an action verb.

■■ 14.1C PREDICATE NOMINATIVES AND PREDICATE ADJECTIVES

Predicate Nominatives

A noun or pronoun can also follow a linking verb and tell more about the subject of a sentence. Such a noun or pronoun is called a **predicate nominative**. (See also Linking Verbs, 12.3B.)

E X A M P L E S

That is an expensive **car**. (The noun *car* follows the linking verb *is* and tells more about the subject, *that.*)
The kitchen is my favorite **room**. (The noun *room* follows the linking verb *is* and tells more about the subject, *kitchen.*)

A **predicate nominative** is a noun or pronoun that follows a linking verb and tells more about the subject of the sentence.

Predicate Adjectives

A linking verb connects the subject of a sentence with a word in the predicate that describes or explains the subject. In the sentence, "Stefan is happy," the adjective *happy* follows a linking verb and tells more about the subject, *Stefan.* Such an adjective is called a **predicate adjective**.

E X A M P L E S

The house seems **empty**.
Shelley looks **terrific**.

A **predicate adjective** is an adjective that follows a linking verb and describes or explains the subject of the sentence.

14.2 TYPES OF SENTENCES

Knowing about independent and subordinate clauses is important in distinguishing the four kinds of sentences: simple, compound, complex, and compound-complex.

▟▟ 14.2A SIMPLE SENTENCES

A **simple sentence** consists of only one independent clause. It is important to remember that *simple* here means that the sentence consists of only one independent clause. It doesn't necessarily mean short and easy. Such a sentence might use many phrases (not clauses) to express a complicated thought. Both of the following sentences are simple sentences. (See also Clauses, 13.2.)

> EXAMPLES
>
> **Wayne sat** down.
> Having reached the end of the long winding road, **Wayne**, tired from days of driving, **pulled** to the side of the road and, leaning against a rock, **paused** to think about his plans.

The second example includes many participial and prepositional phrases, one infinitive phrase, and a compound predicate. Even so, since it includes only one independent clause, it's called a simple sentence.

A **simple sentence** contains only one independent clause and no subordinate clauses.

▟▟ 14.2B COMPOUND SENTENCES

Compound sentences contain two or more independent clauses and can be formed in several ways. The most common type of compound sentence joins two or more independent clauses with a coordinating conjunction: *and, but, or, nor, for,* or *yet.* Two or more independent clauses may also be joined by a semicolon. (See also conjunctions, 12.7.)

> EXAMPLES
>
> The music soared during the party, and the dancers swayed.
> The music soared during the party, and the dancers swayed, but the neighbors objected.
> The music soared during the party; the neighbors, however, objected.

A **compound sentence** has two or more independent clauses.

▉ 14.2C COMPLEX SENTENCES

Complex sentences have only one independent clause, but they also can have any number of subordinate clauses. The following sentences are both complex sentences.

EXAMPLES

The music soared while the dancers swayed. (*The music soared* is the independent clause; *while the dancers swayed* is the subordinate clause.)

Although the neighbors objected, the music soared while the dancers swayed. (*The music soared* is the independent clause. *Although the neighbors objected* and *while the dancers swayed* are subordinate clauses.)

A **complex sentence** has one independent clause and at least one subordinate clause.

▉ 14.2D COMPOUND-COMPLEX SENTENCES

A sentence that has more than one independent clause plus one or more subordinate clauses is a **compound-complex sentence**. It combines a compound sentence and a complex sentence.

EXAMPLE

Although the neighbors objected, the music soared, and the dancers swayed. (*The music soared* and *the dancers swayed* are both independent clauses. *Although the neighbors objected* is a subordinate clause.)

A **compound-complex sentence** has two or more independent clauses and at least one subordinate clause.

14.3 SENTENCE PURPOSES

You can define various types of sentences by examining their structure, and you can also categorize sentences by their purpose. **Declarative sentences** make statements. **Imperative sentences** issue commands. **Interrogative sentences** ask questions, while **exclamatory sentences** express strong feelings or emotions. Read on to find out more.

14.3A DECLARATIVE SENTENCES

Declarative sentences make statements and are the most common sentences.

EXAMPLES

Portia loves Tchaikovsky's Violin Concerto.
Even though I'm a rock fan, I like the concerto, too.

A **declarative sentence** makes a statement.

14.3B IMPERATIVE SENTENCES

Imperative sentences issue a command or a request. They usually imply but do not state the subject *you.*

EXAMPLES

Clean up your room.
Please be seated.

An **imperative sentence** gives a command or makes a request.

14.3C INTERROGATIVE SENTENCES

A sentence that asks a question is an **interrogative sentence**.

EXAMPLES

May Katrinka and I go to the movies tonight?
Did I really hear what I thought I just heard?
How much is this sweater?

An **interrogative sentence** asks a question.

Don't be misled by sentences that seem to ask a question but really make a statement. If a sentence makes a statement, it should end with a period, not with a question mark.

EXAMPLES

I asked my mother whether Katrinka and I could go to the movies tonight.
I wonder how much this hat costs.

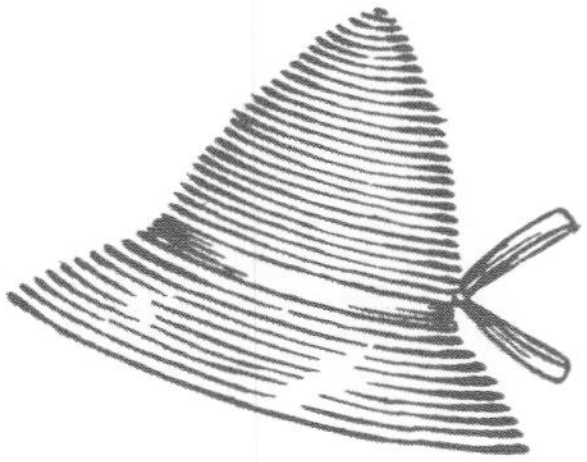

14.3D EXCLAMATORY SENTENCES

Exclamatory sentences express sudden outbursts of emotion. Such sentences end with an exclamation point.

EXAMPLES

How late it is!

What a great game that was!

An **exclamatory sentence** expresses strong feeling or emotion.

14.4 COMPLETE SENTENCES

Effective writing is made up of complete sentences. As you write, ask yourself whether your sentences have a subject, a verb, and express a complete thought. As you write sentences, be on the alert for two problems to avoid: fragments and run-on sentences. Both can weaken your writing.

■■ 14.4A FRAGMENTS

Writers often make the mistake of using fragments of sentences instead of complete sentences. The word *fragment* means "a part broken away from the whole." The "whole" in this case is a complete sentence, which must contain a subject and a verb and express a complete thought. A **sentence fragment** is a group of words that lacks a subject or verb and does not express a complete thought.

A clause is a group of words with a subject and a verb. If a clause doesn't express a complete thought, it can't stand alone. Such a clause is called a **fragment**, as you can see in the following examples.

EXAMPLES

Because my pen stopped working.

While Leo was waiting for the bus.

In each of these examples, the writer has left the reader waiting for the thought to complete itself. The writer could complete each of these fragments by adding an independent clause.

EXAMPLES

Because my pen stopped working, I stopped writing.

The rain began to fall while Leo was waiting for the bus.

After Miriam left the theater, she realized that she had forgotten her purse.

Some fragments are only groups of words. They lack a subject, a verb, or both. Examples in bold-face type follow.

EXAMPLES

I'd like that one. **The one over there.**

Here I am. **Home at last.**

I remember 1987. **My favorite year.**

It's a beautiful car. **Runs like a dream.**

The following examples show each fragment joined with words that make a complete sentence.

I'd like the one over there.

Here I am, home at last.

I remember 1987, which was my favorite year.

It's a beautiful car, and it runs like a dream.

A **sentence fragment** is a group of words that doesn't express a complete thought. Frequently, but not always, a sentence fragment lacks a subject, a verb, or both.

▋▋ 14.4B RUN-ON SENTENCES

A **run-on sentence** consists of one independent clause joined to another without the proper punctuation or a coordinating conjunction.

EXAMPLES

RUN-ON I'm afraid of the dark please turn on the light.

RUN-ON I'm afraid of the dark, please turn on the light.

It's easy to spot run-on sentences. Just remember that two or more independent clauses that are not joined by a conjunction or a semicolon make a run-on sentence. Look at the following examples for some ways to correct the run-on sentences you just read.

EXAMPLES

I'm afraid of the dark; please turn on the light. (Add a semicolon.)

I'm afraid of the dark, **so** please turn on the light. (Add a comma and coordinating conjunction *so*.)

Please turn on the light **because** I'm afraid of the dark. (Link the two sentences with the subordinating conjunction *because*.)

Please turn on the light. I'm afraid of the dark. (Use periods to punctuate the run-on as two separate sentences.)

A **run-on sentence** consists of two or more sentences joined without the proper punctuation or a conjunction.

14.5 EFFECTIVE SENTENCES

Two of the most important keys to good writing are clarity and smoothness. Several techniques are available to help you write sentences that clearly express your ideas and that allow the reader to progress smoothly and easily from one idea to another. These strategies include coordination and subordination, parallelism, and sentence variety. If you use these strategies, you are using sentence combining. This technique joins two or more sentences into one stronger sentence. The new sentence shows how your ideas are related and also makes your writing more interesting and enjoyable to read.

■■ 14.5A COORDINATION AND SUBORDINATION

One way to bring clarity and smoothness to your writing is to show the relationships between ideas in sentences. You can use **coordination** to link sentences. Combining sentences through coordination tells your reader that two thoughts are of roughly equal importance.

> EXAMPLE
>
> **My mother works in a factory,** but **my father has an office at home.**

The two boldfaced parts of the sentence have equal weight—neither is more important than the other. The two clauses are connected by the coordinating conjunction *but*, which helps to show contrast. You might prefer to downplay the contrast and simply add one thought to another

thought; in that case, the conjunction *and* would work better.

> EXAMPLE
>
> My mother works in a factory, **and** my father has an office at home.

If you wish to emphasize choice, you might choose *or* to coordinate your independent clauses.

> EXAMPLE
>
> I'll ask my mother, **or** I'll ask my father.

Coordination occurs when two sentences of equal weight are paired. The resulting sentence contains two independent clauses linked by a coordinating conjunction.

If the ideas in two sentences don't carry equal weight, you should express them in a way that clearly indicates that one idea is more important. This way of combining sentences is called **subordination** and uses subordinating conjunctions instead of coordinating conjunctions.

> EXAMPLES
>
> **Although** I like science-fiction stories, my brother prefers mysteries.
> **Although** my brother prefers mysteries, I like science-fiction stories.

In each case, the subordinating conjunction *although* makes it clear that the main thought of the sentence is expressed in the independent clause, while the subordinate clause plays only a supporting role. Your decision about whether to use coordination or subordination to combine sentences will depend on whether you think two or more ideas are of equal importance (coordination) or whether you think one of the ideas is more important (subordination).

Subordination occurs when two sentences of unequal weight are paired. The resulting sentence usually contains an independent clause and a subordinate clause linked by a subordinating conjunction. The conjunction indicates which clause is more important.

▪▪ 14.5B PARALLELISM

As a writer, you can use the technique of **parallelism** to make your sentences as clear as possible so that your readers can easily follow your ideas. To keep your sentences parallel, state similar ideas in a similar fashion. If you don't use parallelism, your sentences may be harder to follow, or they may simply "feel wrong." Consider the following nonparallel construction. Look carefully to see whether you can find any word or words in the example sentence that need to be changed in order to create parallel construction.

EXAMPLE

To fish and collecting stamps are my main hobbies.

One hobby is stated as an infinitive phrase (*to fish*), while the other is expressed as a gerund phrase (*collecting stamps*). This is not parallel construction. But by using the same grammatical form for each hobby, you can restore the parallelism of the sentence, making the sentence easier and more satisfying to read.

EXAMPLE

Fishing and collecting stamps are my main hobbies.

Following are some examples of faulty— and corrected—parallelism.

E X A M P L E S

FAULTY	The governor's committee recommended a tax increase and cutting the budget.
BETTER	The governor's committee recommended increasing taxes and cutting the budget.
BETTER	The governor's committee recommended a tax increase and a budget cut.
FAULTY	The apple was red, juicy, and tasted good.
BETTER	The apple was red, juicy, and tasty.

Parallelism occurs when two or more thoughts are expressed in the same grammatical form.

14.5C SENTENCE VARIETY

Another valuable technique in creating clear, smooth sentences is to vary the beginning, length, and rhythm of your sentences. Consider the following series of short, choppy sentences.

E X A M P L E

We unpacked the gear. We set up the tent. Ann-Marie started the campfire.

You can achieve sentence variety in at least two ways. You can use subordination to help create a smoother flow between sentences. For example, you can combine these three sentences into two by using the subordinating conjunction *after.*

E X A M P L E

After we unpacked the gear, we set up the tent. Then Ann-Marie started the campfire.

You can combine all three sentences into one by revising the sentences even more. First, use a participial phrase (*after unpacking the gear*) in place of the first sentence. Then link the third sentence by means of the subordinating conjunction *while.*

E X A M P L E

After unpacking the gear, we set up the tent while Anne-Marie started the campfire.

Sentence variety is a technique for creating clear, smooth writing by varying the beginning, length, and structure of your sentences.

▛ 14.5D SENTENCE COMBINING

Often you'll want to combine two or more short sentences into one longer one in order to give your writing a smoother flow. The art of combining sentences can help you avoid a choppy, start-and-stop feeling in your writing. It can also help you communicate the relative importance of different ideas.

> E X A M P L E
>
> My mother is strict. My father is lenient.

The previous sentences seem like two separate bulletins from the newsroom. The reader is left wondering whether the writer wants to show any relationship between these two sentences or whether one idea is more important than the other. Combining the sentences results in better writing.

> E X A M P L E
>
> Although my mother is strict, my father is lenient.

▛ 14.5E LENGTH AND COMPLEXITY OF SENTENCES

Sentence length, like paragraph length, has important effects on writing. The longer the sentences, the more serious and formal your style is likely to be. Short sentences, by contrast, tend to produce a lighter, more informal tone, but don't overdo it. The best advice is to vary sentence length. Unless you're aiming for a profound, weighty tone, avoid sentences that go on and on. At the same time, unless you're writing for beginning readers, don't write too many short, "John loves Mary" sentences in succession. Usually you'll want to create a tone somewhere between grave seriousness and bright cleverness.

Chapter 15 Using Verbs

A s you know, even the most common verbs have many different forms. In fact, the most common verbs are the ones with the most variety in forms. This chapter will help you to know the various forms of verbs so that you can choose the right one for the occasion.

15.1 PARTS OF VERBS

Verbs can be tricky to use correctly. One reason is that they have different forms for different uses. These forms are called **principal parts**–the present, the present participle, the past, and the past participle.

A verb has four principal parts. They are the **present**, the **present participle**, the **past**, and the **past participle**.

▪▪ 15.1A REGULAR VERBS

A **regular verb** is one that forms its past and past participle by adding -d or -ed to the present. All verbs form their present participle by adding -ing. For example, *knock* becomes *knocking*.

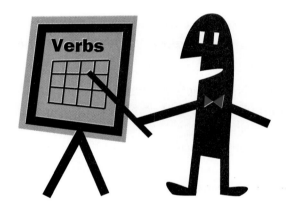

Regular Verbs			
PRESENT	PRESENT PARTICIPLE	PAST	PAST PARTICIPLE
fade	fading	faded	faded
walk	walking	walked	walked
study	studying	studied	studied
stop	stopping	stopped	stopped

Notice that regular verbs may require a spelling change when their form changes. Verbs that end with silent *e*, like *fade*, drop the *e* in the present participle. When a verb ends with a consonant and *y*, like *study*, the *y* changes to *i* in the past and past participle. When a verb ends with one consonant after a short vowel, like *stop*, the final consonant is doubled in all the other principal parts. When in doubt about spellings, look in your dictionary.

■■ 15.1B IRREGULAR VERBS

An **irregular verb** doesn't form its past and past participle by adding -*d* or -*ed* but in some other way. The following lists show six of the ways in which this occurs.

The past and past participle have the same form as the present.

PRESENT	PRESENT PARTICIPLE	PAST	PAST PARTICIPLE
burst	bursting	burst	burst
hit	hitting	hit	hit
let	letting	let	let

Others: cost, hurt, put, set, spread

The past and past participle have the same irregular form.

PRESENT	PRESENT PARTICIPLE	PAST	PAST PARTICIPLE
bring	bringing	brought	brought
buy	buying	bought	bought
catch	catching	caught	caught

Others: feel, find, hold, keep, lay, lead, leave, lose, make, say, sell, send, sit, teach, tell, win

The letter -*n* is added to the past to form the past participle.

PRESENT	PRESENT PARTICIPLE	PAST	PAST PARTICIPLE
break	breaking	broke	broken
choose	choosing	chose	chosen
speak	speaking	spoke	spoken

Others: freeze, steal

The letter - *n* is added to the present to form the past participle.

PRESENT	PRESENT PARTICIPLE	PAST	PAST PARTICIPLE
blow	blowing	blew	blown
draw	drawing	drew	drawn
drive	driving	drove	driven

Others: give, grow, know, rise, see, take, throw

The letter *i* in the present form changes to an *a* in the past and a *u* in the past participle.

PRESENT	PRESENT PARTICIPLE	PAST	PAST PARTICIPLE
begin	beginning	began	begun
drink	drinking	drank	drunk
ring	ringing	rang	rung

Others: shrink, sing, sink, spring, swim

The past and past participle are formed in various other ways.

PRESENT	PRESENT PARTICIPLE	PAST	PAST PARTICIPLE
do	doing	did	done
fall	falling	fell	fallen
bite	biting	bit	bitten

Others: be, come, eat, go, lie, ride, run, tear, wear, write

The most effective way to master the irregular verbs is to read and listen carefully. Nevertheless, a couple of the trickiest pairs deserve special attention.

▦ 15.1C PROBLEM VERBS

You may have found yourself puzzled by the verbs *lie* and *lay*, *sit* and *set*. Many students have. It isn't surprising, because they're hard to keep straight.

lie, lay

The verb *lie* means "to rest or recline." It's never followed by a direct object. Here are its principal parts.

PRESENT	PRESENT PARTICIPLE	PAST	PAST PARTICIPLE
lie	lying	lay	lain

E X A M P L E S

Our cats often **lie** (rest or recline) on the sofa.

Today they **are lying** on the hood of the car.

Bonnie says they also **lay** there yesterday.

They **have lain** on the car for about an hour.

The verb *lay* means "to put or place something." It is usually followed by a direct object. Here are its principal parts.

PRESENT	PRESENT PARTICIPLE	PAST	PAST PARTICIPLE
lay	laying	laid	laid

E X A M P L E S

Please **lay** those textbooks on the desk.

Gary **is laying** the books on the table, Mrs. Brown.

Jen **laid** the books on the windowsill last week.

Sometimes students **have laid** the books on the floor.

sit, set

The verb *sit* is something like *lie*. It means "to rest or recline in a seated position." Like *lie*, it is never followed by a direct object. See the following page for the principal parts of *sit*.

PRESENT	PRESENT PARTICIPLE	PAST	PAST PARTICIPLE
sit	sitting	sat	sat

EXAMPLES

I sometimes **sit** by the window.
My mother **is sitting** there now.
Aunt Concetta **sat** there yesterday.
I **have sat** here for more than an hour.

The verb *set* (just like *lay)* means "to put or place something." It is usually followed by a direct object. Here are its principal parts.

PRESENT	PRESENT PARTICIPLE	PAST	PAST PARTICIPLE
set	setting	set	set

EXAMPLES

Please **set** the table immediately.
My sister **is setting** the table today.
I **set** the table every day last week.
Sid and Aaron **have set** the table
  twice this month.

15.2 VERB TENSE

Verbs express time. The **tense** of a verb shows the time that the verb expresses.

■■ 15.2A SIX TENSES

The tense, or time, of a verb can be present, past, or future. In addition to these three simple tenses, there are three perfect tenses—present perfect, past perfect, and future perfect. As used here, *perfect* means "completed" or "finished."

Here are the six tenses of the irregular verb *sing.* Notice how the principal parts are used to form each tense.

The **present tense** shows action that is happening now.

PRESENT

I **sing** in the shower.

The **past tense** shows action that occurred in the past.

PAST

Gene Kelly **sang** in the rain.

The **future tense** shows action that is going to take place in the future. The word *shall* or *will* goes before the verb.

FUTURE

Whitney Houston **will sing** at the opening game of the World Series. We **will sing** tomorrow.

The **present perfect tense** shows action that occurred in the past and continues in the present. The word *have* or *has* goes before the verb.

PRESENT PERFECT

We **have sung** that song many times. Nan **has sung** "Summertime" since she was five years old.

The **past perfect tense** shows action that occurred before some other action. The word *had* goes before the verb.

PAST PERFECT

You **had sung** in the choir before last week's performance, hadn't you?

The **future perfect tense** shows action that will be completed at some specific time in the future. The words *will have* (or *shall have*) go before the verb.

FUTURE PERFECT

No one **will have sung** "The Star-Spangled Banner" so many times in one year.

15.2B CONJUGATION

To **conjugate** means to list all the singular and plural forms of a verb in its six tenses. The following chart shows the conjugation of the regular verb *walk*.

Conjugation of *walk*		
Present		
	Singular	Plural
first person	I walk	we walk
second person	you walk	you walk
third person	he, she, it walks	they walk

Past		
	Singular	Plural
first person	I walked	we walked
second person	you walked	you walked
third person	he, she, it walked	they walked

Future		
	Singular	Plural
first person	I shall/will walk	we shall/will walk
second person	you will walk	you will walk
third person	he, she, it will walk	they will walk

Present Perfect

	Singular	Plural
first person	I have walked	we have walked
second person	you have walked	you have walked
third person	he, she, it has walked	they have walked

Past Perfect

	Singular	Plural
first person	I had walked	we had walked
second person	you had walked	you had walked
third person	he, she, it had wallked	they had walked

Future Perfect

	Singular	Plural
first person	I shall/will have walked	we shall/will have walked
second person	you will have walked	you will have walked
third person	he, she, it will have walked	they will have walked

The following chart shows the conjugation of the irregular verb *begin*.

Conjugation of *begin*		

Present

	Singular	Plural
first person	I begin	we begin
second person	you begin	you begin
third person	he, she, it begins	they begin

Past

	Singular	Plural
first person	I began	we began
second person	you began	you began
third person	he, she, it began	they began

Future

	Singular	Plural
first person	I shall/will begin	we shall/will begin
second person	you will begin	you will begin
third person	he, she, it will begin	they will begin

Present Perfect

	Singular	Plural
first person	I have begun	we have begun
second person	you have begun	you have begun
third person	he, she, it has begun	they have begun

Past Perfect

	Singular	Plural
first person	I had begun	we had begun
second person	you had begun	you had begun
third person	he, she, it had begun	they had begun

Future Perfect

	Singular	Plural
first person	I shall/will have begun	we shall/will have begun
second person	you will have begun	you will have begun
third person	he, she, it will have begun	they will have begun

The most irregular English verb is *be*. It is a very important word in the language. Here is the conjugation of the verb *be*, the principal parts of which are *be, being, was,* and *been.*

Conjugation of *be*

Present

	Singular	Plural
first person	I am	we are
second person	you are	you are
third person	he, she, it is	they are

Past

	Singular	Plural
first person	I was	we were
second person	you were	you were
third person	he, she, it was	they were

Future

	Singular	Plural
first person	I shall/will be	we shall/will be
second person	you will be	you will be
third person	he, she, it will be	they will be

Present Perfect

	Singular	Plural
first person	I have been	we have been
second person	you have been	you have been
third person	he, she, it has been	they have been

Past Perfect

	Singular	Plural
first person	I had been	we had been
second person	you had been	you had been
third person	he, she, it had been	they had been

Future Perfect

	Singular	Plural
first person	I shall/will have been	we shall/will have been
second person	you will have been	you will have been
third person	he, she, it will have been	they will have been

▪▪ 15.2C AVOIDING SHIFTS IN TENSE

Since tenses show time, be careful not to shift tenses in a way that confuses the time sequence.

When Terry **gave** her speech, everyone **cheers**. (Note: With the verb *gave* in the past, the verb *cheers* can't be in the present tense. Correction: When Terry **gave** her speech, everyone **cheered**.)

15.3 ACTIVE AND PASSIVE VOICE

In addition to tense, verbs have **voice**. The voice of a verb is either **active** or **passive**. It's usually best to use the active voice in your writing.

E X A M P L E S

ACTIVE VOICE: The reader **praised** the book.
PASSIVE VOICE: The book **was praised** by the reader.

The **active voice** shows that the subject is performing the action. The **passive voice** shows that the subject is the receiver of the action of the verb.

Chapter 16 Using Pronouns

As you know, a **pronoun** is a word that takes the place of a noun. That's not all you need to remember, though. Pronouns, like verbs, have different forms and you have to use the exact form that fits what you want to say. Because you need pronouns so often, it's especially important to know how to use the correct form in the correct place. This chapter tells you how.

16.1 CASE

Case is an important part of learning about pronouns. You would never say, "Me went to the store." In this sentence the pronoun *me* sounds childish because it is in the wrong case. All nouns and pronouns have case.

Case is the form of a noun or pronoun that indicates its use in a sentence.

There are three cases in English, the nominative, the objective, and the possessive. A noun or pronoun that acts as a subject or as a predicate nominative is in the **nominative case**.

A noun or pronoun that acts as an object is in the **objective case.** The object may be a direct object, an indirect object, or the object of a preposition.

EXAMPLES

NOUN: Tashi met **Cindy** at the airport. (direct object)

PRONOUN: Phil drove **me** to the hotel. (direct object)

Tashi gave **me** a pencil. (indirect object)

Alex sits behind **me** in class. (object of a preposition)

A noun or pronoun that shows possession or ownership is in the **possessive case.**

EXAMPLES

NOUN: **Cindy's** coat had been left on the seat.

PRONOUN: The pencil is **mine**.

My book is on the desk.

(The pronoun *my* is used as an adjective.)

The following chart shows the three cases of personal pronouns.

Nominative Case					
Singular	I	you	he	she	it
Plural	we	you	they		
Objective Case					
Singular		me	you	him	her	it
Plural		us	you	them		
Possessive Case							
Singular	my	mine	your	yours	his	her	hers	its
Plural	our	ours	your	yours	their	theirs		

16.1A NOMINATIVE CASE

The nominative case of personal pronouns seldom causes problems except in these three situations.

Compound Subjects

If you use the nominative case for one of the pronouns in a compound subject, use the nominative case for the other pronouns.

EXAMPLE

She and **I** went to the beach.

(Hint: Try saying each part separately: *She* went to the beach. *I* went to the beach. Then put the nominatives together in the compound subject.)

Predicate Nominatives

The same rule for compound subjects holds true for predicate nominatives. (See also Predicate Nominatives, 14.1C.)

EXAMPLE

The fastest runners are Luis and **I**.

(When you see a linking verb, such as *are*, use the nominative case.)

In conversation, you'll usually use the objective case for predicate nominatives. "It was *me* in the gym." But avoid this usage in your writing, except in dialogue or direct quotations. (A headline writer for a New York tabloid once ignored this exception. A man, hysterical and in shock, identified a close relative who had died in an accident: "Oh, no! It's her!" he screamed. The tabloid's headline writer dutifully corrected him—"Distraught man screams,'Oh, no! It's she!'")

Pronouns with Noun Appositives

Sometimes a personal pronoun precedes a noun in apposition, as in "You girls must be tired." Such a pronoun is in the same case as the noun. (See Appositives, 20.2G.)

> E X A M P L E
>
> **We** players were excited. (Hint: Try removing the noun: *We* were excited.)

▦ 16.1B OBJECTIVE CASE

Similar questions arise with the objective case as with the nominative case. How do you deal with compound direct objects, indirect objects, and objects of prepositions? How do you choose the correct form with a noun appositive? (See also Direct Objects and Indirect Objects, 14.1B.)

Compound Direct Objects

If you use the objective case for one of the pronouns in a compound direct object, use the objective case for the other pronouns.

> E X A M P L E
>
> Amy will meet **them** and **us** in the mall. (Hint: As with compound subjects, say each part separately: Amy will meet *them* in the mall. Amy will meet *us* in the mall. Then put the two together in the compound direct object.)

Compound Indirect Objects

In using compound indirect objects, follow the same rule as for direct objects. Use the same splitting-the-compound technique to make your pronoun choices.

> E X A M P L E
>
> Gina told **her** and **me** the story. (Gina told *her* the story. Gina told *me* the story. Put the two together.)

Compound Objects of Prepositions

When using compound objects of prepositions, use the same approach as with direct objects and indirect objects.

> EXAMPLE
>
> The Oroville debaters won against **him** and **her**.

16.1C POSSESSIVE CASE

Possessive pronouns are used in three ways: (1) by themselves, (2) before nouns, (3) before gerunds. (See also Gerunds and Gerund Phrases, 13.1B.)

> EXAMPLES
>
> (1) The package on the shelf is **yours**.
> (2) Kathy fed **her** cat.
> (3) **His** arriving late annoyed me.

Notice that possessive pronouns, unlike possessive nouns, do not require an apostrophe.

> EXAMPLE
>
> The book bag is **his**, not **Mary's**.

The personal pronoun *its* can cause errors if you confuse it with the contraction *it's*, for *it is*. Ask yourself whether the *i-t-s* in your sentence means *it is*. If it does, put in the apostrophe. If it doesn't, leave the apostrophe out as in the example that follows.

> EXAMPLE
>
> **It's** true that the car's design is **its** best feature.

16.1D PROBLEM PRONOUNS

Who, Whom, Whose

The pronoun *who* also has three cases—nominative, objective, and possessive.

Nominative: who, whoever
Objective: whom, whomever
Possessive: whose

To decide which case you need, see how the word is used in the sentence. If it is a subject or predicate nominative, use the nominative case. See the examples that follow.

> EXAMPLES
>
> **Who** is calling? (subject)
> Your friend is **who**? (predicate nominative)

If the word is an object, use the objective case.

> **EXAMPLES**
>
> **Whom** did you ask? (direct object).
> (Hint: Change the order of the
> question: You did ask **whom**?)
> For **whom** did you ring? (object
> of the preposition)

The pronouns *whoever* (nominative) and *whomever* (objective) are used in the same way as *who* and *whom*.

> **EXAMPLES**
>
> **Whoever** wants to may stay for dinner.
> You may go to the dance with
> **whomever** you please.

If the word shows possession or ownership, use the possessive case.

> **EXAMPLE**
>
> **Whose** lunch is this?

16.2 PRONOUNS AND ANTECEDENTS

Remember that a pronoun takes the place of a noun. This noun is the pronoun's **antecedent**. The antecedent often appears in the same sentence as the pronoun, but it may occur in a previous sentence.

> **EXAMPLES**
>
> **Lisa** believed that **she** was right.
> The girl was **Andrée Dupres**. **She**
> looked tired.

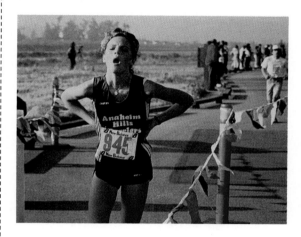

16.2A NUMBER AND GENDER

A pronoun must agree with its antecedent in number and gender. **Number** refers to whether a noun or pronoun is singular or plural. **Gender** refers to whether a noun or pronoun is masculine, feminine, or neuter.

Pronoun Gender		
Masculine	Feminine	Neuter
he, him, his	she, her, hers	it, its

The pronouns *I* and *you* and the plurals *they*, *them*, and *their* don't appear in this chart, because they don't show gender.

Pronoun antecedents are usually easy to identify.

EXAMPLES

Marilyn kept **her** purse in the locker.
The coaches discussed **their** players.

Problems with Pronoun Number

When a pronoun has two or more singular antecedents joined by *and* or *both/and*, use a plural pronoun.

EXAMPLE

Ruth **and** Inga should bring **their** cameras.

You may find it more difficult to decide which pronoun to use with singular antecedents joined by *or*, *nor*, *either/or*, or *neither/nor*. In such cases, use a singular pronoun.

EXAMPLES

Ruth **or** Inga should bring **her** camera.
Neither Ruth **nor** Inga brought **her** camera.

Problems with Pronoun Gender

Gender sometimes raises questions about pronoun usage. You may not know whether the antecedent is male or female, or the antecedent could include both males and females. At one time, people simply used the masculine form with these unclear antecedents. Today they are more likely to use both masculine and feminine forms.

EXAMPLES

Every **juror** had **his** own opinion. (former usage)
Every **juror** had **his** or **her** own opinion. (newer usage)

As with many usage problems, using the plural in the sentence may be the best solution.

EXAMPLE

All twelve **jurors** had **their** own opinion.

▰▰ 16.2B INDEFINITE PRONOUNS AS ANTECEDENTS

When an indefinite pronoun is the antecedent of a personal pronoun, the sense of the sentence will sometimes tell you whether the personal pronoun should be singular or plural. Common sense doesn't always work, though. A few pronouns—*everybody* and *everyone*, for example—are singular even though they seem as if they should be plural. Look at the following chart.

Indefinite Pronouns			
Singular Indefinite Pronouns			
anybody	either	neither	one
anyone	everybody	nobody	somebody
each	everyone	no one	someone

	Plural Indefinite Pronouns		
both	few	many	several

Singular or Plural Indefinite Pronouns				
all	any	most	none	some

A singular indefinite pronoun requires a singular personal pronoun of the correct gender.

E X A M P L E S
....

One of the women talked about **her** Chinese heritage.
Each of the passengers told **his** or **her** story.

A plural indefinite pronoun requires a plural personal pronoun. Plurals create no gender problems.

E X A M P L E S
....

Both of the pilots landed **their** planes in the fog.
Several of the rabbits jumped from **their** cages.

Agreement with an indefinite pronoun that can be either singular or plural depends on the number and gender of the object of the preposition that follows it.

E X A M P L E S
....

Most of the **currency** had lost **its** value.
Most of the **coins** had lost **their** luster.

Chapter 17 Subject-Verb Agreement

You know that every sentence must have a subject and a verb. There's more to a sentence than that, though. Your subject and verb must agree—that is, they must both be either singular or plural. Check the information in this chapter to see about subject-verb agreement.

17.1 SINGULAR AND PLURAL

A singular subject takes a singular verb. A plural subject takes a plural verb.

EXAMPLES

Mike **plays** the sax. (singular subject/singular verb)
Geese **fly** in formation. (plural subject/plural verb)

A **verb** must agree with its subject in number.

▓▓ 17.1A *YOU* AS SUBJECT

The pronoun *you* is an exception to the rule. Whether it is singular or plural, it takes a plural verb.

EXAMPLES

You are the quarterback. (singular *you*/plural verb)
You are the linebackers. (plural *you*/plural verb)

▓▓ 17.1B VERB PHRASES

A **verb phrase** is the main verb plus any helping verbs. In a sentence with a verb phrase, the first helping verb agrees with the subject. (See Verb Phrases, 12.3C.)

EXAMPLES
....

We **should be going** soon.
Jennifer **will be waiting** for us.

Singular and Plural Helping Verbs					
Singular	am	is	was	has	does
Plural	are		were	have	do

EXAMPLES
....

SINGULAR: The sky **is turning** black.
(singular *sky*/singular *is*)

PLURAL: The grapes **are going** sour.
(plural *grapes*/plural *are*)

17.2 COMMON AGREEMENT PROBLEMS

Subjects and verbs must agree in number, so watch out for the following possible problems.

▐▐ 17.2A INTERRUPTING WORDS

When other words separate a subject from a verb, be careful not to let another, closer word determine the number of the verb. Remember that the verb agrees with its subject, not with any interrupting words.

EXAMPLE
....

One of my classmates **takes** chess lessons. (*One* is the subject. *Classmates* is the object of the preposition *of*.)

Don't be distracted even by long interruptions. Go all the way back to the subject to decide on the number of the verb.

EXAMPLE
....

A **friend** of hers, one of three girls who moved from Lansing to Three Rivers, **writes** to her once or twice a year. (singular *friend*/singular *writes*; ignore the interrupting words)

▐▐ 17.2B INVERTED ORDER

Writers don't always put sentences in subject-verb order. In fact, they vary the order as part of their style. Certain kinds of sentences, though, are always written in inverted, or reverse order.

There are three common kinds of inverted sentences. The easiest way to decide on the correct verb form is to reword the sentences in subject-verb order. Questions are almost always inverted.

> EXAMPLE
> ....
> **Has** the **package** from Tokyo **arrived**? (The *package* from Tokyo *has arrived*.)

Sentences beginning with *Here* or *There* are inverted.

> EXAMPLE
> ....
> **There were** a dozen **deer** beside the road. (A dozen *deer were* beside the road. *There* is simply a sentence-starter. **NOTE:** The word *deer* can be either singular or plural. The adjective *dozen* shows that *deer* is plural.)

Writers put some sentences in verb-subject order for effect and save the key word or words for last.

> EXAMPLE
> ....
> Along the path, half hidden from view, **stood** a spectral **horse**. (A spectral *horse stood*.)

A **verb** agrees in number with its subject regardless of the order of the words.

▦ 17.2C COMPOUND SUBJECTS

A compound subject that consists of two or more singular subjects joined by *and* takes a plural verb.

> EXAMPLE
> ....
> A **car** *and* a **truck are** in the driveway.

The matter of compound subjects gets a bit more difficult when *or, either/or,* or *neither/nor* joins the subjects.

If both subjects are singular, the verb is singular.

> EXAMPLE
> ....
> The **car** *or* the **truck** has a flat tire.

If a singular subject and a plural subject are joined by *or* or *nor*, the verb agrees with the nearer subject.

EXAMPLES

Neither **Joan** *nor* her **cousins are going** to Boston.
Neither my **cousins** *nor* **I am going** to Boston.

NOTE: Since the second example is so awkward, it's best to revise the sentence: My **cousins are** not **going** to Boston, and neither **am I**.

17.2D INDEFINITE PRONOUNS

Look back at the list of indefinite pronouns in 16.2B. These pronouns require verbs that match their number. Then note the sets of examples that follow.

A singular indefinite pronoun requires a singular verb.

EXAMPLES

One of the women **is speaking**.
Each of the passengers **was telling** a story.

A plural indefinite pronoun requires a plural verb.

EXAMPLES

Both of the pilots **were landing** in dense fog.
Several of the rabbits **have jumped** from the hutch.

Agreement with an indefinite pronoun that can be either singular or plural depends on the number of the object of the preposition that follows it.

EXAMPLES

Most of the *currency* **is missing**.
Most of the *coins* **are tarnished**.
Most of the *students* **are** in class.

17.2E *DOESN'T* AND *DON'T*

The contraction *doesn't* means "does not" and is singular. The contraction *don't* means "do not" and is plural. By changing such contractions into their original two words, you will see that *doesn't, isn't, wasn't,* and *hasn't* are singular, while *don't, aren't, weren't,* and *haven't* are plural.

EXAMPLES

She **doesn't know** the law. (She *does* not know . . .)
We **don't know** it either. (We *do not* know . . .)

Chapter 18 Using Adjectives and Adverbs

Adjectives and adverbs can add life and sparkle to your sentences. In general, they don't raise puzzling questions of usage. In fact, most of the usage questions about adjectives and adverbs involve the degrees of comparison—the positive, the comparative, and the superlative. Read this chapter for hints about comparison and other facts about adjectives and adverbs.

18.1 COMPARISON OF ADJECTIVES AND ADVERBS

Sarah said, "I got 95 on my math test."

"That's a *high* mark," Thomas replied, "but I got a *higher* one. I got 97."

Ellen, who had been listening to them, said, "You both did well, but I got the *highest* mark in the class. I got 100."

These students were using different degrees of the same adjective to show comparison.

- ◎ The word *high* is the positive degree.
- ◎ The word *higher* is the comparative degree.
- ◎ The word *highest* is the superlative degree.

You can also show comparison with adverbs.

- ◎ A zebra can run **fast.**
- ◎ A cheetah can run **faster.**
- ◎ A racehorse runs the **fastest** over a long distance.

Most adjectives and adverbs show degrees of comparison by changing their form.

The **positive** degree is the basic form of an adjective or adverb. When you use it, you are showing no comparison.

> EXAMPLES
>
> I have a **new** dress. (adjective)
> A turtle moves **slowly.** (adverb)

▚ 18.1A REGULAR COMPARISONS

The **comparative** degree shows the difference between two people, things, or actions.

E X A M P L E S

My sister has a **newer** dress than I have. (adjective)

A gazelle can run **faster** than a zebra. (adverb)

The **superlative** degree shows the highest or best when three or more people, things, or actions are compared.

E X A M P L E S

My aunt has the **newest** car of anyone in our family. (adjective)

A cheetah can run the **fastest** of any animal. (adverb)

One-syllable adjectives and adverbs usually add *-er* and *-est* to form the comparative and superlative degrees.

Regular Comparisons—One-Syllable Words		
Positive	Comparative	Superlative
Adjectives		
strong	stronger	strongest
brave	braver	bravest
tall	taller	tallest
Adverbs		
near	nearer	nearest
soon	sooner	soonest

Two-syllable adjectives and adverbs sometimes add *-er* and *-est*, but most of them add the words *more* and *most*.

Regular Comparisons—Two-Syllable Words		
Positive	Comparative	Superlative
Adjectives		
busy	busier	busiest
careful	more careful	most careful
Adverbs		
quickly	more quickly	most quickly
slowly	more slowly	most slowly

There is no firm rule for deciding whether a two-syllable modifier takes *-er/-est* or *more/most*. Your best guide is your ear. If the construction sounds awkward (*usefuller, jealousest*), use *more* and *most* (*more useful, most jealous*).

Modifiers with three or more syllables add *more* and *most* to form the comparative and superlative degrees.

Regular Comparisons—Three-Syllable Words		
Positive	Comparative	Superlative
Adjectives		
generous	more generous	most generous
Adverbs		
happily	more happily	most happily

■■ 18.1B IRREGULAR COMPARISONS

If you were asked to compare the adjective *good*, you wouldn't say, *"Good, gooder, goodest."* Some modifiers, such as *good*, are compared irregularly. Here's a list showing irregular comparisons of adjectives and adverbs.

Irregular Comparisons		
Positive	Comparative	Superlative
Adjectives		
bad	worse	worst
good	better	best
many	more	most
Adverbs		
badly	worse	worst
well	better	best
much	more	most

These comparisons are complete in themselves. You never add *-er/-est* or *more/most* to any of them.

■■ 18.1C NEGATIVE COMPARISONS

The words *less* and *least* (the opposite of *more* and *most*) are used for negative comparisons.

Negative Comparisons		
Positive	Comparative	Superlative
Adjectives		
generous	less generous	least generous
Adverbs		
happily	less happily	least happily

18.2 PROBLEMS WITH MODIFIERS

Along with questions about the comparison of adjectives and adverbs, a few other problems can arise.

■■ 18.2A DOUBLE COMPARISONS

Use only one method at a time to compare adjectives and adverbs. Don't combine *-er/-est* with *more/most*. It's incorrect to say, "The Sears Tower is *more taller* than the

Empire State Building" or "Of all three ships, the *West Virginia Belle* came the *most nearest* to shore." The following examples show the correct form.

EXAMPLES

The Sears Tower is **taller** (not *more taller*) than the Empire State Building.
Of all three ships, the West Virginia Belle came the **nearest** (not *most nearest*) to shore.

▦ 18.2B DOUBLE NEGATIVES

Always avoid double negatives in your speaking and writing. A double negative is a construction that uses two negative words. The most common negative words are *no* and *not,* but there are others, such as *nothing, nobody, no one, hardly,* and *scarcely.* All *-n't* contractions are negatives. The *–n't* stands for *not.* Don't say, "We *can't hardly wait* until next season" or *"Hasn't she bought no* ticket yet?" The following examples show the correct form.

EXAMPLES

We **can hardly wait** until next year.
Hasn't she **bought** a ticket yet?

▦ 18.2C *GOOD* AND *WELL*

When the catcher in a baseball game tells his pitcher, "You done real good," he means it as praise. The pitcher has won the game,

after all–but the catcher has performed a feat, too. He has crammed three usage errors into a four-word sentence.

The catcher's sentence should have been, "You did very well." In this sentence, *well* is an adverb.

The word *good* is always an adjective.

EXAMPLE

Fernando is a **good** pitcher.

The word *well* may be an adjective or an adverb. As an adjective it has two uses.

EXAMPLES

Tony seems **well**. (He appears to be in good health.)
It's ten o'clock, and all's **well**. (Everything is satisfactory.)

Otherwise, the word *well* is an adverb.

EXAMPLE

Fernando pitched **well** this afternoon.

Chapter 19 Glossary of Usage

If you've listened to both rap lyrics and a presidential address to the nation, you know there is more than one kind of English. Complex as our language is, it can be divided into two broad categories: standard and nonstandard.

Standard English is the language of most writing. It's the form of English most widely accepted throughout the world. Nonstandard English is the language of much casual conversation. It is affected by regional and social influences. It uses expressions that are perfectly acceptable for person-to-person talk with your friends but would be out of place in a school paper, except in quoted dialogue. It might cost you points in a test or cost you a job in an interview.

Standard English is worth mastering. The following glossary deals with some common usage questions, focusing on formal and informal style.

accept, except The verb *accept* means "to receive with approval." The preposition *except* means "other than."

EXAMPLE

I **accept** your explanation **except** for one statement.

advice, advise *Advice* is a noun meaning "a recommendation." *Advise* is a verb meaning "to recommend."

EXAMPLE

My **advice** to you is to **advise** your friend to come with us.

affect, effect   Although both of these words can be used as either nouns or verbs, *affect* is usually a verb, and *effect* is usually a noun. The verb *affect* means "to influence or act upon." The noun *effect* means "a result."

EXAMPLE

The rain may **affect** our game but will have no other **effect**.

all right, alright   Like many usage matters, this involves spelling. Some readers object to the *alright* spelling. To avoid criticism, write *all right*.

EXAMPLE

Do you feel **all right**, Marcia?

all together, altogether   *All together* means "in a group." *Altogether* means "entirely."

EXAMPLE

When we sing **all together**, the result is **altogether** too loud.

a lot   Write this expression as two words, since there is no word *alot*. Avoid *a lot* in formal writing.

EXAMPLE

The bear in our backyard attracted **a lot** of attention. (More formal: The bear in our backyard attracted *much* attention.)

beside, besides   *Beside* means "at the side of." *Besides* means "except for."

EXAMPLES

I stood **beside** Marta at the counter.
No one was there **besides** us.

etc.   The Latin abbreviation *etc.* is short for *et cetera*; it means "and other things." Never use the word *and* with it, since that results in two *and*'s. Avoid *etc.* altogether in formal writing. You may occasionally use *and so forth* to substitute for *etc.*

EXAMPLE

Aldo brought bread, cheese, peanut butter, jelly, **etc.** (Formal: Aldo brought bread, cheese, peanut butter, jelly, *and so forth* for the picnic.)

fewer, less   If you are referring to more than one item, use *fewer*. If you are referring to a single quantity, use *less*.

E X A M P L E

The Bills had **fewer** losses than the Rams, but they seemed to have **less** enthusiasm.

good, well   *Good* is an adjective that modifies nouns and pronouns. *Well* is an adverb that modifies verbs.

E X A M P L E

It was a **good** performance; everyone played **well**.

have, of   Because of the similar sound of the words, writers sometimes use *of* when they should use *have*.

E X A M P L E

We should **have** (not *of*) listened to her.

hear, here   This is the kind of mistake that computer spell checkers cannot find. Both words are spelled correctly, but their uses are different. *Hear* concerns listening. *Here* means "in this place." When in doubt, remember that *ear* is part of the spelling of *hear*.

E X A M P L E

Can you **hear** the speaker from **here**?

in, into   When there is movement from outside to inside, use *into*. Otherwise, use *in*.

E X A M P L E

He walked **into** the lobby and stayed **in** it for two hours.

its, it's   *Its* is a possessive. *It's* is a contraction for *it is*. You can say about your dog:

E X A M P L E

It's sitting in **its** favorite spot.

learn, teach   When you *learn*, you gain knowledge. When you *teach*, you show how.

E X A M P L E S

Ms. O'Neill is the one who **teaches** (not *learns*) us algebra.
We **learn** it well when she **teaches** us.

lie, lay   *Lie* is an intransitive verb and doesn't take a direct object. *Lay* is a transitive verb and does take a direct object.

EXAMPLES

First the trainer taught the dog to **lie** down.

Then she taught him to **lay** his head on his paws.

like, as   Recognize the difference between the preposition *like* and the subordinating conjunction *as*. If the word is followed by a clause, the choice is *as*.

EXAMPLE

The confetti fell **like** snow, but the parade kept moving **as** (not *like*) the grand marshal had ordered.

off, off of   Do not use *off of*.

EXAMPLE

He got **off** (not *off of*) his mountain bike.

passed, past   The verb *passed* is the past tense of *pass*. The word *past* can be a noun ("a time gone by"), an adjective ("ended, just gone by"), or a preposition ("beyond").

EXAMPLES

We **passed** a sign that said, "The **past** is prologue."

Sue has driven **past** the school for the **past** half hour.

raise, rise   *Raise* is a regular verb meaning "to lift something up," "to increase," or "to grow something." It is usually followed by a direct object. *Rise* is an intransitive verb; it doesn't take a direct object. It is also an irregular verb whose principal parts are *rise, rising, rose,* and *risen*. It means "to move upward" or "to get up."

EXAMPLES

Raise the curtain. (*curtain* is a direct object)

The rooster crows when the sun **rises**.

shall, will   You may remember *shall/will* from your study of the conjugation of verbs. Except in certain questions, *will* is always acceptable.

EXAMPLES

Shall we go to the party? (*Shall* makes this question an invitation. *Will* would change the meaning of the question.)
We **will** meet at eight o'clock.

sit, set   *Set* is usually a transitive verb that takes a direct object, and *sit* is an intransitive verb that is not followed by a direct object. (See Transitive and Intransitive Verbs, 12.3D.)

EXAMPLES

Please **set** the table.
It's time for everyone to **sit** down.

than, then   *Than* is a subordinating conjunction used for comparisons. *Then* is an adverb meaning "at that time" or "next."

EXAMPLES

The lake is deeper **than** the river.
We crossed the river and **then** reached the lake.

that, which, who   As relative pronouns, *that* refers to people, animals, or things; *which* does not refer to people; and *who* refers only to people.

EXAMPLES

The girl **that** I met, the swans **that** I saw, and the photos **that** I took are all a part of my memory.
The play, **which** our class put on last week, impressed even Ms. Lee's parrot, **which** watched it from backstage.
We applauded the boy **who** played the trumpet.

their, there, they're   *Their* is a possessive pronoun. It denotes ownership. *There* is an adverb meaning "at that place." It also is used simply as a sentence starter. *They're* is a contraction of *they are*.

EXAMPLES

Their books were right **there** in the closet.
There are witnesses who insist **they're** telling the truth.

them, those *Them* is the objective case of *they*. Don't use it as a subject or an adjective in place of *those*.

EXAMPLE

Those (not *Them*) are delicious grapes, but I liked **those** (not *them)* berries even better.

to, too, two. *To* is a preposition *(to* the library) and also the sign of an infinitive *(to* go). *Too* is an adverb meaning "in addition," "more than enough," or "very." *Two* is a number.

EXAMPLES

Barbara went **to** the store **to** buy a loaf of bread.

We thought there were **too** many decorations **too.**

There were **two** balloons beside the driveway.

when, where Don't use these words directly after a linking verb in a definition.

EXAMPLE

A stampede is a sudden flight of animals, such as cattle. (Not: A stampede is *when* (or *where)* animals, such as cattle, suddenly run away.)

who, whom *Who* is the nominative form of the possessive pronoun. *Whom* is the objective form.

EXAMPLES

Who is going to the movies with us? Nicole said she was going, but I don't know with **whom**.

whose, who's *Whose* is a possessive pronoun. *Who's* is a contraction of *who is*.

EXAMPLES

Who's the player **whose** glove is missing?

Did you find out **who's** starring in the play?

your, you're *Your* is a possessive pronoun. *You're* is a contraction of *you are*.

EXAMPLES

You're the first person on **your** team to set a record.

You're my favorite person.

Chapter 20 Punctuation

T hink of punctuation marks as signals. For example, a traffic signal tells you when to stop, go, or slow down. Suppose you tried to read a paragraph or a story that had no punctuation—no periods, commas, or quotation marks. You'd get lost in no time, with the ideas running into one another. Punctuation marks are signals that help to separate and clarify ideas in writing.

20.1 END MARKS

Every sentence ends with one of three punctuation marks: a period, a question mark, or an exclamation point.

20.1A PERIODS

Always put a **period** at the end of a declarative sentence. A declarative sentence makes a statement.

> E X A M P L E
>
> My family visited the Metropolitan Museum of Art**.**

Use a **period** to end a declarative sentence.

An imperative sentence is one that gives a command or makes a request.

Imperative sentences usually end with a period.

> E X A M P L E S
>
> Enter the music store here**.**
> Please direct me to the country music CD's**.**

Use a **period** to end most imperative sentences.

20.1B QUESTION MARKS

An interrogative sentence is one that asks a question. Use a **question mark** at the end of an interrogative sentence.

EXAMPLES

Where can we find the costume exhibit?
Have you seen the Chinese vases?

Use a **question mark** to end an interrogative sentence.

20.1C EXCLAMATION POINTS

An exclamatory sentence is one that shows strong emotion. Put an **exclamation point** at the end of an exclamatory sentence.

EXAMPLE

What a large museum this is!

Use an **exclamation point** to end an exclamatory sentence.

Sometimes an imperative sentence shows strong emotion. End this kind of sentence with an exclamation point.

EXAMPLE

Don't touch that painting!

Use an **exclamation point** to end an imperative sentence that shows strong emotion.

20.2 COMMAS

When you speak, you naturally pause in certain places to make your meaning clear to your listeners. Similarly, when you write, you use **commas** to separate certain words or to set them off from the rest of the sentence. Like pauses in speaking, commas in writing help make your language clear and understandable.

20.2A ITEMS IN A SERIES

One important use of commas is to separate a series of items. The items may be words or groups of words.

EXAMPLES

Cabbage, broccoli, and cauliflower are all members of the mustard family.
You can boil, steam, or saute vegetables.
Lisa planted flowers along the walk, around the big tree, and in the backyard.

Use a **comma** to separate three or more items in a series.

▦ 20.2B COMPOUND SENTENCES

Another important use of commas is to separate the parts of a compound sentence. Remember that a compound sentence contains two or more independent clauses.

> **EXAMPLES**
>
> Our house is painted blue, but all the other houses on our street are white.
> Andrew dislikes old songs, Rebecca hates rap, but Nick likes all kinds of music.

Use a **comma** to separate the clauses in a compound sentence.

▦ 20.2C SEPARATION OF ADJECTIVES

Commas sometimes separate two or more adjectives that come before a noun.

> **EXAMPLES**
>
> The long, sad movie made us cry.
> We enjoyed the cold, snowy day.

Use a **comma** or **commas** to separate two or more adjectives before a noun if each adjective modifies the noun alone.

However, if the first adjective modifies the combination of the second adjective and the noun, don't use a comma between the adjectives.

> **EXAMPLES**
>
> I'll meet you by the old oak tree.
> Hal owns a fierce brown dog.

If you want to test whether or not to use a comma, put the word *and* between the adjectives. If the *and* sounds silly (fierce *and* brown dog), don't use a comma.

▦ 20.2D INTRODUCTORY ELEMENTS

Use a comma after some words or phrases at the beginning of a sentence. For example, you should set off an introductory word such as *yes, no,* or *well* from the rest of the sentence with a comma. Also use a comma after an introductory phrase.

> E X A M P L E
>
> No**,** you may not read my diary.

Use a **comma** after a word such as *yes, no,* or *well* at the beginning of a sentence.

Imagine saying the example sentences aloud. Wouldn't you pause after *no* and *well*? Thinking about how you would say sentences like these may help you remember where to use commas.

Use a comma after a prepositional phrase (or a series of prepositional phrases) at the beginning of a sentence. Also use a comma after a dependent clause at the beginning of a sentence.

> E X A M P L E S
>
> By the third inning, our team had scored three runs.
> Until the day after tomorrow, Sharon will be busy writing her paper.

Use a **comma** after one or more prepositional phrases that begin a sentence.

20.2E INTERRUPTERS

Sometimes a sentence contains an interrupter, a word or phrase that seems to interrupt the flow of the sentence.

> E X A M P L E
>
> Some sentences, **for example,** contain an interrupter.

The interrupter (*for example* above) is usually not an essential part of the sentence. You could remove the interrupter without changing the sentence's basic meaning. Set off such words or phrases from the rest of a sentence with commas.

> E X A M P L E S
>
> That painting, **in my opinion,** is beautiful.
> This drawing, **however,** shows little skill.

Use **commas** to set off a word or phrase that interrupts the flow of a sentence.

Notice that when expressions of this kind appear at the beginning or end of a sentence, they are also set off with a comma. Here is an example.

> E X A M P L E
>
> **By the way,** have you visited the museum recently?

20.2F DIRECT ADDRESS

In writing, you may address a person directly by name. When you use direct address, set the name off from the rest of the sentence with a comma or commas.

> E X A M P L E S
> ....
>
> **Mrs. Marquez,** what is a quasar?
> Please describe the moon's surface,
> **Elaine.**
> The sun, **Alan,** is merely another star.

Use **commas** to set off the name of a person addressed directly.

20.2G APPOSITIVES

Appositive are words or groups of words that explain or identify the nouns they follow. If an appositive gives extra information about the noun but is not essential to the meaning of the sentence, you should set it off with commas.

> E X A M P L E
> ....
>
> My youngest sister, **Leonie,** is a carpenter.

Notice that the appositive, *Leonie,* gives extra information about the noun *sister.* Without the appositive, the sentence still makes sense:

> E X A M P L E
> ....
>
> My youngest sister is a carpenter.

If you can remove a phrase from a sentence in this way, you probably need to set that phrase off with commas.

> E X A M P L E S
> ....
>
> My best friend, **Yoskiko,** wrote that poem.
> That book belongs to Mr. Greenbaum, **my history teacher.**

Use a **comma** or **commas** to set off an appositive that is not essential to the meaning of the sentence.

Some appositives, on the other hand, are necessary to identify the nouns they follow. Don't use commas to set off this type of appositive.

> E X A M P L E
> ....
>
> Maya acted in the play *Our Town.*

There are many different plays. *Our Town* is a particular play that Maya acted in, so no comma is needed.

20.2H NONESSENTIAL ELEMENTS

A comma or commas are used to set off nonessential elements in a sentence. A nonessential element is a word, phrase, or clause that can be removed from a sentence without changing the basic meaning of the sentence.

> EXAMPLE
>
> The stream, which is very pretty, overflows its banks every spring.

Use **commas** to set off nonessential elements in a sentence.

Don't use commas with an essential element in a sentence. An essential word, phrase, or clause contains information that is needed to identify a person, place, or thing in a sentence.

> EXAMPLES
>
> The stream that passes my house overflows its banks every spring.
> The runner who crossed the finish line first is my sister.

20.2I DATES

When you write a date, use a comma to separate the day and the year. Also put a comma between the year and any words that follow it.

> EXAMPLES
>
> May 28, 1994
> October 5, 1980, is the day I was born.

Place a **comma** between the day and the year in a date. If the date is contained within a sentence, put a comma after the year.

Don't use a comma after the month when only the month and the year are given.

> EXAMPLE
>
> The earthquake took place in September 1993.

20.2J ADDRESSES

When an address appears within a sentence, use commas to separate the parts of the address.

EXAMPLES

My address is 1125 State Street, Minneapolis, Minnesota, and I love to get mail!

We traveled to Paris, France, and Rome, Italy, last summer.

Use a **comma** between street and city names, between city and state names, and between city or state and country names. Also use a comma to separate the last item in an address from the rest of the sentence.

Don't use a comma between an abbreviation for a state name and a ZIP code.

EXAMPLE

My address is 1125 State Street, Minneapolis, MN 70935.

■■ 20.2K LETTERS

Always use a comma after the salutation of a friendly letter.

EXAMPLES

Dear Lucinda,
Dear Aunt Rosita,

Use a comma after the closing of a friendly letter or a business letter.

EXAMPLES

Your friend,
Fondly,
Sincerely yours,

To help you remember to use commas in salutations and closings, think of them as elements that you must set off from other parts of the letter.

Use a **comma** after the salutation of a friendly letter and after the closing of a friendly letter or a business letter.

20.3 SEMICOLONS

Like a comma, a **semicolon** indicates a pause and separates elements in a sentence. In fact, you can think of a semicolon as standing for a longer pause or a stronger separation than a comma does.

▪▪ 20.3A COMPOUND SENTENCES

A compound sentence contains two or more main clauses. You often join the main clauses with a comma and *and, or,* or *but.* However, when you don't use *and, or,* or *but,* you must separate the main clauses with a semicolon.

> E X A M P L E S
>
> José wrote the song**;** we are performing it.
> The melody is nice**;** the words are silly.

Use a **semicolon** to separate main clauses not joined by *and, or,* or *but.*

You can use other transitional words, such as *however, therefore, besides, consequently, nevertheless, furthermore,* and *moreover,* to link the main clauses of a compound sentence. To join the main clauses, use a semicolon.

Use a **semicolon** to separate main clauses joined by a transitional word such as *however, therefore,* or *moreover.*

> E X A M P L E S
>
> I am not fond of folk music**; however,** I love jazz.
> The concert sold out early**; consequently,** I was unable to buy tickets.

(Put a **comma** after transitional words, such as *however* and *consequently*.)

20.4 COLONS

Use a **colon** in the following places: before lists of items (as in this sentence), after the greeting in some letters, and in time expressions written in numerals.

▪▪ 20.4A LISTS OF ITEMS

Within a sentence, a colon often sets off a list of items from the words that come before it. A term such as *the following* often introduces the list.

> E X A M P L E S
>
> Please send the following items**:** two note pads, one box of pencils, and a large eraser.
> The recipe calls for these ingredients**:** flour, sugar, baking soda, eggs, water, and salt.

Don't use a colon after a verb or a preposition.

> ### EXAMPLES
>
> **INCORRECT** Please send: two note pads, one box of pencils, and a large eraser. (colon used incorrectly after a verb)
>
> **CORRECT** Please send two note pads, one box of pencils, and a large eraser.
>
> **CORRECT** The recipe calls for flour, sugar, baking soda, eggs, water, and salt.

▜▛ 20.4B LETTERS

Always use a colon after the greeting in a business letter. In other kinds of letters, use a comma, not a colon.

> ### EXAMPLES
>
> Dear Sir or Madam**:**
> Dear Ms. Jamal**:**

Use a **colon** after the salutation of a business letter.

▜▛ 20.4C TIME

Use a colon with numerals that indicate the time. Place the colon between the hour and the minute.

> ### EXAMPLE
>
> 5:45 A.M.

Use a **colon** between numerals indicating hours and minutes.

20.5 QUOTATION MARKS

Quotation marks are used in many different ways as a form of punctuation.

▜▛ 20.5A DIRECT QUOTATIONS

Direct quotation is the use of a person's own words. A direct quotation lets your readers know that you are telling them exactly what the person said. Put quotation marks around the person's words. Use commas to set off the quotation from the rest of the sentence.

> ### EXAMPLES
>
> President Franklin D. Roosevelt said, "The only thing we have to fear is fear itself."
> "Roosevelt served as President during the Great Depression," said Manuel.
> "Social Security," declared Rhoda, "was Roosevelt's finest achievement."

Use **quotation marks** to enclose a person's exact words.

Be sure to place other punctuation marks correctly. Always place a comma or a period ending a quotation before the quotation mark. Also place a question mark or exclamation point that is part of the person's words before the quotation mark.

EXAMPLES

Mr. Romano asked, "Did you finish the assignment?"
"Watch out!" shouted the construction worker.

If the person's exact words are not a question or an exclamation, place the punctuation mark after the quotation mark.

EXAMPLE

Did the announcer say, "We'll be right back"?

Remember one more point. If you tell what a person says without giving the person's exact words, don't use quotation marks. This kind of quotation is called an indirect quotation.

EXAMPLES

Manuel said that Roosevelt served as President during the Great Depression.
Rhoda claimed that Social Security was Roosevelt's greatest achievement.

Do not use **quotation marks** to enclose an indirect quotation.

20.5B TITLES

Also use quotation marks to enclose the titles of most short pieces of writing. Such pieces include stories, poems, songs, articles, and book chapters.

EXAMPLES

Last week we read the poem "The Raven," by Edgar Allan Poe.
Poe's short story "The Tell-Tale Heart" is terrifying.
For my paper, I found a magazine article entitled "Edgar Allan Poe's Chamber of Horrors."

Use **quotation marks** to enclose titles of stories, poems, songs, articles, and book chapters.

20.6 HYPHENS

Hyphens have two main uses: to indicate a break in a word and to join parts of a word.

▦ 20.6A WORD DIVISION

When a whole word will not fit unbroken at the end of a line, a hyphen shows that the word continues on the next line.

> **EXAMPLE**
>
> The Baseball Hall of Fame was **established** in 1939.

Use a **hyphen** to divide a word at the end of a line.

Always divide a word between its syllables. Use a dictionary to check the correct syllable division.

▦ 20.6B COMPOUND WORDS

A compound word is a word made up of two or more smaller words. In some compound nouns, hyphens join the smaller words.

> **EXAMPLES**
>
> My **sister-in-law** was made a **trustee** of the company.
> Her **great-grandmother** was the first **lieutenant-governor** of the state.

Use **hyphens** in certain compound words.

Many compound words don't contain hyphens. If you wonder about any such words, check your dictionary.

▦ 20.6C NUMBERS AND FRACTIONS

When writing numbers in words, use hyphens for numbers above twenty and below one hundred.

> **EXAMPLE**
>
> **Twenty-seven** girls and **thirty-eight** boys registered for the volleyball tournament.

Use a **hyphen** to join the parts of the numbers twenty-one through ninety-nine.

Sometimes you need to use hyphens in fractions. If a fraction is used as an adjective, it requires a hyphen.

> **EXAMPLE**
>
> This vote requires a **two-thirds** majority.

Use a **hyphen** in a fraction that acts as an adjective.

To tell whether a fraction functions as an adjective, look for a noun after the fraction. In the example above, the fraction *two-thirds* precedes the noun *majority*. The fraction *two-thirds* is an adjective modifying *majority*. Therefore, you need to use a hyphen.

NOTE: Do not use a hyphen in a fraction that acts as a noun.

EXAMPLE

Exactly **two thirds** of the students are here now.

Notice that in this example no noun immediately follows the fraction. The fraction *two thirds* stands by itself and acts as a noun.

20.6D PREFIXES AND SUFFIXES

When you write words that contain prefixes and suffixes, you generally join the prefix or suffix directly with the root word to form a new word. However, you must always use a hyphen to join certain prefixes and suffixes to a root word.

EXAMPLES

The speaker appeared **self-conscious.**
The **ex-president** of the club attended the meeting.
We greeted the **president-elect.**

Use a **hyphen** with the prefixes *self-* and *ex-* and the suffix *-elect.*

20.7 APOSTROPHES

Apostrophes have two important uses. One is to indicate possession. The other is to stand for a missing letter or letters in a contraction.

20.7A POSSESSIVE FORMS OF NOUNS

To show that a person or thing owns something, use the possessive form of the noun that names that person or thing. When writing the possessive form of a noun, remember to use an apostrophe.

Singular Nouns

When writing the possessive form of a singular noun, always add an apostrophe and *s* to the end of the noun.

EXAMPLES

The dog**'s** bone is in the backyard.
Ivy is growing on the building**'s** walls.
The garden is our class**'s** project.
That is Ines**'s** sweater.
His daughter-in-law**'s** name is Viola.

Use an **apostrophe** and *s* to form the possessive of a singular noun.

Sometimes people confuse the possessive form of a singular noun with the plural form of the noun. Because an *s* often appears in both forms, the mistake is understandable.

> E X A M P L E S
>
> **SINGULAR NOUN:** girl
> **PLURAL NOUN:** girls
> **SINGULAR POSSESSIVE:** girl's

To avoid this confusion, remember that possessive nouns need an apostrophe.

Plural Nouns

There are two different rules to remember for forming the possessive of plural nouns. As noted above, many plural nouns end with *s*. To form the possessive of these plural nouns, just add an apostrophe.

> E X A M P L E S
>
> Where is the boys' locker room?
> The Andersons' apartment is on the fourth floor.

Use an **apostrophe** to form the possessive of a plural noun ending with s.

Some nouns have irregular plurals—that is, plurals that don't end with *s*. Treat such a plural noun as if it were a singular noun. That is, add an apostrophe and *s*. Take careful note of the examples that follow.

> E X A M P L E S
>
> That store sells women's clothing.
> The children's mother will be here in a few minutes.

Use an **apostrophe** and s to form the possessive of a plural noun that does not end with s.

20.7B POSSESSIVE FORMS OF PRONOUNS

While all possessive nouns contain apostrophes, the possessive forms of most pronouns do not. Never use an apostrophe in the possessive form of a personal pronoun. Personal pronouns include such words as *yours, hers,* and *its*.

> E X A M P L E S
>
> Is this **your** book? Is this **yours**?
> **Her** hair is brown. **Hers** is brown.

Do not use an **apostrophe** in the possessive form of a personal pronoun.

It's correct to use an apostrophe in the possessive form of one kind of pronoun: an indefinite pronoun. An indefinite pronoun is one that doesn't refer to a specific person or thing. Here are some indefinite pronouns: *anyone, everybody, nobody, one, someone.* Form the possessive of an indefinite pronoun just as if it were a noun–by adding an apostrophe and *s.*

> E X A M P L E S
> ....
> Everyone**'s** plate is empty.
> Someone**'s** dog trampled the flower bed.

Use an **apostrophe** and s to form the possessive of an indefinite pronoun.

■■ 20.7C CONTRACTIONS

Another important use for apostrophes is in forming contractions. A contraction is a word formed by combining two words in a way that leaves out one or more letters. The apostrophe takes the place of the missing letter or letters.

> E X A M P L E S
> ....
> **He is** my brother. **He's** my brother.
> We **do not** give refunds. We **don't** give refunds.
> **It is** time to leave now. **It's** time to leave now.
> I think **we have** won. I think **we've** won.

Use an **apostrophe** to take the place of a missing letter or letters in a contraction.

Since the apostrophe stands for one or more missing letters, be sure to put the apostrophe in the right place. When writing a contraction, ask yourself what letter or letters the apostrophe stands for.

■■ 20.7D SPECIAL PLURALS

A less common use of apostrophes is in forming some special plurals. Use an apostrophe in the plural forms of letters, numbers, and words that stand for themselves, for example, the letter *m*, the number *5*, or the word *and.*

> E X A M P L E S
> ....
> How many *m*'**s** are there in *recommend*?
> These numbers look like *5*'**s**, but they should be *3*'**s**.
> This writer uses too many *and*'**s**.

Use an **apostrophe** to form the plural of letters, numbers, and words that stand for themselves.

20.8 PARENTHESES AND DASHES

Punctuation marks help writers make their meaning clear to the reader in different ways. One important way is to make the relationships between words and between ideas clear. Two kinds of punctuation marks writers use for this purpose are parentheses and dashes.

■■ 20.8A PARENTHESES

Use **parentheses** to set off extra information within a sentence. The information in parentheses is not as important as the main part of the sentence.

> EXAMPLES
>
> Elizabeth Blackwell (1821-1910) was the first woman doctor in the United States.
>
> With her sister, Emily Blackwell (also a doctor), and Marie Zackrzewska, Blackwell founded the New York Infirmary for Women and Children.

Use **parentheses** to set off added information that is not of major importance to the sentence.

When you include parentheses in a sentence, check to see whether you have used them correctly. Removing the words in parentheses should leave a sentence that is still complete and makes good sense.

■■ 20.8B DASHES

Like parentheses, a pair of **dashes** can set off extra information in a sentence. But dashes call more attention to the words set off.

> EXAMPLES
>
> The warp—not the woof—is the lengthwise yarn on a loom.
>
> Please show the yarn—if you can find it—to Mrs. Rodriguez.

Use **dashes** to set off and call attention to extra information in a sentence.

Use a single dash to signal an interruption or a sudden change of thought.

> EXAMPLES
>
> Take a look at this—now, where did I put that thing?
>
> Put the ham in the refrigerator before the dog—whoops, too late!

Chapter 21 Capitalization

Like punctuation marks, capital letters give your readers information about the meaning of your words. For example, a capital letter can mark the beginning of a sentence or signal a proper noun—the name of a specific person, place, or thing. The use of capital letters is called **capitalization**.

21.1 FIRST WORDS AND THE WORD *I*

These may be the two situations in which you use capital letters most frequently in your own writing: when you start a new sentence and when you write the word *I*.

■■ 21.1A FIRST WORD OF SENTENCE

Sentences can end with either a period, a question mark, or an exclamation point. But all sentences begin the same way—with a capital letter.

> EXAMPLE
>
> **T**he first game of baseball was played on June 19, 1846.

Begin every sentence with a **capital letter**.

■■ 21.1B FIRST WORD OF DIRECT QUOTATION

This rule also applies to sentences that are direct quotations. A direct quotation gives a person's exact words.

> EXAMPLE
>
> George Washington said, "**D**iscipline is the soul of an army."

Use a **capital letter** to begin a direct quotation that is a complete sentence.

▪▪ 21.1C THE WORD *I*

Always write the word *I* as a capital letter.

> EXAMPLE
>
> Rachel wrote me a letter, but **I** never received it.

Always **capitalize** the word *I*.

21.2 PROPER NOUNS

A noun is a part of speech that denotes people, places, things, qualities, and acts. Common nouns, like *cat, boy,* or *city,* are used to talk about a whole class of things or any member of that class. A common noun is never capitalized, except when it is the first word in a sentence. Proper nouns, like *Tigger, Jeff,* or *Minneapolis,* refer to specific and unique things, people, or places. A proper noun should always begin with a capital letter.

▪▪ 21.2A NAMES

All proper nouns begin with a capital letter. Many proper nouns are the names of people. Always begin a person's name with a capital letter.

> EXAMPLES
>
> The team captain is **A**ndrea **M**arquez.
> My favorite author is **L**aurence **Y**ep.

Capitalize the names of people.

Initials are a shortened form of people's names. Use capital letters for initials. Also capitalize the abbreviations *Sr.* and *Jr.* that follow some people's names.

> EXAMPLES
>
> The winners are **J. N.** Field and **L. D.** Todd.
> Today's speaker is Harold **M.** Farber, **Jr.**

Names of People

In addition to capitalizing people's names, you should also capitalize the names of groups of people. Groups include nationalities, races, and religions.

> EXAMPLES
>
> Many immigrants in the United States are **M**exicans.
> In South Korea, many of the people are **B**uddhists.
> Several authors contributed articles to the anthology about **A**sians in North America.

Capitalize the names of nationalities, races, and religions.

Names of Places

Like the names of specific people, the names of specific places always begin with a capital letter. For example, you should capitalize the names of streets and highways. Notice that both the actual name and the word *street* or *place* or *highway*–or any similar word–begin with a capital letter.

EXAMPLES

Follow **P**ine **B**oulevard to **H**olter **A**venue.

The house is at the corner of **E**lm **S**treet and **B**ryant **P**lace.

Capitalize the names of streets and highways.

The names of cities and towns, counties, states, and countries begin with capital letters.

EXAMPLES

My home is **G**reenburg, which is in **S**mith **C**ounty.

We drove through **N**ew **H**ampshire and **M**aine and then into **C**anada.

Capitalize the names of towns, cities, counties, states, and countries.

Sections of a country often have names. You should use a capital letter for these names as well.

EXAMPLES

Autumn is magnificent in **N**ew **E**ngland.

The climate of the **S**outhwest is hot and dry.

Capitalize the name of a section of a country.

NOTE: In your writing, you may use points of the compass (east, west, north, south) to indicate direction–not as names of parts of the country. Do not capitalize words like *east* and *west* that simply indicate direction.

EXAMPLE

We headed **southwest** across the plain.

The names of geographical features such as continents, mountains, islands, and bodies of water also begin with a capital letter.

EXAMPLES

The world's largest continent is **A**sia.

The **P**acific **O**cean covers one third of the earth's surface.

The **C**olorado **R**iver flows from the **R**ocky **M**ountains to the **G**ulf of **C**alifornia.

Capitalize the names of geographical locations.

In addition to places on Earth, most names of places in outer space are also capitalized. These include the names of planets and stars.

EXAMPLE

Is that point of light **Venus** or the **North Star**?

Capitalize the names of planets and stars.

Do not capitalize *sun* and *moon*. Do not capitalize *earth* when the word *the* comes before it.

Names of Things

Proper nouns also include names of specific things, such as buildings (the Washington Monument), books (*A Wrinkle in Time*), events (Veterans Day), and organizations (World Wildlife Fund). Only the names of specific things begin with capital letters. Some of the things whose names you should capitalize are described below.

Things That are Built or Made

People give names to many things they make or build, including ships and aircraft, buildings and monuments, and brands of products.

EXAMPLES

Christopher Columbus commanded the *Santa Maria*.
The space shuttle *Columbia* made its first flight in 1981.
Tourists can take elevators to the top of the **Empire State Building** and the **World Trade Center**.
Which brand of soap do you prefer, **Cleanso** or **Washtime**?

Capitalize the names of ships, aircraft, spacecraft, buildings, monuments, and the brand names of products.

Organizations You should also capitalize the names of groups, including organizations, such as the American Red Cross; businesses, such as General Motors; and institutions, such as Cornell University.

If you are concerned about animals, you can contribute to the **H**umane **S**ociety.

We called **M**ountaintop to reserve our flight.

Doctors at **M**emorial **H**ospital treated the child.

Capitalize the names of organizations, businesses, and institutions.

Events   The names of events also start with a capital letter. Events include days of the week, months, and holidays.

EXAMPLES

DAY OF THE WEEK: Sunday
MONTH: February
HOLIDAY: Presidents' **D**ay

In addition, historical events—for example, World War II—should be capitalized.

EXAMPLES

On the fourth Thursday in November, people in the United States celebrate **T**hanksgiving.

The **B**attle of **B**ull **R**un is a famous battle of the **C**ivil **W**ar.

Capitalize the names of events.

Written Works   Written works include books, magazines, stories, songs—anything that someone writes or composes. You should capitalize the names of such works.

Use capital letters for the first word, the last word, and other important words in the name. For example, note the capitalization of this title: *The Wind in the Willows*. The first word, *The*, is capitalized even though it is not an important word. (Unimportant words include prepositions like *in* and *of*, and the articles *a, an*, and *the*.) The important words *Wind* and *Willows* begin with a capital letter, but the unimportant words *in* and *the* do not.

EXAMPLES

I found the poem "**T**he **B**ells" in a book called *The Poems of Edgar Allan Poe*.

Our school newspaper, *Rangeley Review*, ran an article entitled "**N**ew **H**umanities **P**rogram **P**roposed at **R**angeley."

My latest song is "**M**oving in the **F**ast **L**ane."

Notice that the titles of long works, such as books, newspapers, and magazines, are written in italic type. When you write such titles, you should underline them. If you are using a computer and your printer can print in italic type, put such titles in italics instead of underlining them. In contrast, titles of shorter works, such as stories, articles, and songs, are enclosed by quotation marks. (For more information, see 20.5B.)

Capitalize the first word, the last word, and all important words in the titles of books, magazines, newspapers, stories, articles, poems, and musical compositions.

▚ 21.2B TITLES OF PEOPLE

Titles used before people's names begin with a capital letter. Capitalize abbreviations of titles too.

E X A M P L E S
....

Our class met with **M**ayor Poletti and **C**ouncilwoman Stein.
Tomorrow the speakers will be **D**r. Chen and **M**rs. Farber.

Capitalize a title or an abbreviation of a title used before a person's name.

Sometimes a title takes the place of a person's name. For instance, you may address a person directly by using his or her title. When addressing a doctor, you might say, "Hello, Dr. Harper" or "Hello, Doctor." When you write a title alone in direct address, capitalize the title and spell it out completely.

E X A M P L E S
....

What are your orders, **C**aptain?
Yes, **C**oach, we did our push-ups.

Capitalize the title of a person when it is used alone in direct address.

When you write a person's title alone in ways other than direct address, do not capitalize it.

E X A M P L E
....

The mayor and the councilperson spoke about the town's recycling program.

There is one exception. Always capitalize the title *President* when it refers to the incumbent President of the United States.

EXAMPLES

Anita is the president of the stamp club. The **P**resident gave a press conference yesterday in Washington.

Some titles of people show family relationships. For example, the word *aunt* is a title when it comes before a person's name, as in *Aunt Mary*. This kind of title, when it has no name after it, can also indicate a particular person. Words such as *Mother* and *Dad* often stand alone to refer to a person's parents. Capitalize a title like *Aunt* when it comes before a person's name or when it stands alone. Capitalize *Mother* and *Dad* and so forth when they are used alone.

EXAMPLES

Suzanne received a letter from **U**ncle Marcel.
Would you please mail this letter for me, **D**ad?

Capitalize titles showing family relationships when they are used before a name or alone in direct address.

Sometimes words showing family relationships are used without a name but have a possessive noun or pronoun in front of them. Do not capitalize such words of family relationship.

EXAMPLES

Suzanne received a letter from her uncle.
Suzanne's mother mailed the letter.

21.3 PROPER ADJECTIVES

Proper adjectives are adjectives that come from proper nouns.

EXAMPLES

Spain–Spanish
Africa–African

Like the nouns they are based on, proper adjectives should be capitalized.

EXAMPLE

For lunch, Sheila had roast beef on **F**rench bread with **R**ussian dressing.

Capitalize proper adjectives.

Chapter 22 Italics, Numbers, and Abbreviations

Editors of newspapers and magazines rely on guides called style sheets. These style sheets tell the editors how to deal with countless matters of punctuation, capitalization, and spelling. Three of the matters you would find on any style sheet are covered in this chapter—how to use italics, how to write numbers, and how to handle abbreviations.

22.1 ITALICS (UNDERLINING)

In your reading, you may have noticed certain words printed in slanting type, called **italics**. (*This sentence is printed in italics.*) When you write, you use underlining in place of italics. Some uses of underlining follow.

In printed material, words, letters, and numbers that stand for themselves are usually in italics. The titles of certain works are also put in italics. When you write by hand or use a typewriter, you can't use italics, so you use underlining instead. If you have a computer, however, you may choose either underlining or italics. Review how to select underlining and italics in your word processing system. Use either one for the purposes described in this section.

■■ 22.1A WORDS, NUMBERS, AND LETTERS

Use underlining or italics to highlight words, letters, and numbers that stand for themselves. To help you understand how a word may stand for itself, compare the sentences in the examples on the next page.

EXAMPLES

The tire was flat.
The word *flat* has many different
meanings.

In the first sentence, *flat* describes the
tire. In the second sentence, the word *flat*
itself is being discussed.

EXAMPLES

ON A COMPUTER   You used the word *so*
three times in one sentence.
ON A TYPEWRITER   You left out
the <u>h</u> in <u>telephone</u>.
HANDWRITTEN   Is that number a
<u>1</u> or a <u>7</u>?

Underline or use **italics** for words, letters, and
numbers that stand for themselves.

22.1B TITLES

Another use of underlining or italics is to
indicate the titles of some written works.
Generally, underline names of long works
such as books, magazines, newspapers, and
plays. Also underline names of movies and
television series.

EXAMPLES

I read *The Call of the Wild*, a novel by
Jack London.
Time and *Newsweek* are both news
magazines.

Underline or use i**talics** for titles of books
magazines, newspapers, plays, movies, and
television series.

22.2 NUMBERS

You can write numbers in two ways:
spelled out (for example, *five*) or as numerals (for example, *5*). There are several
rules that explain when to write numbers in
numerals and when to spell them out.

22.2A NUMERALS

If you can spell out a number in one or two
words, you should usually do so. For
example, spell out *eleven*, *twenty-five*, and
three million. If a number is longer than two
words, write it as a numeral–for example,
527 or *3,914*.

EXAMPLES

My father is **forty-two** years old.
Teresa received **one hundred** dollars.
There are **5,280** feet in a mile.
Earth is **93,000,000** miles from the sun.

Spell out **numbers** that you can write in one or
two words. Write numbers of more than two
words as **numerals**.

Don't begin a sentence with a numeral. Spell out any number, even one longer than two words, that begins a sentence.

> E X A M P L E
>
> **Three hundred sixty-five** days make one year.

Spell out a **number** at the beginning of a sentence.

If writing a large number in words seems awkward, you can reword the sentence so that the number isn't at the beginning.

> E X A M P L E S
>
> **One thousand two hundred thirty-five** students attend Highpoint Middle School.
> Highpoint Middle School has **1,235** students.

22.2B ORDINAL NUMBERS

Always spell out each ordinal number. **Ordinal numbers** are numbers that show order, such as *first*, *second*, *third*, and so on.

> E X A M P L E S
>
> I am my parents' **second** child.
> Today is my mother's **thirty-fifth** birthday.

Spell out **ordinal numbers**.

22.3 ABBREVIATIONS

Abbreviations are shortened forms of words. Writers use abbreviations in place of whole words to save space or to make writing a word easier. Many abbreviations use capital letters; most end with a period.

22.3A USE OF PERIODS IN ABBREVIATIONS

> E X A M P L E
>
> **Mrs.** Young arrived promptly at 4:30 **P.M.** on Wednesday.

Use a period after most **abbreviations**.

22.3B ABBREVIATION OF SOME TITLES

Abbreviations are useful in notetaking, but avoid using most abbreviations in formal writing. Some abbreviations, however, are customary even in formal writing. For example, titles used before people's names, such as *Mr.* and *Dr.*, are usually abbreviated. In fact, the title *Ms.*, which was coined to be used in place of either *Miss* or *Mrs.*, doesn't stand for any longer word at all!

> E X A M P L E S
>
> **Mr.** and **Mrs.** Han have been married for forty-five years.
> George always appreciated **Dr.** Thurber's thoughtful advice.

Use **abbreviations** for the titles **Mr.**, **Mrs.**, **Ms.**, and **Dr.** when they appear before the name of a person.

Also abbreviate certain words that follow people's names—for example, *Jr.* (Junior) and *Sr.* (Senior).

EXAMPLE

Martin Luther King, **Jr.,** was born in Atlanta in 1919.

Use the **abbreviations Jr.** and **Sr.** after a person's name.

22.3C ABBREVIATIONS FOR TIME OF DAY AND YEAR

When you write the year or the time of day in numerals, it's correct to use abbreviations for the expressions A.M. (before noon), P.M. (after noon), B.C. (before Christ), and A.D. (in the year of the Lord).

EXAMPLES

The train arrived at 8:30 P.M. on Monday.

Julius Caesar was assassinated in 44 B.C. by his political enemies.

King John of England was forced to sign the Magna Charta in A.D. 1215.

Abbreviate the expressions A.M., P.M., B.C., and A.D. when they are used with numbers.

22.3D ABBREVIATIONS WITHOUT PERIODS

Notice that all the abbreviations used so far have periods. Some abbreviations, though, such as those for names of organizations, don't have periods. When you use these abbreviations, write the first letter of the important words in the name without periods or spaces between the letters.

EXAMPLES

United Nations – **UN**

American Federations of Labor – **AFL**

We got our puppy from the **ASPCA**, an organization that helps homeless animals.

The **FBI** posted a list of its most-wanted criminals.

The **IRS** collects taxes.

Write the **abbreviations** of names of many organizations and agencies without periods.

Unit IV Additional Resources

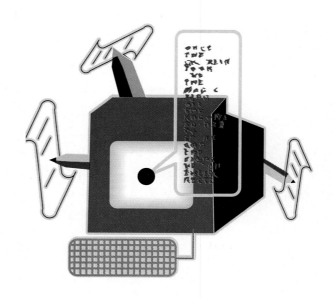

Need help studying for a test? Writing a letter? Doing research for a math or science project? This unit contains information that will help you with these and other problems. Perhaps you need to brush up on taking notes or outlining. Maybe you want some ideas about using a computer for a project. Check out the chapters in this unit to sharpen your skills.

C O N T E N T S

CHAPTER 23 Technology...394

CHAPTER 24 Spelling...405

CHAPTER 25 Vocabulary 418

CHAPTER 26 Letter Writing 428

CHAPTER 27 Test, Study, and Research Skills.........................435

CHAPTER 28 Critical Thinking Skills 455

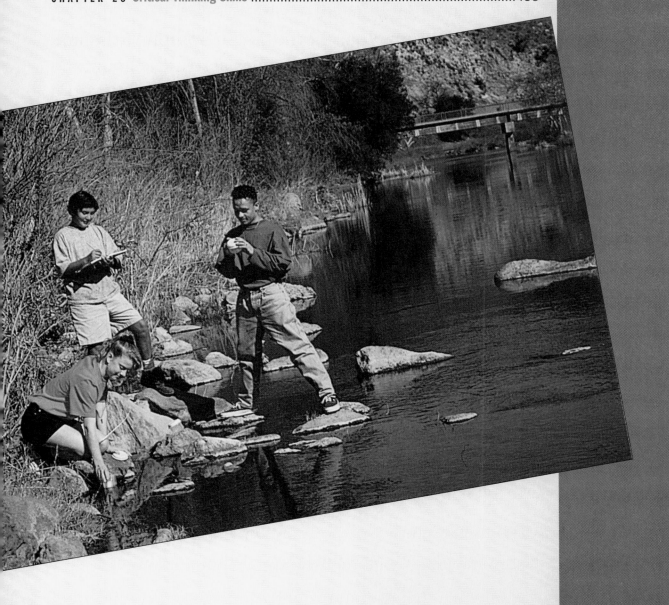

Chapter 23 Technology

Imagine it's 1860. You write a letter to a friend who lives in California and send it the fastest way you can. In just ten days, Pony Express riders traveling on horseback from your home in St. Joseph, Missouri, carry your letter almost two thousand miles across the country.

But you live in the 1990s. You could still mail a letter to a long-distance friend, but you also might make a phone call, send a fax, or use electronic mail. As a result of new technology, communication takes less time and less effort than ever before. Today, with just the touch of a key, you can instantly reach people around the world–if you know which communication tools are available and how to use them.

23.1 USING THE COMPUTER TO WRITE

One of the most important communication tools you'll use is the **computer,** an electronic device that stores, retrieves, and processes information. With a computer in school or at home, you can do everything from researching to writing to creating your own publications.

■■ 23.1A THE WORD ON WORD PROCESSING

With word processing **software,** or a set of electronic instructions that tells the computer what to do, you can type and edit your writing. You **input,** or enter, information into a computer by typing on a **keyboard.** A **printer** can print out information that you input.

Before you start writing with a computer, you'll need to know how to create, name, and store files. You'll also need to know basic word processing skills, including how to type, select, delete, add, save, and print text.

A computer comes in handy throughout the writing process. Before you start, you can use a computer to record the ideas you generate. When you write, you don't have to worry about making errors because you can make changes or corrections in seconds. If you want classmates' feedback and your computers are linked, classmates can read your draft on their own screens and directly input their reactions. When you revise and edit, you can make a **hard copy**, or printout on paper, of your draft; mark it by hand; and input changes. Also, you can use a computer to create a polished copy of your writing. Check out the chart in the next column for ideas on using a computer to write.

Ideas for Using a Computer to Write

Prewriting
freewrite
brainstorm
write and save journal entries
find and organize facts
create an outline

Drafting
expand an outline by inserting writing after headings
scroll through draft to work on different parts
save drafts to revise at another time

Revising
"cut and paste" to move text
search for and replace words or phrases throughout draft
print multiple copies to share with classmates
use networking, or computers that are linked with other computers, to get feedback

Editing
proofread hard copy to spot errors
input changes and corrections
use "spell checker" to find spelling errors
use "grammar checker" to find grammatical errors
use built-in thesaurus to find synonyms

Publishing
choose typefaces, type styles, and type sizes
set margins and center text
arrange text attractively on the page
add borders and rules
determine spacing
use headers or footers to add page numbers
add graphics if software can create them

Once you're satisfied with your writing and how it looks, print out a hard copy. If you'd like to publish electronically, you can share your writing through electronic mail or on a network bulletin board. You might want to create an electronic portfolio by making a file of your best work.

Using a computer to write won't make you a better writer, but you'll be able to produce written work more quickly and more accurately. You can add, delete, and move material easily without rewriting your entire paper.

Also, you can use a computer to store many different writing assignments. If you name files clearly, it'll be easy to find a portfolio and add writing to it. Someday, you might want to use your saved word processing files to create your own publications to share with friends, family members, or classmates.

Word Processing Tips

- ◎ Save often.
- ◎ Double space drafts to allow room for revising and editing.
- ◎ Type one space after a period, not two.
- ◎ Clearly name and organize computer files.
- ◎ Make a **backup copy,** or duplicate copy, by copying files onto floppy disks.

▓ 23.1B DO-IT-YOURSELF DESKTOP PUBLISHING

Have you ever wanted to create a brochure, design a book jacket, make a poster, or publish a newspaper or newsletter? You can create all of these publications–and more–with a computer. **Desktop publishing** is the process of using a computer and software to combine words and art into a publication.

Before you start, think about what you'd like the finished publication to look like. With desktop publishing software, you design the size and shape of your publication. Then you move different word processing, drawing, or picture files to arrange words and art in your design. For example, you might create a newsletter page with a logo and three columns of text, or you might wrap words around a piece of artwork. You also might want to add graphs or maps to a report or article.

There are two ways to add illustrations to your text. First, you can use software. Different programs will enable you to paint or draw illustrations on the computer that you can then paste into your text. Other programs provide you with clip art. Clip art is already drawn and includes images such as animals or decorative borders. You search for the illustration you want, select it, and move it into your text.

A second way to add illustrations is by using a **scanner**, a machine that reproduces images. Software processes those images. Using a scanner and image-processing software, you can insert photographs or original art into your publication.

Desktop publishing allows you to combine illustrations with text. Using a computer and desktop publishing software to publish your writing is less expensive and takes less time than having it printed professionally. It can also be fun to plan, design, and even produce your own publications.

Desktop Publishing Tips

- Look at other similar publications for design ideas.
- Draw sketches first to see how a page might look.
- Experiment with different designs.
- Use italic or boldface type to highlight important information.
- Use drawing software to create charts, graphs, and diagrams.

23.2 STORING AND GETTING INFORMATION

Do you keep copies of your writing to read again and again? Where do you put information you want to save? You might store information in a folder and file it or you might copy it into a notebook. You can also use today's technology to store and retrieve information electronically.

23.2A FROM FLOPPIES TO CD-ROMS

You don't have to leaf through piles of paper anymore. A number of different electronic storage devices can help you get information quickly.

Floppy Disks A floppy disk is a removable 3.5-inch or 5.25-inch disk that stores software and information. With a floppy disk, you can transfer information from one computer to another or make a duplicate copy of information that you want to keep.

Before you use a floppy, you must **format** it, or prepare it for use. To store or get information, you insert a floppy disk into the disk drive of a computer. The **disk drive** holds a disk, gets information from it, and records the information. You can store information on a floppy disk until you no longer need it. Then you can delete what you don't want.

Hard Disks A hard disk also stores information and software. You can also delete information from a hard disk when you no longer want it. A hard disk, however, is located inside a computer and is not removable. In comparison to a floppy, a hard disk can retrieve and save information much faster and can save more information. You can transfer information from a hard disk to a floppy and from a floppy to a hard disk.

CD-ROM Disks CD-ROM (Compact Disc-Read Only Memory) disks are removable disks that can store 300,000 pages of text. To get information from a CD-ROM disk, you need CD-ROM software and either a CD-ROM player or a computer with a CD-ROM drive.

Unlike using floppies or hard disks, you can't store your own files or change information on CD-ROM disks. You can print out information, such as an electronic encyclopedia article stored on a CD-ROM disk, or transfer information to a hard disk.

CD-ROM disks can combine text, sound, graphics, and pictures. While you might research information on CD-ROM disks, you can also use CD-ROM software to make your own multimedia presentations incorporating photographs, sound, text, and video.

Videodiscs Videodiscs, which are the size and shape of phonograph records, can also store large amounts of information. Like CD-ROM disks, videodiscs can combine text, sound, and still and moving pictures. For instance, you might hear a presidential speech or watch news footage of an important event in history. To view a videodisc, you need a special disc player and a TV monitor. Using a directory to find exactly what you want to see, you can use a remote control or a computer to select and view portions of a videodisc.

You can quickly locate and use information that's been electronically stored on floppy disks, hard disks, CD-ROM disks, and videodiscs. Once you know how to retrieve information that is stored electronically, you'll be able to find what you want with a simple keystroke.

Electronic Storage Tips

- ◎ Save files every fifteen minutes or so.
- ◎ Clearly name files for easy retrieval.
- ◎ Make backup copies to prevent the loss of information.
- ◎ Arrange and organize your files to make them easy to find.

▪▪ 23.2B THE BASICS OF DATABASES

Have you ever used a telephone book to look up a phone number? If so, you've used a database. A **database**, which is a large collection of related information, can be created, stored, and read by means of a computer.

Using a Database To use an electronic database, you can **scan**, or browse, for information you want. You can also tell the computer what to look for; the information you've requested will be displayed. You might locate a particular book by searching in an electronic database in your library. Or you might find information by searching an electronic database, such as a telephone book or a dictionary, stored on a CD-ROM disk.

Creating a Database In an electronic database, all the information about a person, a place, or a subject that is grouped together is called a **record**. Each piece of information in a record is stored in a **field**. Suppose your database is a chart. A record would be a row while the fields of your friends' addresses and phone numbers would be columns named "Addresses" and "Phone Numbers." To create a database file, you need a computer and database software. You name

fields and then enter the appropriate information in each field to make a record.

You can easily find information stored in a database. For example, if you want to search in a community resources database to find out which organizations offer help for teenagers, you can instruct the computer to search for the records containing information about teenagers. You can also print out the information you need.

Electronic storage allows you to save, organize, and retrieve information quickly. Whether you're saving your writing on floppies, using databases or CD-ROM disks to do research for a project, or creating a database of magazines where you can submit your own stories, you can use technology to store and get information.

23.3 RESEARCH THE MODERN WAY

Not only can you use technology for writing, publishing, and storing information, but you can also use it for finding information in many public and school libraries. You can use a computer at home or in school to find information, too.

■■ 23.3A TECHNOLOGY IN THE LIBRARY

From photocopiers to laser scanners that read library card bar codes to fax machines that send articles between libraries, technology has changed how you find, borrow, and use library materials. Knowing where to find information and how to use technology in the library are important skills.

Periodicals A library contains books and **periodicals**, or magazines and newspapers. Periodicals can be photographically reduced in size, stored on cards called **microfiche** or on rolls of film called **microfilm**, and read with a mechanical reader. In this way, periodicals are less likely to be misplaced or damaged.

Periodicals—as well as reference works such as an encyclopedia or a world atlas—may also be stored on CD-ROM disks. You can print out articles stored on CD-ROM disks, microfiche, or microfilm.

Nonprint Materials Everything in a library that is not a book or a periodical—filmstrips, movies, cassette tapes, records, videocassettes, and compact disks—is nonprint material. Nonprint materials might come in handy when you do research for a particular project or report.

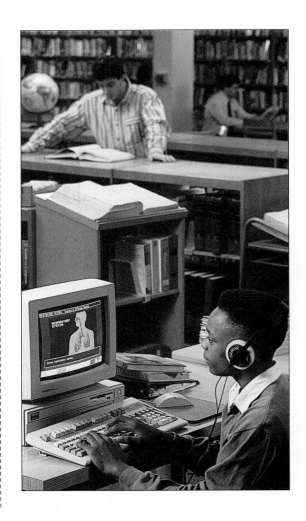

▪▪ 23.3B ON-LINE CATALOGS

How can you get information for your research paper? You can ask a librarian for help or use a card catalog. You might also use an **on-line**, or computerized, catalog that contains a list of books, periodicals, and nonprint materials found in your school or public library, in other libraries in the area, or in libraries throughout the country.

You might search an on-line catalog database for books or periodicals by typing a combination of terms, or **key words**, such as the author's name, the title, or the subject. The computer will display the information you request. You can even search from places other than the library with a **modem**, a computer-telephone connection, and communication software. You might be able to make a phone call to gain access to your library's database 24 hours a day.

Information in an On-Line Catalog
Books
author's name
title
publisher
copyright date
where a book is shelved
whether the book is currently available
which local libraries also have this book
Periodicals
author's name
title of the article
date, volume, and issue of periodical
number of pages in the article
brief summary of what the article is about

While an on-line catalog contains much the same information as a card catalog, it allows you to scan through a list of books more quickly, to search for periodicals, and to print out a list of books or articles. You can find out just about anything you want to in a library—but only if you know where and how to find the information.

On-Line Search Tips

- Find out how to use the on-line catalog system in your library.
- Check key words for correct spelling.
- Use cross-references.
- Narrow the topic if you search by subject.
- Use different key words for on-line searching.
- Follow the on-screen instructions or printed directions.

23.4 USING TECHNOLOGY TO COMMUNICATE

Technology has made it possible to communicate more rapidly over longer distances. Through the use of computers and other devices, people in different communities, cities, and countries can be in touch instantly.

▪▪ 23.4A THE FACTS ABOUT FAX

If you want to reach someone right away, you might send a **telefacsimile**, or **fax**. A sending device called a fax machine scans a document and then changes it into electronic signals that are transmitted over telephone lines. A receiving fax machine converts the document back into readable form and prints out an exact copy. Sending a fax is great for fast person-to-person communication.

▪▪ 23.4B NETWORKING

You can communicate with groups of people by networking. **Networks** are groups of computers that are connected together by cable or by satellite. A network can link as few as two computers in your school or as many as fifteen million computers in different countries.

The purpose of networking is to share resources electronically and to collaborate with other people. Networking allows you to share the following materials.

What Can Be Shared on a Network

◎ software and computer files

◎ computer equipment, such as printers, modems, and scanners

◎ information—by exchanging electronic mail or by tapping into library or commercial databases

Networking can provide you with a link to your classmates, to other students in your community, or even to students around the world.

Electronic Mail Through the use of networks, you can send messages in minutes—computer to computer—by **electronic mail**, or **E-mail**. To send E-mail, you need a computer, a modem, a telephone, and communication software. A modem sends and receives information through the telephone system and allows a computer to "talk" with another computer.

How can you send E-mail to a student in another school? After you create a message on a computer, you can send it to the computer address of the student who will get the message. The message is delivered to an electronic mailbox where it remains until the student reads it. The student can respond to your message whenever he or she wants to.

Bulletin Boards Networks also let you use electronic bulletin boards. To contact others with similar interests, such as students concerned about the environment, you need a modem, computer, communication software, and a telephone. You can call an electronic bulletin board to read messages or to leave a message of your own.

Information Services If you subscribe to an information service, you can make a phone call to get different kinds of information. With a modem, a computer, and communication software, you have access to huge commercial databases that contain up-to-the-minute information, including financial reports, weather forecasts, and news. You can even shop or make travel plans through an information service.

■■ 23.4C TECHNOLOGY FOR THE DISABLED

Technology also helps disabled people read, write, and communicate. For example, special devices help physically impaired people use their voices or eye or muscle movement to operate a computer. People who are visually impaired can use Braille keyboards and Braille printers or speech synthesizers that read text aloud in an artificial voice. Hearing impaired people can communicate by E-mail and electronic bulletin boards.

With the use of technology, you can communicate more easily with others. You can send E-mail or faxes or tap into electronic bulletin boards to share writing or ideas with your classmates and with students in different cities and countries.

23.5 THE SCOOP ON SOFTWARE

Without software, a computer is useless. The following list will help you match the right type of software with the purpose you have in mind. Remember too that some software may be useful in more than one category.

Calculate
• spreadsheet software
• accounting software

Communicate
• multimedia production software
• communication software

Organize
• presentation software
• calendar-making software

Entertain
• games software

Educate	
• math software	• history software
• science software	• reading software
• geography software	• vocabulary software

Research
• CD-ROM software
• database software

Illustrate	
• drawing software	• clip art software
• painting software	• image-processing software

Write and Publish
• word processing software
• desktop publishing software

You've learned how technology can be used to write, publish, research, and communicate. Now take a ride on the information highway! Explore ways that you can use technology to learn and grow.

23.6 DO IT YOURSELF: TECHNOLOGY ACTIVITIES

Technology can help you in many areas of your life. To practice what you've learned in this chapter, choose one or more of the following activities.

1. Use either floppy disks or a hard disk to save and keep your favorite writing assignments and to store ideas for future assignments. Use CD-ROM disks or videodiscs to research different subjects for reports, essays, or magazine or newspaper articles you write.

2. Create a community resource database. Set up fields such as *organization, address, phone number,* and *services.* Enter information to create the first record, the second, and so on. To organize the database, sort information alphabetically, chronologically, or numerically. Add or change information to update your database.

3. Use an on-line catalog to find and print out a list of books and articles about the history of computers. If you search by subject, try different words and phrases, such as *computers* or *computer-history*, until you find what you're looking for. If you get stuck, ask a librarian for help.

4. Create and send an E-mail message from your class to a class in another community, state, or country. You might find out what interests or concerns other students have or share information about projects your classes are working on.

5. Find out what types of software are sold at local computer stores and through mail-order catalogs. Before you buy software, check to see what software will work with the computer you use.

Chapter 24 Spelling

When you write, you have to think about many things: what you want to write about, how to organize your ideas, how to present your thoughts clearly, and more. Spelling may seem like a minor detail, but in fact it is quite an important part of the impression your writing makes. Whether you are writing a school paper, a letter, a job application, or, later in life, a report for work, you will be judged in part by details such as spelling.

Spelling errors can make your writing hard to follow and may give an impression that you are careless and do not take pride in your work. Correct spelling, on the other hand, is a sign that you have put effort into your writing and that it is worth your reader's time. Learning to spell well is a worthwhile investment, and it is something anyone can do with a little effort.

24.1 SPELLING RULES

Although English contains many words that are confusing or difficult to spell, many other words follow simple rules. Learning those rules is a good first step in becoming a good speller. The following pages will show you spelling rules and give you some hints to help you become a better speller than you already are.

▪▪ 24.1A WORDS WITH *IE* AND *EI*

The letters *ie* and *ei* appear in many English words and often are confused. A simple rule tells you when to use *ie* and when to use *ei*. You may already have heard this rhyme.

Put *i* before *e* except after *c*
Or when sounded like *a*
As in *neighbor* and *weigh*.

EXAMPLES

believe, chief, retrieve
ceiling, receipt, receive
eight, veil

There are, unfortunately, exceptions to this rule, but the exceptions are few. If you can memorize them, you've got it made! Here are some of the exceptions: *either, neither, leisure, seize, weird, foreign, height.*

24.1B ADDING PREFIXES

A **prefix** is a word part that can be added to the beginning of a word. For example, *re-* and *over-* are prefixes. When you add a prefix to a word, do not change the spelling of the word.

EXAMPLES

re- + run = rerun
over- + rule = overrule
mis- + spell = misspell

Notice that in some words, such as *overrule* and *misspell,* the prefix ends with the same letter that the main word begins with. People often misspell words of this kind. Remember that the letter must appear twice. Do not change the spelling of the prefix or the main word.

24.1C ADDING SUFFIXES

A **suffix** is a word part that can be added to the end of a word. Adding suffixes and inflectional endings is a bit more complicated than adding prefixes. There are a few rules to learn, but the rules are logical and you may already know them.

Words Ending with *e*

When you add a suffix to a word ending with *e,* follow this rule: If the suffix begins with a vowel, drop the final *e* when you add the suffix.

EXAMPLES

value + -able = valuable
inflate + -able = inflatable
observe + -ant = observant
drive + -ing = driving

Drop the final e before adding a suffix beginning with a vowel. Keep the final e before adding a suffix beginning with a consonant.

If the suffix begins with a consonant, keep the final *e.*

EXAMPLES

use + -ful = useful
care + -less = careless
safe + -ty = safety

NOTE: There are exceptions to these rules–for example, *noticeable, courageous, argument, truly.*

Words Ending with *y*

When you add a suffix or ending to a word with a final *y*, follow this rule: If the main word ends with a consonant and *y*, change the *y* to *i*.

EXAMPLES

happy + -ness = happiness
rely + -able = reliable
beauty + -ful = beautiful
deny + -ed = denied

When a word ends with a consonant and *y*, change the *y* to *i* before adding a suffix or -*ed*.

If the main word ends with a vowel and *y*, do not change the spelling of the main word.

EXAMPLES

enjoy + -able = enjoyable
play + -ful = playful
joy + -ous = joyous
destroy + -ed = destroyed

When a word ends with a vowel and *y*, do not change the *y*.

There are exceptions to these rules. In certain words, don't change *y* to *i* when

you add -*ing*: *denying, relying, hurrying.* And there are other exceptions too–for example, *daily, shyness.*

Words Ending with a Vowel and a Consonant

When a one-syllable word ends with a single vowel followed by a single consonant, follow this rule: Double the final consonant before adding a suffix or ending that starts with a vowel.

EXAMPLES

spot + -ed = spotted
run + -er = runner
sit + -ing = sitting
red + -en = redden

Double the final consonant of a one-syllable word ending with a vowel and a consonant before adding an ending that starts with a vowel.

▪ 24.1D PLURALS OF NOUNS

The following rules will help you spell the plural forms of nouns correctly.

Most nouns form the plural by adding *s* or *es*. Some nouns have irregular plural forms. The spellings of these irregular plurals can be tricky, but you will have less trouble with them if you remember the rules in this section.

EXAMPLES

year	years
class	classes
brush	brushes
fox	foxes

Form the plural of most nouns by adding *s.* But if a noun ends with *s, sh, ch, x, or z,* add *es.*

For words that end with *y*, follow this rule: If a consonant comes before the *y*, change the *y* to *i*, and add *es.*

EXAMPLES

party + es = parties
berry + es = berries
industry + es = industries

To form the plural of a noun ending with a consonant and *y*, change the *y* to *i* and add *es.*

If a vowel comes before the *y*, just add *s.*

EXAMPLES

tray	trays
monkey	monkeys

To form the plural of a noun ending with a vowel and *y*, add *s.*

Most words ending with *f* or *fe* have regular plurals, but some change their spelling in the plural.

EXAMPLES

chief	chiefs
roof	roofs
safe	safes

To form the plural of most words ending with *f* or *fe*, add *s.*

EXAMPLES

leaf	leaves
thief	thieves
loaf	loaves
shelf	shelves
calf	calves

To form the plural of certain nouns ending with *f*, change *f* to *v* and add *es.*

EXAMPLES

wife	wives
knife	knives

To form the plural of certain nouns ending with *fe*, change *f* to *v* and add *s.*

There is no rule to tell you which nouns change *f* to *v* and which don't. You must simply remember those that do change spelling. If you're not sure, consult your dictionary.

Nouns ending with *o* present the same kind of problem. The ones that end with a vowel and *o* are easy to remember. They are regular and just add *s*.

E X A M P L E S

radio + s = radios
rodeo + s = rodeos
patio + s = patios

To form the plural of a noun ending with a vowel and *o*, add *s*.

Words that end with a consonant and *o* are more difficult. Some of them add *s*, and others add *es*. Memorize these words.

E X A M P L E S

Add *s*:	soprano	sopranos
	photo	photos
	silo	silos
	piano	pianos
Add *es*:	tomato	tomatoes
	hero	heroes
	echo	echoes
	potato	potatoes

To form the plural of a noun ending with a consonant and *o*, add *s* or *es*.

Some nouns do not follow any pattern to form their plurals. The plural forms have unusual spelling changes.

E X A M P L E S

man	men
woman	women
child	children
mouse	mice
goose	geese
tooth	teeth

A few nouns are spelled exactly the same way in their singular and plural forms. Once again, you just have to remember these.

E X A M P L E S

sheep	sheep
deer	deer
species	species

24.1E SPELLING HOMOPHONES

Homophones are words that sound alike but have different spellings and meanings. For example, *hear* and *here* are homophones. They are pronounced the same way, but *hear* means "listen to" and *here* means "in this place." Homophones present a special spelling problem, but read on to find ways to combat the homophone problem.

Its and *it's* are homophones that cause a great deal of trouble. *Its* is the possessive form of the pronoun *it*. *It's* is a contraction that stands for *it is*.

> E X A M P L E S
>
> The cat cleaned **its** fur with **its** rough, pink tongue.
> **It's** instinct that guides the cat's behavior.

The following is an easy way to help you spell these words correctly. Remember that in a contraction, an apostrophe stands for a missing letter. The apostrophe in *it's* stands for the missing *i* in *it is*. If you are not sure whether the word you are writing should be spelled *its* or *it's*, try using *it is* instead. If *it is* makes sense in the sentence, you can write *it's*.

There are several other homophone pairs that are made up of one possessive pronoun and one contraction.

Homophone Pairs
their / they're
theirs / there's
whose / who's
your / you're

You can use the same method to help you spell them correctly.

Another kind of homophone pair can be spelled as either one word or two. The pair that most commonly causes confusion is *already* and *all ready*. *Already* means "by this time" or "previously." *All ready* means "completely ready."

> E X A M P L E S
>
> Akira and I have **already** packed.
> We are **all ready** to go.

TIP: The expression *all ready* is made up of two words. The word *all* is an adverb modifying the adjective *ready*. You can delete *all*, and the sentence will still make sense. "We are ready to go." If the correct word is *already,* you cannot remove part of it. "Akira and I have ready packed" does not make sense.

You can use the same method to test the pair *all together* and *altogether*. *All together* means "in a group." *Altogether* means "completely" or "thoroughly."

> E X A M P L E S
>
> The children arrived **all together**.
> The theater is **altogether** too noisy.

You can think of your own ways to remember the spellings of other confusing homophones. For example, to remember the difference between *here* and *hear*, you might say to yourself, "I hear with my ear."

Always proofread your writing carefully. Some homophones are words that you know well–for example, *to, too,* and *two*. If you mix these words up, it may be because of carelessness. With careful proofreading, you can easily spot these spelling errors.

24.2 ONE HUNDRED MOST FREQUENTLY MISSPELLED WORDS

across	doubt	obedient
absence	eighth	occasion
accidentally	embarrass	occurrence
accurate	encourage	opportunity
achievement	enough	parallel
acquaintance	environment	possess
analyze	exaggerate	prejudice
answer	excellent	presence
apologize	exhaust	privilege
attendance	exhibit	quietly
beginning	extraordinary	recommend
behavior	fascinate	responsibility
biscuit	foreign	restaurant
boundary	government	rhythm
bracelet	grammar	safety
business	guarantee	schedule
calendar	guide	scissors
canoe	handkerchief	separate
cemetery	immediately	sergeant
character	interesting	sincerely
chocolate	judgment	succeed
college	knowledge	temperature
column	laboratory	tomorrow
comfortable	length	truly
committee	license	twelfth
congratulate	luxurious	vacuum
conscience	marriage	vehicle
conscious	mathematics	villain
courageous	mileage	vinegar
courteous	muscle	welcome
curiosity	mysterious	whisper
debt	necessary	whistle
describe	noticeable	
despair	nuisance	

Read through the list on this page and decide which of these words are problems for you. Put those words on your own personal spelling list and study them a few at a time.

24.3 STRATEGIES TO IMPROVE SPELLING SKILLS

Some people are better spellers than others. But most people can learn to spell better. It takes some work, but spending just a few minutes a day on improving your spelling skills can really pay off. Here are some suggestions.

- **Keep a list of your own personal spelling demons.** Although some words seem to be difficult for many people, everyone has his or her own spelling "demons"—words that create the most trouble. Keep a list of words you have trouble spelling and use the list as a study tool. For a few minutes every day or as often as possible, review a few of the words on your list. Practice visualizing and writing the words. Add new words to your list as they come up and delete ones that you have mastered. You can keep your list in your writing folder so you can easily look at it when you write.

Use pronunciation clues. When you are not sure how to spell a word, try to sound it out. Use clues in the word's pronunciation to help you spell it. Divide the word into syllables, and pronounce each syllable carefully to yourself. Make sure you have not left out or added any syllables or letters. Look for any familiar word parts, such as prefixes and suffixes.

Try other spellings. It may help you to write the word a few different ways on a piece of scrap paper. If you have seen the word many times in your reading, or if you have been practicing visualizing and writing the word on your personal spelling list, the correct spelling may just "look right."

Develop your own "bag of tricks." Think up memory tricks that will help you remember the correct spellings of words. Memory tricks can help you distinguish between homophones, remind you about letters that aren't pronounced, or simply give you a clue to a spelling you just can't seem to remember. You might remind yourself that there is a *rat* in *separate* or remember that the *principal* is your *pal.*

separate

Use your dictionary. If you can't figure out how to spell a word, don't just guess. If you guess, you won't learn anything, and you may get used to seeing the word spelled the wrong way. Take a minute to look up the word in the dictionary. Even if you're not sure of the spelling, you can figure out enough of it to look up a few different possibilities until you locate the word. Write the word on your own personal spelling list, and go back to it later for review.

While you are reading, notice how words are spelled. If you find a totally unfamiliar word in your reading, you may want to look up its meaning in a dictionary. At the same time, notice the word's spelling. Are there any tricky letters that you might have trouble with? Try to get an image of the word in your mind. You may want to write it a few times.

Read and write as much as you can. The more practice you get in seeing and writing words, the better a speller you'll be.

24.4 SPELLING AND THE WRITING PROCESS

The writing process consists of five stages: prewriting, drafting, revising, editing, and publishing. Although it is helpful to be aware of correct spelling at any stage of this process, the stage when you can focus especially on spelling is the editing stage. It is at this stage that you proofread your work, looking for errors in spelling as well as in grammar and punctuation.

Careful proofreading is a vital part of being a good speller. Here are some strategies you can use to become a better proofreader.

Proofreading for Spelling Errors

1. Look at the words individually. Do you see any of your personal spelling demons? Are there other words whose spelling you're not sure of? Do any words look "wrong"? Have you substituted a homophone of the word you intended?

2. Focus on each problem word. Sound it out to be sure you haven't left out or added letters. Remind yourself of your memory trick for the word. Write it different ways on a separate piece of paper. Get out your dictionary and look up any words you're unsure of.

3. Look at every word carefully, even "easy" ones. People often mix up simple homophones, leave out letters, or transpose letters in a word when they are writing quickly. Now is your chance to catch those careless errors.

Careful proofreading makes a big difference in how your work appears to your audience. Spelling errors are distracting to a reader and could make your writing hard to understand. A well proofread composition shows that you have put care into your work, and that it is worth taking seriously.

24.5 USING TECHNOLOGY

If you do your writing on a computer, you may find that correcting spelling errors is a little easier. First, you may find errors easier to spot in type on a screen than scribbled on a piece of paper. Also, a spelling error can be corrected in seconds without rewriting.

Depending on your word-processing program, you may also have a spell-check feature. A computer with a spell-check program has a dictionary. When you use spell-check, the computer goes through your work searching for letter combinations that are not in its dictionary. It calls out a word it doesn't recognize and offers you correctly spelled words similar to the word it found. This feature obviously can save you a great deal of time and can simplify the proofreading stage.

Beware! Technology does not solve all problems. First, you will not always have your computer with you when you write, so you still have to learn to spell correctly. Continue to be an active speller. Try to figure out the correct spellings of words yourself, since this process helps you become a better speller. If spell-check finds any misspelled words that you missed, record them in your personal spelling list and review them later. Use spell-check only as a backup.

Second, spell-check is by no means foolproof. The computer's dictionary is limited. For example, it does not contain any proper nouns, such as place names. It may not have special vocabulary, such as science terms. In addition, it knows only whether a word is listed in its dictionary, not whether it has been used correctly. If you write *there* when you meant *their,* for example, spell-check will pass it right by. Continue to check for confused homophones and use your own dictionary as you write, to check both spellings and meanings of words. Proofread a hard copy after you use spell-check and before you publish your paper.

24.6 DO IT YOURSELF: SPELLING ACTIVITIES

Learning to spell may not be your favorite pastime, but it does not have to be unpleasant, and it can even be fun. Here are some activities that can help you be a better speller without too much pain. Solutions to help you and some answers are given at the end of this section on page 417.

1. When you work with your personal spelling list, practice one word at a time. Try this method for learning a new word.

- Look at the word.
- Look away and picture the word in your mind.
- Spell the word aloud.
- Write the word.
- Check to see if you have written the word correctly. If not, repeat the above steps until you've gotten it right.
- Write the word again a few more times.

This process will help cement the spelling in your mind, so the next time you'll remember it correctly.

2. Come up with memory tricks for words that you have trouble spelling. Have fun with this! Anything that helps you is fine, even if it seems silly. For practice, see if you can think of some memory tricks that could help you with these problems.

- You confuse the words *capital* and *capitol*.
- You can't remember how many *d*'s and *s*'s there are in *address*.
- You always spell *baggage* incorrectly as *bagage*.

3. Pronounce words carefully to help you spell them. Here are some words that people sometimes misspell because they pronounce them incorrectly.

athlete	(not athalete)
library	(not liberry)
February	(not Febuary)
mischievous	(not mischievious)
introduce	(not interduce)
picture	(not pitcher)
jewelry	(not joolery)
probably	(not probly)
length	(not lenth)
recognize	(not reconize)

To help you spell these words correctly, try the following.

- Look up each word in a dictionary. Check the pronunciation and look at the syllable division.
- On a separate sheet of paper, write each word divided into syllables.
- Carefully pronounce each syllable.
- Circle any letters that you might leave out.
- Underline any syllables that you tend to mispronounce.
- Rewrite each word correctly several times.

4. Familiar word parts such as prefixes and suffixes can help you spell unfamiliar words. For example, the long word *interaction* doesn't look so hard if you divide it into the prefix *inter-* and the familiar word *action*.

To practice finding word parts, write each of these words on a separate piece of paper, and underline each prefix or suffix.

postpone	placement
preexist	overtake
unbelievable	insanely

5. To check whether you remember the rule for spelling words with *ie* and *ei*, try this exercise. Write the words on a separate sheet of paper, and fill in each blank with *ie* or *ei*.

bel__ve	rec__ve
c__ling	rel__f
w__ght	v__l

6. To see how well you know the rules for adding prefixes, join each of the following prefixes and main words. Write the new words on your paper.

un- + known	over- + rule
re- + arrange	un- + natural
im- + mature	mis- + spell

7. To see how well you know the rules for adding suffixes and endings, join each of these combinations. Write the new words on your paper.

agree + -ment	rely + -able
blue + -ish	joy + -less
care + -ful	spin + -ing
move + -able	rid + -ance
beauty + -ful	

8. To check your knowledge of spelling plurals, try the following exercise. On your paper, write the plural form of each of the following nouns.

rash	shelf
glass	knife
candy	patio
alley	tomato
roof	goose
loaf	sheep

9. There are some pronunciation clues that you can use in spelling. One helpful thing to know is that the letters *c* and *g* are pronounced differently before different vowels.

Before *e* and *i*	Before *a, o,* and *u*
c sounds like *s*	*c* sounds like *k*
g sounds like *j*	*g* sounds like *g* as in *go*

For practice, use the above information to answer the following questions:

◉ You want to add the suffix *-able* to the word *notice.* Should you drop the *e*?

◉ When you add the suffix *-ous* to the word *courage,* should you drop the *e*?

◉ Which word is spelled correctly: *picnicing* or *picnicking*?

◉ Why couldn't you spell the word *guess* this way: *gess*?

ANSWERS

2. Possible memory tricks:
   The **capitol** building has a d**o**me on t**o**p.
   Add a **d** to **a dress**.
   Three **g**'s in **baggage**.

4. *post*pone   place*ment*
   *pre*exist   *over*take
   *un*believ*able*   *in*sane*ly*

5. believe   receive
   ceiling   relief
   weight   veil

6. unknown   overrule
   rearrange   unnatural
   immature   misspell

7. agreement   reliable
   bluish   joyless
   careful   spinning
   movable   riddance
   beautiful

8. rashes   shelves
   glasses   knives
   candies   patios
   alleys   tomatoes
   roofs   geese
   loaves   sheep

9. No, dropping *e* would change the sound of *c*.
   No, dropping e would change the sound of *g*.
   The correct spelling is *picnicking*.
   Gess would be pronounced *jess*.

Chapter 25 Vocabulary

Increasing your vocabulary is an ongoing process that will continue throughout your life. Having a good vocabulary is helpful in many ways. It means you will understand what you read more easily and be able to read increasingly more difficult material. It helps you in improving your writing and speaking skills, since having a large variety of words at your command allows you to use more colorful, specific language that will interest your audience. A good vocabulary also helps you do well on standardized tests.

25.1 WORD PARTS

One way to improve your vocabulary is to become familiar with word parts—prefixes, suffixes, and roots—that appear in many different words. Knowing the meanings of these word parts will help you figure out the meanings of the words you see them in.

▪▪ 25.1A ROOTS

The **root** of a word is a base to which other word parts may be added. For example, the word *predict* can be divided into the prefix *pre-* and the root *dict*. Most roots come from Latin or Greek words. The root *dict* comes from a Latin word that means "to say."

Knowing the meaning of some common roots can help you figure out the meanings of words that contain those roots. For example, if you know that *pre-* means "before," you can figure out that *predict* means "say before." Although this is not an exact definition, it does give you a good idea of the meaning of *predict:* "declare in advance" or "foretell."

The following is a list of common roots. The list also contains the meanings of the roots and examples of their use.

Common Roots		
Root	**Meaning**	**Examples**
astr, aster	star	astronaut
cred	belief, trust	credit, incredible
cycl	circle, wheel	bicycle
dict	say	contradict, dictate
duc, duct	lead	conduct
fer	carry	transfer
flect, flex	bend	flexible
grad, gress	step, go	graduate, progress
graph, gram	write	telegraph
hydro, hydr	water	hydrant, hydroelectric
ject	throw	project
log	knowledge	biology
meter	measure	thermometer
miss, mit	send, let go	transmit
ped	foot	pedal, pedestrian
pend, pens	hang, weigh	suspense, pendulum
phon	sound, voice	telephone
port	carry	transport
rupt	break	interrupt, rupture
scope	see, watch	telescope
scrib, scrip	write	inscribe
sphere	round	hemisphere
therm	heat	thermal

Common Prefixes		
Prefix	**Meaning**	**Example**
bi-	two	bicycle
dis-	opposite, away	dislike
fore-	before	forecast
hemi-	half	hemisphere
im-	not	immature
in-	not	incomplete
inter-	between, together	interact
micro-	small	microscope
mis-	badly	misspell
non-	not	nonsense
over-	over, too much	overdo
post-	after	postpone
pre-	before	precook
pro-	forward	proceed
re-	again, back	rewrite, rebound
semi-	half	semicircle
sub-	under	subway
super-	above, more than	supernatural
trans-	across	transfer
tri-	three	triangle
un-	not	unhappy
uni-	one	uniform

■■ 25.1B PREFIXES

A **prefix** is a word part that can attach to the beginning of a word or root. The purpose of a prefix is to modify the meaning of the word or root. For example, the prefix *im-* means "not." If you add *im-* to the word *perfect*, you form a new word that means "not perfect": *imperfect*. Like roots, many prefixes come from Greek or Latin. Knowing their meanings will help you piece together the meaning of a word from its parts. See the following chart.

■■ 25.1C SUFFIXES

A **suffix** is a word part that can be attached to the end of a word or root. Suffixes add to the meaning of the word or root they are attached to. For example, the suffix *-able* means "able to be." If you add it to the root *port*, which means "carry," you form the word *portable*, meaning "able to be carried." Knowing the meaning of a suffix can help you discover the meaning of an unfamiliar word.

Below are some common suffixes with their meanings and examples of their use.

Common Suffixes		
Suffix	**Meaning**	**Examples**
-able	able to be, likely to be	affordable
-ance	act or state of	acceptance
-ant	showing; person who	assistant, expectant
-ence	act or state of	preference
-ent	showing; person who	confident, resident
-fy	make	beautify
-ful	full of	joyful
-ible	able to be, likely to be	collectible
-ic	like, related to	electronic
-ish	like	childish
-ion	act, state, or result of	reflection
-less	without	careless
-ly	manner of	quickly
-ment	act, state, or result of	achievement
-ness	state of	sadness
-ous	full of, having	nervous, furious

25.2 WORD ORIGINS

Every word has a story behind it. A word may have evolved over the centuries from an old form of English, it may have its roots in ancient Greek or Latin, or it may have come into English fairly recently from a language such as Spanish or French.

An **etymology** is a brief history of a word. Most dictionaries contain etymologies. For example, if you look up the word *liberty*, you will find that it originally came from the Latin word *liber*, meaning "free." Knowing the etymology of a word can contribute to your understanding of the word's meaning. Word origins are interesting to investigate and can help you remember words you have learned.

The oldest form of English was **Old English**, a language spoken by Germanic peoples who invaded England in the fifth century A.D. Over the centuries, words from Latin, Greek, French, and other languages enriched Old English as it evolved into the English language that is spoken today. English continues to change, as words from Spanish, Italian, Russian, and many other languages become part of it. In addition, old words may change in meaning, and new words are invented all the time. New words may come from special fields such as science or sports, from the names of people or places, and from many other unexpected sources.

▌▌ 25.2A WORDS FROM OTHER LANGUAGES

You probably know that a sofa is a piece of furniture with a long, padded seat. But did you know that the word *sofa* comes from an Arabic word meaning "long bench"? Many other English words have interesting derivations.

Words from Spanish and French

The word *canyon* comes from the Spanish word *cañón*, which is related to the Spanish word for *street–calle*. You can see that the meaning of *canyon*, "a deep, narrow valley," is similar to that of "street."

Another word that comes from Spanish is *bronco*. *Bronco* means "rough" or "wild." In English, the word *bronco* means "a wild, unbroken horse."

In English, a *souvenir* is something that serves as a reminder. The word comes from the French verb *souvenir*, which means "to remember."

▪▪ 25.2B WORDS FROM NAMES OF PEOPLE AND PLACES

Some words come from names of places. For example, the word *coach* comes from the Hungarian word *kocsi*, which means "of Kocs." Kocs is a village in Hungary where carriages and carts used to be made.

Words from People's Names

Words may also be derived from people's names. The word *guy*, for example, meaning "man" or "fellow," comes from the name Guy Fawkes. Guy Fawkes was a real person who in 1605 tried to blow up the Parliament building in London, England. He was stopped, and British people still celebrate Guy Fawkes Day by burning likenesses of Guy Fawkes.

Another example is *macadam*, a kind of roadway constructed by a special process using pieces of stone held together with cement or asphalt. The word came from the name of the man who invented the process, John L. McAdam.

25.3 SYNONYMS, ANTONYMS, AND HOMONYMS

Synonyms are words that have the same or nearly the same meaning. For example, *talk* and *speak* are synonyms. Part of having a good vocabulary is being aware of synonyms. They allow you to make your writing more varied, interesting, and precise.

WEAK: "The old man **walked** across the road." *(Walked* is not a very descriptive word.)

BETTER: "The old man **hobbled** across the road," or "The old man **shuffl**ed across the road."

A useful tool in helping you find and learn about synonyms is a **thesaurus,** a book that lists synonyms. You can use a thesaurus to find different words that have similar meanings.

Finding similar words is the easy part. What is more difficult to learn is the slight differences in meaning between synonyms. Few synonyms have exactly the same meaning. For example, *hobble* means "walk unsteadily" or "limp." *Shuffle* means "walk without lifting the feet." If you are not sure exactly what meaning a word conveys, look it up in a dictionary before you use it. Be sure the word you choose conveys the image you intended.

Dictionaries are also a source of synonyms. Some entries have one or more synonyms listed at the end. In addition, for some groups of synonyms, dictionaries sometimes give special usage notes under one of the synonyms explaining the slight differences in meaning among them.

Antonyms are words that have opposite or nearly opposite meanings. For example, *fast* and *slow* are antonyms. Using antonyms in the right place can clarify meaning, help create an image, or emphasize a point.

EXAMPLES
....

The teacher rewarded **obedience**, not **unruliness**.

Rebecca appeared even more **frail** beside her **vigorous** cousin.

Most thesauruses list antonyms as well as synonyms, so you can refer to a thesaurus to find antonyms, too. Dictionaries also list antonyms for some words. Note that not every word has an antonym. For example, the word *street* has synonyms but no antonyms.

Homonyms are words that have the same spelling and often sound alike but have different meanings. *Rose* means "stood up" but it also can mean "a kind of flower." *Pitch* means "to throw a baseball," but it also can mean a hard-selling advertisement.

Homonyms can cause confusion when you read. Sometimes you may see a familiar word that does not make sense to you in a particular sentence because you are not aware of another, different meaning. Whenever this happens, use your dictionary to find the appropriate meaning of the word.

25.4 DENOTATION AND CONNOTATION

The **denotation** of a word is its basic meaning, the meaning you would find if you looked it up in a dictionary. A word may have an additional layer of meaning, or connotation. **Connotation** is the suggested meaning or feeling attached to a word. For example, the denotation of the word *home* is "house" or "place where someone lives." For most people, this word has an additional connotation of comfort and safety.

Be aware of the fact that many synonyms, which have similar denotations, may have very different connotations. Often, one word has a **positive connotation**—that is, has a good feeling attached to it, whereas its synonym has a **negative connotation**—a bad feeling. *Clever* and *crafty* are similar in meaning, but *clever* has a positive connotation and *crafty* has a negative connotation.

Using a word with a particular connotation can have a strong effect on your audience. People who write speeches and advertisements take advantage of this fact.

For example, a car is not simply described as "well designed" or "fast." It is said to be "sleek, swift, and powerful."

Note that if you use a word with a connotation different from the one you intended, the result can be confusing, insulting, or unintentionally funny. If you tell your friend she's *stingy*, she might think you're putting her down for not being generous. But if you are using *stingy* to show that you really admire how *thrifty* she is—that is, how she manages to buy things on sale and save her money—then you're praising her.

25.5 CONTEXT CLUES

The **context** of a word consists of the words or sentences that surround the word. If you don't know the meaning of a word, context can often help you. You just have to know how to look for context clues. Context clues can be definitions, examples, comparisons, or other words or phrases that reveal information about the unknown word.

■■ 25.5A DEFINITIONS

Sometimes you will be lucky enough to find the definition of a word written right after it. Writers sometimes provide a definition if they want to clarify the meaning of a particular word.

EXAMPLE

At the Mexican restaurant, Casey ordered *burritos, soft flour tortillas filled with shredded beef and beans.*

▩ 25.5B EXAMPLES

Examples are another kind of context clue. An example doesn't state a word's meaning as obviously as a definition does, but it can reveal information.

> EXAMPLE
>
> In the distance he could make out some kind of *edifice*, possibly a *church* or a *mansion*.

From the examples *church* and *mansion*, you see that an *edifice* is a "large building."

▩ 25.5C COMPARISON AND CONTRAST

Another kind of context clue is a comparison. A **comparison** compares an unfamiliar word with something else more familiar. The comparison may include a synonym of the unfamiliar word.

> EXAMPLE
>
> The *adagio* section of the concerto was like a *slow, graceful dance*.

This clue suggests that *adagio* means "slow and graceful." You can also find a clue to the meaning of an unfamiliar word in a contrasting statement. A word such as *although*, *but*, or *not* is a hint to look for a contrast. The **contrast** may include an antonym of the unknown word.

> EXAMPLE
>
> *Although* the weather service had predicted *inclement* weather, the day was *calm* and *sunny*.

Here you can tell that *inclement* must be the opposite of "calm and sunny," and, in fact, the word means "severe" or "stormy."

▩ 25.5D GENERAL IDEA OR TONE

Sometimes you may not find a specific clue like the ones described above, but the whole sentence or paragraph in which an unfamiliar word appears helps you figure out its meaning.

> EXAMPLE
>
> The *ferocious* storm struck the boat with howling wind and waves that were forty feet high.

The whole sentence gives you a sense of what *ferocious* must mean: "fierce and violent."

25.6 MULTIPLE MEANINGS

Some words have more than one meaning. For example, a *grave* is a place where a corpse is buried, but *grave* also means "important" or "serious." If you know only one meaning of a word, you may be confused to see it used differently. The following examples show a word with multiple meanings used in different ways.

EXAMPLES

The carpenter used a *bolt* to fasten the back of the chair and the seat. (*Bolt* here means "a metal pin for fastening objects.")

Sara was afraid the horse would *bolt* suddenly and run away with her. (*Bolt* here means "to dash or dart off.")

If you encounter a word that doesn't seem to make sense in a sentence, the word may have a meaning that you're not aware of. You may be able to figure out the intended meaning using context clues. If not, look up the word in your dictionary, and go through all of its possible meanings until you find the one that makes sense in that context.

25.7 STRATEGIES TO INCREASE VOCABULARY

There are many strategies you can use on an ongoing basis to increase your vocabulary. The following are some suggestions.

Tips for Increasing Your Vocabulary

◎ When you encounter an unfamiliar word in your reading, don't skip over it. Take the time to find out what it means. Notice how it is used. This process will help you get to know the word and absorb it into your vocabulary so that you will remember it the next time you encounter it.

◎ If someone uses a word you don't understand in a conversation or in class, don't be embarrassed to ask its meaning. That's how you learn.

◎ Try to figure out an unfamiliar word's meaning by using context clues. Make a practice of looking for all types of context clues whenever you see a word you don't know.

◎ Remember that words may have multiple meanings.

25.8 DO IT YOURSELF: VOCABULARY ACTIVITIES

Being able to express yourself is important. A good vocabulary is one of the strongest tools you use in your communicating. See the next page for some spelling activities that will help improve your vocabulary.

1. Following are some words made up of word parts from the lists on pages 419 - 420. Figure out the meanings of the words by putting together the meanings of the parts.

EXAMPLE

Sample: regress   *re*. means "back" and *gress* means "go," so *regress* means "go back."

hemisphere   cyclic
thermometer   incredible
portable   reflection

2. For practice in using context clues, read the following sentences. See how many context clues you can find. Use them to help you figure out the meanings of the words in boldface type.

Half the people in the experiment will receive the new medication; however, the other half will receive a **placebo,** such as a sugar pill.

This coat is as **impervious** to rain as an underground cave is to sunlight.

Sandra came up with a scheme to win the student election. She spread rumors about one of the other candidates, spray-painted over her opponents' campaign posters, and convinced her friend on the student newspaper to write a great editorial about her. Of course, when these **machinations** were discovered, she was disqualified.

3. Work in groups to practice using a thesaurus to help you learn and use precise synonyms. Follow these steps.

- Write a sentence that contains a vague or general word.
- Look up the word in your thesaurus.
- Write a list of synonyms for the general word.
- Each synonym has its own special nuance of meaning. Decide which word fits exactly what you want to say.
- If you're not sure of the exact meanings of the words in your list, look them up in a dictionary. Write a brief definition of each word. Then choose the word you want to use.
- Rewrite your sentence substituting the more precise word.

Using words precisely and correctly is a key skill in communicating your ideas. For example, the word *nice* is a general word that doesn't say very much. Instead of calling a person "nice," you should use a more precise word. You can look up *nice* in a thesaurus to find a list of synonyms including *pleasant, pleasing, agreeable, cordial, amiable,* and *cheerful.* If you looked up these synonyms in a dictionary, you would find, for example, that *pleasant* means "having pleasing manners or appearance," while *amiable* means "friendly and sociable." You would pick the word that suggests the meaning you want to convey.

It is the subtle nuances of meaning that make synonyms interesting. Using them correctly allows you to bring more precision and flair to your writing.

4. To check your understanding of words with multiple meanings, read the following sentences. The word *stick* appears in each sentence. Write a definition for each use of the word.

- The dog will fetch a *stick*.
- Be careful not to *stick* yourself with the pin.
- The stamp would not *stick* to the envelope.

5. Decide which word in each pair below has a positive connotation and which has a negative connotation.

lazy/relaxed
courageous/reckless
stubborn/determined
rash/spontaneous
generous/spendthrift
thorough/fussy

ANSWERS

1. *Hemi-* means "half" and *sphere* means "round," so *hemisphere* means "half of something round."
Therm means "heat" and *meter* means "measure," so *thermometer* means "something that measures heat."
Port means "carry" and *-able* means "able to be," so *portable* means "able to be carried."
Cycl means "circle" and *-ic* means "like," so *cyclic* means "like a circle."
In- means "not," *cred* means "belief," and *-ible* means "able to be," so *incredible* means "not able to be believed."
Re- means "back," *flect* means "bend," and *-ion* means "act of," so *reflection* means "act of bending back."

4. First sentence: a branch or piece of wood. Second sentence: pierce with something pointed. Third sentence: hold firmly; adhere.

5. lazy, negative; relaxed, positive
courageous, positive; reckless, negative
stubborn, negative; determined, positive
rash, negative; spontaneous, positive
generous, positive; spendthrift, negative
thorough, positive; fussy, negative

Chapter 26 Letter Writing

Letter writing is a useful form of communication because it has so many different purposes. You can write personal letters to friends, family members, or acquaintances. You can write business letters to get jobs, information, goods, or services.

Although telephone calls can accomplish much day-to-day communication, letter writing is still very important. You can communicate detailed information—such as numbers, the correct spelling of names, and complicated stories—more accurately in a letter than in a telephone call. You can draft, revise, and edit a letter to make sure it says exactly what you want it to say. During a telephone call, you have no opportunity to correct or revise what you say before your audience hears it. In addition, a letter provides a written record of your communication. Now that people can send letters by fax machines and computers as quickly as they can make telephone calls, the advantages of letters are even clearer than ever.

Just in case you *still* think letters are not important anymore, consider this: The U.S. Postal Service handles more than 90,000,000,000 (ninety *billion*) pieces of first-class mail every year!

26.1 PERSONAL LETTERS

Personal letters are usually of two different kinds. One kind is the informal, friendly letter you write to someone close to you. The other kind is the social letter that you write to someone with whom you feel you should be a little more polite and formal, like the parents of a friend.

26.1A FRIENDLY LETTERS

A friendly letter can be about anything. It often sounds much like a conversation you would have with the person you're writing to. Using a proper format is less important in friendly letters than in more formal letters. Still, friendly letters usually include the basic parts of a letter: the **date**, a **salutation** (a "hello"), the **body** of the letter, and a **signature** (your name). Friendly letters almost always include a **closing** just before the signature. The following example of a friendly letter contains all of the basic letter parts.

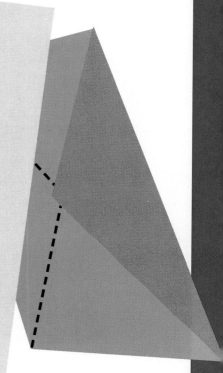

Salutation
Dear Kasha,

Date Monday, January 12

Body

I'm sorry I was a pain today at your house. I'll be honest. The problem was seeing you with the puppy your parents gave you during the holidays. I wanted a pet, too, but my parents wouldn't let me have one. I was jealous. I just couldn't tell you to your face because my feelings were so strong. Writing this letter has helped me get my feelings under control. I'm going to put this in your locker in the morning. I hope we are still best friends.

Closing Sorry,
Signature Dawn-Ann

▪▪ 26.1B SOCIAL LETTERS

You usually write a social letter for a specific reason. Maybe you are thanking someone for a gift or for inviting you for a visit. Maybe you want to respond to an invitation or send holiday greetings to a distant relative. In these situations, you want to sound a little more polite and formal but still friendly.

On invitations, you often see the letters *R.S.V.P.* This is an abbreviation for the French phrase *répondez s'il vous plaît,* which means "reply, please." People put *R.S.V.P.* on an invitation if they need to know whether you're coming, so it's polite to respond as soon as possible.

A formal social letter has all the same parts as a friendly letter: the date, a

Heading/Return Address 25 Zinnia Drive
Maple Falls, CT 06123
Date September 13, 1994

Salutation
Dear Mr. and Mrs. Janson,
Body
Thank you very much for inviting me to the Labor Day cookout you had for all the kids in the neighborhood. I had a great time meeting David and all his friends. It is a wonderful thing to be included when you've just moved to a new town. I look forward to spending more time with you and David.

Closing Gratefully,
Signature John Wallace

salutation, the body, a closing, and your signature. In addition, a formal social letter has a **heading** or **return address**, which is your address. The heading is a courtesy to the person receiving the letter. It provides your address in a handy place in case the person wants to write back to you.

26.2 BUSINESS LETTERS

Business letters are more formal than social letters. You often write a business letter to someone you've never met to request information or ask about a product or service. For a business letter to be effective, it should convey its message very clearly, and its appearance must be very neat. If at all possible, you should type a business letter or generate it on a computer. You should also keep a copy of any business letter—a carbon copy, a photocopy, or an electronic copy on a computer.

A business letter has all the parts a social letter does, with three additions. First, below the return address and above the salutation, you should put an **inside address**, which includes the name, title, organization, and address of the person you are writing to. Second, in addition to signing your name, you should type your name below your signature. Third, if you send along something with your business letter, such as a résumé or a copy of a disputed bill, you should add the word *enclosure* at the bottom of the letter and tell what you have included.

There are two basic formats for business letters: the **block** format and the **modified block** format. In the block format, every part of the letter begins at the left margin. There is an extra blank line between paragraphs, but paragraphs are not indented. In the modified block format, the heading, date, closing, signature, and enclosure note are typed to the right of an imaginary line running down the middle of the page. There is an extra blank line between paragraphs, and paragraphs are indented.

26.2A LETTERS OF APPLICATION

Although there are many different kinds of business letters, one of the most important is a **letter of application**. You write a letter of application when you're applying for a job, for admission to a school, or for a prize or award. A letter of application is a formal business letter, but in it you should give the reader a feeling for who you are and why you should be considered.

In this sample letter of application, you can see all the parts of a business letter, and you also can see how a business letter typed in the block format looks.

9 Rose Way   **Heading/return address**
Albuquerque, NM 88234
June 10, 1995   **Date**

Richard Percy   **Name**
Chairperson   **Title**
National Teen Instrumental Musician Awards   **Organization**
1600 Melody Lane   **Address**
Kansas City, MO 64112

Dear Mr. Percy: **Salutation**
Body
I am writing to apply for a National Teen Instrumental
Musician Award. Enclosed you will find my application form,
letters of recommendation, and a cassette tape of my audition.

My instrument is the alto saxophone. During the seven years I
have been studying the sax, I have made good progress with
this difficult instrument. My audition tape reveals the feeling I
have developed for saxophone music.

I would be honored and excited to receive a National Teen
Instrumental Musician Award. The master classes that are
part of the award would give me valuable help in becoming an
accomplished saxophonist, which is my goal.

I look forward to hearing from you on the announcement date.

Sincerely,   **Closing**
Rachael Greco   **Handwritten signature**
Rachael Greco   **Typed signature**

Encl: Application form   **Enclosure note**
      Letters of recommendation (2)
      Cassette tape

⬛⬛ 26.2B OTHER BUSINESS LETTERS

The other main category of business letters includes letters that concern information for goods and services. If you are writing to request information or to place an order for goods or services, the letter should be very direct, formal, and polite.

If you are writing a letter of complaint, you should avoid showing anger or frustration. Businesses want their customers to be satisfied, and they respond to letters of complaint. Your message should be clear and to the point. A letter that is brief is better than one that goes into too much detail.

In the sample letter of complaint, the writer first explains the problem, and then makes her request.

In this letter, you see how a business letter in a modified block format looks.

Heading/return address   9 Rose Way
Albuquerque, NM 88234
Date   March 13, 1995

Customer Service Department
Universal Musical Equipment Catalogue   **Inside Address**
82739 East Park Road NW
Seattle, WA 98777

Dear Sir or Madam: **Salutation** (Use a formal salutation when you don't know the person's name.)

Body

Last month I ordered a package of 12 reeds for an alto saxophone from your catalogue. When they arrived last week, they were all brittle and chipped. I am returning them with this letter.

Your catalogue offers a money-back guarantee on all merchandise, so I would appreciate your refunding my payment as soon as possible.

Thank you for your assistance in this matter.

Closing   Sincerely,
Handwritten signature   *Rachael Greco*
Typed signature   Rachael Greco

Encl: Package of 12 reeds   **Enclosure note**

26.3 MECHANICS

Look over the sample letters carefully and notice the punctuation and capitalization used. You should use a comma after the salutation in personal letters, but you use a colon after the salutation in business letters. In both, use a comma after the closing.

26.4 ENVELOPES

The format for addressing envelopes is the same for personal and business letters, except that you are usually expected to type the envelopes for business letters.

Your name and address appear in the upper left-hand corner of the envelope. The name and address of the person to whom you are writing are placed just right of center in the middle of the envelope. See the example that follows.

Tyrone Pell
198 Thomas Jefferson Road
Montclair, NJ 07405

Roger Watkins, Director
Summer Theater Institute
41 East 42nd Street, Suite D
New York, NY 10036

26.5 DO IT YOURSELF: LETTER-WRITING ACTIVITIES

1. You are getting an important award. There is going to be a big award ceremony, and you want your favorite aunt to be there. The problem is she lives in another state, quite far away. You told her about the award on the phone, but you want to write a letter—a special, personal invitation to persuade her to come and see you receive the award. Write a letter to your aunt, using the appropriate friendly letter conventions.

2. You are doing research for a report about the origins of place names. You've read that there is a booklet called "The Naming (and Misnaming) of America," which you can get free from the U.S. Department of the Interior. Write a letter asking for a copy of it. Here is the address:

U.S. Department of the Interior
Geological Survey
1200 South East Street
Arlington, VA 22202

3. You had a *big* birthday party at which you got presents from everyone. One of your parents' friends gave you a T-shirt you really love. Write a letter thanking that person for the gift.

Chapter 27 Test, Study, and Research Skills

....

Have you ever wondered why some people always seem to know the answers to questions in class, make wonderful reports, and always do well on tests? Is it because they are basically smarter than other people? Probably not. People aren't born knowing everything they ever need to know in life. Life is a continuing process of learning, and the people who seem to learn best are the ones who have good and effective learning skills. With a little thought and effort, anyone can become a more effective learner. The information in this chapter can help you improve your skills.

27.1 TEST-TAKING SKILLS AND STRATEGIES

From the time you started school, you've probably been taking tests. Those tests took different forms, but they all had the same purpose: to measure your knowledge and abilities. Tests can reveal where you are in the process of developing skills. They are also an important way for your teachers to evaluate how you are doing. All too often, however, tests cause fear and anxiety in students. Often this fear of test taking is caused by not knowing how to prepare for a test. Worrying about a test can hurt your performance. The easiest way to avoid needless fear and nervousness is to realize that test taking is a skill that can be mastered by any student. Learning the basic techniques of test taking will help you approach your tests with a more relaxed and confident attitude. That's half the battle.

The first commandment of test taking is NEVER CRAM. Trying to shovel several weeks' worth of knowledge into your brain in a single frantic evening is a recipe for sure disaster. Aside from the toll it takes on your nerves, cramming isn't a very effective way to learn.

◨ 27.1A PREPARING FOR TESTS

When a test is coming up, keep the following guidelines in mind:

1. **Begin preparing well in advance.** What is "well in advance"? That depends on how much material the test covers. A useful rule of thumb is that you should begin studying no later than four days before a short test and no later than ten days before a more comprehensive exam. At the early stages of preparation, your main task will be making sure you know the date of the test, the format, and what material will be covered. Knowing these things will enable you to plan your study time much more effectively.

2. **Assemble all your study materials.** Make a list of all the items you will need to study for the test: class notes, homework assignments, textbooks, reading notes, quizzes, and so on. Gather all these materials into one spot where you will have ready access to them.

3. **Decide which of your materials is the most important, and tackle that first.** Usually the most important study material will be your class notes or your textbook. Begin reading and reviewing this material, trying to focus on the key points and themes that came up in class discussions. If you are studying your textbook, make notes or outline the information so you have it in a concise form, which you can review easily and often. After several days of working with your class notes or your textbook, you can begin to review any other materials you have gathered.

4. **Begin to test yourself.** After a few days of reviewing, you should begin to test yourself. There are several ways to do this. First, you might think up a list of likely questions and see how well you can answer them in writing. If your test involves memorizing rules or facts, you can simply close your book or put away your notes and see whether you can write out the rules or facts in question. At this stage, you must be absolutely honest with yourself. If you don't *really* know something you need to know, go back to your materials and study until you do. At this stage, as at all other stages of studying, it is important not to set rigid limits to your studying time. You should be prepared to spend as much time as necessary to master the material.

5. **Consider working in a group.** If you think you would absorb more of the material by working with classmates or friends, arrange a time to get together to review the material and test one another. This method

works well for some but not for everyone. On the one hand, the group can sometimes come up with ideas that individuals would not have thought of alone. On the other hand, if some members are not as serious and focused as you are, a group can be a distraction. The wisest course is to begin studying on your own; if you feel you might benefit from working with a group, try that method. Be sure that you and the other group members have first done some studying on your own so that you will have some useful information and ideas to exchange. Starting from scratch in a group most likely will not be very helpful.

6. **Get plenty of rest the day before the test.** People who cram all night are likely to be too tired mentally to communicate what they have learned. If you start studying well in advance, you can get to bed early and approach the test with an alert, refreshed mind and a relaxed attitude.

7. **Eat a good breakfast the day of the test.** Don't sleep so late that you have to rush out without eating a well-balanced breakfast. Studies have shown that test takers with a good supply of "fuel" usually fare better than those who are "running on empty."

If you follow these seven steps, you will have gone a long way toward assuring yourself a positive and productive test-taking experience. Now let's move on to consider the various kinds of tests and the best methods for approaching each one.

27.1B OBJECTIVE TESTS

The most common kind of classroom test is the **objective test**. Such tests are called *objective* because they require you to give a brief, correct answer.

Multiple Choice

Objective tests come in a variety of formats, but the most common is the **multiple-choice test.** The questions in such tests usually consist of incomplete statements that require completion. Or they may be questions to which there is only one correct answer. The student must choose the best answer from three or four choices.

EXAMPLE

César Chavez led a labor-organizing movement for
a. automobile workers.
b. steel workers.
c. migrant farm workers.
d. office workers.

Students of United States history will recognize *c* as the correct answer. The only sure-fire method for answering such a question is to be so well acquainted with the material that you will not be misled by the incorrect answers. Sometimes the best answer may not leap out at you immediately, even if you know the material well. In such a case, there are a few guidelines you can follow to increase your chance of choosing the correct answer:

1. **Read the question carefully.** If you misunderstand the question, you'll probably have trouble answering it correctly.

2. **Read all the answers thoroughly and carefully.** Even if you come upon an answer that seems right, there may be another choice later on that is even better.

3. **Ignore answers that seem completely wrong.** This strategy helps you narrow the possible choices and focus on right answers.

When the correct choice is not immediately obvious to you, following these three steps will give you a better chance of identifying the correct answer.

Fill in the Blank

Another common objective test format is the **fill-in-the-blank** type.

E X A M P L E

Most of the workers organized by Chavez originally came from_____.

It is important to keep in mind that the answers to such questions must be correct both factually and grammatically. Here, the single word *Mexico* would be correct.

Short Answer

The **short-answer question** is also widely used.

E X A M P L E

What is a boycott, and how was it used by the United Farm Workers in its labor struggle?

Your answer to such a question should be thorough but concise. (Remember, you are supposed to give a *short* answer, not write an essay.) Writing your answer as a complete sentence will increase the likelihood that your answer is thorough. For a good answer to this question, see the next example.

E X A M P L E

A boycott is a refusal by one group to buy a particular product or have any dealings with a certain group. The United Farm Workers, under the leadership of César Chavez, was successful in organizing a nationwide consumer boycott of grapes in order to pressure the major grape growers into recognizing their union.

Analogies

You'll find that **analogies** often show up on standardized tests, such as the test you take to gain admission to a school or college. Analogy questions test your ability to understand the relationships between words and abstract ideas. An analogy typically asks you to identify the relationship between two pairs of items.

EXAMPLE

LIGHT:DARK::
a) small : tiny
b) tall : short
c) icy : wintry
d) sleepy : cranky

The correct answer is *b* since none of the other pairs of words are opposites. See the following analogies that deal with other kinds of relationships.

1. **Cause and effect:**
   rainstorm : flood : : victory : celebration
2. **User and instrument:**
   carpenter : hammer : : artist : paintbrush
3. **Synonyms:**
   freedom : liberty : : happiness : gladness
4. **Traits or features:**
   monster : scary : : grass : green
5. **General type and specific example:**
   shelter : house : : entertainment : circus

Since most analogy questions are multiple-choice, the guidelines for dealing with multiple-choice items apply here as well.

Reading-Comprehension Tests

Another important area that is covered by many standardized tests is **reading comprehension**. This type of test measures your ability to understand and remember material that you have read. The test asks you to read a passage and then answer multiple-choice questions about the passage. These questions might involve recalling specific facts from the passage, drawing conclusions, or identifying main ideas.

EXAMPLE

Television influences children in many important ways. The average child in the United States watches about 6,000 hours of television before he or she enters the first grade. That's about 20 percent of a preschooler's waking life. So before a child has even learned to read or write, his or her view of the world has been strongly shaped by television. Since most young children prefer to watch cartoons, their attitudes are influenced by typical Saturday mornings in front of the tube, with images of violence in the programs and junk food in the commercials. What can we expect of a society whose youngest members are programmed to accept conflict, violence, and advertising as a way of life–even before they have been taught their ABC's?

1. What would be the best title for the preceding paragraph?
   a) The Benefits of Children's Television
   b) Why We Need Censorship
   c) The Dangers of Junk Food
   d) Television and Young Children

2. Which of the following words best describe the author's attitude toward the television-viewing habits of young children?
   a) enthusiastic
   b) indifferent
   c) troubled
   d) sarcastic

3. What percentage of the average preschooler's waking hours are spent in front of the television?
   a) fifty percent
   b) twenty percent
   c) most
   d) seventy-five percent

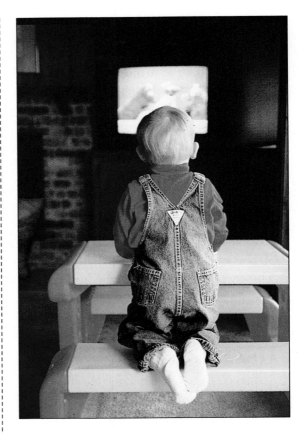

The paragraph focuses on children's television, but it certainly does not view it favorably, so the correct answer to Question 1 cannot be *a*. The paragraph mentions junk food, but that is not the main topic, and there is no mention of censorship at all. The best answer to this question is *d*.

Which choice for Question 2 best describes the author's attitude? Although the author is not happy about the impact of television on youngsters, he or she does not express his or her views in a sarcastic way, so *c* is the best answer to Question 2.

Question 3 simply asks you to recall a fact from the passage. Since *c* is not expressed as a fraction, it cannot be the correct answer. The time spent by children, according to the writer, is 20 percent, so *b* is the correct response.

A useful approach to most passages of reading comprehension is to read the questions before you read the passage. Then you will be able to anticipate the key points as you read the passage. You should read the passage thoroughly once. Multiple readings are not likely to improve your comprehension and will just waste time. For additional guidelines, see the section on multiple-choice items on page 437.

27.1C ESSAY TESTS

An essay test is a written test designed to assess your understanding of important ideas as well as your ability to see relationships among ideas.

The basic study techniques discussed on pages 436–437 apply as much to essay tests as they do to objective tests. Your first step in preparing for an essay test is to follow the seven steps explained in Test-Taking Skills and Strategies.

There are also some special kinds of preparation that you can use for essay tests. Once you feel that you know the material well, you should make a list of the major topics and themes. You can usually do this by looking over the chapter and section titles in your textbook or class notes. Using these topics as a starting point, try to write some questions you think your teacher might ask. Then write out sample answers to your questions in essay or outline form. This will give you practice in organizing your material and will help you practice your writing skills.

When you take an essay test, read the questions carefully. Be sure you understand their content. Also look for key words that tell you how you should structure your answer. Some important words to look for are *compare, contrast, explain, tell why, list, review, describe, show,* and *trace.* Each of these words suggests a different way to organize your answer. Remembering what these key test terms mean can help you write effective answers on essay tests.

> ### K E Y   T E R M S
>
> **compare:** show similarities
> **contrast:** show differences
> **explain:** inform about facts or give directions
> **tell why:** give reasons
> **list:** give examples or reasons
> **review:** summarize
> **describe:** create a vivid picture in words
> **show:** demonstrate logically
> **trace:** discuss origin and development

If you have time, make a brief outline of the key ideas you want to include. If time is short, try to plan your answer in your head before you start writing.

As you write, follow the basic form of essay writing discussed in the section on writing paragraphs, Chapter 10. You should have a clearly stated main-idea sentence in your opening paragraph. Follow up with one or more paragraphs in which you provide evidence and support for your main idea. In these supporting paragraphs, be as specific as you can. Avoid vague, general statements. Give specific examples and thoroughly define all key terms. End your answer with a concluding paragraph in which you restate your main idea.

Budget your time carefully. In order to pace yourself, bring a watch or use the classroom clock. Limit the time you spend on organizing and outlining so that at least half of the test time is left for actually writing your essay. Proofread your essay if you have time.

Below is a sample essay question that you might find on an American history test.

EXAMPLE

Sample Essay Question
Discuss the significance of the Cuban missile crisis of 1962. Do you think that the outcome was a victory or defeat for United States foreign policy?

A possible answer to the question appears in the next example.

EXAMPLE

Answer 1
In the fall of 1962, the United States government announced that there were Soviet missiles in Cuba, pointed at cities in the United States. This information started a series of events that brought the world face to face with the real possibility of all-out nuclear war between the United States and the Soviet Union. But President John F. Kennedy managed to save the world from destruction without sacrificing the honor or the interests of the United States.

The Soviets said that Fidel Castro, the Communist leader of Cuba, had asked them to put the missiles there to protect Cuba from United States aggression. In 1961, the United States had backed an invasion of Cuba by Cuban exiles. President Kennedy believed that Cuba, a Communist country only ninety miles off the coast of Florida, was a threat to national security and having the missiles there made it even worse. He was determined to get the Soviets to remove them.

When the United States demanded that the Soviets move their missiles out of Cuba, they refused to because the United States had missiles in Turkey that were pointed at cities in the Soviet Union. But President Kennedy and Nikita Khrushchev, the leader of the Soviet Union, managed to reach an agreement. The Soviets would move the missiles out of Cuba if the United States removed their missiles from

Turkey and pledged never to invade Cuba. This was a good agreement because it seemed to be an even exchange. Kennedy and Khrushchev had both gotten the other person to do something. But Kennedy really won, because the United States got more than it gave up. The missiles in Turkey were already obsolete, and the United States never intended to invade Cuba anyway. The Cuban missile crisis was a major victory for President Kennedy. By showing strong will and good judgment, he eliminated a threat to national security and avoided a nuclear disaster.

The following is another possible response to the same question.

EXAMPLE

Answer 2

Kennedy won a major victory in the Cuban missile crisis. The Soviets were trying to take over the world at the time, and they had to be stopped. Kennedy really showed them who was boss, and Khrushchev had to get out of Cuba and stay out. Let this be a big lesson to dictators and aggressors everywhere.

It is clear that the author of the first

answer has mastered the important facts relating to the question. But instead of just reciting a random series of facts, the writer has organized them in a way that shows their relevance to the question. The writer clearly states the main idea in the opening paragraph and uses the other paragraphs to support and develop the main idea. Then the writer restates and summarizes the main point in the last paragraph. By contrast, the second sample answer does not show real familiarity with the relevant facts or the ability to organize them in a coherent way.

There are two keys to success on essay tests: 1) know the relevant information, and 2) use your essay-writing skills to communicate the information in an organized way.

27.2 TAKING NOTES

You can increase your understanding of the books you read by taking notes. Taking notes helps you pick out the most important material and organize your thoughts. It also reinforces your reading comprehension by forcing you to engage in a sort of instant review of the material as you write it down.

Note taking can be useful in day-to-day reading, in studying for tests, and in doing research for term papers. You can take your notes on ordinary note paper, but many people prefer to use 4 x 6 note cards. Such cards let you shuffle and organize your notes more easily.

When a passage in your reading strikes you as especially important, write the topic of the passage at the top of a card and then summarize the contents of the passage. As you write, be sure that you think through the essential meaning of the passage so that you can rewrite it in your own words in a condensed form. Doing this will increase your understanding of the material.

EXAMPLE

Passage
You may know that human senses aren't very sharp, compared with those of other animals. This is partly because many people live in towns, where sounds are louder. When most of the sounds you hear are loud, after a while you don't pay attention to soft sounds. In wildlands, most sounds are soft, so you have to learn to hear them.

Also, some other animals hear better than we do, some see better, some have a better sense of smell, and some can move more quickly, silently, and carefully than people can. Wild animals have developed sharp senses and fast feet to help keep them from becoming another animal's dinner. Humans have developed a big brain

for the same reason.
(from *Take a Hike! The Sierra Club Kid's Guide to Hiking and Backpacking*, by Lynn Foster, Sierra Club/Little, Brown and Company, 1991: page 139)

EXAMPLE

Note Card
SENSES: ANIMALS VS. HUMANS
Human senses are not as sharp as most animals' senses. Animals rely on their senses to protect them from predators. Humans use their brains for the same purpose.

27.2A PARAPHRASING AND SUMMARIZING

Restating an author's ideas in your own words is called **paraphrasing**, and it is one of the most important note-taking skills. If you are gathering information for a research paper, you should give authors credit for their ideas even if you are not quoting them directly. For the proper method of citing sources in a research paper, see pages 448-450.

Students who fail to master the art of paraphrasing, however, run the risk of **plagiarism**. It is plagiarism to use an author's ideas or exact words in your writing without giving credit to the author. Your teacher can easily detect plagiarism.

It's important to learn how to benefit from the ideas of others without claiming these ideas as your own—either intentionally or unintentionally.

Occasionally it is helpful to write down an author's exact words in your notes. When you do this, put the entire passage in **quotation marks** so that you don't mistake the passage for a paraphrase when you return to your notes later on. If you are working on a research paper, including direct quotations from various experts can lend an air of authority and vividness to your paper. Just remember to use quotation marks and to identify the source of each quotation.

Summarizing is another important note-taking skill. Summarizing is really just paraphrasing in a shortened form. You might want to present an idea from the book you are reading in a few key words. In such a case, you paraphrase the passage so that it is at least half as long as the original. The passage below is followed by examples of paraphrasing, summarizing, and quotation.

EXAMPLE

Original Passage

For the first 50 years of recorded sound, starting with Thomas Alva Edison's playback of "Mary Had a Little Lamb," all recordings were acoustic. Absolutely no electronic equipment was involved at any stage—unless you want to count the light bulbs used to see what was going on. Recording relied entirely on the acoustic energy of a performer's voice or musical instrument going directly into the microphone. One lone microphone, responding to this very close voice or instrument, caused a stylus to etch the physical track of the sound waves directly onto a hard wax record as the performance was actually occurring. (Laura Dearborn, *Good Sound*)

EXAMPLE

Paraphrase: Beginning with Edison's recording of "Mary Had a Little Lamb," the first half-century of recording used no electronic equipment; the recordings were made acoustically. The musician's or singer's performance was fed into a microphone that transmitted the sound waves it captured into a needlelike device called a stylus. The stylus translated the sound waves into the grooves that it engraved onto a hard wax disc.

Summary: No electronics in recording for first fifty years. Sound waves from music fed directly into microphone, then transmitted directly onto a hard wax disc by a stylus.

Quotation: According to Laura Dearborn, "For the first 50 years of recorded sound, starting with Thomas Alva Edison's playback of 'Mary Had a Little Lamb,' all recordings were acoustic."

27.3 MEMORIZING

Once you have a complete set of notes, you can begin drafting your research paper or studying for a test. If you are using your notes to study for a test, you need to memorize the key material. There is no single best way to memorize, but there are some basic techniques that can make your task simpler and more efficient.

1. **Memorize key concepts.** Use chapter titles, outline topics, or headings from your notes to make a list of the most important concepts and topics. Concentrate on learning the key points about these topics. Be *selective*. Focus on only those major concepts and facts that you think your teacher is likely to ask about. Trying to memorize every fact and detail is an impossible task. Keep in mind that all tests, essay or objective, are designed to evaluate your grasp of important material, not every last detail.

2. **Test yourself.** This step is like a rehearsal. After you have reviewed the most important concepts and facts, test your mastery of the subject. One good method is to *write out* what you consider to be the essential things you need to know. Then compare your written self-test with your notes to see what gaps still exist. If there are gaps, review that material further. You can also recite the material aloud, but it's harder to keep track of what you've said than what you've written down.

3. **Use memory games.** Memory games, sometimes known as **mnemonic devices**, are especially useful with short, manageable chunks of material. You can make up words that consist of the first letters of key concepts; you can think of associations between various concepts. (For example: *photosynthesis* has the word *photo* in it; *photo* means "light." Light comes from the sun. So photosynthesis involves sunlight.) Be careful. If you try to use memory games to help you recall too much information, you may have trouble remembering your own memory games! The trick with mnemonic devices is not to use them too often.

27.4 OUTLINING

Outlining is another useful method for organizing your notes for studying or research. With this method you can group key themes, topics, and facts in a logical order. Each main topic is numbered with a Roman numeral, and subtopics and details are arranged logically under the main topics. If you are reading about history, the order of your outline might be chronological. In other subjects, you might organize the information by cause and effect or order of importance.

Origins of Ancient Greece

I. The Pre-Hellenic Civilizations
  A. Minoan Civilization on Crete, 4000-1600 B.C.
  B. Waves of Invading Tribes, Starting 1600 B.C.
    1. Achaeans
    2. Arcadians
    3. Ionians
  C. Mycenaean (Late Hellenic) Period, 1500-1100 B.C.
    1. Achaean dominance
    2. Heroic (Homeric) Age
      a. Agamemnon of Mycenae
      b. Nestor of Pylos
      c. Trojan War
  D. Dorian Invasion, 1100 B.C.

II. The Hellenic States
  A. The Formation of City-States, 1000-499 B.C.
    1. Introduction of coined money, 680 B.C.
    2. Overthrow of aristocrats by middle-class tyrants after 650 B.C.
  B. Age of Colonization, 750-500 B.C.
  C. Aristocracy in Sparta
    1. Influence of ideas of Lycurgus
    2. Emergence of aristocratic-military regime
  D. Democracy in Athens
    1. Overthrow of monarchy in 683 B.C.
    2. Solon's democratic reforms of 594 B.C.
    3. Struggle between nobility and middle class
    4. Victory of Cleisthenes and middle class, 500 B.C.
      a. Council of 500
      b. Popular assembly (ecclesia)

The sample outline deals with history and is basically chronological. Notice, however, that there are other forms of classification used. Under the heading "Aristocracy in Sparta," for example, the subcategories are topical rather than chronological. In making your own outlines, choose a basic scheme of classification that works best for your subject—chronological, cause and effect, or order of importance—but be flexible enough to combine or mix the schemes where necessary. The order of numbers and letters is the same for all outlines: Roman numeral, capital letter, Arabic number, lowercase letter, Arabic number with parentheses, and lowercase letter with parentheses.

27.5 BIBLIOGRAPHICAL FORMS

If you are using your notes or outline for a research project, you must be able to cite, or credit, your sources. After all, if you are borrowing ideas from other people, fairness and honesty dictate that you give them proper credit. Citing sources also makes your writing more authoritative and persuasive because you can show that it is based on the findings of recognized experts in the field.

First you will need to cite your sources in the body of your report. The three main methods for doing this are parenthetical citations, endnotes, and footnotes. Ask your teacher which style of citation would be best for your report. Remember that you should cite both paraphrased ideas and direct quotations.

Parenthetical Citations

Parenthetical citation is the simplest method of citing sources, and it is the method preferred by many teachers. A parenthetical citation is inserted right after the sentence or passage that includes a quotation or an idea borrowed from a source. It consists of the author's last name and the page of the work where the quotation or idea was found.

EXAMPLE

Johann Sebastian Bach is considered by everyone to be a very important composer. The period during which he lived and wrote is often called the Age of Bach. But during his lifetime, he was better known as an organist than a composer and his fellow musicians (and even his sons) called him the Old Whig because they thought his music was old-fashioned (Sommer 4).

If two books by Elyse Sommer had been listed in the bibliography, the parenthetical citation would have included a shortened version of the name of the book so the reader would know which one was being quoted:

EXAMPLE

(Sommer, *Kids' World Almanac* 4).

Someone who wanted more information about the source of these facts about Bach would look for the Works Cited list or the bibliography. The complete information of the source would be found there.

If you use parenthetical citations, a **Works Cited list**, a list of your sources, is the last page of your report. A works cited page can give authority to your work because you list the books and articles you read in the process of researching your paper.

Bibliographies

A Works Cited list and a **bibliography** are nearly the same, and they follow exactly the same format. There is one small but important difference between them: A Works Cited list includes only those books and periodicals mentioned in the parenthetical citations, whereas a bibliography lists all works the writer consulted, regardless of whether or not they showed up in the paper. In your list of works cited, list all your sources alphabetically, with the authors' last names appearing first. For each entry, indent all lines after the first. If you cite more than one work by the same author, after the first entry replace the author's name with three dashes.

E X A M P L E

Works Cited

Bardeche, Maurice, and Robert Brasillach. *History of Motion Pictures.* New York: Norton, 1938. [two authors]

Crowther, Bosley. *The Lion's Share.* New York: Dutton, 1967. [one author]

- - -. *The Great Films: Fifty Golden Years of Motion Pictures.* New York: Putnam, 1967. [another book by same author, Bosley Crowther]

"Isn't That Special?" *New York*

8 Nov. 1993:20. [unsigned magazine article]

It's a Wonderful Life. Dir. by Frank Capra. Turner Entertainment, 1993. [film or videotape]

Knight, Arthur. "Motion Picture." *The World Book Encyclopedia.* 1988. [signed article in encyclopedia]

Rafferty, Terrence. "The Current Cinema: City of Demons." *The New Yorker* 26 July 1993: 79-81. [signed magazine article]

Endnotes and Footnotes

You can also acknowledge a source by using an **endnote** or a **footnote**. To create an endnote or a footnote, place a number after the sentence or phrase whose source you wish to cite. Put the number right after the last punctuation mark and raise it by a half line. Here's the Bach citation as an endnote or a footnote within the text.

E X A M P L E

Johann Sebastian Bach is considered by everyone to be a very important composer. The period during which he lived and wrote is often called the Age of Bach. But during his lifetime, he was better known as an organist than a composer and his fellow musicians (and even his sons) called him the Old Whig because they thought his music was old-fashioned.[1]

To identify a work from which you borrowed information, prepare either endnotes or footnotes. The form of each kind of note is the same—only the position is different. An endnote is found in a list titled *Notes* on the last page of a report. A footnote is placed at the bottom (or "foot") of the page on which it appears.

E X A M P L E

¹Elyse Sommer, *The Kids' World Almanac of Music: From Rock to Bach* (New York: World Almanac/ Pharos Books, 1991) 4.

When you prepare footnotes, you'll need to leave enough space at the bottom of each page for that page's footnotes.

An endnote or a footnote for a book should include the following: (1) the author's name (first name first) followed by a comma; (2) the book title (italicized or underlined); (3) the city of publication, followed by a colon and the name of the publishing house and the year of publication (all these should be in parentheses); (4) the page number of the citation followed by a period.

E X A M P L E

¹Arthur Knight, *The Liveliest Art* (New York: The New American Library, 1957) 152.

Periodicals are cited in footnotes as follows: (1) the author's name, followed by a comma; (2) the title of the article in quotation marks and followed by a comma (the comma goes *inside* the quotes); (3) the title of the periodical in italics or underlined (followed by the volume number if it's a scholarly journal) and followed by a colon; (4) the date; (5) the page number.

E X A M P L E S

²Carl Dreyer, "Thoughts on My Craft," *Sight and Sound* 25 (Winter 1955-56): 128-29.
³Irving Howe, "Dreiser and the Tragedy," *New Republic* 22 August 1964: 28.

After you have cited a work once, you don't need to give all the information when you cite the same work again. For example, if the person writing the report about Bach were to cite *The Kids' World Almanac of Music* again, the footnote would look like what follows.

E X A M P L E

² Sommer 15.

27.6 USING THE LIBRARY/MEDIA CENTER

Your library is like a theme park of the human mind and spirit. Here the great ideas and accumulated knowledge of humankind lie before you like undiscovered lands awaiting your arrival. Your passport is your library card. Best of all, it's all free. Great scientific discoveries, the heroes and villains of great literature and cinema, the priceless classics of great music, the hopes and conflicts of the world as chronicled in newspapers and magazines—all this at your fingertips. All you need to do is walk through the door. Here are a few tips on finding your way around.

In most libraries, fiction books are arranged alphabetically by the author's last

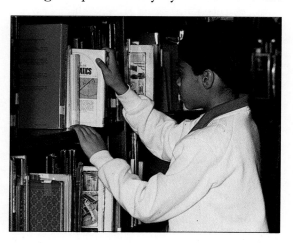

name. If an author has written more than one work of fiction, then the titles are arranged alphabetically under the author's name.

School libraries usually arrange nonfiction books by the **Dewey Decimal System.** This system assigns every book a coded number called a **call number**. The numbers indicate subject matter. The chart below shows how books are arranged in the Dewey Decimal System.

DEWEY CLASSIFICATION OF NONFICTION		
Numbers	*Subject Areas*	*Examples of Subdivisions*
000-099	General Works	encyclopedias, handbooks
100-199	Philosophy	psychology, ethics, personality
200-299	Religion	Bibles, mythology, theology
300-399	Social Sciences	government, law, economics
400-499	Languages	dictionaries, grammars
500-599	Science	general science, mathematics
600-699	Technology	engineering, inventions
700-799	The Arts	music, theater, recreation
800-899	Literature	poetry, dramas, essays
900-999	History	biography, geography, travel

Many libraries catalog their books by computer. This form of storing information about books is sometimes called an

on-line catalog. The computer allows you to look for books by typing in the names of authors or titles, or subjects. Once you have typed in the kind of information you desire, a list of books will appear, along with other useful information such as call numbers, number of copies available, loan period, and location.

Some libraries still use the traditional **card catalog**, a set of cabinets with small drawers that contain cards that provide information about all the books in the library. Like the on-line catalog, the card catalog lists books in three categories: *author, title,* and *subject.* Although it cannot provide as much information as a computer, the card does furnish the basics: call number and subject matter.

An author card, a subject card, and a title card are essentially the same. The first line of the author card (right next to the call number) lists the author's name on the author card and the subject's name on the subject card.

Your search for books will be much easier if you are familiar with the main parts of a book.

Parts of a Book

1. **Title page**: The first page, which gives title, author, publisher, and place of publication.
2. **Copyright page:** Overleaf of title page, which gives year the book was copyrighted and any copyright updates.

3. **The preface, foreword, and introduction:** Sections in which the author, editor, or publisher explains the nature and purpose of the book and acknowledges those who have helped produce it.
4. **Table of contents:** A list of the chapters and subsections of the book with their page numbers.
5. **Appendix:** Additional information not found in the main portion of the book.
6. **Glossary:** Alphabetical listing of difficult words or technical terms that appear in the book.
7. **Bibliography:** Alphabetical listing (by author) of works consulted in writing the book.
8. **Index:** Alphabetical listing of all topics and people mentioned in the book, along with page numbers; this is a far more detailed listing than the table of contents.

Periodicals–magazines and newspapers–can also be found in on-line and printed indexes. Many libraries have computer terminals connected to periodical indexes that allow you to search for any topic in any time period.

The standard printed source for periodicals is the *Readers' Guide to Periodical Literature.* This guide indexes about 175 periodicals alphabetically by author and index.

Sifting through the vast resources of a library is easier if you are acquainted with the main reference works. You are probably familiar with some of these, such as encyclopedias and dictionaries. A listing of useful reference works follows.

Encyclopedias feature articles on a wide variety of topics, listed alphabetically. Popular encyclopedias include *The World Book Encyclopedia, Encyclopaedia Britannica, Collier's Encyclopedia,* and *Compton's Encyclopedia.*

Biographical references contain summaries of the lives of notable people, living and dead. These references are sometimes arranged according to the fields in which these people gained their recognition, for example, *Current Biography, Dictionary of American Biography, Contemporary Authors, Everyman's Dictionary of Literary Biography,* and *Who's Who in America.*

Almanacs are published once a year and contain vast amounts of statistical information about events during the preceding year, as well as other useful data. Popular almanacs include: *The World Almanac and Book of Facts; The Information Please Almanac,* and *Book of Facts.*

Atlases contain maps and other information about world geography. Examples include *Hammond Ambassador World Atlas, Atlas of World Cultures, National Geographic Atlas of the World, Times Atlas of the World,* and *National Atlas of the United States of America.*

27.7 DO IT YOURSELF: STUDY-SKILLS ACTIVITIES

1. You have been reading *Tuck Everlasting* in English class. Today was the last day spent on it in class. A week from today you are going to be tested on the entire book. List the days between now and the day of the test. Then plan what you will do between now and then to prepare for that test. When will you start studying? What will you do each day?

2. Imagine that you had to answer this essay question: Why does an essay test provide a better measure of a student's knowledge and abilities than any of the most commonly used objective tests? Plan and outline your answer to this question, using information in Section 27.1.

3. Paraphrase the following passage:

The people in the audience were unhappy and upset. They were sure that the man on the stage would soon become ill and probably die when he ate the tomato. For hundreds of years before this day in the year 1830, everyone had believed that tomatoes were unsafe to eat because they were poisonous. One man, however, Colonel Robert Johnson of Salem, New Jersey, was certain this fear of eating tomatoes was based on a false belief. In fact, he was sure that this juicy red fruit was a safe and nourishing food. As Colonel Johnson began to bite into a tomato, the audience gasped and a few people even fainted. A few minutes later when the tall, healthy man began to eat another tomato, the audience clapped their hands and cheered. Americans had been introduced to one of their all-time favorite foods.

4. Recall the strategies you read about in 27.3. How could you use these strategies to help you remember important information about these concepts? (If these concepts are new to you, learn about them in an encyclopedia before you get started.)

  geology
  stalactite
  hieroglyphics
  stalagmite

5. To practice your skills in preparing Works Cited entries, create a Works Cited list for everything you read for an entire week. Use the entries in 27.5 as your model for citing all the books and magazine articles you read.

6. Try this with a classmate. Make a list of things you'd like to know. They can be things you're really curious about or weird things you think it might be fun to find out. For everything you dream up, your partner should think of library resources you could use. When you have listed ideas for every item on your list, go to the library and test out the ideas.

Chapter 28 Critical Thinking Skills

You might be surprised at how many times a day you use critical thinking. For example, when you're deciding what to have for lunch in the cafeteria, how do you make that decision? If you feel like having a salad but the lettuce looks wilted, you draw the conclusion that the salad might not taste very good. If you've eaten in the cafeteria many times, you might know that the grilled cheese sandwich is usually cooked to perfection. Your experience might help you make the generalization that the grilled cheese is always good, so you order it. Both generalizing and drawing conclusions are important critical thinking skills that can help you be as happy with your writing as you are with your lunch.

28.1 OBSERVATION

Observation is the cornerstone of all critical thinking. You must look carefully at the material you're working with in order to evaluate it correctly. Consider yourself a human camera, noticing what is in front of you and selecting its important details. By being aware of this information–in your life as well as in your writing–you'll be able to analyze it in the best possible way.

28.2 DETERMINING CAUSE AND EFFECT

Let's pretend you've just dropped onto Earth from Mars. Everything is new to you. Nothing seems to make sense. Later, you begin to observe a few interesting but unexplainable events. For instance, you notice that at a certain time of the year, the weather turns from warm to cool. When it starts to get cool, many birds begin flying away, all in the same direction. You realize that the cool weather must have something to do with all the birds being in the air. The weather is the **cause** of an **effect**, bird migration. That effect can, in turn, become the cause of another effect—more birds in the warm climates of the South.

Understanding causes and effects is important when you're writing. For example, your teacher might ask you to observe a scientific experiment and write a short paper about it. First, of course, you'll have to observe the experiment and take good notes. Then you might want to look at the evidence and decide whether there are any cause-and-effect relationships. Did one chemical cause a reaction? Note the name of the chemical and describe *how* it caused the reaction. Then explain in detail *what* the change—the effect—looked like.

Sometimes an effect has more than one cause. Suppose you're reading about acid rain, a form of pollution in rainwater. You might discover that acid rain has several causes: factory emissions, vehicle emissions, fertilizers, coal-burning furnaces, and de-icer chemicals on winter roadways. Always inspect an effect for having more than one cause.

Cause-and-Effect Checklist
Here is a checklist you can follow to make sure that when you use cause and effect, you have every base covered.

- Do all the effects in your paper have a well-explained cause—or causes?
- Have you adequately explained how the cause produces the effect?
- Are the effects you've discussed actually the result of the cause you've described?
- Have you placed the cause and the effect together so that the connection is obvious and easily understood?

28.3 ORDERING INFORMATION

Organizing information in a logical way is very important in writing. If you're explaining to someone how to build a model airplane, but you explain the steps in the wrong order, what do you think the plane will look like? Other types of organizing in your writing are just as crucial.

Ways of Organizing Information
Chronological order refers to the way events occur over time. This kind of order is important when you're writing a biography. Your writing will be clearer if you explain the events of the person's life in the order in which they occurred. It might be confusing, for example, to write about your subject's college years before you've explained the person's childhood.

Spatial order has to do with the arrangement of things in space. You might want to describe a large room where something happened. Usually the best way to do this is to write as if you are scanning the room in an orderly way, for example, from left to right, from right to left, or from front to back.

Order of importance is the sequence of ideas. In working with this type of ordering, you must first lay out all the important facts you'll discuss. Perhaps you're writing a persuasive essay about lowering the driving age. You'll probably have several ideas that you think will convince your reader that your position is correct. It's up to you to decide which ideas are the strongest and which ideas you think will be the most persuasive. Rank the points you want to make from the strongest to the weakest. Then decide what order to put them in. You may decide to open strongly by using your most persuasive points first. If you decide to close strongly, you'll save the best points until the end of your essay and build up to them. Whatever the order, making decisions about the importance of ideas allows you to control how the information in your paper is organized.

28.4 DRAWING CONCLUSIONS

Put on your detective hat. You're about to solve an important case. Before you is the evidence.

- The hall is dark as you enter.
- There are low whispers to the left in the living room.
- Rustling paper can be heard in the far corner.
- As you creep in, all becomes silent.
- Your mom wished you a happy birthday this morning and gave you a present, but no party was planned.

Based on the evidence, what do you think is happening in the living room? What conclusion have you drawn from the evidence? When you write, be sure you wear your detective hat. Writing has a lot in common with investigating, and especially with drawing conclusions.

A good conclusion is usually the result of a series of observations. For example, if you see a little girl on a playground crying, it wouldn't be logical to reach the conclusion that she's a crybaby, based on your one observation. However, if the same little girl is crying every time you see her, you might logically conclude that she's a crybaby.

Sometimes a conclusion is based on a chain of reasoning. For example, you may have noticed that your mother is always in a good mood on Monday morning and that she doesn't seem to mind bringing home work from the office. You've heard her talking about her job at social gatherings. You know that people who like their jobs generally act this way, so you might conclude that she likes her job.

28.5 MAKING INFERENCES

You make an inference when you make a reasonable assumption based on known facts. For example, if you hear a siren on the street outside your home, you might infer that an emergency vehicle is going by. Similarly, if an author describes a story character as having "shifty eyes and an evil laugh," you'll probably infer that the character is going to be one of the bad guys.

When making an inference, ask yourself the questions that follow.

- Is my inference based on sound reasoning—or on personal prejudice or fear? (For example, an insecure person might see a group of people laughing and wrongly infer that they're laughing at her.)
- What other logical explanation or conclusion could I have reached? Why is the inference that I chose the most logical?
- How does the context of the situation support my inference? For instance, if

you're reading about a track meet, you'll infer that a character's competitive attitude is natural.

28.6 MAKING GENERALIZATIONS

After a beautiful spring and summer, you think back over the flowers that bloomed in the city's garden. You remember that in the early spring there were a few types of flowers growing—-crocuses, jonquils, and some hyacinths. Later, in June and July, there were thirty or forty different types of flowers blooming. You might make a **generalization** about your observation by stating that there were more flowers in bloom in June than there were in April and May. Because you've based your observation on facts, your generalization is probably correct. Generalizing allows you to make statements about things based on observation and reasoning.

Guidelines for Making Generalizations

- Make sure your generalization is limited to the facts you're dealing with. If you are writing about basketball rules for students your age, don't make a generalization that applies to all basketball players everywhere.

- Be sure you understand all the facts and cause-and-effect relationships. For example, suppose that a basketball team from a particular school usually wins its games. Does it win because it has better players? Because it has a great court to practice on? Because it gets more practice? Or because it has a good coach?

- Make sure you apply your reasoning in a valid way. If you generalize that what is true in one situation is also true in another, make sure that the two situations are reasonably alike.

28.7 EVALUATING INFORMATION

You've learned to compare sale promotions in math class. You know that a ten-percent price reduction on a stereo might still mean more money out of your pocket than a low, low price at another store. This type of reasoning is called **evaluation.** You consider information at hand and then make a decision based on the facts and based on your own reasoning.

In your writing, you evaluate information presented to you as well. Perhaps you've interviewed experts on endangered species. Now you're going to write a report about those animals. You realize some people think that some species of wildlife should not be protected because saving them would put people out of work. In writing your report, you'll want to evaluate arguments on both sides of the controversy. Then you'll make a recommendation based on the facts you've gathered.

28.8 POINT OF VIEW

Think about watching a space shuttle launch on television. You saw the ignition and blastoff clearly, didn't you? How do you think the event looked from inside the control tower or from an observation point at the launch site? Depending on where you view an event–from which **point of view**–the event will look slightly different.

This is also true when it comes to people. Characters in a book, for example, would tell the same story quite differently because each character "sees" the events from a different perspective. When you're writing a story, it's important to keep this in mind. As the author, you must decide from which point of view you want to tell your story. If you're writing a humorous story about the day you adopted your dog, would it be funnier from your point of view or from the dog's? Maybe your new puppy got mud all over the house and made your mother angry. Would the story be funny told from your mom's perspective? Probably not!

28.9 DISTINGUISHING BETWEEN FACT AND OPINION

Everyone has had the experience of mistaking opinion for fact. A popular movie star might endorse a breakfast cereal or a political cause. It's up to you to determine whether what the star says is actually fact or merely an opinion.

It's also important to know when information comes from a biased point of view. This means that the person giving the information has a particular reason for wanting you to believe something. For example, advertisers want you to believe that their products are wonderful so they'll make sales.

Which of the following statements are fact, and which are opinion?

- *Multigram Plus* provides 90% of all the vitamins and minerals you need every day. There's not a better thing you can do for your body than eat a bowl of *Multigram Plus* for breakfast. (first sentence, *fact*; second sentence, *opinion*)
- *Melancholy Murder* is better than the best Agatha Christie mystery. (*opinion*)
- Many types of whales, including orca, humpback, and giant finback, either live or migrate to the Sea of Cortes. Altogether more than 850 species of marine life inhabit those waters. (*facts*)

In your own writing, being able to distinguish between facts and opinions is vital. Make sure the evidence you cite in a paper is based on fact, not opinion or what you *wish* were true. Your writing will be believable if you follow these suggestions.

- Make sure you find out the sources of information. Is the source an expert, or is it someone whose information might be inaccurate or biased?
- Decide whether information is fact or opinion—and whether it comes from a biased source.
- Be alert for any exaggeration of facts.
- Be able to state why each point in your paper is true.

28.10 STEREOTYPING

Stereotyping occurs when you draw conclusions about other people based on your opinions of the groups the other people belong to. To assume that someone will act or think in a certain way because she's a woman, or because he's a man, or because of his or her race, religion, hometown, job, and so on, is to use a **stereotype.** It is an unfair and unrealistic way of looking at people. People are more complicated–and more interesting–than any stereotype.

As you write, evaluate your judgments to be sure you aren't using stereotypes. It might be helpful to make a list of common stereotypes before beginning a writing project. That way you can be aware of the pitfalls to avoid.

28.11 CLASSIFYING

When you were younger, did you ever match blocks by color or shape? Your game was a simple form of classifying. Now you do more sophisticated kinds of classifying. In science class, you might classify plants and animals. In English class, you might classify words by their function in a sentence, for example, as nouns, verbs, or direct objects. To **classify** is to put things with similar or like characteristics together in groups.

When you gather information for a paper, you arrange all the material under different headings, grouping similar facts and details together. Classifying is important to good writing. When you write a topic sentence and include relevant details, you're classifying the details under the topic that they support.

If you are writing a scientific paper about wasps, for example, you'll want to make sure you group the information about wasps under the correct headings. Organize your information first in an outline and refer to your outline as you write to be sure you are presenting all the information in a logical fashion.

EXAMPLE

Wasps
I.   Wasps as insects
      A. Number of legs
      B. Body type
      C. Color
II.   Nest-building methods of different species
      A. Social wasps build nests for entire colonies
          1. Paper wasps
          2. Hornets and yellow jackets
      B. Solitary wasps have individual nests built by females
          1. Potter wasps
          2. Mud-dauber wasps

When you write from an outline, you can convert the major heads into topic sentences and use the information in the subheads to write the details of the paragraph. When you read over your paper during the revision stage, use your outline again to be sure your classifications are correct.

28.12 COMPARE AND CONTRAST

When you **compare** and **contrast,** you look at what's similar and different about two things. For example, you might write a paper about Russia before and after the break-up of the Soviet Union. You might look at several factors, such as family life, economics, and politics in your paper. For each factor, you want to find out how conditions changed and how they remained the same.

Comparing and contrasting can also be used in other kinds of writing. Let's say you've chosen pandas as a topic for an informative essay. You might describe what they look like, where they live, and what their system of family life is like. As part of your paper, you can compare how wide-ranging their habitat once was in contrast to what it is today. Because of the destruction of their habitat, the panda's territory has been much reduced. You'd be using comparison and contrast as a part of your overall discussion.

28.13 PURPOSE AND AUDIENCE

Whenever you write, you must keep in mind your purpose for writing and your audience. The tone of your writing, its form and content, and the way you present your material depends on why and for whom you're writing.

For example, if you're interested in catching people's attention and convincing them to buy a product, would you write an advertisement in a few words or a persuasive essay? An ad with interesting illustrations and bold type would probably catch people's attention. A persuasive essay takes time to read, so it probably wouldn't be as good at attracting attention.

It's a good idea to think through your purpose before you write your first word. Be sure you can state simply, in one sentence, what you hope to accomplish by your writing. Remember to include the reader in your planning as well. By thinking about both, you increase the chances that your writing will accomplish its purpose and be read by its intended audience.

Similarly, when you're reading someone else's writing, ask yourself these questions.

- What is the author's purpose for writing? Is it to entertain? To inform? To persuade?
- Might the author have a hidden

purpose? For example, when political candidates write about social reform, they might also be trying to make themselves look good so they will win votes in a future election.

- Who seems to be the author's intended audience?
- How well has the author's purpose succeeded with me?

28.14 DO IT YOUR-SELF: CRITICAL THINKING ACTIVITIES

1. Think of an idea for improving your city or town that you would like to suggest to an elected official. For example, you might suggest having a street fair or holding weekend roller-skating sessions in the city hall parking lot. Once you've come up with an idea, make a list of the facts and reasons you could use to persuade someone that your idea should be adopted. Number your ideas to show the order of importance, using *1* for the idea you think is the strongest and most persuasive.

2. Create an outline to show how you would organize the following information into a report.

- *The Wonderful Wizard of Oz*, by L. Frank Baum, was first published in 1900.
- The movie *The Wizard of Oz* was released in 1938.
- Baum made the story into a musical comedy for the stage in 1901.
- Baum wrote thirteen sequels to *The Wonderful Wizard of Oz*.
- The musical *Babes in Toyland*, which opened in 1903, was based on the story line of *The Wizard of Oz*.
- The movie starred Judy Garland as Dorothy.
- The movie and the original stage show have completely different songs.
- *The Wiz* is a rock musical based on the movie.
- *The Wiz* opened in New York in 1975.

3. Each topic listed below is followed by three sources of information. Decide which source you think would be the best authority and which source is most likely to be biased.

Damage to environment caused by an oil spill

oil company responsible for the accident

an environmental group

the director of the Environmental Protection Agency

Benefits of restoring a city's downtown district

- local historical society
- downtown merchants
- people owning homes in nearby neighborhoods

The best sources of protein

- people who are vegetarians
- cattle ranchers
- nutritionists

The nature and habits of wolves

- the encyclopedia
- an animal rights group
- a study of wolves in classic literature

4. Find an advertisement in a magazine or newspaper. Look for one that has a great deal of print and explains the benefits of the product. Read the ad and categorize each statement as *fact* or *opinion*. Then look at the statements again. For the statements you identified as *fact*, mark those that might be influenced by bias.

5. Your purpose and audience influence the form, content, and tone of your writing. Think about the following purposes and audiences and decide which kind of written product would be most appropriate—a friendly letter, a business letter, a persuasive essay, a report, or another method.

- You want to tell other students about a new book you've read.
- You want to inform the school that your English class wants to put on a play.
- You want to ask the mayor for permission to "adopt" a public garden.
- You want to get students involved in a Neighborhood Watch program.

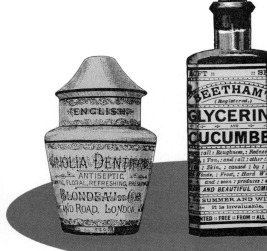

Literary Terms and Techniques

ABSTRACT TERM A word or phrase that stands for an idea or something else that cannot be perceived by one or more of the five senses. *Life, liberty,* and *the pursuit of happiness* are all abstract terms.

ACRONYM A word formed by combining the first letters or syllables of several words. *Sonar,* for example, is an acronym for "**so**und **na**vigation and **r**anging."

ACT A major division of a play. Full-length plays often have two to five acts, which are further divided into scenes. A short play may have only one act.

ALLEGORY A work of fiction or a play in which most of the characters, events, and settings work together to teach a moral lesson. A *fable* is one simple kind of allegory.

ALLITERATION The repetition of sounds in words near one another, especially consonant sounds at the beginning of words. The expression "suffering succotash" uses alliteration.

ALLUSION A brief reference in a work to something outside the work. The writer assumes that the reader will know the allusion. Allusions are often made to history, literature, current events, music, art, mythology, and religion. For example, the title of Stephen Vincent Benét's story "By the Waters of Babylon" is an allusion to a verse from the Bible that contains that phrase.

AMBIGUITY The possibility that a situation can be interpreted in more than one way. Sometimes writers intentionally create ambiguity in a work to encourage readers to speculate about its meaning.

ANALOGY A logical comparison between two things that are alike in some ways but not in others.

> ### EXAMPLE
> The state of Florida is like the letter J tilted on its side. Near the top of the J is the city of Pensacola; near the bottom, the city of Miami.

ANALYSIS The process of studying a subject by separating it into its basic parts.

ANECDOTE A brief story that recounts a real-life event and is told to entertain or inform.

ANTAGONIST   In a plot with a conflict, the person or force that opposes the main character, or *protagonist*. In Jack London's "To Build a Fire," the antagonist is the frozen landscape in which the protagonist struggles to survive.

ANTONYM   A word whose meaning is the opposite (or nearly the opposite) of another word. *Day* and *night* are antonyms.

APHORISM   A brief, memorable statement that makes a clear point or observation.

> E X A M P L E
>
> Injustice anywhere is a threat to justice everywhere.
>
> —Martin Luther King, Jr.

APOSTROPHE   Language addressed to an imaginary or absent listener. The "listener" may be a person, thing, or idea.

> E X A M P L E
>
> Sail on, O Ship of State!
> —Henry Wadsworth Longfellow

ARCHAISM   Language used in the past but rarely used now. The words *thee* and *thou* are archaisms.

ASSONANCE   The repetition of vowel sounds in words near one another. The expression "sweet dreams" uses assonance.

ATMOSPHERE   The primary mood of a work of literature. Pace and descriptions of setting often help establish atmosphere.

AUDIENCE   The person or persons who read, hear, or view a work.

AUTOBIOGRAPHY   An account of a person's life written by that person. For example, the book *Barrio Boy* is Ernesto Galarza's autobiography.

BALLAD   A brief poem that narrates a single episode and is written to be sung. A *folk ballad* is an anonymous ballad that has been passed down orally.

BIOGRAPHY   An account of a person's life written by someone other than that person. *Harriet Tubman: Conductor on the Underground Railroad* is author Ann Petry's biography of Tubman.

CAUSE AND EFFECT   A relationship between events in which one event sets off (causes) another event.

CHARACTER   A person (or another creature that behaves like a person) in a work of literature. *Flat characters* have only one or two personality traits. *Dynamic characters* have several sides to their personalities and are more like real people; they change and grow as a result of plot events and interaction with other characters. *Static characters* remain the same throughout a work.

CHARACTERIZATION   A writer's development of a character's personality. *Direct characterization* states opinions about a character's personality: "Juana was shy but sincere." *Indirect characterization* provides details from which readers infer the character's personality. These details may include the character's actions, speech, and thoughts, as well as descriptions of the character's physical appearance and relations with other characters.

CHRONOLOGICAL ORDER　The time order in which actions or events happen. Most plots unfold in chronological order, although some are told out of order.

CLICHÉ　A phrase or expression used so often that it has lost its imaginative impact. *White as snow* and *cold as ice* are examples.

CLIMAX　In a plot, the point of highest tension or emotional involvement.

COHERENCE　The quality of having all ideas in a written work relate to one another.

COLLOQUIALISM　A word, phrase, pronunciation, or grammatical usage that is characteristic of informal speech but is discouraged in formal or written English. The term "a lot" is a colloquialism.

COMEDY　A drama or another work that treats characters and events in a humorous or lighthearted way and usually has a happy ending.

COMPARISON AND CONTRAST　An examination of two subjects in order to show their similarities and differences.

CONCRETE POETRY　Poetry in which the shape or appearance on the printed page reflects the subject or meaning. In Maxine Kumin's "400-Meter Freestyle," for example, the lines of the poem resemble laps in a swimming pool.

CONCRETE TERM　A word or phrase that stands for something that can be perceived by one or more of the five senses. *Sun* is a concrete term; *happiness* is not.

CONFLICT　The struggle between opposing forces around which the events of a plot focus. The conflict may be between two characters (person against person); it may be between a character and nature; or it may be a personal struggle within a character (person against self).

CONNOTATION　The feeling that a reader or listener gets from a word. For instance, *slender* and *skinny* mean basically the same thing, but *slender* has a more positive, or pleasing, connotation.

CONSONANCE　The repetition of consonant sounds in words near one another, especially at the end of the words. The expression "figh**t** i**t** ou**t**" uses consonance.

COUPLET　A two-line poem or stanza, or two consecutive rhymed lines within a poem.

> E X A M P L E
>
> But if the while I think on thee, dear friend,
> All losses are restored, and sorrows end.
> —Shakespeare, "Sonnet Thirty"

DENOTATION　The precise meaning of a word, as opposed to its connotation. For example, the denotation of the word *sunshine* is "light from the sun." The connotation of the word is "warmth and cheerfulness."

DÉNOUEMENT   The outcome of the plot. The conflict is resolved in the dénouement.

DESCRIPTION   Writing that creates a mental picture of a person, place, or object by providing details about its qualities and appearance.

DIALECT   The form of a language used in a particular region or by a particular group of people. Dialects may differ in vocabulary, pronunciation, and/or grammar.

DIALOGUE   Conversation between characters in a work of literature.

DIARY   A person's day-to-day account of his or her thoughts and experiences. *Anne Frank: The Diary of a Young Girl* is one famous example.

DRAMA   Type of literature written to be performed by actors playing the roles of characters in front of an audience. A drama is also called a *play*. Like stories, dramas usually have a *plot* in which a conflict is resolved. Most dramas contain *dialogue* for the actors to speak and *stage directions* that tell them how to move and speak. The play also gives instructions about scenery and costumes. Many older plays have dialogue written in poetry.

DRAMATIC POETRY   Poetry that reveals character through speech and consists mainly

or entirely of dialogue or a long speech by one person.

EDITORIAL   A short newspaper or magazine essay expressing an opinion, generally that of the publication's editor or editorial board.

ELEGY   A serious poem mourning a death or another great loss.

EMPHASIS   Prominence given to the most important ideas.

END-STOPPED LINE   A line of poetry that ends with a natural pause, usually indicated by punctuation. In the following example, both lines are end-stopped.

> EXAMPLE
>
> Papa was on the front porch.
> Mama was in the kitchen.
>   —Sandra Cisneros,
>   "Twister Hits Houston"

ENJAMBMENT   Lines of poetry in which there is no pause from one line to the next.

> EXAMPLE
>
> Do you remember
> How you won
> That last race . . . ?
>   —Frank Horne, "To James"

EPIC   A long narrative poem that celebrates heroic achievements in grand language. The *Odyssey* is an epic.

EPIGRAM   A brief, witty poem or saying.

> E X A M P L E
>
> Three may keep a secret if two of them are dead.
>
> —Benjamin Franklin

EPIGRAPH   A quotation at the start of a book, poem, or section of a work–for example, at the begining of a chapter.

EPISODE   An incident in a story, novel, play, or narrative poem.

EPITAPH   Words or a poem inscribed on a tombstone or another memorial for the dead. New England graveyards are famous for humorous epitaphs.

> E X A M P L E
>
> Here lies the body of John Mound, Lost at sea and never found.

EPITHET   A nickname that helps describe a person or a literary character. The word *King* in *Nat "King" Cole* is an epithet; so is the phrase *Empress of the Blues*, often used to describe blues singer Bessie Smith.

ESSAY   A short piece of nonfiction on a particular topic. A *narrative essay* recounts a series of events, usually in chronological order. A *descriptive essay* presents a portrait of a person, place, or thing. An *expository essay* provides information or explains something. A *persuasive essay* tries to make readers think, feel, or act in a certain way.

EXAGGERATION   Language that makes something seem greater or more extreme than it really is. Exaggeration is a useful tool of persuasion and of humor. The giant characters in the Paul Bunyan stories are examples of exaggeration.

EXPOSITION   Writing that explains or informs. Examples of exposition include recipes, instructions, and most school textbooks. The term *exposition* is also applied to the section of background information that often opens a story or novel.

FABLE   A brief story or narrative poem that teaches a moral and often includes animal characters. Famous examples include Aesop's fables and the fables in the *Panchatantra* from the literature of India.

FACT   An item of information that can be shown to be accurate.

FAIRY TALE   A traditional story that contains magical events and supernatural characters, such as elves, giants, witches, or fairies. "Jack and the Beanstalk" and "Snow White" are examples.

FANTASY   Fiction that features characters and settings that could never occur in the real world. *Alice in Wonderland* is an example.

FICTION   Literature that features invented characters and events and often takes place in invented settings. Novels and short stories are two common forms of fiction.

FIGURATIVE LANGUAGE   Language that is used to stir the reader's imagination or to persuade the reader. Figures of speech do not present factual information. Examples of figurative language, called *figures of speech*, include *simile, metaphor, hyperbole, symbol*, and *personification*.

FLASHBACK In a plot, an event that interrupts the normal chronological order to show what happened at an earlier time.

FOLKLORE The traditional literature, beliefs, customs, songs, and dances of a culture.

FOLKTALE An anonymous traditional story that was passed down orally before being written down. The stories about Anansi the spider are examples of folktales. Folktales include *tall tales, fairy tales, fables, legends,* and *myths*.

FORESHADOWING Hinting at future developments in a plot, usually to build suspense and encourage readers to keep reading.

FRAME A story in which another story unfolds; also called a *frame story*. The story of Scheherazade in *The Thousand and One Nights* is a famous example of a frame story.

FREE VERSE Poetry that has no meter (pattern of stressed and unstressed syllables).

EXAMPLE

Primer Lesson

Look out how you use proud words.
When you let proud words go, it is
    not easy to call them back.
They wear long boots, hard boots;
    they walk off proud; they can't
    hear you calling–
Look out how you use proud words.
                            –Carl Sandburg

HAIKU Japanese form of three-line poem in which the first and third lines have five syllables each and the middle line has seven syllables.

EXAMPLE

There a beggar goes!
Heaven and earth he's wearing
For his summer clothes.
    –Kikaku, TR. Harold G. Henderson

HOMOPHONE A word with the same pronunciation as another word but with a different meaning and often a different spelling. *Sea* and *see* are homophones.

HUMOR Written or spoken language that attempts to make others laugh.

HYPERBOLE A phrase or expression that uses exaggeration to make a point or achieve humor. The hyperbole in the following example makes the point that the punter kicked the ball a long distance.

EXAMPLE

The Falcons' punter *kicked the ball a mile!*

IDIOM An expression that means something different from its actual, word-for-word meaning. "Chew the fat" and "shoot the breeze" are idioms.

IMAGE A word or phrase that appeals to one or more of the five senses. The use of images is called *imagery*. Notice that the images in the next example appeal to the senses of smell, sight, and touch.

> EXAMPLE
>
> My grandmothers . . .
> Smelling of soap and onions and
>   wet clay
> With veins rolling roughly over
>   quick hands . . .
> —Margaret Walker, "Lineage"

INVERTED ORDER   The placement of words in a sentence so that the subject follows the verb.

> EXAMPLE
>
> Into the blue sky over Albuquerque
> V   S
> flew hundreds of hot-air balloons.

IRONY   The effect on an audience (readers or viewers) when they become aware of the difference between the way things seem and the way they really are. In *situational irony,* what seems likely to happen is not what actually happens.

> EXAMPLE
>
> A young boy who is left home alone winds up stopping two adult robbers.

In *dramatic irony,* what a character believes is true is not what the reader or audience knows is really true.

> EXAMPLE
>
> Little Red Riding Hood thinks she is talking to her grandmother but we know it is the wolf in disguise.

In *verbal irony,* words that seem to mean one thing really mean the opposite.

> EXAMPLE
>
> A baseball fan remarks, "I just love lots of homework on the opening night of the World Series."

JARGON   The special vocabulary used by people in a particular profession or activity. Examples of computer hackers' jargon are *hard drive, boot up,* and *default.*

JOURNAL   A day-to-day written account of a person's experiences and impressions. A journal is usually less personal than a diary and may focus on just one area of the writer's experience. For example, a gardener may keep a journal of his or her activities in the garden.

LEGEND   A traditional story based in history and usually focusing on an actual hero, but handed down orally and usually much exaggerated over time. The stories about King Arthur are examples of legends.

LIGHT VERSE   Poetry that is not serious in tone or subject. *Limericks* and *nursery rhymes* are examples of light verse.

LIMERICK   A humorous five-line poem that follows a strict pattern of rhythm and rhyme.

472

A cheerful old bear at the zoo
Could always find something to do.
When it bored him to go
On a walk to and fro,
He reversed it and walked
 fro and to.

LYRIC POETRY Poetry that focuses on the expression of thoughts and feelings. It differs from *dramatic poetry*, which portrays a character, and *narrative poetry,* which tells a story. Lyric poems are usually shorter than narrative poems or dramatic poems.

MAGIC REALISM Writing that uses realistic details and an ordinary tone to describe characters or events that could not exist in the real world. These characters and events express truths about a political situation or a culture. Contemporary Latin American writers like Nobel Prize winner Gabriel García Marques often use magic realism.

METAMORPHOSIS A change in shape or form of a character or plot in myths and fairy tales. For example, in "The Frog Prince," a frog is kissed and turns into a handsome prince.

METAPHOR A figure of speech that implies a comparison between two unlike things. A metaphor differs from a *simile,* which directly states the comparison with a word such as *like* or *as. Happiness is a warm puppy* is a metaphor. (*Happiness is like a warm puppy* is a simile.)

METER A regular pattern of syllables of stressed and unstressed syllables in a line of poetry. Notice, for example, the pattern of stressed syllables (marked ´) and unstressed syllables (marked ˘) in the stanza that follows:

"Ring out the old, ring in the new,
Ring happy bells, across the snow:
The year is going, let him go:
Ring out the false, ring in the true.
　　　　　–Alfred, Lord Tennyson,
　　　　　　"Ring Out, Wild Bells"

MONOLOGUE A long speech by one person.

MOOD The emotional quality of a story, poem, or play. The mood may be created by the setting, the dialogue, the writer's use of language, or other elements. Examples of mood include *sad, cheerful, suspenseful.*

MOTIVATION The reason or reasons that a character acts or speaks in a certain way.

MYSTERY A story, novel, or play in which something is unknown or secret until near the end. The stories and novels that feature the detective Sherlock Holmes are famous examples of mysteries.

MYTH An anonymous traditional story that uses gods and goddesses, spirits, or other supernatural elements to try to explain why things are the way they are. For example, the Greek myth about Phaethon attempts to explain why the sun seems to move across the sky.

NARRATION   Writing that recounts a series of events, usually in chronological order. Short stories, novels, narrative essays, and narrative poems are all narration.

NARRATIVE POETRY   Poetry in which the main purpose is to tell a story. "The Highwayman" by Alfred Noyes is a narrative poem.

NARRATOR   The person recounting events in a novel, short story, or other narrative work. The narrator may or may not be in the story.

NEOLOGISM   A word or phrase newly introduced into the language; for example, a "fax" machine. Science and current events are two sources of neologisms.

NONFICTION   Prose written about real people and events or other factual information.

NOVEL   A book-length work of fiction.

ODE   A long poem that focuses on thoughts and feelings, usually about an important subject.

ONOMATOPOEIA   Words whose sound suggests their meaning. The words *hush* and *buzz* are examples.

OPINION   A personal view or judgment on an issue.

ORAL LITERATURE   Literature that has been passed from storyteller to storyteller over many generations; sometimes called *orature*. Myths, legends, folktales, and folk ballads are four common kinds of oral literature.

OXYMORON   A phrase consisting of two words that seem to be opposite. The term "sad comic" is an oxymoron.

PACE   The speed or tempo suggested by a piece of writing. Writers often use action and speech to quicken the pace and use description to slow it down.

PARADOX   A situation or statement that seems impossible yet is true. For example, the statement *There is nothing as loud as silence* is a paradox. Since silence can be used to express strong disapproval it can indeed be "loud."

PARAGRAPH   A group of sentences that develop a single idea. Unified paragraphs include a topic sentence that states the main idea and supporting sentences that develop that main idea.

PARALLELISM   The use of similar grammatical structures to express similar ideas. Parallelism emphasizes ideas and helps make them memorable.

E X A M P L E

... a nation *of the people, by the people,* and *for the people* ...
                                    –Abraham Lincoln

PARAPHRASE   To restate in your own words the writing or ideas of others. A *paraphrase* (noun) is any piece of writing that makes such a restatement.

PARODY   A work that humorously imitates the style and content of another work. For example, the lines below are part of a parody of "Twinkle, Twinkle, Little Star."

Twinkle, twinkle, little bat!
How I wonder what you're at!
                            —Lewis Carroll

PERSONIFICATION   Writing or speech in which something that is not human performs actions usually done by human beings. For example, the following lines suggest that rain is capable of kissing and singing.

Let the rain kiss you . . .
Let the rain sing you a lullaby.
          —Langston Hughes, "April Rain Song"

PERSUASION   Writing or speech that tries to convince readers to think, feel, or act in a certain way.

PLOT   The sequence of events in a story, novel, or play. Usually the events unfold in *chronological order*, although *flashbacks* sometimes interrupt the time sequence. A plot usually centers on one or more conflicts, or struggles, that a main *character* must face. In a short story, the conflict is frequently introduced after a section of background information called the *exposition*. After the conflict is introduced, complications are added in the *rising action* that builds to a *climax*, the point of highest tension or emotional involvement. After the climax, the *falling action* leads to a *resolution*, or *dénouement*, in which the outcome of the conflict is revealed and the loose ends are tied together.

POETRY   Writing that expresses thoughts, feelings, and experiences in language that is more concentrated and imaginative than prose (the language of stories, novels, and essays). Poets are especially careful with *diction*, or word choice, and with the connotations and sounds of the words they choose. Poetry often uses devices such as *alliteration*, *rhyme*, and *meter*.

POINT OF VIEW   The vantage point from which a story, novel, or other narrative work is told. In the *first-person point of view*, the narrator is a character in the work who uses first-person pronouns like *I* and *me*. In the *third-person point of view*, the narrator refers to all characters with third-person pronouns like *she* and *he*. The third-person point of view may be *limited* to the thoughts and experiences of one character. In other works, it may be *omniscient*, presenting the thoughts and experiences of many characters and providing information that no character could know.

PROSE   Writing that is not poetry. Novels, stories, and essays are written in prose. Prose may be *expository* (give information), *narrative* (tell a story), *descriptive* (paint a word picture and appeal to the five senses), or *persuasive,* (try to convince the reader or listener to agree).

PROTAGONIST   The main character who undergoes the conflict in a drama or a work of fiction; also called the *hero* or *heroine.*

PROVERB   An anonymous saying passed down orally that usually offers advice or makes a wise observation about human behavior.

> E X A M P L E
>
> One picture is worth a thousand words.
>
> —Chinese proverb

PUN   A humorous play on words, usually involving homophones.

> E X A M P L E
>
> Seven days of hiking make one week (weak).

PURPOSE   What a writer hopes to accomplish by writing or speaking.

REALISM   The attempt in writing or another art to depict life as it really is lived.

REFRAIN   A line or lines repeated regularly in a poem or song. Ballads often include refrains.

RHYME   The repetition of similar sounds at the ends of words; for example, *shaken* and *taken, shake it* and *take it.* Rhyme that is not exact is called *approximate rhyme, imperfect rhyme, near rhyme, slant rhyme,* for example, *love* and *prove.* Rhyme that occurs at the ends of lines of poetry is called *end rhyme;* rhyme within a line is called *internal rhyme.* Below is an example of internal rhyme.

> E X A M P L E
>
> Once upon a midnight dreary, while I pondered, weak and weary . . .
>
> —Edgar Allan Poe, "The Raven"

RHYME SCHEME   The pattern of end rhymes in a poem. To identify a poem's rhyme scheme, you can assign a new letter to each new rhyming sound. For example, the following stanza has the rhyme scheme *abab.*

> E X A M P L E
>
> The night is darkening round me,   A
> The wild winds coldly blow;   B
> But a tyrant spell has bound me   A
> And I cannot, cannot go.   B
>
> —Emily Brontë, "Spellbound"

RHYTHM   The alternation between stressed and unstressed syllables in poetry or other writing. In the example on the next page, stressed syllables are marked (ˊ) and unstressed syllables are marked (ˇ).

> ### EXAMPLE
>
> Break, break, break,
> On thy cold gray stones, Ŏ Séa!
> —Alfred Lord Tennyson,
> "Break, Break, Break"

RIDDLE   A puzzle in the form of a question. The answer to a riddle often involves a *pun*.

> ### EXAMPLE
>
> *Question:* When is a door not a door?
> *Answer:* When it's ajar.

SATIRE   Literature that makes fun of the evils or follies of people or society. *Gulliver's Travels* is a famous satire.

SCENE   Full-length plays usually have two to five acts, which are each further divided into scenes. Each scene usually has a different setting (time and/or place).

SCIENCE FICTION   Fiction that explores the possible consequences of scientific or technological advances or discoveries. Ray Bradbury, Ursula LeGuin, and Samuel Delany are popular science-fiction writers.

SETTING   The time and place in which a work occurs. Many works often have a general setting–Puerto Rico in the 1960s, for example–as well as more specific settings–for instance, Friday evening in Manuela's house in the city of San Juan.

SHORT STORY   A work of fiction intended to be read in one sitting. Important elements of a short story include plot, characterization, setting, point of view, and theme.

SIMILE   A figure of speech that compares two seemingly unlike things and directly states the comparison with a word such as *like* or *as*.

> ### EXAMPLE
>
> My heart is like a singing bird.
> —Christina Rossetti, "A Birthday"

SLANG   Highly informal language that consists of new words or new meanings for old words. Slang terms eventually either enter the language or fade from fashion. For example, few people today use the 1960s slang terms *mod* (for modern) and *boss* (for very good).

SONNET   A fourteen-line poem with a strict pattern of meter and, usually, rhyme. Sonnets are typically serious lyric poems that express strong emotion. For example, "Design" by Robert Frost is a sonnet.

SPEAKER   In a lyric poem, the voice that communicates to the reader. The speaker may or may not be the poet.

STANZA   Groups of lines into which a poem is divided. For example, a poem may consist of three groups of four lines each. Each group has the same rhyme scheme. Poems that do not use stanzas generally use *verse paragraphs* (with indents) or *free verse*.

STEREOTYPE   A character who occurs again and again in literature and who behaves in predictable ways; also called a *stock character.* The *local football star* and the *country doctor* are examples.

STYLE   An author's characteristic way of writing. Elements of style include subject matter, word choice, tone, the use or the lack of imagery, figurative language, and devices such as rhythm, rhyme, and alliteration.

SUBPLOT   A less important or less developed plot in addition to the main plot. Longer works like novels and full-length plays often have subplots.

SUSPENSE   A feeling of anticipation as an audience wonders what will happen next and what will happen at the end of a story or play. Pace and foreshadowing often help build suspense.

SYMBOL   A person, place, event, or object that stands for something beyond its literal meaning, usually something abstract. For example, the American flag is a symbol of the United States. The use of symbols is called *symbolism.*

SYNONYM   A word that has the same or nearly the same meaning as another word. *Dusk* and *twilight* are synonyms.

TALL TALE   A brief, humorous tale that achieves its humor chiefly through exaggeration. "Three Strong Women" is a Japanese tall tale.

THEME   The general idea or attitude toward life expressed in a work of literature. A theme may be directly stated in a work. More often, however, it is implied through details such as symbols, setting, the title, characters' personalities and motivation, and conflict. For example, in *Anne Frank: The Diary of a Young Girl,* the theme is faith in the goodness of people.

THESIS STATEMENT   A sentence or two presenting the main idea of an essay.

TONE   The attitude that a writer conveys toward his or her subject, characters, or audience. The tone of a work may be sad, angry, serious, or lighthearted, among other choices.

TOPIC SENTENCE   A sentence that states the main idea of a paragraph.

TRAGEDY   A serious drama or another serious work that ends with the downfall of the main character.

UNDERSTATEMENT   Language that makes something seem smaller, weaker, or less important than it really is. The use of *not bad* to mean "very good" is an example of understatement.

POSTAL SERVICE ABBREVIATIONS

Alabama	AL	Montana	MT
Alaska	AK	Nebraska	NB
Arizona	AZ	Nevada	NV
Arkansas	AR	New Hampshire	NH
California	CA	New Jersey	NJ
Colorado	CO	New Mexico	NM
Connecticut	CT	New York	NY
Delaware	DE	North Carolina	NC
District of Columbia	DC	North Dakota	ND
Florida	FL	Ohio	OH
Georgia	GA	Oklahoma	OK
Guam	GU	Oregon	OR
Hawaii	HI	Pennsylvania	PA
Idaho	ID	Puerto Rico	PR
Illinois	IL	Rhode Island	RI
Indiana	IN	South Carolina	SC
Iowa	IA	South Dakota	SD
Kansas	KS	Tennessee	TN
Kentucky	KY	Texas	TX
Louisiana	LA	Utah	UT
Maine	ME	Vermont	VT
Maryland	MD	Virgin Islands	VI
Massachusetts	MA	Virginia	VA
Michigan	MI	Washington	WA
Minnesota	MN	West Virginia	WV
Mississippi	MS	Wisconsin	WI
Missouri	MO	Wyoming	WY

Index

....

A

a, an, 308

abbreviations, 390-391; postal service, 478; state, 479

abstract term, 465

accept, except, 360

acronym, 465

action verb, 304-305

active voice, 344

act of play, 465; scene, 476

actors. *See* cast

address: comma with, 371-372; envelope, 434; inside letter, 431; return, 430

address, direct: comma, 369-370

adjective, 307-309; and adverb, 356-359; comma separating, 368; comparison, 223, 356-359; position, 308; predicate, 327-328; proper, 309, 387

adjective clause, 320

adjective phrase, 315

adverb, 309-311; and adjective, 356-359; comparison, 356-359; interrogative, 310; negative, 310-311; or preposition, 311

adverb clause, 321

adverb phrase, 315

advertising: copywriting and layout, 35-36, 37; public service poster, 199; senses employed, 82

advice, advise, 360

affect, effect, 361

agreement of subject-verb. *See* subject-verb agreement

allegory, 465

alliteration, 465

all right, alright, 361

all together, altogether, 361, 410

allusion, 465

almanac, 453

already, all ready, 410

ambiguity, 465

an, a, 308

analogy, 465

analysis, 465

anecdote, 144, 465

antagonist, 466

antecedent: indefinite pronoun as, 350-351; pronoun, 196, 302, 349-351

antonym, 422, 466

aphorism, 466

apostrophe, 377-378; defined, 466; special plurals, 379

application letter, 431-432

appositive: comma, 370; noun, 347

archaism, 466

article, definite and indefinite, 308

as, like, 295, 363

assonance, 466

atlas, 453

atmosphere, 466

audience: defined, 466

audience identification, 12; writing for, 12, 25, 181, 211, 214, 218-219, 221, 225, 245; book review, 211; critical thinking, 462-463; demonstration speech, 152; description, 79; descriptive speech, 92, 94; editorial, 173-174; explanatory chart, 163; expository essay, 140; graphic design, 36, 37; news report, 276, 277; oral presentation, 27, 30; personal narrative, 46; persuasive speech, 190, 195; photo essay, 98; public service poster, 200, 203; publishing, 25; reader's theater, 66; research paper, 254, 268, 269; tall tale, 122, 123; videotape, 280-281, 285

autobiography, 49, 466

B

ballad, 466

be, 343

begin, 342-343

beside, besides, 361

bibliographical forms, 448-451

bibliography, 449-450

bibliography card, 259, 260, 263

biography, 49, 466; reference, 453

body: book review, 217; demonstration speech, 156; drafting ideas, 18, 84; editorial, 178, 180-181; expository essay, 144-145; notes, 48; personal letter, 429; personal narrative, 51; persuasive speech, 194; research paper, 261

body language, 26

book: parts of, 452; reference, 453

book jacket, 240-247; design effect, 243, 245; flaps and flap copy, 242, 244-245; illustration, 243-244; spine, 242

book review, 208-225; judgment, 215; rating, 210-211

brainstorming, 9, 10; expository essay, 138, 139, 152, 173, ; reader's theater, 61; research paper, 253, 254

business letter, 431-432; format, 431; kinds, 431-432

C

camcorder, 278, 281, 282

campaign, 199, 200, 201, 202

capitalization, 381-387; checklist, 22; first words, 381, 382; names of person, place, thing, 382-386; organizations and events, 385; research paper, 267; titles of people, 386-387; written works, 385-386

caption, 126, 131, 132, 133

card catalog, 452

case: nominative, 345-346, 347; objective, 345-346, 347; possessive, 347-348; pronoun, 345-349

cast, actors, 65, 66, 232

cause and effect: defined, 466; determining, 455-456

CD-ROM disk, 398; library research, 400

character: defined, 466; protagonist, 475

characterization: defined, 466

characters, 108, 109; book review, 213; creating, 111-112

chart, 135, 141, 145, 189, 193; campaign, 201; explanatory, 160-167, 283; rating, 210-211; vocabulary, 419

checklist: demonstration speech revision, 157; editing, 22, 88; editorial revision, 182; expository essay revision, 146; personal narrative revision, 53; research paper, 264-265, 267; short story editing, 115; short story revision, 114; spelling, 411; tall tale, 123, 125. *See also* evaluation

chronological order, 15, 48, 143, 447-448, 457, 467

citation, 263, 264; bibliographical forms, 448-451; endnote and footnote, 450-451; parenthetical, 448-449; works cited page, 266

classifying, 461-462

clause, 319-321; adjective, 320; adverb, 321; independent, 319-320; noun, 321; relative pronouns, 320; subordinate, 319; subordinating conjunction, 321

cliché, 115, 195, 196, 294, 295, 467

climax in plot, 467

closing. *See* ending

clustering, 9, 11, 120, 152, 172

coherence, 467

collage, 40, 41, 68-73

colloquialism: defined, 467; versus formal diction, 157, 298

colloquial language, 155

colon, 373-374

comedy, 467

comma, 367-372; nonessential elements, 371; personal narrative, 56

common noun, 300

community place: description, 76-89; photo essay, 96-101; public service poster, 198-205

comparison: adjectives, 223, 356-359; adverbs, 356-359; context clue, 424; critical thinking, 462; degree of, 356, 357; double, 358-359; irregular, 358; negative, 358; regular, 357-358

comparison and contrast: context clue, 424; critical thinking, 462; defined, 467

complaint letter, 432

complete predicate, 324

complete subject, 323

complex sentence, 329

compound-complex sentence, 329-330

compound direct object, 347

compound indirect object, 347

compound object of preposition, 347

compound predicate, 325

compound preposition, 311-312

compound sentence, 328-329; comma, 367-368; semicolon, 372-373

compound subject, 324-325, 346, 354-355

compound words, 376

computer, 394-397; desktop publishing, 396-397; information storage and retrieval, 397-400; library research, 400-401; networks, 402; spelling aid, 413-414; word processing, 395-396

concluding sentence, 293; expository essay, 147

conclusion: drawing, 457-458. *See also* ending

concrete language, 112; poetry, 467; term, 467

conflict: defined, 467; external and internal, 47, 113; short story, 108, 109

conjugation of verb, 341-343

conjunction, 312-313; coordinating, 311-312; correlative, 312; subordinating, 313, 321

connotation, 297; defined, 467; positive and negative, 423

consonance, 467

context clue, 423-424; comparison and contrast, 424; definition of word, 423-424; example, 424; tone or general idea, 424

contraction, apostrophe, 378

coordinating conjunction, 311-312

copywriting, 35

correlative conjunction, 313

couplet, 467

credits, 285, 448

Critical Thinking:
   activities, 463-464;
   audience and purpose, 462-463;
   book review, 212-214;
   cause and effect, 455-456;
   classifying, 461-462;
   comparison and contrast, 462;
   drawing conclusions, 457-458;
   evaluating, 459;
   fact and opinion, 460-461;
   generalizing, 458-459;
   inferring, 458;
   movie review, 230;
   observation, 455;
   organizing, 456-457;
   point of view, 460;
   skills, 455-464;
   stereotyping, 461

cues, 65, 66, 234, 235

cut and paste: book jacket, 245; layout, 35-36, 37; revising, 21

D

dashes, 380

database, 398-399; field, 399; record, 399; scan, 399

date: comma with, 371; personal letter, 429

declarative sentence, 330; period, 366

definition of word, 423-424

degree of comparison: comparative, 356, 357; positive, 356; superlative, 356, 357

demonstration speech, 135, 150-159

demonstrative pronoun, 303

denotation, 297, 467; vocabulary, 423

dénouement, 468

dependent clause. *See* subordinate clause

description, 74, 75; community place, 76-89; defined, 468; paragraph, 289-290; person, 81; speaking project, 90-95

descriptive essay, 74

descriptive speech, 90-95

design. *See* graphic design

desktop publishing, 396-397; scanner, 396

Dewey Decimal System, 451

dialect, 468

dialogue: defined, 468; proofreading, 116; reader's theater, 58, 63; short story, 112; videotape preparation, 282-283

dialogue tag, 112, 116

diary, 49, 468

diction, 297

dictionary, 422

direct address: comma, 369-370; title capitalization, 386, 387

direct object, 326-327; action verb, 306

direct quotation, 257, 258, 265, 374; capitalization, 382

disabled, technological advances for, 403

displaying: book jacket, 247; explanatory chart, 167; graphic design, 37; photo essay, 101; public service poster, 205; self-portrait and collage, 72; storyboard, 133

doesn't, don't, 355

doodling, 33-34

double comparison, 358-359

double negative, 359

drafting, 9, 16-19; book review, 218-221; computer, 395; demonstration speech, 153-157; description, 83-84; descriptive speech, 93; editorial, 177-181; explanatory chart, 164-165; expository essay, 144-145; graphic design, 35; movie review, 233-235; news report, 274-275; personal narrative, 49-52; persuasive speech, 192-194; photo essay, 98-100; public service poster, 202-203; research paper, 262-264; self-portrait and collage, 71; short story, 110-113; storyboard, 131; tall tale, 121-122; videotape preparation, 282-283

drama: act, 465; comedy, 467; defined, 468; reader's theater, 58-67; scene, 476; tragedy, 478
dramatic poetry, 468

E

editing, 9, 21-25; book jacket, 246-247; book review, 223-224; computer, 395; description, 87-89; editorial, 183-184; explanatory chart, 166; expository essay, 147-148; movie review, 237; news report, 275-276; personal narrative, 55-56; persuasive speech, 195-196; photo essay, 98-100; public service poster, 204; research paper, 266-267; short story, 115-116; style sheet, italics, numbers, and abbreviations, 388-391; tall tale, 123; videotape, 284
editorial, 169, 468; writing, 170-185
effect, affect, 361
electronic or E-mail, 402
elegy, 468
emphasis, 468
encyclopedia, 453
ending: book review, 217, 221; drafting, 19, 84; editorial, 181; expository essay, 145, 147; letter writing, 372, 429; notes, 48-49; oral presentation, 29; personal narrative, 52; persuasive speech, 194; punctuation marks, 366-367; research paper, 261, 264; short story, 113; storyboard, 132

endnote, 450-451
end-stopped line, 468
enjambment, 468
envelope, 434
epic, 468
epigram, 468
epigraph, 469
episode, 469
epitaph, 469
epithet, 469
essay, 469
essay, expository, 136-149
essay test, 441-443
etc., 361
etymology, 420-421
evaluate, 206, 207; audience, 254; book review, 212, 213, 216; movie review, 231-232; topic, 254-255
evaluation: book jacket, 247; book review, 225; critical thinking, 459; demonstration speech, 159; description, 89; descriptive speech, 95; editorial, 185; explanatory chart, 167; expository essay, 149; library research, 256; movie review, 239; news report response, 277; personal narrative, 57; persuasive speech, 197; photo essay, 101; public service poster, 205; reader's theater, 67; research paper, 269; self-portrait and collage, 73; short story, 117; storyboard, 133; tall tale, 125; videotape, 285; visual communication project, 37

events, capitalization of, 385

exaggeration, 469. *See also* hyperbole

except, accept, 360

exclamation point, 367

exclamatory sentence, 331; exclamation point, 367

exhibiting. *See* displaying

explanation, 134-135; videotape preparation, 282-283, 284

explanatory chart, 160-167; videotape, 283

exposition: defined, 469; essay, 136-149; paragraph, 291

expository essay, 136-149

expository writing, 135; paragraph, 291

external conflict, 47, 113

F

fable, 469

fact, 168, 469; editorial, 172, 175-176; opinion and, 460-461

fact-finding, 175-176

fairy tale, 469

fantasy, 469

fax, 402

feedback: description, 85; graphic design, 36

fewer, less, 361

fiction, 102, 469

figurative language, 86-87, 469; mixed metaphor, 295

first person, 110, 121; point of view, 296

flashback, 113, 470

floppy disk: disk drive, 397; format, 397

focus question, 255, 256

focus statement, 255, 256

folklore, 470

folktale, 470

footnote, 450-451

foreshadowing, 470

format: book review, 224; letter writing, 429-531; works cited page, 266

frame (story), 470

free verse, 470

freewriting, 10; explanatory chart, 163; personal narrative, 44-45; short story, 107

French language, 421

G

gender, pronoun, 349, 350

generalizing, 458-459

gerund phrase, 317-318

glossary of usage, 360-365

good, 358

good, well, 359, 362

grammar checklist, 22

graphic design, 32-37

graphic images, 31, 32, 35

graphic organizer, 176, 191-192

H

haiku, 470

have, of, 362

hear, here, 362, 409

here, 354

homonym, 422

homophone: defined, 470; spelling, 409-410

humor, 470; comedy, 467; limerick, 472; parody, 474; pun, 475

hyperbole, 86, 118, 470

hyphen, 375-377; word division, 376

I

I, capitalization, 381, 382

idiom, 470

image, 471

image collecting: photo essay, 99; VCR, 278-285

imperative sentence, 330; period, 366

in, into, 362

indefinite pronoun, 303; as antecedent, 350-351; possessive form, 378; singular and plural, 355

independent clause, 319-320

indirect object, 327

indirect quotation, 374-375

inferring, 458

infinitive, 318

infinitive phrase, 318

information gathering, 13, 93; chart, 141, 164; fact-finding, 175-176; networking, 402-403; news report, 272; report, 248, 249

information storage and retrieval: CD-ROM disk, 398; database, 399-400; floppy disk, 397; hard disk, 397; videodisc, 398

interjection, 313

internal conflict, 47, 113

interrogative pronoun, 304

interrogative sentence, 330-331; question marks, 366-367

interrupting word, 353; comma use, 369

interview, 49; news report, 270, 271, 272-273; self, 47; videotape, 283, 285

into, in, 362

intonation, 30

intransitive verb, 306-307

introduction: book review, 217, 218-219; comma use, 56, 368-369; demonstration speech, 154-155; drafting ideas, 18, 83; editorial, 179; expository essay, 144; letter-writing punctuation, 372, 373; notes, 48; personal letter, 429; personal narrative, 49-50; persuasive speech, 193; reader's theater, 63; research paper, 261, 262; short story, 110-111; videotape, 283

inverted order, 353-354, 471

inverted pyramid, 274-275

irony, 471

irregular comparison, 358

irregular verb, 338-339; conjugation, 342, 343

italics, 388-389

its, it's, 362, 409-410

J

jargon, 471

journal, 49, 471

journal keeping, 4-5

Journal Writing, 5, 8, 11, 41, 75, 103, 134, 169, 207, 249

judgment statement, 216, 217

K

key words, 401

L

lay, lie, 339, 362-363

layout, 35-36

learn, teach, 362

legend, 472

less, fewer, 361

letter writing, 428-434; activities, 434; business, 431-433; colon, 374; comma, 372; envelope, 434; personal, 429-430; punctuation and capitalization, 433

library research, 250, 254; Dewey Decimal System, 451; media center, 451-453; microfiche and microfilm, 400; nonprint material, 400; on-line catalog, 400-401, 452; research paper, 256-259; technological advances, 400-401

lie, lay, 339, 362-363

light verse, 472

like, as, 295, 363

limerick, 472

linking verb, 305

listening: to movie review, 235-236, 237; to news report, 270, 276-277; to speaker, 31, 92, 93; to speech, 195

literary terms and techniques, 465-478

lyric poetry, 472; speaker, 477

M

magic realism, 472

main clause. *See* independent clause

main-idea statement, 177-178, 262

mapping. *See* clustering

media, 33, 279; library, 451-453

medium: book jacket illustration, 243-244; graphic images, 32-33; self-portrait and collage, 71; videotape, 279

memoir, 49

memorizing technique, 446-447

metamorphosis, 472

metaphor, 86, 472; mixed, 295

meter, 472

mnemonic device, 446-447

modem, 401

modifier, problems with, 358-359

monologue, 472

mood, 472

motivation, 473

movie review, 226-239; delivery, 236-237

movie theater, 229

mystery, 473

myth, 473

N

names: capitalization, 382-387; epithet, 469; words from, 421

narration: defined, 473; paragraph, 290; personal narrative, 40, 41, 42-57; voice-over, 282

narrative poetry, 473

narrator, 58, 63, 64, 110, 473

negative, double, 359

negative comparison, 358

neologism, 473

networking, 402-403; bulletin boards, 402-403; electronic or E-mail, 402; information services, 403

news report, 270-277; delivery, 277; lead, 272, 274, 275; rating, 277

nominative case, 345; compound subject, 346; noun appositive, 347; predicate nominative, 346-347

nonfiction, 102, 473

nonstandard English, 360

not, -n't, 359

note cards: book review, 214-215, 217; demonstration speech, 154, 156; explanatory chart, 164; expository essay, 142; library research, 257, 258, 259, 260, 263; movie review, 233-234, 236; oral presentation, 28; persuasive speech, 190-191; skill in using, 444; tall tale drafting, 121

notes: endnote and footnote, 450-451; news report, 273, 274-276; organizing, 48-49; skill in taking, 443-446

noun: abstract and concrete, 300; as adjective, 308; collective, 301; compound, 300-301; compound and collective, 300-301; concrete, 300; possessive form, 377-378; proper and common, 299-300, 309; spelling of plural, 407-409

noun clause, 321

novel, 473

number, pronoun, 349

numbers and fractions: hyphen, 376; style sheet, 388-390

O

objective case, 345-346; compound direct object, 347; compound indirect object, 347; compound object of preposition, 347

objective test, 437-441

observation: critical thinking, 455; role of senses, 79-81, 82

ode, 473

of, have, 362

off, off of, 363

Old English, 420

omniscient point of view, 110, 296

on-line catalog, 400-401, 452; key words, 401

onomatopoeia, 473

opening. *See* introduction

opinion, 168-169, 473; book review, 220; editorial, 172; fact and, 460-461; movie review, 226, 227, 228; persuasive speech, 186, 188;

testing, 175

oral literature, 473

oral presentation. *See* speaking; speech

orature, 473

order: chronological, 15, 48, 143, 447-448, 457, 467; of importance, 15, 143, 457; inverted, 353-354; spatial, 15, 457

ordinal numbers, 390

organizations: abbreviation, 391; capitalization, 385

organizing ideas, 14-16; critical thinking, 456-457; description, 81-82; explanatory chart, 165; expository essay, 142; graphic organizer, 176, 191-192; notes, 48-49; reader's theater, 62; research paper, 260-261; sequence chain, 98

outlining, 15-16; sequence chain; expository essay, 143; movie review, 232-233; order, 143; research paper, 260-261; research tool, 446-447; steps in the process, 143. *See also* chart

oxymoron, 473

P

pace: defined, 473; oral presentation, 29-30; personal narrative, 51

paradox, 473

paragraph, 288-293; concluding sentence, 293; defined, 473; descriptive, 289-290; expository, 291; narrative, 290; persuasive, 288-289; supporting sentence, 292; topic sentence, 291-292; transitional sentence, 292-293; types, 288-291

parallelism, 334-335, 474

paraphrase, 257, 474; note-taking, 445-446

parentheses, 380

parenthetical citation, 448-449

parody, 474

participial phrase, 316-317

participle, 315-316; or verb, 316; past, 316, 337-340; present, 316, 337-340

parts of speech, 299-313

passed, past, 363

passive voice, 344

past participle, 316, 337-340

peer response: personal narrative, 45, 52; persuasive speech, 197; tall tale, 125

period, 366; abbreviation, 391

periodical, 453

person: capitalization of name, 383; capitalization of title, 386-387; observation and description, 81

personal narrative, 40, 41

personal pronoun, 302; possessive form, 378

personification, 474

persuasion: defined, 474; editorial, 169; paragraph, 288-289; speech presentation, 186-197

photo essay, 74; community place, 96-101

phrase, 314-318; adjective, 315; adverb, 315; gerund, 317-318; infinitive, 318; participial, 316-317; prepositional, 314-315; verb, 306, 352-353; verbal, 315-318

places: capitalization, 383-384; words from names of, 421

plagiarism, 257, 258, 445

planning. *See* drafting; prewriting

play. *See* drama

plot, 108, 474; book review, 213; building, 113; climax, 467; dénouement, 468; flashback, 113, 470; foreshadowing, 470; subplot, 477

plural, formation of: apostrophe, 378-379

poetry: concrete, 467; couplet, 467; defined, 474; dramatic, 468; enjambment, 468; epic, 468; free verse, 470; haiku, 470; light verse, 472; limerick, 472; lyric, 472; meter, 472; narrative, 473; ode, 473; refrain, 475; rhyme, 475; rhyme scheme, 476; rhythm, 476; sonnet, 477; stanza, 477

point of view: critical thinking, 459; defined, 475; first person, third person, 296-297; personal narrative, 50; short story, 110; tall tale, 121-122

possessive case, 346; usage, 347-348

possessive form: noun, singular and plural, 377-378; pronoun, personal and indefinite, 378

possessive pronoun, 302-303; personal and indefinite, 378

postal service abbreviations, 478

poster, public service, 198-205

practice: demonstration speech, 153; descriptive speech, 94-95; movie review, 233-234; persuasive speech, 194-195; speaking, 29-30

predesigning, 32-34

predicate: complete, 324; compound, 325; simple, 323-324

predicate adjective, 327-328

predicate nominative, 327, 346-347

prefix: adding, 406; hyphen, 377; vocabulary, 419

prepositions: compound, 311-312; or adverb, 312; speechwriting, 236

prepositional phrase, 314-315; adjective, 315; adverb, 315

present participle, 316, 337-340

press kit, 229, 230

prewriting, 9, 10-16; book review, 210-217; computer, 395; description, 78; editorial, 172; expository essay, 138-143; personal narrative, 44-49; research paper, 252-261; short story, 108-109; storyboard, 130

principal parts of verb, 337-340

problem pronouns: *who, whom, whose,* 348-349

problem verbs, 339-340; *lie, lay,* 339; *sit, set,* 340

pronoun, 345-351; antecedent, 196, 302, 349-351; case, 345-349;

gender, 349, 350; number, 349; possessive form, 302-303, 378; problem, 348-349; reflexive, 302; relative, 320; types, 301-304

proofreading: checking, 148; dialogue, 116; spelling, 413; techniques, 22-25

proper adjective, 309; capitalization, 387

proper noun, 299, 300, 309; capitalization, 382-387

prose, 475

protagonist, 475

proverb, 475

publishing, 9, 25; book review, 224; computer, 395, 396-397; description, 89; editorial, 184-185; expository essay, 148-149; personal narrative, 56-57; research paper, 268; short story, 116-117

pun, 475; riddle, 476

punctuation, 366-380; apostrophe, 376-379; checklist, 22; colon, 373-374; comma, 56, 367-372; dashes, 379-380; dialogue, 116; end marks, 366-367; hyphen, 375-376; letter writing, 372, 373, 433; parentheses, 379; quotation marks, 374-375; semicolon, 372-373

purpose: critical thinking, 462-463; defined, 475; sentence, 330-331

Q

question mark, 366-367

quotation: direct, 257, 258, 265, 374, 382; epigraph, 469; indirect, 374-375

quotation marks, 265, 374-375; note-taking, 445, 446

R

raise, rise, 363

reader, writing for, 12, 25, 181, 211, 214, 218-219, 221, 225, 245

reader's theater, 40, 41; writing and performing, 58-67

reading: book review, 214-215; comprehension test, 439-440

realism, 475

redundancy, 295

reference works, 453

refrain, 475

regular comparison, 357-358

regular verb, 337-338; conjugation, 341, 342

rehearsing: news report, 275-276; reader's theater, 64-66; tall tale, 122-123

repetition, 296

report, 248, 249; research paper, 250-269

research, 248; bibliographical forms, 448-451; memorizing technique, 446-447; note-taking, 443-446; outlining, 447-448; skill, 435-454; technological advances, 400-401. *See also* library research

research paper, 250-269; on-line catalog, 400-401. *See also* library research revising, 9, 20-21; book jacket, 246; book review, 222-223; computer, 395; demonstration speech, 157-158; description, 85-87; descriptive speech, 94; editorial, 181-183; explanatory chart, 165-166; expository essay, 145-147; graphic design, 36; movie review, 235-236; news report, 275-276; personal narrative, 53-55; persuasive speech, 194-195; photo essay, 98-100; public service poster, 203; research paper, 264-266; script, 64-66; self-portrait and collage, 72; short story, 114-115; speaking, 29-30; storyboard, 132; tall tale, 122-123; videotape, 284

rhyme, 475

rhyme scheme, 476

rhythm, 476

riddle, 476

rise, raise, 363

R.S.V.P., 430

run-on sentence, 332-333; expository essay, 148

s

salutation. *See* introduction

satire, 476

scanner: database, 399; desktop publishing, 396; fax, 402

scene of play, 476

science fiction, 476

script: movie review, 232, 234; news report, 271, 274-276; reader's theater, 58, 59-60, 62, 63, 64-66; videotape, 279-280, 282, 284

self-portrait, 40, 41, 68-73

semicolon, 372-373

senses: observation, 79-81, 82; sensory detail, 144

sentence, 322-336; complete, 331-333; effective, 332-336; fragment, 331-332; length and complexity, 336; parallelism, 334-335; parts of, 322-328; purposes, 329-331; structure, 183; supporting, 292; transitional, 292-293; types, 328-330; types in paragraph writing, 291-293; variety, 335-336

sentence combining, 336; coordination, 333-334; speech writing, 158; subordination, 334

sequence chain, 98, 99

series, items in: colon, 373; comma, 367

setting, 109, 476; book review, 213; development, 112

shall, will, 340-341, 363

short story, 103, 476; writing project, 104-117

showing: and telling, description, 87; and telling, videotape, 282

signature, personal letter, 429

simile, 86, 476

simple predicate, 323-324

simple sentence, 328

simple subject, 323

sit, set, 340, 364

sketching, 34; book jacket illustration, 244; storyboard, 130, 131

slang, 195, 196, 476; speechwriting, 235

software, 395; CD-ROM, 398; technological advances, 403-404

sonnet, 477

source: citation, 448-451; credits, 285, 448; news report, 272, 273

Spanish language, 421

spatial order, 15, 457

speaker: listening to, 31, 92, 93; lyric poetry, 477

speaking, 26-27; delivery, 30-31; getting started, 27-29; persuasion, 192-193; projection, 66; revision and practice, 29-30. *See also* speech

Speaking Projects:
demonstration speech, 150-159;
descriptive speech, 90-95;
ideas for, 61, 62, 93, 120, 152, 189, 228, 271;
movie review, 226-239;
news report, 270-277;
persuasive speech, 186-197;
reader's theater, 58-67;
tall tale, 118-125

speech: delivering, 94, 95, 158-159, 197; demonstration, 135, 150-159; descriptive, 90-95; parts of, 299-313; persuasive, 186-197

spelling, 405-417; activities, 414-417; book jacket, 246-247; checklist, 22, 411; *ie* and *ei*, 405-406; explanatory chart, 166; homophones, 409-410; improvement strategies, 411-412; misspelled word list, 411; poster, 204; prefix, 406; rules, 405-410; spell-check, 413-414; storyboard, 133; suffix, 406-407; vocabulary activities, 426-427; writing process and, 413

stage directions, 66

standard English, 360

stanza, 477

state abbreviations, 478

stereotype, 461, 477

still photo, 282

storyboard, 103, 126-133

storytelling, 102-133; oral literature, 473; short story, 104-117; tall tale, 118-125

student model, 43-44, 59-60, 69, 77, 91, 97, 105-107, 119-120, 127-129, 137-138, 151, 161, 171-172, 187-188, 199, 209, 227, 241, 251-252, 271, 279-280

style: book review, 213. *See also* writing style

style sheet, 388-391

subject finding, 10-11; description, 78; developing ideas, 13; narrowing, 12, 140; persuasive speech, 189-190; public service poster, 20-202; research paper, 252

subject of sentence, 322-323; complete, 323; compound, 324-325; position, 325-326; simple, 323 subject-verb agreement, 352-355; problems, 353-355; singular and plural, 352-353

subordinate clause, 319

subordinating conjunction, 313, 321

subplot, 477

suffix: adding, 406-407; *e* ending words, 406; hyphen, 376; vocabulary, 419-420; vowel and consonant ending, 407; *y* ending words, 407

summary, 257, 258; conclusion, 19, 264; note-taking, 445-446

suspense, 477

symbol, 477

synonym, 421-422, 477

T

tall tale, 103, 118-125, 477; delivery, 123-124

tape recording, 125

tape-recording, 237, 238

teach, learn, 362

technological advances, 394-404; activities employing, 404; communication, 401-403; computer use, 394-397; information storage and retrieval, 397-400; research, 400-401; software, 403-404; spelling aid, 413-414

TelePrompTer, 228

telling: and showing, description, 87; and showing, videotape, 282

tense: future, 340-343; future perfect, 340-343; past, 340-343; past perfect, 340-343; present, 340-343; present, book review, 223; present, script revision, 64; present perfect, 340-343; shift in, 343; usage, 223; verb, 88, 340-344

test-taking, 435-443; essay test, 441-443; objective test, 437-441; preparation for, 436-437, 453-454

than, then, 364

that, which, who, 364

the, 308

their, there, they're, 364

them, those, 364-365

theme, 477; book review, 213

there, 354

thesaurus, 422

thesis statement, 477. *See also* main-idea statement

things, capitalization of, 384-386

third person, 110, 122; point of view, 296

time indication: abbreviation, 391; colon, 374

title: abbreviation, 390-391; capitalization, 385-387; quotation marks, 375; style sheet, 389

to, too, two, 365, 410

tone, 297-298, 477; book review, 213; context clue, 424

topic: demonstration speech, 152, 153, 154; descriptive speech, 92; editorial, 173, 174-175; explanatory chart, 162-163; expository essay, 142; narrowing, 254-255; outlining, 447-448; personal narrative, 46; photo essay, 98; research paper, 252-255. *See also* subject finding

topic sentence, 478; expository essay, 142; paragraph, 291-292

tragedy, 478

transitions: comma, 373; description, 85; descriptive speech, 93; editorial, 184; expository essay, 145; personal narrative, 54, 55; sentences, 292-293; videotape, 283

transitive verb, 306-307

U

understatement, 478

usage: adjective and adverb, 356-359; adjectives in comparisons, 223; checklist, 22; cliché, 115; colloquial versus formal diction, 157, 298; figurative language, 86-87; glossary of, 360-365; present tense, 64, 223; pronoun, 345-351; pronoun antecedent, 196, 349-351; slang, 235; verb, 337-344; verb tense, 88. *See also* style

V

VCR, 280; voice-over, 282

verb, 304-307, 337-344; agreement with subject, 352-355; conjugation, 341-343; irregular, 338-339, 342, 343; principal parts, 337-340; problem, 339-340; regular, 337-338, 341-342; tense, 88, 340-344; voice, 344

verbal, 315-318; gerund, 317; infinitive, 318; participle, 315-316

verbal phrase, 315-318

verb phrase, 306, 352-353

VHS tape, 280

videodisc, 398

videotape, 229, 230; preparation, 278-285

visual aids, 154

Visual Projects:
book jacket, 240-247; explanatory chart, 160-167; graphic design, 32-37; ideas for, 70, 98, 162, 200, 279; photo essay of community place, 96-101; public service poster, 198-205; self-portrait or collage, 68-73; storyboard, 126-133; videotape, 278-285

vocabulary, 418-427; context clue, 423-424; denotation and connotation, 423; increasing strategy, 425; jargon, 471; multiple meaning, 424; prefix, 419; root of word, 418; spelling activities, 426-427; suffix, 419-420; synonyms, antonyms, and homonyms, 421-423

voice, active and passive, 344

voice-over, 282

W

walk, 341-342

webbing. *See* clustering

well, good, 359, 362

when, where, 365

who, which, that, 364

who, whom, 365

who, whom, whose, 348-349

whose, who's, 365

will, shall, 340-341, 363

word choice: tone, 298; usage glossary, 360-365

word meaning, 418-419; vocabulary, 418-427

word origin. *See* etymology

word processing, 395-396; backup copy, 396; hard copy, 395; input, 395; keyboard, 395; printer, 395; software, 395; spelling aid, 413-414

writing process, 9-25; spelling and, 413; stages of, 9

Writing Projects:
book review, 208-225; describing community place, 76-89; editorial, 170-185; expository essay, 136-149; ideas for, 48, 107, 130, 139, 173, 211, 253 personal narrative, 42-57; research paper, 250-269; short story, 104-117

writing style, 294-298, 477; capitalization, 385-386; italics, numbers, and abbreviations, 388-391; style sheet, 388-391

Y

you, 352

your, you're, 365

ACKNOWLEDGMENTS

PHOTOGRAPHY

3 Bob Daemmrich/Tony Stone Images; **5** Will McIntyre/Photo Researchers, Inc.; **6-7** L. Kilvoord/The Image Works; **13** Nancy Sheehan/© D.C. Heath; **17** Steven Frame/Stock Boston; **23** Elena Rooraid/PhotoEdit; **25** Richard Hutchings/PhotoEdit; **31** Melina Freedman; **38-39** Mark Antman/The Image Works; **41** Colby College Museum of Art, in memory of Dorothy Emmons Whitchurch.; **42** Myrleen Ferguson/PhotoEdit; **47** David Young-Wolff/PhotoEdit; **50, 55** Tony Freeman/PhotoEdit; **65, 66** Mary Kate Denny/PhotoEdit; **67** David Young-Wolff/PhotoEdit; **68** Schalkwijk/Art Resource, NY; **71** Jeff Isaac Greenberg/Photo Researchers, Inc.; **74** David Young-Wolff/PhotoEdit; **75** Thomas Dimock/The Stock Market; **76** Bob Daemmrich/The Image Works; **82** Tony Savino/The Image Works; **91** David Young-Wolff/PhotoEdit; **100** Richard Hutchings/PhotoEdit; **103** Bob Daemmrich/Stock Boston; **104** Tony Freeman/PhotoEdit; **113** Michael Newman/Photo Researchers, Inc.; **124** Richard Hutchings/PhotoEdit; **131** David Young-Wolff/PhotoEdit; **135** Nancy Sheehan; **140** Mary Kate Denny/PhotoEdit; **147** Mary Kate Denny/PhotoEdit; **149** Bob Daemmrich/The Image Works; **150** Mary Kate Denny/PhotoEdit; **153** Richard Hutchings/PhotoEdit; **156** Bob Daemmrich/The Image Works; **160** Lynn M. Stone/The Image Bank; **162** Tony Freeman/PhotoEdit; **163** David Young-Wolff/PhotoEdit; **175** Karen R. Preuss/The Image Works; **181** Bob Daemmrich/Stock Boston; **186** David Young-Wolff/PhotoEdit; **188** Joe Sohm/The Image Works; **192** David Young-Wolff/PhotoEdit; **196** Skjold/The Image Works; **198** Bob Daemmrich/The Image Works; **203** David Young-Wolff/PhotoEdit; **204** Bill Bachmann/The Image Works; **207** *Mother and Child*, Elizabeth Catlett, 1970. Cedar, 36"h. ©SEMA, Courtesy of the artist.; **208** Gabe Palmer/The Stock Market; **215** Michael Newman/PhotoEdit; **221** Mary Kate Denny/PhotoEdit; **225** Tony Freeman/PhotoEdit; **226** Stephen Fris/Stock Boston; **234** Tony Freeman/PhotoEdit; **238** Bob Daemmrich/The Image Works; **239** Michael Newman/PhotoEdit; **240, 249, 250** David Young-Wolff/PhotoEdit; **257** Jeff Dunn/Stock Boston; **275** Tony Freeman/PhotoEdit; **284** Bill Bachmann/Stock Boston; **287** Ken O' Donoghue/© D.C. Heath; **289** David Perry Lawrence/The Image Bank; **290** FPG International; **292** *l* David Burnett/The Stock Market; *r* Gabe Palmer/The Stock Market; **296** Richard Mackson/FPG International; **298** *t* Stephen Simpson/FPG International; *b* Jim Pickerell/The Image Works; **300** Zefa/H. Armstrong Roberts; **302** Joe Van Os/The Image Bank; **303** Myrleen Ferguson/PhotoEdit; **304** Steve Dunwell/The Image Bank; **306** Hank deLespainasse/The Image Bank; **307** Whitney Lane/The Image Bank; **309** Peter Beck/The Stock Market; **315** Jose L. Pelaez/The Stock Market; **316** Michael Nelson/FPG International; **321** David Young-Wolff/PhotoEdit; **323** Frank Siteman/Stock Boston; **324** Harald Sund/The Image Bank; **326** Peter Menzel/Stock Boston; **330** Arthur Tilley/FPG International; **339** Kay Chernush/The Image Bank; **341** Karl A. Gehring/LGI Photo Agency; **342** Mark Antmann/The Image Works; **347** Michael Newman; **349** Tony Freeman/PhotoEdit; **357** Jurgen Vogt/The Image Bank; **363** Joseph Nettis/Photo Researchers, Inc.; **365** Schneps/The Image Bank; **368** Kevin Forest/The Image Bank; **370** Scott Snow/The Image Bank; **371** Dr. Morley Read/Science Photo Library/Photo Researchers, Inc.; **377** Margot Granitsas/The Image Works; **378** John Coletti/Stock Boston; **380, 381** The Bettmann Archive; **383** George Randall/Photo Researchers, Inc.; **384** NASA; **386** Steven Burr Williams/The Image Bank; **387** Joseph Sohm/Chromosohm/The Stock Market; **391** PhotoWorld/FPG International; **392-393** David Young-Wolff/PhotoEdit; **400** Gabe Palmer/The Stock Market; **412** Bob Daemmrich/Stock Boston; **414** D. Lada/H. Armstrong Roberts; **417** USDA; **422** Alan L. Detrick/Photo Researchers, Inc.; **440** Gordon R. Gainer/The Stock Market; **451** Frank Cezus/FPG International; **460** Jim Pickerell/FPG International

ILLUSTRATION

Michael Bartolis Project Opener logos, Terms to Know logos, 337, 394, 404, 414, 453, 458

John Hersey 6, 8, 26, 38, 40, 74, 102, 134, 168, 206, 248, 286, 392

John Rumery 9

Lauren Scheuer 295, 297, 299, 305, 313, 316, 318, 319, 320, 334, 338, 351, 353, 366, 373, 379, 397, 399, 408, 412, 420

David Shepherd 294, 297, 306, 312, 313, 317, 328, 340, 344, 345, 352, 362, 385, 427, 454